Art and Answerability

University of Texas Press Slavic Series, No. 9
Michael Holquist, General Editor

ART AND ANSWERABILITY

Early Philosophical Essays
by M. M. Bakhtin

Edited by Michael Holquist and Vadim Liapunov
Translation and Notes by Vadim Liapunov
Supplement translated by Kenneth Brostrom

UNIVERSITY OF TEXAS PRESS, AUSTIN

Second paperback printing, 1995

Requests for permission to reproduce material from this
work should be sent to Permissions, University of Texas
Press, Box 7819, Austin, Texas 78713-7819.

∞ The paper used in this publication meets the
minimum requirements of American National Standard for
Information Sciences—Permanence of Paper for Printed
Library Materials, ANSI Z39.48-1984.

The publication of this book has been supported by a grant
from the National Endowment for the Humanities, an
independent federal agency.

Library of Congress Cataloging-in-Publication Data

Bakhtin, M. M. (Mikhail Mikhaĭlovich), 1895–1975.
    Art and answerability : early philosophical essays / by
M. M. Bakhtin ; edited by Michael Holquist and Vadim
Liapunov ; translated and notes by Vadim Liapunov ;
supplement translated by Kenneth Brostrom.
        p.   cm. — (University of Texas Press Slavic series ;
no. 9)
    Translated from the Russian.
    Includes bibliographical references.
    ISBN 0-292-70411-9. — ISBN 0-292-70412-7 (pbk.)
    1. Aesthetics. 2. Philosophy. 3. Literature—Philosophy.
I. Holquist, Michael, 1935– . II. Liapunov, Vadim, 1935– .
III. Title. IV. Series.
BH39.B29 1990
111'.85—dc20   89-70718

Светлой памяти
Михаила Михайловича Бахтина

Contents

INTRODUCTION: THE ARCHITECTONICS OF ANSWERABILITY

I

There is a story to the effect that Queen Victoria was so delighted by *Alice in Wonderland* that she left a standing order for the author's next book. The following year (1866) she was not at all amused when she received a formidably technical treatise on logic called *Condensation of Determinants* by Charles Lutwidge Dodgson, which was, of course, Lewis Carroll's real name.[1] Anglophone readers of Bakhtin may experience something like Queen Victoria's chagrin when they start working their way through the works in this third volume of Bakhtin translations to appear in the University of Texas Press Slavic Series.[2] The essays assembled here are all very early and differ in a number of ways from Bakhtin's previously published work. Readers will probably first suspect that they are encountering a "new Bakhtin" in the style of these essays. One reason why Bakhtin has so quickly become popular with so many (and varied) readers is that they have found him easy to read, at least by comparison with other theorists now competing for attention. These texts, by contrast, are extremely difficult and make demands on the reader's erudition, powers of synthesis, and sheer patience not encountered in the books that have defined Bakhtin's achievement in the recent past. In addition, many of their terms and concepts are currently unfashionable. At a time when "the author" has long been presumed dead, and when the words "hero" and "aesthetics" have a certain anachronistic ring to them, a long monograph called "Author and Hero in Aesthetic Activity" will require of its readers an extra degree of imagination and sympathy. Obviously, we believe the extra effort will be well repaid, first of all because these texts make possible a deeper understanding of Bakhtin's previously published books.

A major topic in these works is "architectonics," a term that in Bakhtin's thought is constantly taking on new meaning in the different contexts in which it is invoked. But at this preliminary state, architectonics can be understood as concerned with questions of building, of the way something is put together. Architectonics provides the ground for Bakhtin's discussion of two related problems in these essays. The first is how relations between living subjects get ordered into categories of "I" and "another." The second is how authors forge the kind of tentative wholeness we call a text out of the relation they articulate with their heroes. More particularly, architectonics also provides a conceptual armature for his later, more partial readings of specific works and authors, in all of which, in one way or another, the relation of parts to wholes figures prominently. In his disputations with other schools (such as Formalism in the early text included here called "The Problem of Content, Material, and Form in Verbal Art," or, in his last years, when indicating weaknesses in Structuralism), Bakhtin's argument usually includes the charge that his opponents have not completely theorized their position. He criticizes their lack of philosophical thoroughness largely because they fail to provide their particular pronouncements with an overarching conceptual framework of the kind he had provided in these early works for his own subsequent studies of more highly particularized subjects.

Aesthetics, another major topic of these essays, is treated by Bakhtin as a subset of architectonics: architectonics is the general study of how entities relate to each other, whereas aesthetics concerns itself with the problem of consummation, or how parts are shaped into wholes. Wholeness, or consummation, is always to be understood here as a relative term: in Bakhtin, consummation is almost literally in the eye of the beholder. As will become clearer in what follows, wholeness is a kind of fiction that can be created only from a particular point of view. When invoking the term, one should always keep in mind the twin questions: "consummated— by (for) whom?" and "consummated—when?" Consummated wholes may be of one kind or another, but for Bakhtin, who sought to make loopholes into (almost) metaphysical categories, their wholeness can never be absolute. A major irony, amidst a host of other ironies, is that these texts that wrestle with the problem of

wholeness are themselves incomplete, raising first of all the problems of their genre. What shall we call these fragments? In what
follows I shall refer to them as "essays," because—although they
are parts of larger texts, they are not as they now stand full-fledged
works. They also have the quality of essays because they are
clearly attempts to test out, to contest, to try the propositions
they engage.

How to shape heterogeneous parts into a (positionally) consummated whole is a problem Bakhtin seeks to resolve at various levels. One of the more important of these is the kind of whole we
consummate when we shape the life of another person into a biography. It may, then, help to place these essays in Bakhtin's own
oeuvre if we remember the kind of biography it has become conventional to consummate for Bakhtin himself. Bakhtin's mature
career is usually divided into the following chapters. In the early
Nevel'/Vitebsk period (1919–1924), he wrote a number of philosophical works, chiefly in the area of a broadly conceived notion
of aesthetics. This was followed by a Leningrad period (1924–
1929) during which he completed manuscripts—some of which,
published under the names of his friends, continue to arouse dispute over his authorship—devoted to a wide range of particular
figures and topics. After his arrest in 1929 there is a long period of
exile and a return to the provinces (1930s to 1960s) during which
he worked on the history and theory of the novel. Bakhtin's late
period (roughly from the mid-1960s to his death in 1975) included
the appearance of many of his formerly unpublished manuscripts,
a move to Moscow, and work on several of the philosophical topics that had preoccupied him in his youth. He returned, in other
words, to the problems he first laid out for himself in the essays
included here, all written in the five years between 1919 and 1924.

In the spring of 1918, Bakhtin finished his studies in classical
philology at the University of Petersburg. Like many others, he
sought relief from the chaos that followed in the immediate wake
of the revolution by going into country districts where food and
fuel were more abundant. He ended up in the western provinces,
where he quickly became a member of a small group of intellectuals who feverishly threw themselves into the debates, lectures,
demonstrations, and manifesto writing that characterized life at
that extraordinary time. It was in this atmosphere of immense intellectual and political intensity that Bakhtin sought to think
through for himself some of the problems then of most concern to

philosophers, such as (to name only a few) the status of the knowing subject, the relation of art to lived experience, the existence of other persons, and the complexities of responsibility in the area of discourse as well as in the area of ethics.

Bakhtin had already immersed himself in philosophy from a very early age, particularly in ancient Greek, Hellenistic, and modern European philosophy. Thanks to his unusually well-educated German governess, he not only grew up speaking German at home, but even began his reading of the Greek classics in German translation. He read the German systematic philosophers, as well as Buber and Kierkegaard, while still a gymnasium student in Vilnius and Odessa. At the university, he trained as a scholar in the Greek and Latin classics as they were taught in the old German philological tradition, in which the studies of literature and language were inextricably bound to each other. But Tadeusz Zielinski, his eminent professor of classics, emphasized in addition the need to know the whole spectrum of classical civilization, including philosophy. After leaving the university, Bakhtin moved to the west Russian town of Nevel', where he immediately fell in with a group of young people passionately devoted to study and disputation of the latest developments in philosophy. In Nevel' and later in Vitebsk, Bakhtin was surrounded by intense philosophical debates. These took place not only in his study circle, but in public forums organized by the local party committee. Thus, while Bakhtin was still unusually young to be addressing the subjects in these essays—he wrote them all between the ages of twenty-three and twenty-eight—he had already been saturated in philosophical thinking for some time. The particular school that dominated the academic study of philosophy in Europe during these years and was of great importance to the young Bakhtin was Neo-Kantianism. Since these essays draw heavily on Neo-Kantian concepts and terminology, a few words about Neo-Kantianism may be in order.[3]

By 1918, Neo-Kantianism had been the dominant school of philosophy in Germany for almost fifty years. From roughly the 1870s until the 1920s, most professors of philosophy in Germany defined themselves by taking a position vis-à-vis Kant. During this period, most Russians considered Germany to be the home of true philosophical thought. Chairs at the leading universities not only in Germany but in Russia as well were held by Neo-Kantians of one kind or another. They were particularly well entrenched at

Petersburg University during the years when Bakhtin was a student there.[4] Although Neo-Kantianism was a widespread phenomenon that included several philosophies that were highly varied in their concerns, the one feature of Kant's thought they all had to confront was the master's formulation of the mind's relation to the world, the innovation that was at the heart of his "Copernican revolution." In Kant's view, his predecessors had either, like Leibniz, overemphasized the role of intellectualized appearances, thus diminishing the role of the world outside the mind, or, like Locke, had gone too far in the opposite direction by sensualizing concepts, making the mind merely a receptor of information provided by sensations from the world. Kant's breakthrough was to insist on the necessary interaction—the dialogue as Bakhtin would come to interpret it—between mind and world. Kant argued that what we call thought is really a synthesis of two forms of knowledge, sensibility and understanding. Sensibility may be taken roughly to mean what empiricists such as Locke or Hume assumed to be the sole basis of knowledge, the realm of physical sensation. And Kant's use of understanding is roughly what rationalists, such as Leibniz, assumed to be the sole basis of knowledge, the realm of concepts in the mind. The ability to think, which Kant assumed to mean the ability to make judgments, requires *both* forms of knowledge, which he triumphantly brought together in his "transcendental synthesis": a priori concepts, he argued, do exist *in* the mind, but they can be used actively to organize sensations from the world *outside* the mind. The world, the realm of things-in-themselves, really exists, but so does the mind, the realm of concepts. Thought is the give and take between the two.

Those who came after Kant interpreted this synthesis in various ways. The particular Neo-Kantianism in which the young Bakhtin steeped himself was founded in the late nineteenth century at Marburg University by Hermann Cohen.[5] Cohen radically revised the mind/world relation as Kant had defined it. He emphasized the trancendental aspects of Kant's synthesis, pursuing the quest for a oneness so immaculate that it made him a hero to other seekers after purity, such as the young Pasternak, who in 1912 traveled to Marburg to sit at the feet of the great man. It was the same lust for unity in Cohen that inspired another Russian, Lenin, to attack him as a particularly militant idealist.[6] What attracted Pasternak and repelled Lenin was Cohen's opposition to the potential dualism in Kant's account of how internal thought relates to the external world. Cohen had a remarkably precise mind, and his philosophy is a model of systematicness that sought to unify all operations of consciousness. Roughly stated, his method for doing so was to abandon Kant's thing-in-itself in order to declare a "logic of pure knowing" in which there is only a realm of concepts:[7] the world exists as the subject of thought, and the subject of thought, no matter how material it might appear, is still always a subject that is *thought*.

Bakhtin's connection with the Marburg school was relatively direct, in that his closest friend during the years he was in Nevel' and Vitebsk was Matvei Isaevich Kagan, who returned to Nevel' from Germany almost simultaneously with Bakhtin's arrival there from Petrograd. Kagan was a man of remarkable intellect who commanded the respect of all who came into contact with him. Originally fleeing to Germany to escape persecution as a Jew and to pursue study in mathematics and physics, he had taken up the study of philosophy with Cohen in Marburg. Kagan's move from the exact sciences to philosophy was not unusual in the years just before World War I, when scientists such as Hermann von Helmholtz sought to reinterpret Kant through the logic of mathematics and the workings of the human nervous system, or when physicists such as Ernst Mach applied what they had learned about the nature of matter and energy in the laboratory to the great questions of metaphysics. The Marburg school was the version of academic Neo-Kantianism most concerned with uniting new discoveries in the sciences with the study of philosophy, so Kagan felt quite at home in the old German university on the heights above the river Lahn. But Kagan's budding career as a philosopher in Germany was interrupted by the outbreak of the war in 1914; during the next four years, he was held as an enemy alien (although Cohen himself had intervened on his behalf). He was released for repatriation to Russia only after the signing of the treaty of Brest Litovsk in 1918. The enthusiasm of Bakhtin and his friends for German philosophy was given new depth and impetus by Kagan's return.

Two general aspects of Marburg Neo-Kantianism that played an important role in the composition of these essays should be emphasized. The first of these is the Neo-Kantian desire to relate traditional problems in philosophy to the great new discoveries about the world and nature being made in the exact and biological sciences on the cusp of the nineteenth and twentieth centuries. Bakhtin himself was intensely interested in science, particularly the new physics of Max Planck, Albert Einstein, and Niels Bohr, and current developments in physiology, particularly the study of the central nervous system, an area in which Petersburg was one of the world centers. His closest friends were either lapsed mathematicians such as Kagan or, in later years, scientists such as the biologist (and historian of science) Ivan Kanaev. This aspect of his activity will perhaps explain the attention paid to questions of perception and materiality in these essays. They share in the general effort of thinkers in the early years of the twentieth century to come to grips with the new problems raised by theoretical physics and the new physiology for anyone concerned with the traditional issues of how mind relates to body, and how physical matter relates to such apparently immaterial entities as relations between things. There is a certain lack of clarity about these issues in Bakhtin's philosophy, deriving in some measure from ambiguities inherent in the treatment of the same topics in contemporary science. At a time when Einstein was taking the first steps toward redefining what had appeared to be static physical objects as forms of volatile energy, it is perhaps not surprising that matter—while still being a basic category—did not have the kind of certainty that was unproblematically assumed in traditional (binary) distinctions between matter and mind, or body and soul.

A second aspect of the Marburg school's activity that proved to be important in Bakhtin's development was the emphasis of its founder on unity and oneness. Bakhtin was not merely a passive receptor of Neo-Kantian ideas, of course, and one of the most important ways he demonstrates his independence from Cohen, even at this early stage, is by resistance to the idea of an all-encompassing oneness, or *Allheit*. In this, Bakhtin is perhaps best understood as a figure who is trying to get back to the *other* side of Kant's synthesis, the world, rather than the mind (and in particular the rational mind), the extreme to which Cohen tended. The Kantian concept of the heterogeneity of ends is much closer to Bakhtin's work than the Neo-Kantian lust for unity. The essays in this collection can thus be seen as an attempt to rethink the possibility of wholeness in terms more complex than those provided by the Marburg school (or by other philosophers of the early nineteenth century, as we shall see below). Kant's definition of relation between mind and world had the effect of defining the knowing subject as a maker of sense out of the otherwise inchoate matter of the world. In his obsession with perception as an act of *authoring* in these essays, Bakhtin is closer to Kant himself than he is to Cohen, insofar as he rethinks the problem of wholeness in terms of what is an essentially aesthetic operation. In these essays, the individual subject is conceived as similar to the artist who seeks to render what is *not* an artwork in itself (independent of the artist's activity) into something that *is* the kind of conceptual whole we can recognize as a painting or a text. Cohen's lust for unity with its attendant rationalism was not what drew Bakhtin to the sage of Marburg. It was rather his emphasis on process, the radical "ungivenness" of experience, with its openness and energy—the loopholes in existence—that attracted Bakhtin.

II

During all the years he was in Nevel' and Vitebsk, Bakhtin was constantly writing. We know from references in contemporary journals, newspapers, and personal correspondence that between 1918 and 1924 he worked on several projects. Some of these were not published and have been lost, such as a monograph (possibly two) sometimes called "Patterns of Verbal Creation" and at other times "Aesthetics of Verbal Creation." Other projects, such as a book on Dostoevsky begun at this time, were later published in revised form.

This anthology contains three pieces from the years in Nevel' and Vitebsk: "Art and Answerability," a very short piece that appeared on September 3, 1919, in the one and only edition of the Nevel' journal *Day of Art*, which is the only piece by Bakhtin to be published under his own name until the Dostoevsky book came out ten years later. It was lost in these obscure provincial pages until republished in 1977.[8]

"The Problem of Content, Material, and Form in Verbal Art" was scheduled for publication (but did not appear) in 1924. It actually saw the light of day in 1975, the year Bakhtin died.[9] It seems to have been put together in the form we now have sometime in 1923, although it appears to be closely related to the material on verbal creativity Bakhtin was writing at least two years earlier. "The Problem of Content, Material, and Form in Verbal Art" is difficult to date with any precision, but it can reasonably be speculated that it was begun fairly early in Nevel' and that Bakhtin continued to work on it after his move to Vitebsk (1920) until he left for Leningrad in 1924.

Another fragment, provisionally entitled by its Russian editors "Toward a Philosophy of the Deed," was published for the first time only in 1986 and will appear in translation in the next volume of the Texas Slavic Series;[10] its composition would seem to precede "Author and Hero in Aesthetic Activity," which was published in two parts: a long monograph under that title was included in an anthology of Bakhtin's writings that appeared in 1979.[11]

The textual history of Bakhtin's early works is obviously quite complicated—suffice it to say that they all come at the same set of problems from different angles. Thus, it is extremely difficult to discuss any one of them without reference to the others, which is why in the remainder of these remarks I shall not only refer to the works included in the present volume, but shall allude from time to time to the forthcoming translation of "Toward a Philosophy of the Deed."

Why are these essays important? And for whom? A full answer to the first question will, I hope, emerge in the reader's encounter with the texts themselves; I shall offer some partial preliminary answers in what follows. The second question—for whom are these pieces important?—can be answered more readily: the material in this volume was first of all important for Bakhtin himself. It is the precondition for his later work, insofar as it contains many, if not most, of the ideas he would spend the rest of his life exploring, revising, or even contradicting. These essays are also important because, with their appearance, any opinion of Bakhtin formed on the basis of his previously published work must now be modified or discarded.

For Bakhtin, these pieces preserved the fundamental principles of the dialogism that guided his work throughout an unusually long working career.[12] They date from 1919–1924, the so-called philosophical period of his life, or, in other words, from his first years as a mature thinker—although Bakhtin, who was born in 1895, was still only in his twenties when they were written. Some idea of the value Bakhtin himself attached to these early works may be gathered from the special care he accorded the notebooks in which he wrote "Author and Hero in Aesthetic Activity." In general, Bakhtin was notoriously cavalier about his manuscripts;

yet for fifty years—through his frequent moves, his arrest, and exile—he kept with him the yellowing pages of the schoolboy notebooks containing the manuscript of "Author and Hero."

But if these pieces are so important, why was their publication so long delayed? Why did "Author and Hero" appear, in fact, only in 1979—and "Philosophy of the Deed" even later? There are both historical and personal reasons for the fifty-year interval separating the act of writing from the event of publishing these works. In the first decades after the revolution, there could be no question of publishing material so likely to evoke the dreaded charge of "idealism." Some idea of the difficulties Bakhtin had to confront can be gathered from the fate of "The Problem of Content," another piece included here, which was calculated at the time to be a less provocative work than "Author and Hero." Thus, Bakhtin submitted it, and it was actually accepted for publication. But even this relatively "safe" piece was suppressed, when *Russkij sovremennik*, the journal in which it was to appear, was closed down by the government before the essay could see the light of day. It was only when he was close to death, and reassured by the fame his republished Dostoevsky and Rabelais books had brought him, that Bakhtin revealed to his friends the existence of his earlier manuscripts.[13] In 1972, he turned over what was left of his work to two young scholars of the Gor'ky Institute of World Literature, Vadim Valerianovich Kozhinov and Sergei Georgievich Bocharov.

But in addition to the external difficulties that kept Bakhtin from attempting to publish his earlier work, there are reasons for their delayed appearance inherent in his own philosophy and character. As any reader of these essays will quickly become aware, various differences between works that are "consummated" (*zavershën*) as opposed to those that are "unconsummated" (*nezavershën*) are a major concern in Bakhtin's thought. In the case of "Author and Hero," we have a text that is "unconsummated" not only in the sense that it is still patently at the first stage of composition (portions of it are merely notes or fragments intended to be fleshed out at a later date): it is also "unconsummated" according to Bakhtin's own architectonic/aesthetic definition of completedness. At this stage of his career, Bakhtin had not yet gained that distanced point of view, that position of "outsideness" (to use another key concept from these essays themselves) vis-à-vis the concept of dialogue that would come to guide his work in the years to come. Bakhtin is already "Bakhtin" here, but it is in the nature of his own complex views on biography-as-task that not *all* of Bakhtin should be here yet. In fact, in one of the last notes he made to himself just before his death, he himself admits to an unfinished quality in the actual formulation of his ideas; he acknowledges his "love for variation and for a diversity of terms in dealing with the same phenomenon." But he is also aware that there is a "well-known *internal* unconsummatedness of many of my thoughts [because my ideas have always been] in a state of becoming." And he adds that "it is sometimes difficult to distinguish between the one kind of unconsummatedness and the other."[14]

It is particularly difficult to draw such a line in these early essays. But we now have certain advantages that Bakhtin himself lacked as he—a constant meditator on the meaning of borders—surveyed his career. We have the architectonic privilege of being outside Bakhtin's achievement, to a degree he himself—by the conditions he laid down in his own work—could never be. With the appearance of these major early texts, the profiles of his work take on a new clarity; something like a canon has now emerged, and we are enabled an excess of seeing vis-à-vis his work that opens new possibilities for consummating it. The question now becomes: what shall we make of this gift of otherness?

Some will feel less addressed by this question than others, and it is possible, of course, simply to avoid it. One need not have an image of Bakhtin's total oeuvre in order to appropriate isolated aspects of it. But for those concerned with understanding Bakhtin in his own right, the texts in this anthology will pose problems of a certain urgency. Taken together, they provide a general theory of human subjectivity, in which various kinds of perception play a major role in order better to distinguish the specificity of aesthetic perception. But as the reader will soon discover, "aesthetics," as Bakhtin conceives the topic, is far more capacious than is usually thought, including fundamental questions of epistemology, ethics, and, indeed, ontology (although one would like to see the ontological assumptions ruling Bakhtin's work treated at greater length than is the case in the existing fragments).

These essays are only part of a great untitled work Bakhtin never finished, a project we have called "The Architectonics of Answerability" for reasons internal to the remaining fragments. It was to have been "a first philosophy," a "philosophy of the act-deed, and not of the deed's product."[15] Aristotle argued that philosophy was superior to history because it could generalize about what might be, whereas historians were condemned to what had actually been. In this (and in other ways), Bakhtin defines himself as an anti-Aristotelian, for it is precisely what is realized as opposed to possibility that Bakhtin most honors. Thus, although I have talked about Bakhtin's "theory," I do so only for want of a better word: "theory" is a term that must be invoked with great caution in a Bakhtinian context, for Bakhtin's work is—particularly in these essays—militantly opposed to most conceptions of—precisely—theory. His achievement can be called theoretical only in the sense that all grand *anti*-theories are inevitably implicated in what they oppose. A large part of these essays is devoted to a new definition of the human subject. But it is precisely the radical *specificity of individual humans* that he is after: a major paradox in all Bakhtin's work is that he continually seeks to generalize about uniqueness. There is a very real sense in which the *necessity* of doing so is what his work is about. What might be called theoretical tact, the positing of problems in precisely the right measure of generality and specificity, is an obsessive item in Bakhtin's thought, early and late.

The lack of such tact is often the basis for his criticisms of other theorists. In many of his books devoted to a single problem, he almost invariably characterizes his entrance into the conversation about the problem with the same prescription: a plague-on-all-your-houses gesture that points to the need for balance of a kind that Bakhtin argues has heretofore been missing and that he will now provide. Often, this entrance into the dialogue takes the form of the "Goldilocks" formula as she intervenes in the patterns of the three bears: "Not too hot, not too cold, but just right!" Thus, to take only the best-known example, in a much-quoted instance from the 1929 "Voloshinov" book *Marxism and the Philosophy of Language,* there is an initial discrimination made between scholars such as Saussure who are too general (abstract objectivists) and others who are too limitedly specific, such as Vossler (subjective idealists); Bakhtin/Voloshinov's concept of meta- or translinguistics is then proffered as avoiding both extremes. Bakhtin opens his 1952 discussion of "The Problem of Speech Genres" by proclaiming the staggering diversity as well as the overwhelming specificity of language use: "All the diverse areas of human activity involve the use of language." How, then, is one to say anything general about something so unique in all its instances? By positing a subject that can—up to a certain point—be theorized without doing violence to the very heterogeneity it seeks to meditate: in the case of this late essay (as in his earlier work on language), that subject is "the utterance." The value of making such a move is that it, in its turn, opens up a further field of generalizable propositions that still maintain contact with diversity: "Each separate utterance is individual, of course, but each sphere in which language is used develops its own *relatively stable types* of these utterances. These we may call *speech genres.*"[16]

These—and all Bakhtin's other attempts to find a workable dialogue between general formulations and the specific data that give them rise—are prefigured in the works that make up the present volume. But in these early essays, the extremes of generality and specificity Bakhtin posits are greater, and therefore the problem of how they relate to each other is more openly addressed. He does this in two ways.

First, in "Author and Hero in Aesthetic Activity," Bakhtin works out his own position by defining it against existing schools of "expressionist" and "impressionist" aesthetic thought that—in what is perhaps the first of his "Goldilocks" scenarios—err in the first instance by being overly "internal" and subjective (Lipps or Volkelt), and in the second by focusing too exclusively on external formal features (the Formalists).

Second, and more interestingly, by addressing a number of criticisms against theory itself, Bakhtin attempts—theoretically—to work through the dilemma of how to generalize the need to be specific. Kant had sought to rein in the speculative hubris of the Western philosophical tradition by demonstrating the limits of metaphysics. His value for Bakhtin is that the hardheaded citizen of Königsberg (in an example Bakhtin quotes) had insisted 100 Thalers in thought were not equal to 100 Thalers in experience. It is this call to intellectual modesty in Kant, and its implications as worked out in Neo-Kantianism, that draws Bakhtin back again and again to the three great *Critiques,* especially *The Critique of Pure Reason* and *The Critique of Practical Judgment.*

But in order to purge metaphysics, Kant had been forced to resort to a transcendentalism of his own, and it is this tendency in Kant and other thinkers that Bakhtin most strenuously opposes. Bakhtin's thought is a "philosophy of the deed" insofar as he again and again draws a distinction between experience and *reflection* on experience, or cognition. "The discovery of an a priori, transcendental element in our understanding did not open an exit from the interior of our understanding . . ." Kant's transcendental subject is the positing merely of "a gnoseological subject,"[17] because "epistemological reflection has nothing to do with the individual form of experiencing an object . . . it has to do with the transcendent forms of the object (and not of the experience) . . ." It is the transcendentalized Kant Bakhtin is still setting himself against in such later essays as his monograph on the chronotope, where he makes the point that he is "employing the Kantian evaluation of the importance of [time and space] in the cognitive process, but [I] differ from Kant in taking them not as 'transcendental,' but as forms of the most immediate reality."[18] What Bakhtin means by his apparently casual reference to the difference between a "transcendental" level and the level of "immediate reality" (*samaja real'naja dejstvitel'nost'*) is made clearer in these early essays in those places where Bakhtin distinguishes between *all* cognitive levels of awareness and the kind of *situated* awareness individual human beings experience in the unique sites they occupy in the world at a particular time and in a particular place.

In "Author and Hero in Aesthetic Activity" the distinction is first of all charted in terms of visual perception. If two persons look at each other, one sees aspects of the other person and of the space we are in that the other does not and—this is very important—*vice versa:* "As we gaze at each other, two different worlds are reflected in the pupils of our eyes."

The implications of the difference between these two worlds reverberate throughout these essays, but at a first appropriation this expression signifies that I can see things you do not, such as parts of your body and details of the room or landscape your angle of vision denies you; the same, of course, can be said of you as you regard me from the position you occupy. Each of us has an "excess of vision" relative to the other. We can, conceivably, construct an image of the situation that will fill in the details we cannot actually see. At this level of generality, the positions we occupy are *convertible:* in describing things in this way, Bakhtin is at—*we* are at—the level of cognition that generalizes the subject. For cognition, "there is no absolutely inconvertible relationship of *I* and *all others*; for cognition, '*I* and the *other*,' inasmuch as they are being thought, constitute a relationship that is relative and convertible, since the cognitive *subiectum* as such does not occupy any determinate, concrete place in being." But for a particular person, in a particular place at a particular time, and thus constrained by all the conditions peculiar to such a unique placement, "the interrelationship of 'I—the other' is not convertible for me in lived life in any concrete way." Since it is not convertible, it must be viewed perspectively.

If the central role of architectonics in these essays is not recognized, Bakhtin's obsession with simultaneity of various kinds can all too easily be misread as (yet another example of) a mechanical concern for binary oppositions.[19] But what is essential for Bakhtin is not only the categories as such that get paired in author/hero, space/time, self/other, and so forth, *but in addition the architectonics governing relations between them.* What counts is the simultaneity that makes it logical to treat these concepts *together.* The point is that Bakhtin honors *both* things and the relations between them—one cannot be understood without the other. The resulting simultaneity is not a private *either/or,* but an inclusive *also/and.* In other words, the logic of Bakhtin's simultaneity is—dialogic. But conceiving architectonics dialogically does not eventuate in the simplistic pluralism some of Bakhtin's more liberal (and less informed) readers have wanted to see in his work. Invoking two more key Bakhtinian terms, we may say that wholes are never *given,* but always *achieved;* work—the struggle to effect a whole out of the potential chaos of parts—is precisely what, in fact, architectonics theorizes.

The overwhelming general significance of architectonics must be remembered, then, in any discussion of the specific terms shaping Bakhtin's practice. It is only slightly less vital to keep in mind that architectonics is intended to describe an *activity:* the relations it orders are always in a state of dynamic tension. Architectonics is like architecture insofar as it is about building wholes through the manipulation of relations between parts. But architecture suggests the creation of static structures. The matter of architectonics is active in the sense that it is always in process (architecture is only one instantiation of architectonics, and aesthetics, as we shall see, is another)—not in any of the actual materials it employs to erect relations in themselves exclusively; even though such materials may be the most abstract categories, such as "being" or "relation" itself, they can still be treated as *entities.* When conceived as *in themselves,* they are like the stone and wood deployed by the architect insofar as they are—outside architectonics—inert. Therefore their materiality must be thought in relation to the ends of which their physical aspect is only a (dialogic) part. In other words, they must be conceived as having not merely a physical presence as things in themselves, but also a relation to *other* things. The invisible relation between them, the immaterial lineaments of the simultaneities that bind them— these are also the stuff of architectonics. Being, as Bakhtin never tires of repeating in these essays, is in its essence active: architectonics names the body of techniques by which its sheer flux may be erected into a meaningful *event.*

The specific subset of architectonics that most occupies Bakhtin in these essays is the aesthetic event. He distinguishes here between a "general aesthetics" that lays down the conditions for all aesthetic events and a "special aesthetics" that accounts for the distinctive qualities of the material used in a given art form within those conditions. As befits a thinker so preoccupied with architectonics, Bakhtin advances his argument by constantly making discriminations between these different levels of relations.

The aesthetic, as defined here, is a category that has less to do with the traditional concern of aestheticians for "beauty" than it has to do with the mysterious concepts of "isolation," "outsideness," and "consummation." The activity of perception—understood as the activity of a subject engaged in making sense out of the world by fixing the flux of its disparate elements into meaningful wholes—is treated by Bakhtin as the activity of creating a text, much as authors make texts out of the givenness of the world outside art. Aesthetics in Bakhtin's sense always entails perceiving an object, a text, or even a person as something actively fashioned into the whole of the object it is. This shaping or finishing-off or, as it is rendered in this translation, this *consummation* is then treated as an act of authorship. It will perhaps come as something of a surprise to casual readers of *Rabelais and His World* that not all totalizing strategies are inherently bad. The positive, creative aspect of aesthetic consummation can be grasped only by rethinking authorship, one reason why it is a key concept in these essays. The general aesthetic Bakhtin provides is grounded in the primal condition that holds for all perception of any kind, a condition that might be called the first law of human perception: whatever is perceived can be perceived only from a uniquely situated place in the overall structure of possible points of view. The enabling condition for having a point of view on anything is to be able to see—and one can see only from a particular place. The a priori from which the rest of Bakhtin's thought flows is the assumption that each of us occupies a situation in existence that, for the time we occupy such space, is ours and ours alone: what I see is not the same as what anyone else sees. Perception, how I "see" the world, is always refracted, as it were, through the optic of my uniqueness. Bakhtin calls this uniqueness of vision my "excess of seeing" insofar as it is defined by the ability I have to see things others do not.

He metaphorizes this condition in the encounter of two people looking at each other: "at each given moment, regardless of the position and the proximity to me of this other human being whom I am contemplating, I shall always see and know something that he, from his place outside and over against me, cannot see him-self: parts of his body that are inaccessible to his own gaze (his head, his face and its expression), the world behind his back, and a whole series of objects and relations, which in any of our mutual relations are accessible to me but not to him."

It will be obvious from this example that Bakhtin differs from many other thinkers now in fashion in that he does not begin by rejecting the intuitive sense of things held by most of his readers, who will feel that they are individuals precisely because—for better or worse—they are the keepers of their own uniqueness. We approach here the eye of the Bakhtinian needle: there are some, steeped in current orthodoxies about the death of the subject, who will sniff the brimstone of a thoroughly discredited existen-tialism in all this and pass on. Those with more patience will soon perceive, however, that the human subject defined in this way is not condemned to subjectivism, the prison-house not of language, but of the ego: a first implication of recognizing that we are all unique is the paradoxical result that we are *therefore* fated to need the other if we are to consummate our selves. Far from celebrating a solipsistic "I," Bakhtin posits uniqueness of the self as precisely that condition in which the necessity of the other is born.

But in order to perceive the fatedness of alterity, we must grasp the role of simultaneity in human perception. The "ever-present *excess* of my seeing, knowing, and possessing in relation to any other human being is founded in the uniqueness and irreplace-ability of my place in the world . . . only I—the one-and-only I—occupy in a given set of circumstances this particular place at this particular time; all other human beings are situated outside me." The dialogical paradox of this formulation is that *every* human being occupies such a determinate place in existence: we are all unique, but we are never alone. Bakhtin's enterprise is founded on the situatedness of perception and thus the uniqueness of the person, but it abhors all claims to oneness. It is not only the case that from my unique situation in space and time I am able to see things you do not: it is also—and simultaneously—the case that from the vantage of *your* uniqueness you can see things that *I* cannot.

Rimbaud was not the first to discover that *Je est un autre.* In virtually all traditional societies of the kind that used to be called "primitive," and in most previous stages of our own culture, the otherness of the self has been axiomatic. As a distinguished anthropologist has recently said, "The awareness that 'I is another' is an awareness only a self-interested age obsessively concerned with the autonomy of the individual would regard as paradoxically strange and counter-intuitive."[20]

Bakhtin's formulation of the self/other problem is especially insistent about the need always to negotiate relations among unique individuals. We not only interrogate each other, we interlocate each other, and it is the interlocative or dialogic self that is the subject of Bakhtin's architectonics. The interlocative self is one that can change places with another—that *must,* in fact, change places to see where it is. A logical implication of the fact that I can see things you cannot, and you can see things that I cannot, is that our excess of seeing is defined by a lack of seeing: my excess is your lack, and vice versa. If we wish to overcome this lack, we try to see what is there *together.* We must share each other's excess in order to overcome our mutual lack.

In his later work—most comprehensively in *Marxism and the Philosophy of Language* and the monograph on speech genres—Bakhtin will explore the complexities of reciprocity as they manifest themselves in the formal categories of quotation (in written language) and turn-taking (in spoken language). But in these early essays he explores the condition that such discursive markers manifest in the more abstract terms of time, space, and value.

The specific reciprocity Bakhtin explores in these essays is the interlocative relation of "I" to "another" in lived experience. The fatedness of the self/other distinction as it cuts across all human perception is the basis in these essays for Bakhtin's exploration of "author" to "hero." Aesthetics is the struggle to achieve a whole, but a whole that must first of all be understood as a purely positional or relative construct: the question must always be asked: by and for whom is this whole consummated? Second, such a whole is never a seamless oneness, insofar as it is always a negotiated relation between "two powers and . . . two interdependent systems of laws established by those powers; every constituent in the artistic whole is determined in terms of two value-systems, and in every constituent these two systems are in a state of intense and essential axiological interaction—they are the two paired powers that endow every constituent of the whole and the entire whole itself with the axiological weight of an event." These two powers instance themselves in manifold ways along several different axes, the most basic of which all inhere in features that define the difference between perception from the self and perception from the other.

These terms are currently freighted with so much excess ideological weight that it is difficult to approach any fresh use of them with innocent eyes; but it will perhaps help if we keep in mind that "self" and "other" are not for Bakhtin mysterious categories in which the delusion of immediacy slumbers. Rather, in his use they are the most comprehensive terms for modeling the heterogeneous factors that mandate perception as an event that can only be reciprocal. These essays consist largely of hierarchically ordered catalogues of the attributes that define differences between self-perception and other perception. We shall now hastily review the more important of these attributes, in order to give some idea of their scope and consequences.

III

First of all, a warning is in order. These attributes occur in pairs; to avoid the tedium of constantly repeating that each of them should not be treated as a neatly structuralizable binary opposition, I have not said as much every time. Therefore, it should be kept in mind throughout this survey that what is at issue is not the paired categories as such, but rather the reciprocal simultaneity that yokes each of these pairings in dialogue not only with each other, but with other categories as well.

Discussion has already begun—and these essays will add fuel to the argument—as to which particular -ism, of those that currently occupy our attention, may most readily accommodate Bakhtin's somewhat eccentric oeuvre. But he is indisputably Neo-Kantian at least in this: for all his reservations about "epistemologism," Bakhtin's major concern is to make sense—and use—of the individual subject's perception of the world. Architectonics is the key to Bakhtin's philosophical anthropology because at the heart of all human action is the problem of achieving wholeness of one kind or another out of parts of different kinds. But the basic difference is between self-perception and other perception. This division cannot be overcome; it can only be mediated. Architectonics is how particular differences flowing from this *Urdifferenz* are negotiated into specific relations. Bakhtin's account of architectonic activity is, thus, radically perspectival and situational.

Everything must be approached from the point of view of—point of view. And point of view is always situated. It must first of all be situated in a physical body that occupies time and space, but time and space as embodied in a particular human at a particular time and in a particular place: the main thrust of Bakhtin's whole architectonics is captured in his dictum that architectonics is the ordering of meaning; "as the intuitionally necessary, nonfortuitous disposition and integration of concrete, unique parts and moments into a consummated whole, [architectonics]— *can exist only around a given human being as a hero*" (emphasis added).

In other words, we always conceive the world intentionally, as it relates to the desires and purposes of human beings, without whose ends things would indeed be "in themselves." The subject as "I" literally embodies in a meaningful particularity that is *otherwise* a limitless generality, for thought in itself is always potential, and therefore not inherently limited: it contains "the energy of extraspatial and extratemporal infinitude, in relation to which anything concrete is merely fortuitous; a thought can provide no more than the direction for seeing something concrete, but a direction that is infinite, a direction incapable of *consummating* a whole." An important way in which the potential infinity of thought bears on the actual finitude of my being is the relation my consciousness bears to the moment of my birth and the moment of my death. As a body that was born into the world at a particular time and place, and that will pass away in an equally specific time and place, I literally embody a unique slice of time/ space. As the means, therefore, of particularizing the otherwise

infinitely general aspects of time/space, I become the instrument
for assigning specific value to abstract time and space. In themselves, they have no value, for value is always *for* someone:
"Strictly speaking, geography knows no far or near, here and
there. . . . And history, likewise, knows no past, present, and future. . . . The time of history is itself nonreversible, of course, but
within it all relations are fortuitous and relative (and reversible),
for there is no absolute center of value [of the kind provided by the
situatedness of the individual subject]."

But there is a problem here: as the precondition for architectonically ordering the world, there are important differences between the way I order my own place in it and the way I order the
place of others who are—from my place in existence—*not* the
same kind of center for specifying value that I am. While it is my
mortality that permits me to embody time and space as particular
values, the activity that is my "self" works as if it were co-termi-
nous with consciousness, which—insofar as it comes after birth
and expires before death—means it is manifested as a perpetual
present, without beginning or end. The other, however, I perceive
as limited in time: I can see his beginning and end, and even the
repeatable rhythms of behavior that fix him as an activity identical with his physical body. So, at least, it manifests itself to me;
not only temporally, but spatially I perceive those who are not me
in completely different terms. I see the world from a "horizon":
the world gives itself as immediately around me, as circumscribed
by the unique angle of my vision, as a surrounding full of specific
meanings determined by my own ends. The other, however, I see
as existing in an "environment": the world is the same for him as
it is for others, for it is not conditioned by the uniqueness of his
intentionality (as is my horizon). The other is in the world at
large, including all other beings and things, while I exist in a
world that enfolds me in a unique relation to my ends and is thus
experienced as having an intimacy and reality different from that
of the "environment" in which others are consummated as finite
entities.

In its own terms, my self is not reducible to the temporal or
spatial restraints that make consummation of the other possible.
From itself, in its own terms, it cannot be consummated. Yet it
must be, for only that which is consummated can be perceived.
Long before Sartre, but with overtones that (as we shall see) nevertheless are *post*-Sartrean, Bakhtin makes use of terms we now as-

sociate with *Being and Nothingness* (*pour-soi, pour-les-autres,* etc.), as in his discussion of how the self is forced to perceive itself in the categories of the other. I clothe my inner body, says Bakhtin, in the time, space, and values that are the same I use for others, but behind the I-for-others that results from such appropriation, my I-for-myself, as the enabling condition of my existence, continues to act as the seat of perception and ground of action, and thus in a time/space that is always open, so long as I consciously inhabit the site of its unique place in existence.

In both cases, notice, I consummate—or give finished form to—another. It is this fact that induces Bakhtin to make one of his bolder hypotheses: to treat the activity of perception as the structure of authoring. I give shape *both* to others and to my self as an author gives shape to his heroes. As Bakhtin began his career by announcing, life is not art, and art is not life, but the two cannot be separated from each other. Unlike Plato in the "Phaedrus" and Paul Ricoeur in a number of influential essays treating meaningful action as a text,[21] Bakhtin does not believe writing rescues the event from its spatial limitations in a particular site or its temporal limitations in mere memory. The textualization that the work of art accomplishes needs *itself* to be rescued from the sterility and fixity of its formal manifestation: it is as an "event that we must understand and know the work of art," that is, as "an effective moment in the unitary and unique event of being, and not as a thing—an object of purely theoretical cognition devoid of the validity or force of an event, devoid of any weight with respect to value." Long before Derrida's *Of Grammatology,* Bakhtin was working against the ideology of literacy.

The activity of shaping is not the same operation in lived experience as it is in more mediated expressions. But both activities are driven by a perceptual mandate to consummate. It is aspects of the dialogic need to give form to experience that are shared with the need to give life to forms, that account for the urgency Bakhtin assigns aesthetics in these essays. The relation of author and hero in a literary text, when re- or co-authored by readers, that is, when appropriated by them as the tensile relation of an "I" to another, serves as a particularly clear-cut paradigm of what Bakhtin means by the architectonics of answerability: for I give life to the text by seeking to find the appropriate balance of relations (architectonics as aesthetics) between author and hero in the lived experience of my reading. "Every word in narrative

literature expresses a reaction to another reaction, the author's reaction to the reaction of the hero; that is, every concept, image,
and object lives on two planes, is rendered meaningful in two
value-contexts—in the context of the hero and in that of the author." It is the reader's reaction to reactions in the work of art that
transforms a text into an event by giving it meaning.

It is the meaning or, in other words, the particular configuration of time, space, and values that I construct through architectonically shaping relations between author/hero as self/other—as
they are both other to myself as reader—for which I, in the
unique place I occupy in existence, am answerable. The author,
insofar as he becomes in such a reading a subject, is—like all
other subjects—not an identity, that is, not coincidental with the
biological figure whose name appears in the slot conventionally
reserved for authors. He is the author only in the event of the artwork—only as he can be perceived or shown to be a function of
the relation between author and hero in the event of a particular
reader's reading (co-authoring) of that particular text. There are, of
course, relations between the formal elements of the text—de-
ployment of pronouns, the tense and aspect of verbs, discursive
style of dialogue—and the time, place, and historically instanced
writer involved in the text's first production (which was already a
reading), but these are highly mediated and of an extraordinary
complexity. Since all texts are conceived by Bakhtin to be utterances, and all utterances are linked to each other in the great het-
eroglot dialogue of dialogues constituted by all that has been said
and all that will be said in history, the "origin" of a text is always
only another link in the long chain of its possible transmissions.

IV

The general theory of authoring proposed by Bakhtin in these essays raises new possibilities for perceiving Bakhtin himself as an
author. If we take these early essays of Bakhtin seriously, we ourselves are called upon to consummate, or co-author, his work.
And in order to do so, we are compelled to treat him as a character
or—again in his sense of the word—to treat him as a hero—in
other words, as a subject who is aesthetically consummated by
another: some way must be found to perceive wholeness amidst
the variety of his several works. The difficulty of doing so is com-

pounded by the equally strict Bakhtinian expectation that no whole should homogenize the variety of its parts—it should not, in other words, reduce their heteroglossia to the level of a mono-logue. The dual asymmetry of this demand is not a double bind, nor is it a binary opposition—it is the complex form of simul-taneity not only at the heart of Bakhtin's argument in these es-says, but in the circling, spiraling style of the particular form that argument assumes. The paradox that obssesses Bakhtin here is one that his readers cannot avoid: we must *do* what these essays are *about*. In other words, if we read Bakhtin, we must find a way to generalize his own particularity.

There are at least three directions this undertaking might as-sume: to specify more precisely the particular role of Bakhtin in the "Bakhtin circle"; to understand Bakhtin's relation to other thinkers in the past who have wrestled with some of the same issues he engages; and, finally, to place him in relation to current work on the topics he explores. An introductory essay is not the appropriate place to pursue any of these itineraries very far, but an attempt will be made to indicate what the outlines, at least, for further work in the first two of these directions might be. I shall conclude this essay by suggesting why I avoid the temptation of seeking to formulate a place for Bakhtin in current theory. Suffice it at this point to say that to do so would be to author inevitable inaccuracies: insofar as Bakhtin is still a "living" figure, any statement of his current status is ineluctably a gesture toward a future that cannot be known from the place of contemporaneity.

These early works cannot help but add fuel to the debate about Bakhtin's role in those texts claimed by some to be his that were published under the names of his friends Ivan Kanaev, Pavel Med-vedev, and Valentin Voloshinov. The debate has increasingly be-come a sport only for the initiated, requiring a highly detailed knowledge of the whole Bakhtinian canon, plus an immersion in the lives and worlds of the men involved.[22] Arguments for the sole authorship of Medvedev and Voloshinov based on considerations of style will be strengthened by patent disparities between these early philosophical texts and the later "deuterocanonical" works. Others will find fresh cause for their belief in Bakhtin's major role in the disputed texts' composition. This is not the place to re-hearse arguments for both sides, but any position one assumes now will have to take into consideration Bakhtin's complex the-ory of authorship as it is laid out in these essays. I myself continue to believe Bakhtin played the major role in such texts as *The Formal Method* and *Marxism and the Philosophy of Language*, adopting Medvedev and Voloshinov as co-authoring others (in the sense in which he uses that term in "Author and Hero in Aesthetic Activity") who permitted him to gain a position of outsideness on the subjects treated, a transgredience he would not have achieved without them.

Other thinkers Bakhtin engages in these essays have various degrees of importance in his later work. The concern here for obscure aestheticians of expressionism will in later texts be translated into more interesting attacks on specific versions of idealist ideologies, such as his criticisms of Vossler and (especially) Saussure. Although the Marburg school will become less and less important for Bakhtin in later years, Cohen's emphasis on Kant's distinction between what is given and what is created will play a role in Bakhtin's work until the end.[23]

Another philosopher who figures prominently in these essays and who will continue to shape Bakhtin's thinking is Bergson. Bakhtin's emphasis here on the body, with his very important distinction between "inner" and "outer" body, cannot be understood without reference to the concept of body in Bergson, particularly in *Matter and Memory* (1896). Bergson is important because of his general project of seeking to retrieve for philosophy the problem of mind/body relations that in the waning years of the last century was falling into the hands of the psychologists—indeed, into the hands of many of the same psychologists against whom Bakhtin, too, will take arms. Bergson's attempt to think the materiality of the human body as a philosophical problem is important for Bakhtin in the degree to which it seeks to overcome Cartesian dualism through a series of stratagems that we can now recognize as dialogic. On the one hand, Bergson recognizes that the body is first of all an object among other objects; thus, it may serve as the orientation point for making judgments about the location of things: "the size, shape, even the color of external objects is modified according as my body approaches or recedes from them; that the strength of an odor, the intensity of a sound, increases or diminishes with distance; finally, that this very distance represents, above all, the measure in which surrounding bodies are insured, in some sort, against the immediate action of my body . . . [images of external objects] take rank in an order corresponding to the growing or decreasing powers of my body."[24]

The physical body is important, then, as occupying a unique place in existence. But the sheer physicality of my body cannot be understood as the locus of my existence without *also* taking into account the fact that as a living organism I must, whether I will it or not, pay *attention to life*.[25] I cannot be indifferent to my surroundings. Thus, the body is best understood as the center of my actions. Bergson goes so far as to define psychosis not as "an inward disorder, a disease of the personality," but as precisely "the breaking of the tie which binds this psychic life to its motor accompaniment, a weakening or impairing of our attention to outward life" (*Matter and Memory*, pp. xvii–xix). But insofar as my body is the center of *action* (what Bakhtin calls a deed), "it cannot give birth to a representation" (*Matter and Memory*, p. 5). The body, then, is dependent on activity *other* than its purely physical functions (as they are usually understood, at any rate), for shaping the world into coherent images. A total description of an act would have to include a body, objects (or images of objects) external to it, and *a change in the relations* between the body and the other images. Furthermore, "I see plainly how external images influence the image that I call my body: they transmit movement to it. And I also see how this body influences external images: it gives back movement to them" (*Matter and Memory*, p. 5). The mind (or soul, as Bergson calls it) plays a role in this activity since a judgment must be made first of all about what is influencing what—is it my body that opens the door, or does the door get pushed open knocking me down? Second, and more importantly, of course, once the brute direction of influence is decided, the *effects* of such influence must be evaluated. In this sense the body is but a privileged image, providing for the exercise of choice among possible reactions.

But the body is an image that *is* after all privileged, and Bakhtin attempts in these essays to answer why it should be so. Although close to Bergson in many ways, Bakhtin is dissimilar in the emphasis he assigns to different aspects of the same problem. Thus, Bakhtin concentrates less on body/mind oppositions (for him, they are less oppositions than differing stages of a continuum), preferring rather to highlight the self/other distinctions in which he sees the body's privilege residing. The emphasis on otherness in these essays puts Bakhtin squarely into the tradition of much modern thought. Even an incomplete list of thinkers who have dealt with the problem would have to include minimally Edmund

Husserl,[26] Max Scheler,[27] Maurice Merleau-Ponty,[28] and Jacques Lacan.[29] Three figures of particular importance in understanding Bakhtin's place in this tradition are Martin Buber, Jean-Paul Sartre, and Martin Heidegger. The connection with Buber has already received some attention,[30] so I shall not dwell on it here, except to say that both Buber and Bakhtin owe an obvious debt to Hermann Cohen's meditation on the otherness of God.[31] It is equally obvious that both insist on the ethical need to treat the other person not as "you" but as a "thou." But both Cohen (at least in his last phase, after his move to Berlin in 1912, when he was working on *The Religion of Reason Out of the Sources of Judaism*) and Buber rely heavily on Torah and Jewish midrashic tradition for their inspiration and authority. This context makes for a number of inevitable differences between them and Bakhtin's essentially Russian Orthodox frame of reference when he deals with matters that have occupied religious thinkers of the past. Of course, the whole emphasis on architectonics and aesthetics in these early Bakhtin essays is quite different in its implications from anything in Cohen or Buber.

We know that Bakhtin had read Buber by the time he came to write these early essays. But two thinkers whose work he could not have known in the years he was writing them would seem to bear a much closer relation to the concerns of these essays than does Buber. Heidegger's *Being and Time* was published only in 1927, eight years after the last of the pieces included in this anthology, and Sartre's *Being and Nothingness* did not appear until 1943, two decades after Bakhtin had completed these essays. Yet the surface similarities between the main outlines of Bakhtin's initial project and the Heidegger and Sartre books are striking, extending in some cases even to the same terminology. Before surveying some of those parallels, it will perhaps be useful to ask why they should be there at all—despite the fact that, at the time he was working on these essays, Bakhtin could not possibly have read the relevant texts by either Heidegger or Sartre, since neither had yet been published. The beginnings of an answer are to be found, I believe, in the urgent sense of a general crisis animating the work of each of these men, and the specific means each chose to meet that crisis. Bakhtin is working in the immediate aftermath of World War I and the Bolshevik Revolution; Heidegger writes his book in the shadow of the same war and during the extended political and economic anxiety we call the Weimar Republic; and Sartre finishes his masterpiece during the Nazi occupation of France. In addition, each thinker was unusually sensitive to the new challenges to metaphysics raised by contemporary science and technology. Each was convinced that there could no longer be any question of doing philosophical work as usual.

What disturbed these three thinkers (among others, of course) was the combined negative effect that events in their lifetime were having on traditional ideas about the nature of individual human existence. In ancient Greek or later Christian versions of the soul, as well as in secular Enlightenment ideas about the exalted "nature of Man," a certain importance, if not always dignity, attached to human existence. But any privilege that might still have clung to being human was swept away after the sheer indiscriminateness of the military slaughter that went on from 1914 to 1918, to say nothing (in the case of Sartre) of the radical dehumanization dramatized in Hitler's death camps and torture cellars. The effects of these horrors can be traced in the urgency with which Bakhtin, Heidegger, and Sartre felt they had to do philosophy in a different way. They sought to avoid the abstractness and the exclusive dependence on rationality that had characterized Western metaphysics, which seemed to have very little to do with the world as they found it.

The specific way they chose to go about the task results in some dramatic similarities among them: each sought to rethink the particularity of the individual human subject outside traditional categories for doing so. The self/other relation as it is experienced in the immediacy of unique lives becomes the subject of their investigation, much as truth, justice, and the good had been the subject of earlier thinkers. The self/other relation is a topic whose pursuit has built into it a certain number of ineluctable moves, such as an analysis of the self's relation to a body, the problem of mirror images, or a phenomenology of the gaze. All these topics raise questions about the perception of time and space. In these essays (and at this level of generality), Bakhtin can be observed going through precisely these moves, as, later, Heidegger and Sartre will. Of course, there are considerable differences among the three, and we shall also look at these as we briefly survey their work in relation to each other.

Heidegger's goal of getting at Being through the particular kind of being that human existence constitutes led him to reject Kantian transcendental categories for *existentials*, or the determinants of Being in lived experience. One direction that further work on relations between Bakhtin and Heidegger might well take would be to conceive the various constituents of Bakhtin's architectonics, such as consummated/unconsummated, or inner/ outer bodies, as existentials in the Heideggerian sense. Heidegger's definition of the individual human as *Dasein* is predicated on the assumption that being-there means being-in-the-world, which is always a being-with. Like Bakhtin, Heidegger emphasizes worldliness, and the degree to which self-knowledge comes through others: "Knowing oneself [*Sichkennen*] is grounded in Being-with, which understands primordially",[32] in his "Being-there-too" (*Auch-da-sein*) we have an almost precise parallel with Bakhtin's "And-I-also am" (*i ja esm'*). Heidegger's preoccupation with the time-drenched nature of mortality—the span between birth and death in a particular being-there—as the basis for uncovering meaning in human existence has its analogue in Bakhtin as well.

In discussing the value of time and space, Bakhtin says, "Once you annihilate the moment constituted by the life of a mortal human being, the axiological light of all rhythmic and formal moments will be extinguished. The point here is not, of course, the mathematically determinate duration of a human life, for that duration could be shorter or longer; the only important thing is that a life and its horizon have terminal limits—birth and death. It is only the presence of these terminal points, along with everything conditioned by them, that creates the emotional-volitional tonality of time's passage in a circumscribed life . . . even eternity and limitlessness acquire their axiological meaning only in correlation with a life that is determined."

Parallels between terms used by both thinkers such as "proximity," "on-handness," and many others will be clear enough. But such similarities should not mask differences between the two that are fundamental. The first of these would have to be the emphasis each attaches to embodiment. Heidegger's focus on human existence is motivated by his stated intention to uncover the nature of Being. Having exposed a local instance of being in *Being and Time*, he proposed in the follow-up volume to engage Being more globally. That follow-up volume, of course, was famously never written. Some of the force of Bakhtin's argument against theory *as such* might well be brought to bear on Heidegger's particular strategy of using human existence as a means to theorize Being.

Bakhtin's own course is the reverse of this: he begins with a general account of time, space, and value in human experience, but spends the rest of his life seeking to specify these existentials in studies of particular instances. This turn is perhaps dictated by the more restricted focus of Bakhtin's work in its first stage when compared with early Heidegger: the latter opens his career as a seeker after the ontic; by contrast, even in his most technically "philosophical" pieces, Bakhtin for better or worse does not rise to that level of concern. His architectonics does engage questions of time, space, and value, but there is never any presupposition of an underlying stratum of Being prior to the human experience of them.

There are significant and fairly obvious parallels between these essays and Sartre's *Being and Nothingness*. The most important of these would once again be the general emphasis on being in the world, the role of bodies,[33] the determining power of the other's gaze, and the distinction between being-for-myself and being-for-others. The particular way Sartre conceives consciousness as an emptiness that must be filled,[34] and identity as a task that must be performed, constitutes a further similarity to Bakhtin's early work. But once again, the overarching aim of Sartre's undertaking in *Being and Nothingness*, which may roughly be stated as the attempt to understand the difference between people (who may be *for themselves*) and things (which are only *for others*), makes for differences as well. Primary among these would be the underlying assumption of privilege that Sartre assigns to the in-itselfness of things: Sartre's conscious subject knows himself only as a constantly unrealized project, and others only as a constraint on his own (potential) freedom. The Sartrean subject looks suspiciously like Hegel's *Geist,* insofar as both seek an end to division and struggle and long for the stillness that is inherent in things that are unburdened by the demands of consciousness. As his novel *Nausea* makes clear, Sartre's subject is sick because he desires the condition of being a god, having the attributes *both* of a for-itself and of an in-itself. In Bakhtin, there are no things in themselves, no possibility of an actual object understood as an it-itself; thus, the dialogic subject, existing only in a world of consciousness, is free to perceive others not as a constraint, but as a possibility: others are neither hell nor heaven, but the necessary condition for both.

As a result of Sartre's adversative definition of the other, he had the greatest difficulty in forging a politics, particularly the theory of collective social action to which his last work was devoted.[35] While there is perhaps a greater opening toward such an enterprise in Bakhtin's less restricted version of the other, the lack of a more carefully considered treatment of conflict and power relations in self/other dealings is something of a limitation in Bakhtin's thought as well, particularly in these early works, in which questions of class and gender distinctions are also absent.

V

Perhaps, therefore, the most significant thinker with whom Bakhtin's name has been coupled might still prove to be Karl Marx. The difficulty of conceiving relations between the two are notorious. It is well known that Bakhtin was, like his hero Dostoevsky, a very complicated sort of Christian—as these essays make more manifest than any of his other writings. We now know that the official reason given for Bakhtin's arrest in 1929 was his membership in Voskresenie (Resurrection), an organization of intellectuals who sought to synthesize the principles of Christianity and Marxism. However, in the years just after the revolution, he opposed Bolshevik speakers in public debate on several issues of the day. Yet, in some of the books published under his own name (such as his Dostoevsky monograph), he invokes Marx at some critical points in his argument. In the books published under the names of Medvedev and Voloshinov, Marxism is not only invoked: claims of strengthening or even expanding the scope of Marxist analysis are made. The "authorship question" is thus intertwined with the "Marx question."[36]

The problem is complicated by the fact that these essays—more than any of his other published works—manifest not only Bakhtin's immersion in West European philosophy, but his situatedness in Christian tradition as well. In these early essays, those principles are complicated by a vocabulary that derives not only from philosophy, but from religion. But Bakhtin's relation to the philosophy of religion (which is not the same thing as religion itself) is as idiosyncratic as his relation to a theory of social action. Unlike theology, which might deal with "souls," Bakhtin deals with "the *problem* of the soul." The soul is, of course, one of Christian theology's basic categories; so it is difficult to conceive what Christians will make of Bakhtin's claim that—from the point of view of methodology—the soul has nothing to do with ethics or psychology; in fact, "in my relationship to myself, I have nothing to do with the soul." Rather, "The problem of the soul, from a methodological standpoint, is a problem in aesthetics."

This conclusion will seem less startling if we remember that aesthetics has its own shade of meaning in Bakhtin. It is a key concept in these essays, discussed at more length below. Suffice it at this point that, for Bakhtin, aesthetics is a form of embodying lived experience, for consummating action so that it may have the meaningfulness of an event: "for everything that is aesthetically valid encompasses not a void, but the persistent . . . directedness to meaning on the part of an *act-performing life.*" Or again: "before assuming a purely aesthetic position in relation to the hero and his world, an author must assume a lived-life position, a purely cognitive-ethical position."

With the publication of these essays, then, the strategies by which Bakhtin might be appropriated to Marxism are complicated. For those who would assimilate Bakhtin to—as well as for those who would separate him from—Marxist thought, the least problematic strategy would seem to be to invoke Bakhtin through the agency of a "Bakhtin circle" exclusively; to assume, in other words, that only those texts published under the names of Medvedev and Voloshinov that are *self-proclaimedly* Marxist (and, it can be argued, were not written by Bakhtin) may be incorporated into an authentic Marxist framework.

But for those who *do* accept Bakhtin's major role in the disputed texts' composition, things are not quite so simple—but neither is the resulting contribution to Marxist thought, which might prove to be more useful and interesting than any deriving from the first strategy. Separating a Marxist Voloshinov or Medvedev from a non-Marxist Bakhtin (who, after all, is admitted by all parties to be the major theorist of the three) is ultimately less convincing than to assume a role for them all. These essays open new possibilities for rethinking Bakhtin's relation to Marx. It can now be argued that Bakhtin himself was wrestling with many of the same questions that preoccupied Marx, as these early texts make clear.

This is a possibility that cannot be explored at proper length in an introductory essay. But a dialogue between Bakhtin and Marx might prove to be of the greatest value: seeing one in the light of the other may, for instance, lead to a better understanding of a Bakhtinian social theory that is otherwise only implicit. Conversely, Bakhtin may help to provide what has often felt to be lacking in Marx: a more complex theory of the individual subject in such otherwise collectivist phenomena as class struggle. A beginning might be made in the recognition that Bakhtin and Marx are both seeking to understand the complexities of "value," "exchange," and "otherness" (in particular, various forms of alienation).

The all-pervasiveness of axiology, a theory of values, is self-evident in these essays. In Bakhtin's philosophical anthropology, to be human is *to mean.* Human being is the production of meaning, where meaning is further understood to come about as the articulation of values. In *Capital,* Marx's dismissal of "vulgar economists" is based on his argument that they have not perceived the deep structure of social relations among people engaged in production. For Marx, value always shows "a relation between persons as expressed as a relation between things."[37] It is at the level of social relations that the true meaning of value and exchange must be sought, the level that underlies the surface phenomena of commodities and prices that only formally manifest relations among people.

The significance of understanding Marxist value in these terms is that doing so illuminates a like undertaking in Bakhtin, who is also trying to come to grips with the categories of value and exchange at a level more essential than their surface manifestation. The general categories dominating Bakhtin's early work—time/space, self/other, consummated/unconsummated—are the formal means by which specific values get expressed. Dialogue, in Bakhtin's conception of it, is a way to conceive nonidentity; in other words, it is a recognition of the constant need for exchange—and exchange is fueled by differences in value. It is in seeking to work through the complexities of such issues that the utility of perceiving early Bakhtin through the optic of his later work—and vice versa—makes itself felt. For instance, the centrality of the self/other distinction in these early essays will make some readers uneasy. On the other hand, otherwise sympathetic readers of *Marxism and the Philosophy of Language* have wondered why Bakhtin/Voloshinov spent so much time (and at such a structurally critical point in the text) on the topic of quotation, the formal means by which we set off our own speech from that of others. Much effort is expended discriminating among Lorch's concept of *erlebte Rede*, Lerch's *uneigentliche direkte Rede*, and the more traditional *style indirect libre*. But in light of Bakhtin's total oeuvre, it seems clear that his lifelong preoccupation with the question "who is talking" is his specific way of intervening in ongoing debates about the subject. How we set off words in the category of *direct speech*—a term that, after Bakhtin, must always have a certain irony about it—from the category of *indirect speech* is the defining formal gesture by which we set ourselves off from others.

The movement from Bakhtin's analysis of self/other relations in these early essays to his meditation on the social consequences of speech relations (i.e., quotational and turn-taking strategies) in his later work reveals two more areas of concern he shares with Marx: a quest for the deep structure of work and an attempt to grasp the relation to value of physical labor. In order for this claim to have any meaning, a few words are in order about Bakhtin's dialogically conceived notion of knowledge as a form of quotation and, therefore, of understanding as a form of labor.

Dialogism conceives knowing as the *effort* of understanding, as "the active reception of speech of the other" (*aktivnoe vosprijatie chuzhoj rechi*," *Marxism and the Philosophy of Language*, p. 115; Eng. p. 117). The adjective is all-important here: "*active* reception" means that quoting is never simply mechanical repetition, but constitutes *work*—it is a labor. A new book by James Lynch, director of the Psychophysiological Laboratory at the University of Maryland's medical school, provides evidence that calling dialogue "work" is not just a metaphor (or not only a metaphor): in a series of imaginative experiments, Lynch has shown a direct corollary between blood pressure levels and the activities of talking and listening. Since 1904, when the modern technique of measuring blood pressure was developed, physicians have insisted their patients *not talk* while being tested, because talking had the effect of raising "normal" levels. Lynch recognized that "normal" blood pressure in this equation simply meant those levels that were recorded while the patient was "not communicating"; what interested him was transgression of what most doctors considered "normal" effects—the ways in which the act of verbal communication created different effects in the cardiovascular system.

With the exception of Pavlov, who in his last years posited a relation between the motivated signs of language and the signals of the human body's electrochemical system, Lynch seems to have been the first scientist to recognize that "no other hydraulic or hydrostatic system known to physics [is] influenced by simple conversations."[38]

That *talk* should have effects on the working of the body's machinery is a discovery having social implications that go beyond whatever general significance they might have for the mind/body problem: talking alters a "person's relationship to the social environment in a way quite different from when one [is] silent in the same environment."[39] What is significant about this apparent truism is that it indicates the power of speech to effect a bond between entities that are separated in every other way. Homeostasis, as the governor of systems whose totality represents the inner workings of each single organism, would seem to be the most powerful indicator of the degree to which we are all cut off from each other within our somatic monads. When my hand is cut, my body bleeds but yours does not, therefore we say "I" am the subject of the wound. It is not surprising, therefore, that the internal working of the individual body has often been the ground on which traditional ideologies of unique selfhood have been erected.

The discovery that talking has homeostatic effects registered in the individual body has important implications as well for attempts to conceive the speaking subject; the speaker may not "possess" the meaning of his words, but he is at the very least in a relation to those words that is not shared by others who do not at that moment experience the work of their production. Conceiving understanding as a form of quotation implies that meaning is always rented. The physiological effects of the work of talk register where, at any particular moment, energy in the chain of communication is concentrated: one is responsible for the kinetic as well as semantic effect of words.

What is now being suspected by American scientists was long ago taken as an a priori by Russian philosophers. Bakhtin's particular contribution to these developments lies in the degree to which he insists that the physical labor of communication is the particular effort to construct conceptual simultaneities. He goes much further than psychophysiologists in defining the power of language to bridge gaps, for in *Marxism and the Philosophy of Language* he sees talk as animating simultaneity both within and *between* organisms. Moreover, as opposed to a scientist such as Lynch, Bakhtin assumes talk is within them all the time: there is, in other words, never any "silence," or at least there is none in the sense Lynch intends when he invokes the word. There may be a difference between the cardiovascular response of someone who is talking, in the sense of producing sound waves, and someone who is not talking, in the sense of *not* producing sound waves. But that difference is one of different *degrees* of speech participation, not an absolute cutoff between speech and nonspeech. Consciousness is an activity, the deed of actively responding to others' speech both in listening and in talking. The physiological changes recorded by Lynch may be interpreted not as registering an absolute difference between "talkers" and "nontalkers," but rather as registering differences between levels of otherness in language, kinetic distinctions between words of the other requiring less effort from the body and words we seek to mark as our own requiring more effort: "self," in the sense of *alter* is a project requiring work.

From the perspective of dialogism, the mercury the scientist sees rising in the manometer and the increased speed of the pulse heard through a stethoscope may be said to render palpable the labor not just of talk, but of quotation. Bakhtin insists that quotation is labor, for we cannot transmit another's words, either to another or to ourselves, without in some way working on them. The question "who is talking" with regard to any utterance is also the question "how many are talking?" And since dialogism assumes all words are double-voiced, the answer is always—at least—two: for we call forth, and are ourselves summoned by, the words of others, which we make our own (always in dialogism a relative term) through borders we build around them. The principles governing structures that we erect to set off "our" words from the words of others constitute the architectonics of answerability.

There is, then, in Bakhtin's aesthetic an emphasis on the primacy of lived experience in all its bewildering specificity. It is an emphasis that accords with the most classical Marxist emphasis on the priority of historical experience vis-à-vis all ideational representations of it, as in the programmatic statement of Marx and Engels themselves in *The German Ideology:* "The production of notions, ideas, and consciousness is from the beginning directly interwoven with the material activity and material intercourse of human beings, the language of real life."[40]

If there is to be any productive cross-fertilization between Bakhtin and Marx, it would now seem to have to assume the form of inscribing a Marxist emphasis on politics, economics, and social theory into dialogism's obsession with the personhood of individuals and the metalinguistics in which utterance is a deed. With these essays, at least the tools for such a labor become available.

VI

In the last five years of his life, Bakhtin began to fill his notebooks with sketches for articles on the question of author and hero, self and other, and the relation of art to life. He returned, in other words, to the same subjects that had engaged him in these fragments from his youth. But in Bakhtin's conception of things, there can be no repetition as such: texts, insofar as they are not natural signs, such as fingerprints, are utterances and therefore links in the great chain of speech communication. Their appropriation by another is a new event.

I shall not conclude by attempting to suggest what the entrance of these texts into current discussion might portend, for such an "analysis usually fusses about in the narrow space of small time, that is, in the space of the present day and the recent past and the imaginable—desired or frightening—future . . . there is no understanding of evaluative nonpredetermination, unexpectedness, as it were, 'surprisingness,' absolute innovation, miracle . . ."[41] What can be said is that the texts in this new anthology constitute a particularly significant event, because with them we have for the first time something like a complete Bakhtin, a whole utterance, as it were. Readers may now enter into dialogue with Bakhtin (even to dispute him) at the higher level of a second consciousness, that is, with "the consciousness of the person who understands and responds: herein lies a potential infinity of responses, languages, codes. Infinity against infinity."[42]

Notes

1. The story is unfortunately apocryphal. It was current during Lewis Carroll's lifetime, driving the author in a note appended to the preface of his *Symbolic Logic* (1896) to deny "such an absolute fiction." See Roger

Lancelyn Green's revision of *The Lewis Carroll Handbook,* by Sidney Herbert Williams and Falconer Madan; further revised by Denis Crutch (Folkestone, England: Dawson, 1979). p. 182.

2. All have been published by the University of Texas Press, Austin and London. The first was *The Dialogic Imagination: Four Essays by M. M. Bakhtin,* ed. Michael Holquist, trans. Caryl Emerson and Michael Holquist, 1981. The second was *Speech Genres and Other Late Essays,* ed. Caryl Emerson and Michael Holquist, trans. Vern McGee, 1987.

3. One indication of the school's current obscurity is that relatively little attention is paid to it: there is really no good synthetic or historical account covering the different subgroups of Neo-Kantians, so anyone interested in pursuing relations between them and Bakhtin is compelled to go through the (mostly untranslated) works of such thinkers as Hermann Cohen or Paul Natorp.

4. See Katerina Clark and Michael Holquist, "The Influence of Kant in the Early Work of M. M. Bakhtin," *Literary Theory and Criticism (Festschrift for René Wellek),* ed. Joseph P. Strelka (Bern: Peter Lang, 1984), pp. 299–313.

5. Paul Natorp and Ernst Cassirer are the other leading members of the school, although it could be argued that Cassirer's work after the twenties sets him apart in significant ways from basic "Marburgian" tenets. But he never abandoned the Marburgian obsession with the precise sciences of physics and mathematics.

6. V. I. Lenin, *Materializm i empirokritisizm,* in *Polnoe sobranie sochinenij* (Moscow: Nauka, 1947), vol. 18, pp. 326–327.

7. Cf. his *Logik der reinen Erkenntnis* (Berlin: B. Cassirer, 1902).

8. *Voprosy literatury,* no. 6 (1977), 307–308. It was reprinted in subsequent anthologies of Bakhtin's works in 1979 and 1986.

9. In the 1975 anthology of Bakhtin's works, *Voprosy literatury i estetiki* (Moscow: Khudozhestvennaja literatura, 1975), pp. 6–71. Also included in the 1986 anthology, *Literaturno-kriticheskie stat'i* (Moscow: Khudozhestvennaja literatura, 1986), pp. 26–89.

10. In *Filosofija i sociologija nauki i texniki: Ezhegodnik, 1984–1985,* pp. 80–138.

11. In *Estetiki slovesnogo tvorchestva.*

12. Given Bakhtin's passionate insistence on particularity, an "-ism" invoked to name his own achievement must have a certain awkwardness about it. Nevertheless, now that we have something approaching a Bakhtinian canon or oeuvre, it would seem useful to have a comprehensive term to name the principles that hold together Bakhtin's heterogeneous studies. Given the importance dialogue has in Bakhtin's thought, it is not surprising that "dialogism" is emerging as the term most likely to provide the needed synthesis.

13. Nevertheless, when Vadim Kozhinov went back to Mordovia in 1972 in order to reclaim the manuscripts, he was horrified to find them

moldering away among the rats in a Saransk lumber room. Several pages of these unfinished fragments, according to Bakhtin's own pagination, were missing, compounding the difficulty of "consummating" them as texts. A small group of devoted young people worked for a long time to decipher the notebooks and prepare typed manuscripts from them: anyone interested in Bakhtin owes a great debt to S. M. Aleksandrov, G. S. Bernstein, and, above all, L. V. Deryugina.

14. M. M. Bakhtin, *Literaturno-kriticheskie stat'i*, ed. S. G. Bocharov, V. V. Kozhinov (Moscow: Khudozhestvennaja literatura, 1986), p. 531.

15. M. M. Bakhtin, "K filosofii postupka," p. 122.

16. "The Problem of Speech Genres," in *Speech Genres and Other Late Essays*, p. 201.

17. M. M. Bakhtin, "K filosofii postupka," p. 86.

18. "Forms of Time and the Chronotape in the Novel," in *The Dialogic Imagination*, p. 85.

19. Bakhtin's reservations about Structuralism, with its emphasis on mechanical constructs, are apparent in two later essays, "The Problem of the Text in Linguistics, Philosophy, and Other Human Sciences," and "Answer to a Question from the Editors of *Novyj Mir*," both translated in *Speech Genres and Other Late Essays*.

20. James Fernandez, "Exploded Worlds—Text as a Metaphor for Ethnography (and Vice Versa)," *Dialectical Anthropology* 10 (1985), 23.

21. Paul Ricoeur, "The Model of the Text: Meaningful Action Considered as a Text," *Social Research* 11/2 (1971), 529–562; and "Metaphor and the Main Problem of Hermeneutics," *New Literary History*, 6/1 (1974), 95–110.

22. For the latest (but certainly not the last) exchange in this debate, which—while I myself still accept Bakhtin's major role—is probably ultimately unanswerable in any form that will definitively meet the objections of both sides, see the forum in *Slavic and East European Journal* 30/1 (Spring 1986): 96–102. References to other articles devoted to the debate are also to be found in the forum.

23. For more extended treatment of Bakhtin's relation to Neo-Kantianism, see Clark and Holquist, "The Influence of Kant in the Early Work of M. M. Bakhtin," pp. 299–313.

24. Henri Bergson, *Matter and Memory*, trans. Nancy Margaret Paul and W. Scott Palmer (London: George Allen and Unwin, 1911), p. 6.

25. For a more elaborate account of Bakhtin's relation to Bergson as Bakhtin himself conceived it, see the articles on Vitalism he wrote under the name of his friend Ivan Kanaev: I. I. Kanaev, "Sovremennyj vitalizm," *Chelovek i priroda* (1926), I: 33–42; II: 9–23.

26. Especially in those parts of the *Cartesian Meditations* where Husserl concerns himself with the danger of his phenomenological subject devolving into solipsism, leading him to meditate on the otherness of others. Cf. Husserl's insistence on the "original pairing" of ego and alter

ego (Edmund Husserl, *Cartesian Meditations: An Introduction to Phenomenology*, trans. Dorion Cairns [The Hague: Martinus Nijhoff, 1960], pp. 91–113, esp. p. 112, and those parts of the *Meditations* where he concentrates on the different experience of being embodied in me and in the other, esp. pp. 117–123).

27. Scheler's work on sympathy is the relevant text here. See Max Scheler, *The Nature of Sympathy*, trans. Peter Heath (Hamden, Conn.: Archon, 1970).

28. Merleau-Ponty is especially concerned with thinking through the role of physical bodies in self/other distinctions. See Maurice Merleau-Ponty, *Phenomenology of Perception*, trans. Colin Smith (London: Routledge and Kegan Paul, 1962).

29. Especially in his classic essay on "the mirror stage." See: "The Mirror-Stage as Formative of the Function of the I," in *Ecrits: A Selection*, trans. Alan Sheridan (New York: Norton, 1977), pp. 1–7. See also the Neal H. Bruss essay on Bakhtin and Lacan, which appeared as an appendix in the first edition of the Bakhtin/Voloshinov book on Freud: V. N. Voloshinov, *Freudianism: A Marxist Critique*, trans. I. R. Titunik (New York: Academic Press, 1973).

30. See Katerina Clark and Michael Holquist, *Mikhail Bakhtin* (Cambridge, Mass.: Harvard University Press, 1984), pp. 23, 79–81. A more extensive treatment has been provided by Nina Perlina: "Bakhtin and Buber: The Concept of Dialogic Discourse," *Studies in Twentieth Century Literature* 9 (1984): 13–28.

31. See especially Cohen's essays on the distinctiveness of the Hebrew concept of deity in *Reason and Hope: Hermann Cohen's Jewish Writings*, trans. Ewa Jospe (New York: Norton, 1971).

32. Martin Heidegger, *Being and Time*, trans. John Macquarrie and Edward Robinson (New York: Harper and Row, 1962), p. 161.

33. Jean-Paul Sartre., *Being and Nothingness: An Essay on Phenomenological Ontology*, trans. Hazel Barnes (New York: Philosophical Library, 1956), pp. 303–359.

34. See especially another work of Sartre's, *Transcendence of the Ego: An Existentialist Theory of the Ego*, trans. Forrest Williams and Robert Kirkpatrick (New York: Farrar, Straus, and Giroux [Noonday Press], 1957). But the emphasis on transcendence of the ego indicates precisely where Bakhtin would diverge from Sartre in conceiving the self.

35. See Jean-Paul Sartre, *Critique of Dialectical Reason*, trans. Alan Sheridan-Smith (London: New Left Books, 1976).

36. In some of my previous attempts to come to grips with the question of Bakhtin's relation to Marx, I now believe I oversimplified matters to an unjustifiable degree. There can be little doubt that certain phrases associated with Bolshevik jargon of the time, which occur even in texts signed by Bakhtin himself, were indeed introduced for purposes of protective coloration. An example of this would be his use of the highly

marked phrase *"kulak-bloodsucker"* (*kulak-miroed*) in an essay of 1929 ("Predislovie," in L. Tolstoy, *Polnoe sobranie khudozhestvennykh proizvedenij*, ed. K. Khalabaev and B. Eikhenbaum [Moscow: Gosizdat, 1929]), vol. 11, p. viii.). But such historicist details should not obscure Bakhtin's more fundamental relation to Marxist thought independent of Bolshevik practice, especially in light of these early essays, as I try to suggest here.

37. Karl Marx, *Capital* (Chicago: Charles H. Kerr, 1919), vol. 1, p. 85n.

38. James J. Lynch, *The Language of the Heart: The Body's Response to Human Dialogue* (New York: Basic Books, 1985), p. 49.

39. Ibid., p. 178.

40. Karl Marx and Frederick Engels, *The German Ideology* (Moscow: Progress Publishers, 1976), p. 42.

41. "Toward a Methodology of the Human Sciences," *Speech Genres*, p. 167.

42. "From Notes Made in 1970–1971," in *Speech Genres*, p. 136.

Art and Answerability

ART AND ANSWERABILITY

A whole is called "mechanical" when its constituent elements are united only in space and time by some external connection and are not imbued with the internal unity of meaning. The parts of such a whole are contiguous and touch each other, but in themselves they remain alien to each other.

The three domains of human culture—science, art, and life—gain unity only in the individual person[1] who integrates them into his own unity. This union, however, may become mechanical, external. And, unfortunately, that is exactly what most often happens. The artist and the human being are naively, most often mechanically, united in one person; the human being leaves "the fretful cares of everyday life" and enters for a time the realm of creative activity as another world, a world of "inspiration, sweet sounds, and prayers."[2] And what is the result? Art is too self-confident, audaciously self-confident, and too high-flown, for it is in no way bound to answer for life. And, of course, life has no hope of ever catching up with art of this kind. "That's too exalted for us"—says life. "That's art, after all! All we've got is the humble prose of living."

When a human being is in art, he is not in life, and conversely. There is no unity between them and no inner interpenetration within the unity of an individual person.

But what guarantees the inner connection of the constituent elements of a person? Only the unity of answerability. I have to answer with my own life for what I have experienced and understood in art, so that everything I have experienced and understood would not remain ineffectual in my life. But answerability entails guilt, or liability to blame. It is not only mutual answerability that art and life must assume, but also mutual liability to blame.

The poet must remember that it is his poetry which bears the guilt for the vulgar prose of life, whereas the man of everyday life ought to know that the fruitlessness of art is due to his willingness to be unexacting and to the unseriousness of the concerns in his life. The individual must become answerable through and through: all of his constituent moments must not only fit next to each other in the temporal sequence of his life, but must also interpenetrate each other in the unity of guilt and answerability.

Nor will it do to invoke "inspiration" in order to justify want of answerability. Inspiration that ignores life and is itself ignored by life is not inspiration but a state of possession. The true sense, and not the self-proclaimed sense, of all the old arguments about the interrelationship of art and life, about the purity of art, etc.— that is, the real aspiration behind all such arguments—is nothing more than the mutual striving of both art and life to make their own tasks easier, to relieve themselves of their own answerability. For it is certainly easier to create without answering for life, and easier to live without any consideration for art.

Art and life are not one, but they must become united in myself—in the unity of my answerability.

Notes

Note: This article appeared in the miscellany *Den' iskusstva* [The Day of Art], published in Nevel', September 13, 1919. It is the earliest known publication by Bakhtin. On Bakhtin's life in Nevel', see Katerina Clark and Michael Holquist, *Mikhail Bakhtin* (Cambridge, Mass.: Harvard University Press, 1984), pp. 38–45.

1. Cf. Kant, *The Metaphysics of Morals*, introduction (section 4): "A person is the *subiectum* whose actions are capable of imputation. The moral personality is, therefore, nothing else but the freedom of a rational being under moral laws (whereas the psychological personality is merely the capacity to become conscious of the identity of one's self in the various conditions of one's existence)." On the problematics of "person," see W. Pannenberg, *Religion in Geschichte und Gegenwart*, 3rd ed. (Tübingen: 1961), vol. 55, cols. 230–235; and Max Müller and W. Vossenkuhl, *Handbuch philosophischer Grundbegriffe* (Munich: 1973), vol. 4, pp. 1059–1070. Cf. also Helmut Dahm, *Vladimir Solovyev and Max Scheler* (Dordrecht: D. Reidel, 1975), pp. 43–52.

2. The quotations are from the closing quatrain of A. S. Pushkin's 1828 dialogue-poem (in fifty-five freely rhymed iambic tetrameters) *Poet i tolpa* [The Poet and the Crowd]:

Not for the fretful cares of everyday life,
Not for the pursuit of profit, not for warfare
Are we born—but for inspiration,
For sweet sounds and for prayers.

These lines conclude the Poet's final response to the importunate demands of the Crowd that he should use his gift for teaching them useful moral lessons.

AUTHOR AND HERO IN AESTHETIC ACTIVITY

The Problem of the Author's Relationship to the Hero

For a proper understanding of the author's architectonically stable and dynamically living relationship to the hero,[1] we must take into account both the essentially necessary[2] foundation of that relationship and the diverse individual characteristics that it assumes in particular authors and in particular works. In the present inquiry, we shall limit ourselves to an examination of the essentially necessary foundation of the author-hero relationship. Beyond that, we shall only outline some of the modes and types of its individuation and, finally, we shall verify our conclusions by an analysis of this relationship in works by Dostoevsky, Pushkin, and others.[3]

Enough has been said, perhaps, about the fact that every constituent[4] of a work presents itself to us as the author's reaction to it and that this reaction encompasses both an object and the hero's reaction to that object (a reaction to a reaction). In this sense, the author intonates[5] every particular and every trait of his hero, every event of his life, every action he performs, all his thoughts and feelings, just as in life, too, we react valuationally to every self-manifestation on the part of those around us. These reactions in life, however, have a scattered character, that is, they are reactions to isolated self-manifestations of a human being and not to the whole that he is, not to all of him. And even in the case where we give a complete definition of a human being as a whole—that is, where we define him as a kind, a vicious, or a good person, or as an egoist, etc.—such definitions express the practical position we assume in relation to him in our lived life: they not so much define him as propose a prognosis of what we can and what we cannot expect from him. Or they may simply be a matter of chance impressions of the whole or, finally, a spurious empirical generalization. In life, we are interested not in the whole of a human being, but only in those particular actions on his part with which we are compelled to deal in living our life and which are, in one way or another, of special interest to us. And, as we shall see below, least of all are we ourselves able or competent to perceive in ourselves the given whole of our own personality.

In the work of art, on the other hand, the author's reactions to particular self-manifestations on the part of the hero are founded on his unitary reaction to the *whole* of the hero: all particular self-manifestations of the hero have significance for the characterization of this whole as moments or constituent features of it. What makes a reaction specifically aesthetic is precisely the fact that it is a reaction to the *whole* of the hero as a human being, a reaction that assembles all of the cognitive-ethical determinations and valuations of the hero and consummates[6] them in the form of a unitary and unique whole that is a concrete, intuitable[7] whole, but also a whole of meaning.

This comprehensive reaction of the author to the hero is founded on a necessary principle and has a productive, constructive character. Indeed, any relationship founded on a necessary principle has a creative, productive character. What in life, in cognition, and in performed actions we call a determinate object acquires its determinateness, its own countenance, only through our relationship to it: it is our relationship that determines an object and its structure, not conversely. It is only where our relationship to an object ceases to be founded on a necessary principle (becomes a matter of whim, as it were), where, in other words, we depart from our principled relationship to things and to the world—only then are we confronted by the determinateness of an object as something foreign and independent. The object's determinateness begins to disintegrate for us and we ourselves fall under the domination of the contingent, with the result that we lose ourselves and we lose the stable determinateness of the world as well.

An author, too, does not immediately find a noncontingent vision of the hero, a vision founded on a necessary principle of creation; his reaction to the hero does not immediately become a productive reaction founded on a necessary principle, nor does the whole of the hero immediately arise from the author's unitary valuational relationship to the hero. Before the countenance of the hero finally takes shape as a stable and necessary whole, the hero is going to exhibit a great many grimaces, random masks, wrong gestures, and unexpected actions, depending on all those emotional-volitional reactions and personal whims of the author, through the chaos of which he is compelled to work his way in order to reach an authentic valuational attitude. In order to see the true and integral countenance of someone close to us, someone we apparently know very well—think how many masking layers must first be removed from his face, layers that were sedimented upon his face by our own fortuitous reactions and attitudes and by fortuitous life situations. The artist's struggle to achieve a determinate and stable image[8] of the hero is to a considerable extent a struggle with himself.

Insofar as this process conforms with psychological laws, it cannot be studied by us directly. We meet with it only to the extent to which it precipitates itself in a work of art. That is, we have to do with the ideal history of this process, its history on the plane of meaning,[9] and with the ideal, meaning-related laws governing this history. What the temporal causes of such a process may have been or how it may have proceeded psychologically is entirely a matter of conjecture, but in any case this does not concern aesthetics.

An author tells us this ideal history only in the work he has produced and not in "the author's confession," if there be such, or in his observations on the process of his own creative activity. Everything an author says in this regard must be treated with extreme caution, for the following reasons.

The comprehensive reaction that produces the whole of an object is actively performed or actualized but is not experienced as something determinate; its determinateness consists precisely in the product it brought into being, that is, in the object to which it has given form. An author reflects the hero's emotional-volitional position, but not his own position in relation to the hero; his own position is something he actualizes—it is objective, that is, actualized in an object, but does not itself become an object of examination and reflective experience. An author creates, but he sees his own creating only in the object to which he is giving form, that is, he sees only the emerging product of creation and not the inner, psychologically determinate, process of creation. And, in fact, such is the nature of all active creative experiences: they experience their object and experience themselves *in* their object, but they do not experience the process of their own experiencing. The actual work of creation *is* experienced, but this experiencing neither hears nor sees itself; it sees and hears only the product that is being created or the object to which it is directed. The technical aspects of creation, craftsmanship, may be a matter of conscious knowledge, but, once again, only in the object. As a result, the artist has nothing to say about the process of his creative activity: the process of creation is altogether *in* the product created, and the artist has nothing left to do but to refer us to the work he has produced. In our own analysis, we shall in fact look for it nowhere else.

When, on the other hand, an artist undertakes to speak about his act of creation independently of and as a supplement to the work he has produced, he usually substitutes a new relationship for his actual creative relationship to the work: his actual creative relationship, which was not experienced by him within his own soul but was actualized in a work (was not experienced by him but was an act of experiencing the hero), is replaced by his later and more receptive relationship to the already created work. At the time an author was creating, he experienced only his hero, and he put his whole essentially necessary relationship to the hero into the image of the hero. When, on the other hand, he begins to speak about his heroes in an "author's confession" (as do Gogol' and Goncharov),[10] he voices his present relationship to them as already created and determined: he conveys the impression they produce on him now as artistic images and gives utterance to the attitude he now maintains toward them as living, determinate persons from a social, moral, or other point of view; they have already become independent of him, and he himself has become independent of himself as their active creator, that is, has become a particular individual, critic, psychologist, or moralist.

It should be quite obvious, moreover, how unreliable must be the evidence provided by an author's comments on the process of creating a hero, if we take into account all the chance factors that inevitably affect what an author-as-person has to say about his own heroes, that is, if we take into account such factors as the critical response to his work, his own present world view (which could have changed considerably), his aspirations and pretensions (cf. Gogol'), various practical considerations, and so on. Such authorial evidence has enormous biographical value; it may acquire aesthetic value as well, but only after [undecipherable] of the artistic meaning of a work has been illuminated. The author-as-creator will help us to gain insight into the author-as-person, and only after that will the author-person's comments about his creative activity acquire illuminating and complementary significance. It is not just the heroes created who break away from the process that created them and begin to lead a life of their own in the world, but the same is equally true for their actual author-creator. This is why it is necessary to emphasize the creatively productive character of an author and of his comprehensive reaction to a hero. An author is not the bearer of inner lived experience, and his reaction is neither a passive feeling nor a receptive perception. An author is the uniquely active form-giving energy that is manifested not in a psychologically conceived consciousness, but in a durably valid cultural product, and his active, productive reaction is manifested in the structures it generates—in the structure of the active vision of a hero as a definite whole, in the structure of his image, in the rhythm of disclosing him, in the structure of intonating, and in the selection of meaning-bearing features.

Only when we have understood this essentially necessary, comprehensive, creative reaction of the author to the hero, only when we have understood the *principle* of seeing the hero that engenders the hero as a determinate whole, determinate in all its constituents—only then will it be possible to introduce strict order into the form-and-content determination of the various types of the hero, only then will it be possible to endow them with univocal meaning and to set up a noncontingent systematic classification of them. Complete chaos still holds sway in this regard in the aesthetics of verbal art and especially in literary history. At every step in this field, one encounters indiscriminate mingling of different points of view, different levels of approach, different principles of evaluation.

Consider, for example, such distinctions and determinations as the following: positive and negative heroes (the author's attitude toward the hero); autobiographical and objective heroes; idealized and realistic heroes; "heroization," satire, humor, irony; the epic, dramatic, lyrical hero; character, type, *personage*; the hero of romantic adventure. Or consider the notorious classification of type parts in the theater: the juvenile lead (lyrical or dramatic), the *raisonneur*, the *naïf*, etc.

All these classifications and determinations of the hero are not ordered, not validated at all in relation to each other, and, in point of fact, there *is* no single principle for ordering and validating them. Furthermore, these classifications are usually combined uncritically to produce hybrids. The most serious attempts to approach the hero in a principled manner are offered by the biographical and sociological methods. But these also lack a sufficiently deepened formal-aesthetic understanding of the fundamental creative principle in the author-hero relationship, substituting for it various psychological and social relations and factors that are passive and transgredient[11] to the creating consciousness: the hero and the author cease to be constituents of a work as an artistic whole, and instead become constituents of a prosaically conceived unity of psychological and social life.

The most common practice even in serious and conscientious literary-historical scholarship is to draw biographical material from literary works or, conversely, to explain a given work through biography. Moreover, when doing so, purely factual justifications, i.e., mere coincidence between the facts of the hero's and the author's lives, are taken to be perfectly sufficient. One selects excerpts that lay claim to some sort of meaning, while completely ignoring the whole of the hero and the whole of the author. As a result, one also ignores the most essential constituent, namely, the form of the relationship to the event, the form of experiencing it within a whole of life and the world.

Such factual juxtapositions and reciprocal explanations are particularly preposterous in the case of the author's and the hero's world views, when the abstract content of certain ideas of the author is juxtaposed with corresponding ideas of the hero. Thus, Griboedov's sociopolitical statements are juxtaposed with corresponding statements of his hero, Chatsky,[12] and it is then asserted that their sociopolitical outlook is either identical or similar; or Tolstoy's views, for example, are juxtaposed with those of his hero, Levin.

As we shall see, however, there can be no question of any properly theoretical correspondence or agreement between an author and a hero, for the relationship here is of a completely different order. What is constantly ignored in all such juxtapositions is that the whole of the author and the whole of the hero belong to different planes—different in principle; the very form of the relationship to an idea and even to the theoretical whole of a world view is ignored. It happens again and again that one actually starts disputing with the hero as one would with the author, as if it were really possible to quarrel or to agree with *what exists*.[13] That is, one ignores the *aesthetic confutation*.

It can happen, of course, that the author puts his own ideas directly into the mouth of the hero from the standpoint of their theoretical or ethical (political, social) validity,[14] in order to convince us of their truth and in order to propagandize them. But in that case we are no longer dealing with a relationship to the hero based on an aesthetically productive principle of relating to the hero. Moreover, what usually takes place in such a case is that the idea, in spite of the author's will and consciousness, is modified so as to conform to the *whole* of the hero—not to the theoretical unity of the hero's world view, but to the *whole* of his personality, a whole within which his world view (besides his exterior, his deportment, the perfectly determinate circumstances of his life) constitutes only *one* moment. In other words, what takes place nevertheless is what we call an incarnation of meaning in existence rather than a validation and demonstration of the truth of an idea. If, on the other hand, such a modification fails to take place, what we get is a prosaism that remains undissolved throughout the whole of a work, and only when we have understood the fundamental, aesthetically productive principle of the author's relationship to the hero will we be able to explain such a prosaism, as well as to discover and take into account how the idea being incarnated—being integrated into the whole of the hero—*diverges* from the idea that has a purely theoretical validity for the author, i.e., in what *direction* the idea is modified.

All this is not to deny the possibility that the juxtaposition of the author's and the hero's biographies and their world views *could* be productive for literary history as well as for aesthetic analysis. We are merely denying the validity of the completely unprincipled, purely factual approach to this matter that at present prevails over all others, which is based, first, on confounding the author-creator (a constituent in a work) with the author-person (a constituent in the ethical, social event of life),[15] and, second, on failing to understand the creative principle in the author's relationship to a hero. The result is miscomprehension and distortion or, at best, what we get is an account of the bare facts, an account of the author's ethical, biographical personality, coupled with a failure to understand the *whole* of a work and a hero. For in order

to make use of a source, it is necessary to understand its crea-
tional structure. And when a work of art is to be utilized as a biographical source, the methods of source-criticism customary in
the historical sciences are completely inadequate, for what they
fail to take into account is precisely the structure specific to a
work of art—this has to be the philosophical precondition [unde-
cipherable]. It must be said, however, that literary history, on the
whole, suffers considerably less from the specified methodological fault in the dealing with works of art than does the aesthetics
of verbal creation[16]—a domain in which historical-genetic formations play an especially pernicious role. (At a later point, we shall
have to return to a closer examination of the classifications of the
various types of hero cited earlier, as well as to an assessment of
the biographical and sociological methods.)

The situation is somewhat different in the case of general philosophical aesthetics; here the problem of the author-hero relationship is posed in principle, although not in its pure form. What we
have in mind is, first, the idea of empathy (*Einfühlung*)[17] as a
form-and-content principle in the aesthetic relationship of an
author/contemplator to an object in general and to a hero in particular (Lipps[18] provides the fullest validation of this principle),
and, second, the idea of aesthetic love (cf. Guyau's[19] idea of social
sympathy and, on an entirely different plane, Cohen's[20] idea of
aesthetic love). But these two [undecipherable] conceptions are
too general, too unspecific in character, both with regard to the
particular arts and with regard to the special object of aesthetic
vision—the hero (in Cohen there is more specific differentiation).
Moreover, even on the plane of general aesthetics we cannot accept either the first or the second of these principles fully, although both contain a good deal of truth. We shall have to take
into account both of these standpoints in the course of our inquiry. In the present context, we cannot enter into a general examination and assessment of them.

The aesthetics of verbal creation would, as a matter of fact, gain
a great deal if it were oriented more to general philosophical aesthetics rather than to literary history's quasi-scientific, genetic
generalizations. It is unfortunate but true that major developments in the domain of general aesthetics have failed to exert any
influence upon the aesthetics of verbal creation. Even more: there
actually exists a peculiar fear of any deeper philosophical scru-
tiny. This explains the fact that in our discipline the conception

and formulation of fundamental problems remain on an exceptionally low level.

What we have to do now is give a very general definition of the author and the hero as correlative moments in the artistic whole of a work and then provide no more than a general formula for their mutual relationship—a formula to be specifically differentiated and deepened in the following chapters of our inquiry.

The author is the bearer and sustainer of the intently active unity of a consummated whole (the whole of a hero and the whole of a work) which is transgredient to each and every one of its particular moments or constituent features. As a whole which consummates the hero, this whole is in principle incapable of being given to us from within the hero, insofar as we "identify" ourselves with the hero and experience his life from within him.[21] The hero cannot live by this whole, he cannot be guided by it in his own lived experiences and actions, for it is a whole that descends upon him—is bestowed upon him as a gift—from another active consciousness: from the creative consciousness of an author. The author's consciousness is the consciousness of a consciousness, that is, a consciousness that *encompasses* the consciousness and the world of a hero—a consciousness that encompasses and *consummates* the consciousness of a hero by supplying those moments which are in principle transgredient to the hero's consciousness and which, if rendered immanent, would falsify this consciousness. The author not only sees and knows everything seen and known by each hero individually and by all the heroes collectively, but he also sees and knows *more* than they do; moreover, he sees and knows something that is in principle inaccessible to them. And it is precisely in this invariably determinate and stable *excess*[22] of the author's seeing and knowing in relation to each hero that we find all those moments that bring about the consummation of the whole—the whole of each hero as well as the whole of the event which constitutes their life and in which they jointly participate, i.e., the whole of a work.

Indeed, the hero lives his life cognitionally and ethically: he orients his actions within the open ethical event of his lived life or within the projected world of cognition.[23] The author, on the other hand, orients the hero and the hero's own cognitive-ethical orientation within a world of being that is in principle consummated, that is, within a world which derives its value, independently of the yet-to-be[24] meaning of the event of a lived life, purely from the concrete manifoldness of its already existing makeup. If I am consummated and my life is consummated, I am no longer capable of living and acting. For in order to live and act, I need to be unconsummated, I need to be open for myself—at least in all the essential moments constituting my life; I have to be, for myself, someone who is axiologically[25] yet-to-be, someone who does not coincide with his already existing makeup.

The hero's consciousness, his feeling, and his desire of the world (his object-directed emotional and volitional attitude or posture) are enclosed on all sides, as if within a band, by the author's *consummating* consciousness of the hero and his world; the hero's self-utterances are encompassed and permeated by the utterances of the author about the hero. The hero's vital (cognitive-ethical) interestedness in the event of his own lived life is encompassed by the author's *artistic* interestedness in the hero and his life. In this sense, aesthetic objectivity aims in a direction different from that of cognitive and ethical objectivity. Cognitive and ethical objectivity is the impartial, dispassionate evaluation of a given person and a given event from the standpoint of an ethical and cognitive value which is or is held to be universally valid or tends toward universal validity. By contrast, the center of value for aesthetic objectivity is the *whole* of the hero and of the event of his lived life,[26] and all values that are ethical and cognitive must be subordinated to that whole. Aesthetic objectivity, in other words, encompasses and comprises cognitive-ethical objectivity. It should be clear, therefore, that cognitive and ethical values can no longer function here as the moments which bring about the consummation of the whole of a hero and his life. In this sense, the consummating moments are transgredient not only to the hero's actual consciousness but also to his potential consciousness—his consciousness extended in a dotted line, as it were: the author knows and sees more not only in the direction in which the hero is looking and seeing, but also in a different direction, in a direction which is in principle inaccessible to the hero himself; it is precisely this position that an author must assume in relation to a hero.

In order to find in a given work the author so conceived, it is necessary, first, to single out all those moments or constituent features which bring about the consummation of the hero and the event of his life and which are in principle transgredient to his consciousness, and, second, to determine the active, creatively intent, and essentially necessary[27] unity of all such consummating moments. The living bearer and sustainer of this unity of consummation is the author, who stands over against the hero, who is, in turn, the bearer of the open unity of the event of a lived life—a unity incapable of being consummated from within itself. All of the moments that actively consummate the hero render the hero passive, the way a part is passive in relation to the whole which encompasses and consummates it.

The general formula for the author's fundamental, aesthetically productive relationship to the hero follows directly from what has been said. It is a relationship in which the author occupies an intently maintained position *outside* the hero[28] with respect to every constituent feature of the hero—a position *outside* the hero with respect to space, time, value, and meaning. And this being-outside in relation to the hero enables the author (1) to collect and concentrate *all* of the hero, who, from within himself, is diffused and dispersed in the projected world of cognition[29] and in the open event of ethical action; (2) to collect the hero and his life and to complete him to the point where he forms a *whole* by supplying all those moments which are inaccessible to the hero himself from within himself (such as a full outward image, an exterior, a background behind his back, his relation to the event of death and the absolute future, etc.); and (3) to justify and to consummate the hero independently of the meaning, the achievements, the outcome and success of the hero's own forward-directed life.

Such a relationship of the author to the hero removes the hero from the open unitary and unique event of being[30] which encompasses both him and the author-as-person and within which he, as a person, would stand beside the author—as the author's partner in the event of lived life, or against the author—as the author's antagonist, or, finally, inside the author—as the author himself. That is, such a relationship places the hero beyond mutual surety, collective liability, and solidary responsibility and gives birth to him as a new human being on a new plane of existence—a plane of existence where the hero himself is incapable of being born for himself and through his own power; or, in other words, it invests or embodies the hero in that new flesh which is not essential and does not exist for the hero himself. This is [undecipherable] the author's outside position in relation to the hero, the author's loving removal of himself from the field of the hero's life, his clearing of the whole field of life for the hero and his existence, and—the compassionate understanding and consummation of the event of the hero's life in terms of real cognition and ethical action by a detached, unparticipating beholder.

This relationship of the author to the hero (which we have formulated here in an extremely general form) is a deeply vital and dynamic relationship: the author's position of being situated outside the hero[31] is gained by conquest, and the struggle for it is often a struggle for life, especially in the case where the hero is autobiographical, although not only there. For sometimes it is difficult to take up a stand outside one's partner as well as outside one's antagonist in the event of life; not only being *inside* the hero but also being axiologically *beside* him and *against* him distorts seeing and lacks features that can render him complete and consummate him. In all these cases, the values of life are more precious than the bearer of life. The author experiences the hero's life in value-categories that are completely different from those in which he experiences his own life and the life of other people living together with him (the actual participants in the unitary and open ethical event of being); he determines the sense of the hero's life in a value-context that is completely different.

Now we shall say a few words about three typical cases of deviation from the author's direct relationship to the hero. They occur when the hero coincides in life with the author, i.e., when he is essentially autobiographical.

According to the direct relationship, the author must take up a position outside himself, must experience himself on a plane that is different from the one on which we actually experience our own life. Only if this condition is fulfilled can he complete himself to the point of forming a whole by supplying those values which are transgredient to life as lived from within oneself and thus can consummate that life. He must become another in relation to himself, must look at himself through the eyes of another.

To be sure, in life, too, we do this all the time: we evaluate ourselves from the standpoint of others, and through others we try to understand and take into account what is transgredient to our own consciousness. Thus, we take into account the value of our outward appearance from the standpoint of the possible impression it may produce upon the other, although for ourselves this value does not exist in any immediate way (for our actual and pure self-consciousness). We take into account the background behind our back, that is to say, all that which in our surroundings we do not see and do not know directly and which has no direct axiological validity[32] for us, although it is seen and known by others and has validity for others; all that, in other words, which constitutes the background, against which, as it were, others perceive us axiologically, against which we stand forth for them. Finally, we also anticipate and take into account what will happen after our death—the outcome of our life as a whole (no longer for us, of course, but for others). In short, we are constantly and intently on the watch for reflections of our own life on the plane of other people's consciousness, and, moreover, not just reflections of particular moments of our life, but even reflections of the whole of it. And while seeking to catch these reflections, we also take into account that perfectly distinctive value-coefficient with which our life presents itself to the other—a coefficient which is completely different from the coefficient with which we experience our own life in ourselves.

But all these moments or constituents of our life that we recognize and anticipate through the other are rendered completely immanent to our own consciousness, are translated, as it were, into its language: they do not attain any consolidation[33] and self-sufficiency in our consciousness, and they do not disrupt the unity of our own life—a life that is directed ahead of itself toward the event yet-to-come,[34] a life that finds no rest within itself and never coincides with its given, presently existing makeup. If, however, these reflections do gain body in our life, as sometimes happens, they begin to act as "dead points," as obstructions of any accomplishment, and at times they may condense to the point where they deliver up to us a double of ourselves out of the night of our life; but we shall return to this below.

All these moments that can consummate us in the consciousness of the other lose their consummating power by being anticipated in our own consciousness, and as such they merely extend our consciousness in its own direction. Even if we succeeded in encompassing the whole of our consciousness as consummated in the other, this whole would not be able to take possession of us and really consummate us for ourselves: our consciousness would take that whole into account and would surmount it as just one of the moments in its own unity (which is not a unity that is *given* but a unity that is set as a *task*[35] and, in its essentials, is *yet-to-be*). The last word, that is, would still belong to our own consciousness rather than to the consciousness of another, and our own consciousness would never say to itself the word that would consummate it. After looking at ourselves through the eyes of another, we always return—in life—into ourselves again, and the final, or, as it were, recapitulative event takes place within ourselves in the categories of our own life.

In the case of an author-person's aesthetic self-objectification into a hero, this return into oneself must not take place: for the author-other, the whole of the hero must remain the ultimate whole; the author must be separated from the hero—from himself—totally, and one must define oneself purely in terms of values for the other, or, rather, in oneself one must come to see another, and do so utterly. For the immanence of a possible background to consciousness is by no means equivalent to the *aesthetic* conjunction of the hero's consciousness with a background, where the background must shape the contours of his consciousness in its entirety, no matter how deep and inclusive it may be. That is to say, even if the hero's consciousness were conscious of the entire world and rendered the entire world immanent to itself, the *aesthetic* standpoint would still have to provide his consciousness with a background that is transgredient to it. Or, in other words, the author would have to find a point of support outside that consciousness, in order that it should become an aesthetically consummated phenomenon—a hero. And, similarly, my own exterior as reflected through the other is by no means directly equivalent to the *artistic* exterior of a hero.

If the author loses this valuational point of support *outside* the hero, then his relationship to the hero can typically assume three general forms, each one of which includes the possibility of numerous variations. Without anticipating at this point what will be dealt with later, we shall merely outline these three typical cases in terms of their most general features.

The *first* case: the hero takes possession of the author. The hero's emotional-volitional attitude toward objects, the cognitive-ethical position he assumes in the world, is so authoritative for the author that he cannot see the world of objects through any other eyes but those of the hero, and cannot experience in any other way except from within the event that is the hero's life. The author is unable to find any convincing and stable axiological point of support *outside* the hero.

Of course, in order that there should be any artistic whole at all, even if it is an unconsummated whole, it is necessary to find consummating features of some kind, and, consequently, it is also necessary to take a stand in some way outside the hero (who usually is not alone, and the relations we have pointed out apply, therefore, only to the main hero). Otherwise, the result will turn out to be a philosophical treatise or a confession (in the sense of a self-accounting) or, finally, the given cognitive-ethical tension may find its resolution in the performance of ethical actions or deeds purely within the context of lived life. But these points of support *outside* the hero on which the author is still compelled to rely are not founded on a necessary principle and have a fortuitous and insecure character. That is to say, these unstable supports of the author's position outside the hero usually change throughout the course of a work, for they are assumed merely in relation to some particular given moment in the hero's development, and then the hero goes on once again to dislodge the author from his temporarily assumed position, and the author is compelled to search around for another such position. Frequently, the author is provided with such contingent points of support by the other characters: by projecting himself into their emotional-volitional attitudes toward the autobiographical hero, the author tries to free himself from the hero, that is, ultimately, from *himself*. The moments of consummation in this case have a scattered and unconvincing character. Sometimes, when the struggle is hopeless from the very outset, the author may be content with those conventional points of support outside the hero which are provided by purely technical, narrowly formal features in the telling of a story or in the composition of a work: the work turns out to be merely contrived rather than created, and the style (understood as the totality of convincing and powerful devices of consummation) degenerates into a conventional "manner."

It should be emphasized that the point at issue here is not the author's *theoretical* agreement or disagreement with the hero. In order to find a nonarbitrary point of support outside the hero, it is by no means necessary or sufficient to find a well-founded theoretical refutation of the hero's views. An intensely self-interested and confident disagreement is a standpoint no less extra-aesthetic than a self-interested solidarity with the hero. Rather, what must be found is that particular position in relation to the hero from which the hero's entire world view—in all its depth, and with all its rightness or wrongness, its good and evil, impartially—would become merely a moment within the intuitable, concrete *exis-*

tential whole of the hero. That is, the author must move the very center of value from the hero's existence as a compelling *task*[36] into his existence as a beautiful *given;* instead of hearing and agreeing with the hero, the author must see all of him in the fullness of the present and admire him as such. At the same time, however, the cognitive-ethical validity of the hero's attitude as well as the agreement or disagreement with that attitude are not lost—they preserve their significance, except that now they become no more than constituents within the whole of the hero; the admiration is meaningful and intent; both agreement and disagreement are valid moments within the author's integral position in relation to the hero, without exhausting the content of that position.

In our case, this unique position (the only position from which it is possible to see the whole of the hero as well as the world enframing, delimiting, and profiling that whole from outside) fails to be attained outside the hero in any convincing and stable manner by the author's full power of vision. One consequence of this is that the artistic whole exhibits the following peculiarity characteristic for the case we are considering: the background, the world behind the hero's back, is unelaborated and is not distinctly seen by the author/contemplator; instead, it is presented suppositionally, uncertainly, from within the hero himself, the way the background of our own life presents itself to us. Sometimes the background is totally absent: outside the hero and his own consciousness there is nothing that has any stable reality. The hero is not connatural[37] with the background that sets him off (the surroundings, the communal way of life, nature, etc.), he does not combine with it to form an artistically necessary whole; he moves against this background as a living human being moves against a background of lifeless and immobile stage scenery. There is no organic fusion of the hero's outward expressedness in being (his exterior, his voice, his comportment, etc.) with his inward cognitive-ethical position; his outward expressedness envelops him like a mask that is neither unique nor essential, or it fails to attain any distinctness at all, and the hero does not present himself to us *en face* but is experienced by us only from within. The dialogues between *whole* human beings (in which their faces, their facial expressions, their dress, and the setting beyond the bounds of a given scene are necessary, artistically significant constituents)[38] begin to degenerate into self-interested disputations in which the center of value is located in the problems debated. And, finally, the consummating moments are not unified: the author lacks any unitary countenance—it is either a scattered countenance or a conventional mask. This type includes almost all of Dostoevsky's heroes, some of the heros of Tolstoy (Pierre, Levin),[39] Kierkegaard, Stendhal, and other writers whose heroes tend, in part, toward this type as their ultimate limit. (The theme is not dissolved throughout the whole.)

The *second* case: the author takes possession of the hero, introduces consummating moments into him, and the author's relationship to the hero thus becomes, in part, the hero's own relationship to himself. The author's reflection is put into the soul or mouth of the hero; the hero himself begins to determine himself.

A hero of this type may develop in two directions: (1) The hero is not autobiographical, and the author's reflection[40] introduced into him provides the unity which actually consummates him. If it was the form that suffered in the first case we analyzed, then in the present case what suffers is the realistic convincingness of the hero's emotional-volitional attitude within the event of his own lived life. Such is the hero in "Pseudo-Classicism":[41] in his own life-position he maintains, from within himself, that purely artistic, consummating unity which the *author* imparts to him. He remains faithful, that is, to the aesthetic principle determining him from without in every expression of himself from within—in every act, in every facial expression, feeling, word. The heroes of such Russian "Pseudo-Classicists" as Sumarokov, Kniazhnin, or Ozerov[42] often express with great naiveté the moral-ethical idea which consummates them and which they embody not from their own, but from the *author's* standpoint. (2) The hero is autobiographical. After assimilating the author's reflection, the author's comprehensive formative reaction to him, the hero turns it into a moment of his own self-experience and thus surmounts it. A hero of this kind is not capable of being consummated: he surpasses within himself any comprehensive determination of himself from outside as inadequate to himself; he experiences consummated wholeness as a limitation of himself and opposes to it an inexpressible inner mystery of some kind. "You think that all of me is here?"—he seems to say—"You think that you see all of me there is to see? On the contrary! What is most vital in me you can neither see, nor hear, nor know." A hero of this kind is, for the author, infinite, i.e., he is reborn again and again, requiring ever again new forms of consummation which he himself then destroys through his own self-consciousness. Such is the hero in Romanticism: the Romantic is afraid to give himself away in his own hero and leaves some inner loophole in the hero through which he could slip away and rise above his own consummatedness.

Finally, the *third* case: the hero himself is his own author, and, as such, himself interprets his own life aesthetically—he plays a role, as it were. A hero of this kind, as distinct from the infinite hero of Romanticism and the unredeemed hero of Dostoevsky, is self-contented and surely consummated.

The relationship of the author to the hero that we have characterized here only in the most general terms is complicated and diversified by those cognitive-ethical determinations of the whole of the hero which, as we have seen earlier, are indissolubly fused with the purely artistic form given to him. Thus, the hero's object-directed emotional and volitional attitude may be cognitively, ethically, and religiously authoritative for the author: the hero is "heroicized." This same attitude may be exposed as unrightfully claiming a validity it does not possess: the hero is satirized, "ironicized," and so forth.

Any consummating moment, any feature that is transgredient to the hero's self-consciousness, can be utilized in any of these directions (satirical, heroic, humorous, etc.). Thus, it is possible to satirize through *outward appearance,* that is, to limit, to ridicule the cognitive-ethical validity of an attitude by way of its outward, determinate, and all-too-human expressedness in being. On the other hand, it is also possible to "heroicize" through outward appearance—consider, for example, the monumentality of outward appearance in sculpture. The *background* (the invisible and the unknown that occurs behind the hero's back) can render comical the life and the cognitive-ethical pretensions of a hero: a very small man shown against the vast background of the universe; minuscule knowledge combined with self-confident certainty in this knowledge—against the background of a boundless and profound ignorance; one man's certainty in his own centrality and exclusiveness—in juxtaposition with an equally self-confident certainty on the part of others. In all of these cases, the aesthetically utilized background comes to serve as a factor of unmasking or "debunking." But the background not only deprives; it can also provide: the background can also be used for the purpose of "heroicizing" a hero who appears and acts against that background. As we shall see later, however, both satirizing and "ironicizing" still presuppose the possibility that the constituents with which they work may be self-experienced, i.e., they possess a lower degree of transgredience.

What we shall have to demonstrate next is that all constituents of aesthetic consummation are axiologically transgredient to the hero himself or, in other words, that they are not organic in his self-consciousness and do not participate in the world of his life as lived from within himself, i.e., they do not participate in the world in which the hero lives independently of the author. We shall have to demonstrate that these constituents are not experienced as aesthetic values by the hero *in himself*, and, finally, we shall have to establish their interconnection with the external constituents of form—with image and rhythm.[43]

If there is only one unitary and unique participant, there can be no *aesthetic* event. An absolute consciousness, a consciousness that has nothing transgredient to itself, nothing situated outside itself and capable of delimiting it from outside—such a consciousness cannot be "aestheticized"; one can commune in it, but it cannot be seen as a *whole* that is capable of being consummated. An aesthetic event can take place only when there are two participants present; it presupposes two noncoinciding consciousnesses. When the hero and the author coincide or when they find themselves standing either next to one another in the face of a value they share or against one another as antagonists, the aesthetic event ends and an *ethical* event begins (polemical tract, manifesto, speech of accusation or of praise and gratitude, invective, confession as a self-accounting, etc.). When there is no hero at all, not even in a potential form, then we have to do with an event that is *cognitive* (treatise, article, lecture). And, finally, when the other consciousness is the encompassing consciousness of God, a *religious* event takes place (prayer, worship, ritual).

The Spatial Form of the Hero

1. [*The Excess of Seeing*]

When I contemplate a whole human being who is situated outside and over against me, our concrete, actually experienced horizons[44] do not coincide. For at each given moment, regardless of the position and the proximity to me of this other human being whom I am contemplating, I shall always see and know something that he, from his place outside and over against me, cannot see himself: parts of his body that are inaccessible to his own gaze (his head, his face and its expression), the world behind his back, and a whole series of objects and relations, which in any of our mutual relations are accessible to me but not to him. As we gaze at each other, two different worlds are reflected in the pupils of our eyes. It is possible, upon assuming an appropriate position, to reduce this difference of horizons to a minimum, but in order to annihilate this difference completely, it would be necessary to merge into one, to become one and the same person.

This ever-present *excess* of my seeing, knowing, and possessing in relation to any other human being is founded in the uniqueness and irreplaceability of my place in the world. For only I—the one-and-only I—occupy in a given set of circumstances this particular place at this particular time; all other human beings are situated outside me.

Cognition surmounts this concrete outsideness of me myself[45] and the outsideness-for-me of all other human beings, as well as the excess of my seeing in relation to each one of them, which is founded in that position of outsideness.[a] Cognition constructs a unitary and universally valid world, a world independent in every respect from that concrete and unique position which is occupied by this or that individual. For cognition, there is no absolutely inconvertible relationship of *I* and *all others;* for cognition, "*I* and the *other*," inasmuch as they are being thought, constitute a relationship that is relative and convertible, since the cognitive *subiectum*[46] as such does not occupy any determinate, concrete place in being.

However, this unitary world of cognition cannot be *perceived* as a unique concrete whole, charged with the manifold qualities of being, the way we perceive a particular landscape, dramatic scene, *this* particular building, etc. For what the actual perception of a concrete whole presupposes is that the contemplator oc-

---

[a] Correlative with this excess, there is a certain deficiency, for precisely that which only I see in the other is seen in myself, likewise, only by the other. But this is not essential for us in the present context, because the interrelationship of "*I*—the *other*" is not convertible for me in lived life in any concrete way.

cupies a perfectly determinate place, and that he is unitary and *embodied*. The world of cognition and every constituent in it are capable of being thought, but they are not capable of actually being perceived. Similarly, a given inner lived experience and inner whole can be experienced concretely—can be inwardly perceived—either in the category of *I-for-myself* or in the category of the *other-for-me*, i.e., either as *my own* lived experience or as the lived experience of *this* particular and unique *other* human being.

Aesthetic contemplation and ethical action cannot abstract from the concrete uniqueness of the place in being that is occupied by the *subiectum* of ethical action as well as by the *subiectum* of artistic contemplation.

The excess of my seeing in relation to another human being provides the foundation for a certain sphere of my own exclusive self-activity, i.e., all those inner and outer actions which only I can perform in relation to the other, and which are completely inaccessible to the other himself from his own place outside of me; all those actions, that is, which render the other complete precisely in those respects in which he cannot complete himself by himself. These actions can be infinitely varied, depending on the variety of those life situations in which I and the other find ourselves at any given time. But no matter how great the variety of situations, the excess of my self-activity is invariably present in them all, at all times, under all circumstances. Moreover, the composition of this excess tends toward a certain stable constancy.

We are not concerned in the present context with those actions which, by virtue of their outward sense, involve myself and the other within the unitary and unique event of being,[47] and which are directed toward the actual modification of the event and of the other as a moment in that event; such actions are purely *ethical* actions or deeds. Our concern is only with actions of *contemplation*—*actions* of contemplation, because contemplation is active and productive. These actions of contemplation do not go beyond the bounds of the other as a given; they merely unify and order that given. And it is these actions of contemplation, issuing from the excess of my outer and inner seeing of the other human being, that constitute the purely *aesthetic* actions. The excess of my seeing is the bud in which slumbers form, and whence form unfolds like a blossom.

But in order that this bud should really unfold into the blossom of consummating form, the excess of my seeing must "fill in" the horizon of the other human being who is being contemplated, must render his horizon complete, without at the same time forfeiting his distinctiveness. I must empathize or project myself into this other human being, see his world axiologically from within him as *he* sees this world; I must put myself in his place and then, after returning to my own place, "fill in" his horizon through that excess of seeing which opens out from this, my own, place outside him. I must enframe him, create a consummating environment for him out of this excess of my own seeing, knowing, desiring, and feeling.

Let us say that there is a human being before me who is suffering. The horizon of *his* consciousness is filled by the circumstance which makes him suffer and by the objects which he sees before him. The emotional and volitional tones which pervade this visible world of objects are tones of suffering. What I have to do is to experience and consummate him aesthetically (ethical actions, such as assistance, rescue, consolation, are excluded in this case). The first step in aesthetic activity is my projecting myself into him and experiencing his life from within him.[48] I must experience—come to see and to know—what *he* experiences; I must put myself in *his* place and coincide with him, as it were. (How this projection of myself into him is possible and in what form— the psychological problem of such projection—we shall not consider here. It is enough for our purposes that such projection, within certain limits, is possible in fact.) I must appropriate to myself the concrete life-horizon of this human being as he experiences it himself; a whole series of features accessible to me from my own place will turn out to be absent from within this other's horizon. Thus, the person suffering does not experience the fullness of his own outward expressedness in being; he experiences this expressedness only partially, and then in the language of his inner sensations of himself. He does not see the agonizing tension of his own muscles, does not see the entire, plastically consummated posture of his own body, or the expression of suffering on his own face. He does not see the clear blue sky against the background of which his suffering outward image is delineated for me. And even if he were able to see all these features—if, for example, he were in front of a mirror—he would lack the appropriate emotional and volitional approach to these features. That is, they would not occupy the same place in his own awareness that they do in his contemplator's. During the time I project myself into him, I must detach myself from the independent significance of all these features that are transgredient to his consciousness, and I must utilize them merely as a directive, as a means for projecting myself into him. In other words, the outward expressedness of such features is the path by which I penetrate him and almost merge or become one with him from within. But is this fullness of inner merging the ultimate goal of aesthetic activity, for which outward expressedness is only a means and performs only an informative function? Certainly not. Aesthetic activity proper has not even begun yet.

The life situation of a suffering human being that is really experienced from within may prompt me to perform an ethical action, such as providing assistance, consolation, or cognitive reflection. But in any event my projection of myself into him must be followed by a *return* into myself, a *return* to my own place outside the suffering person, for only from this place can the material derived from my projecting myself into the other be rendered meaningful ethically, cognitively, or aesthetically. If this return into myself did not actually take place, the pathological phenomenon of experiencing another's suffering as one's own would result—an infection with another's suffering, and nothing more.

Strictly speaking, a pure projection of myself into the other, a move involving the loss of my own unique place outside the other, is, on the whole, hardly possible; in any event, it is quite fruitless and senseless. When I project myself into another's suffering, I experience it precisely as *his* suffering—in the category of the *other*, and my reaction to it is not a cry of pain, but a word of consolation or an act of assistance. Referring what I myself have experienced to the *other* is an obligatory condition for a productive projection into the other and cognition of the other, both ethically and aesthetically. Aesthetic activity proper actually begins at the point when we *return* into ourselves, when we *return* to our own place outside the suffering person, and start to form and consummate the material we derived from projecting ourselves into the other and experiencing him from within himself. And these acts of forming and consummating are effected by our *completing* that material (that is, the suffering of the given human being) with features *transgredient* to the entire object-world of the other's suffering consciousness. These transgredient features no longer have the function of informing but have a new function, the function of *consummating*. The position of his body which had first informed us about his suffering and which led us to his inward suffering now takes on a purely plastic value, becomes an expression which embodies and consummates the suffering expressed, and the emotional and volitional tones of this expressedness are no longer the tones of suffering. The clear blue sky that enframes him becomes a pictorial feature which consummates and resolves his suffering. And all these values that consummated the image of the other were drawn by me from the excess of my seeing, volition, and feeling.

It should be kept in mind that the constitutive moments of projecting oneself into the other and of consummating the other do not follow one another chronologically; we must emphasize that the sense of each is different, although in living experience projection and consummation are intimately intertwined and fuse with one another. In a verbal work, every word keeps both moments in view: every word performs a twofold function insofar as it directs my projection of myself into the other as well as brings him to completion, except that one constitutive moment may prevail over the other.

Our most immediate task is to examine those plastic-pictorial, spatial values which are *transgredient* to the hero's consciousness and his world, transgredient to his cognitive-ethical stance in the world, and which *consummate* him from outside, from another's consciousness of him—the consciousness of the author/contemplator.

2. [Outward Appearance]

The first matter we must consider is the exterior or outward appearance as the totality of all expressive, "speaking" features of the human body. How do we experience our own exterior? And how do we experience outward appearance in the other? On what plane of lived experience does the aesthetic value of outward appearance lie? Such are the questions we shall now take up.

There can be no doubt, of course, that my own exterior is not part of the concrete, actual horizon of my seeing, except for those rare cases when, like Narcissus, I contemplate my own reflection in the water or in a mirror. My own exterior (that is, all of the expressive features of my body, without exception) is experienced by me from *within* myself. It is only in the form of scattered fragments, scraps, dangling on the string of my inner sensation of myself, that my own exterior enters the field of my outer senses, and, first of all, the sense of vision. But the data provided by these outer senses do not represent an ultimate authority even for deciding the question of whether *this* body is or is not mine. That question is decided only by my inner self-sensation. And it is again my self-sensation that imparts unity to the scattered fragments of my outward expressedness, translating them into its own inner language. This is the case in actual perception: in the outwardly unified world that I see, hear, and touch, I do not encounter my own outward expressedness in being as an outwardly unitary object among other objects. I am situated on the boundary, as it were, of the world I see. In plastic and pictorial terms, I am not connatural with it. While my thought can place my body wholly into the outside world as an object among other objects, my actual seeing cannot do the same thing; my seeing, that is, cannot come to the aid of thinking by providing it with an adequate outward image.

If we turn to our creative imagination, to our dreams or fantasies about ourselves, we shall easily ascertain that they do not work with my outward expressedness and do not evoke any outward, finished image of it. The world of my active fantasies about myself is disposed in front of me, just as is the horizon of my actual seeing; I enter this world as its leading actor, i.e., as the one who conquers all hearts, wins extraordinary glory, and so forth. Yet in doing so, I lack any representation of my own outward image, whereas images of *other* participants in my fantasy, even the most secondary ones, present themselves to me at times with remarkable clarity and completeness—down to expressions of surprise, delight, fright, love, or fear on their faces. Yet the one to whom this fear, delight, and love pertain, that is, myself, I do not *see* at all: myself I *experience* from within myself. Even when I dream about the admiration that my exterior calls forth in others, I do not have to represent it to myself; I represent to myself only the result of the impression it makes on others. In regard to its plastic and pictorial aspects, the world of fantasy is quite similar to that of actual perception. Here, too, the leading actor is not expressed outwardly and exists on a different plane from that of the other participants; while they are expressed *outwardly*, he is experienced *from within.*[* 49] In this respect, fantasy does not fill the lacunae of actual perception; it has no need to do that.

The difference in the planes on which persons exist in fantasy is particularly clear-cut when it has an erotic character: the longed-for heroine attains the highest degree of outward distinctness that our representation is capable of achieving; but the hero—the dreamer himself—experiences himself in his desires and his love from within himself and remains quite unexpressed outwardly. The same divergence of planes occurs in the dreams we have in our sleep. Yet when I begin to recount my fantasy or my dream to another person, I have to transpose the leading actor to the same plane as that of the other participants (even when the story is told in the first person). And, in any case, I have to take into account the fact that all the participants in the story, including myself, will be perceived by the listener on one and the same plastic-pictorial plane; because all of them are, for him, *others.* It is precisely in this that the difference lies between the world of artistic creation and the world of dreaming as well as that of actual life. In the world of artistic creation, all the participants are equally expressed on one and the same plastic and pictorial plane of seeing, whereas in life and in dreams the main hero—I myself—is never expressed outwardly and requires no outward image. The first task an artist must accomplish is to invest with outward bodiliness this leading actor of life and of dreaming about life. Sometimes, when uneducated people read a novel nonartistically, artistic perception is replaced by dreaming; this is, however, not free dreaming, but a passive form of dreaming that is predetermined by the novel. Such a reader projects himself into the main hero, disregards all the features that consummate the hero (the hero's exterior, first of all), and experiences the hero's life as if he were himself the hero of that life.

One can, of course, make the attempt to visualize one's own outward image in imagination, to "feel" oneself from outside, to translate oneself from the language of inner self-sensation into that of outward expressedness in being. But this is far from easy to do. It requires a special and unusual effort; and this difficulty and effort are quite unlike those we experience when trying to recall the not-too-familiar and half-forgotten face of another person. What is involved is less a matter of having an insufficient memory of our own outward appearance than it is a matter of a certain fundamental resistance exerted by our outward image. One can easily ascertain by way of self-observation that the initial result of such an attempt will be the following: the visually expressed image of myself will begin to assume unsteady definition alongside myself as I experience myself from within; it will just barely detach itself from my inner self-sensation in a direction ahead of itself; it will shift slightly to the side and, like a bas-relief, separate from the surface of my inner self-sensation, without breaking away from it entirely. I shall become slightly "doubled," but shall not come apart completely: the umbilical cord of my self-sensation will continue to connect my outward expressedness in being with my inner experience of myself. A certain renewed effort is required in order to visualize myself distinctly *en face* and to break away completely from my inner self-sensation.

And when we succeed in doing this, we shall be struck by the peculiar *emptiness, ghostliness,* and an eerie, frightening *solitariness* of this outward image of ourselves. What accounts for this? It is explained by the fact that we lack any emotional and volitional approach to this outward image that could vivify it and include or incorporate it axiologically within the outward unity of the plastic-pictorial world. All of my emotional and volitional reactions that apprehend and axiologically structure another person's outward expressedness in being (admiration, love, tenderness, compassion, hostility, hatred, and the like) are directed ahead of myself out into the world and are not immediately applicable to myself as I experience myself from within. My own inner *I*— that wills, loves, feels, sees, and knows—I structure from within myself in terms of entirely different value-categories, and these are not directly applicable to the outward expressedness of myself. However, my inner sensation of myself and my life for myself remain present in me as the one who is imagining and seeing: they are not present in me as the one who is imagined and seen. Nor do I find in myself any immediate vivifying and incorporating emotional-volitional reactions to my own exterior—whence its emptiness and solitariness.

In order to vivify my own outward image and make it part of a concretely viewable whole, the entire architectonic of the world of my imagining must be radically restructured by introducing a totally new factor into it. This new factor that restructures the architectonic consists in my outward image being affirmed and founded in emotional and volitional terms *out* of the other and *for* the other human being.

For, from within myself, there is only my own inner affirmation of myself, which I am unable to project upon my outward expressedness (as detached from my inner self-sensation), and that is why it confronts me as axiologically empty, lacking any affirmed foundation. Something like a transparent screen has to be inserted between my inner self-sensation (the function of my *empty* seeing) and my outwardly expressed image: the screen of the other's possible emotional-volitional reaction to my outward manifestation—his possible enthusiasm, love, astonishment, or compassion for me. And looking through this screen of the other's soul (which is thus reduced to a means), I vivify my exterior and make it part of the plastic and pictorial world.

This possible bearer of the other's axiological reaction to me should not become a determinate human being, for, if that were to happen, he would immediately exclude my outward image from the field of my representation and assume its place: I would see him with his outwardly expressed reaction to me, when I would already be in my normal position on the boundaries of the field of vision; and, in addition, he would, as a participant with a definite role, introduce an element of a particular *story* into my dream, whereas what is really needed is an author who does not himself participate in the imagined event.

The point at issue here is precisely how to accomplish the task of translating myself from inner language into the language of outward expressedness and of weaving all of myself totally into the unitary plastic and pictorial fabric of life as a human being among other human beings, as a hero among other heroes. One can easily substitute for this task another task which is entirely different in kind, namely, the task accomplished by discursive thought: thinking has no difficulty at all in placing *me* on one and the same plane with all *other* human beings, for in the act of thinking I first of all abstract myself from that unique place which I—as this unique human being—occupy in being; consequently, I abstract myself from the concretely intuited uniqueness of the world as well. Hence, discursive thought is unfamiliar with the ethical and aesthetic difficulties of self-objectification.

Ethical and aesthetic objectification requires a powerful *point d'appui* outside itself; it requires some genuine source of real strength out of which I would be capable of seeing myself as another.

Indeed, when we contemplate our own exterior—as a living exterior participating in a living outward whole—through the prism of the evaluating soul of a possible other, then this soul of the other—as a soul lacking any self-sufficiency, a soul-slave, as it were—introduces a certain spurious element that is absolutely alien to the ethical event of being. For, inasmuch as it lacks any independent value of its own, what is engendered is not something productive and enriching, but a hollow, fictitious product that clouds the optical purity of being. What occurs here is something in the nature of an optical forgery: a soul without a place of its own is created, a participant without a name and without a role—something absolutely extrahistorical. It should be clear that through the eyes of this fictitious other one cannot see one's true face, but only one's mask-face.* 50 This screen of the other's living reaction must be bodied and given a founded, essential, authoritative independence and self-sufficiency: it must be made into an answerable author. A negative precondition for this is my complete disinterestedness with reference to him: upon returning into myself, I must not exploit his evaluation once again for my own sake. In the present context, we cannot delve into these questions more deeply, since we are dealing only with outward appearance (cf. the narrator, the self-objectification through a heroine, and so forth). But it should be clear that outward appearance as an aesthetic value is not an immediate moment in my self-consciousness: it lies on the boundary of the plastic and pictorial worlds. For, as the leading actor in my own life, actual as well as imagined, I experience myself on a plane that is fundamentally different from the one on which I experience all other active participants in my life and in my imagining.

A very special case of seeing my exterior is looking at myself in a mirror. It would appear that in this case we see ourselves directly. But this is not so. We remain within ourselves and we see only our own reflection, which is not capable of becoming an immediate moment in our seeing and experiencing of the world. We see the *reflection* of our exterior, but not *ourselves* in terms of our exterior. The exterior does not encompass all of me—I am in front of the mirror and not in it. The mirror can do no more than provide the material for self-objectification, and even that not in its pure form. Indeed, our position before a mirror is always somewhat spurious, for since we lack any approach to ourselves from outside, in this case, as in the other, we project ourselves into a peculiarly indeterminate possible other, with whose help we then try to find an axiological position in relation to ourselves; in this case, too, we try to vivify ourselves and give form to ourselves— out of the other. Whence that distinctive and unnatural expression of our face which we see on it in the mirror, but which we never have in our lived life. This expression of our face as reflected in a mirror is made up of several expressions whose emotional and volitional directedness derives from entirely different planes: (1) the expressions of our actual emotional and volitional attitude which we are actualizing at a given moment and which are justified within the unitary and unique context of our life; (2) the expressions of the evaluation on the part of the possible other, expressions of the fictitious soul without a place of its own; and (3) the expressions of our own relationship to that evaluation on the part of the possible other, such as satisfaction or dissatisfaction, being pleased or displeased. For our own relationship to our exterior does not, after all, have an immediately aesthetic character; it pertains only to its possible effect on others—namely, on the immediate observers. That is, we evaluate our exterior not for ourselves, but *for* others *through* others. Finally, these three kinds of expression may also be joined by an expression which we would *like* to see on our own face—again, of course, not for ourselves, but for the other. For we almost invariably attitudinize a bit before a mirror, giving ourselves one expression or another that we deem to be essential or desirable.

All these different expressions contend with one another and can enter into a random symbiosis on our face as reflected in a mirror. In any case, what is expressed here is not a unitary and unique soul—a second participant is implicated in the event of self-contemplation, a fictitious other, a nonauthoritative and unfounded author. I am not alone when I look at myself in the mirror: I am possessed by someone else's soul. More than that. At times, this other soul may gain body to the point where it attains a certain self-sufficiency. Vexation and a certain resentment, with which our dissatisfaction about our own exterior may combine, give body to this other—the possible author of our own exterior. Distrust of him, hatred, a desire to annihilate him become possible. In trying to fight against another's potential, comprehensively formative evaluation, I consolidate it to the point of giving it self-subsistence, almost to the point where it becomes a person localized in being.

To purify the expression of the reflected face is precisely the first task to be accomplished by an artist working on his self-portrait. And this task is achieved only by his authoritative and essentially necessary author: it is the author-artist as such overcoming the artist-as-person. It seems to me, however, that a self-portrait can always be distinguished from a portrait by the peculiarly ghostly character of the face: the face does not, as it were, include within itself the full human being, does not encompass all of him entirely. For me, there is something eerie about the forever-laughing face of Rembrandt in his self-portrait[51] or the strangely alienated face of Vrubel'.[52]

It is much more difficult to provide an integral image of one's own exterior in the *autobiographical* hero of a verbal composition, where one's exterior is involved in the many-sided movement of a *fabula* and must cover the whole human being. I am not aware of any finished efforts of this kind in a major work of art. There are, however, numerous partial attempts, such as Pushkin's portrait of himself as a boy,*[53] Tolstoy's Irtenev as well as his Levin,[54] Dostoevsky's man from the underground, and others. In verbal creation, completeness of outward appearance in purely pictorial terms does not exist and, in fact, is not possible, for it is interwoven here with various other features of a whole human being (these features will be analyzed below).

A photograph of oneself also provides no more than material for collation, and once again we do not see ourselves here—we see only our own reflection without an author. True, it no longer reflects the expression of a fictitious other, i.e., it is purer than the reflection in a mirror; nevertheless, it is fortuitous, artificially received, and does not express our *essential* emotional and volitional stance in the ongoing event of being. It is merely raw material, completely incapable of being incorporated into the unity of my life experience, because there are no principles for its inclusion.

Our portrait, when painted by an artist who is authoritative for us, is an entirely different matter. In this case, what I have is indeed a window into a world in which I never live; this is truly a seeing of oneself in the other's world through the eyes of a pure and whole other human being—the artist; a seeing as divination that has an inherent tendency to predetermine me. For outward appearance must encompass, must contain within itself, and must consummate the whole of my soul—my unitary emotional and volitional cognitive-ethical stance in the world. For me, outward appearance fulfills this function only in the other: I am incapable of feeling *myself* in my own exterior, of feeling myself encompassed and expressed by it, since my emotional and volitional reactions attach to objects and do not contract into an outwardly finished image of myself. My exterior is incapable of becoming *for me* a constituent in a characterization of myself. In the category of *I,* my exterior is incapable of being experienced as a value that encompasses and consummates me. It is only in the category of the *other* that it is thus experienced, and I have to subsume myself under this category of the other in order to be able to see myself as a constituent in the unitary pictorial-plastic external world.

Outward appearance must not be taken in isolation when considered in relation to verbal works of art. A certain incompleteness of the purely pictorial portrait is compensated here by a series of features which are directly associated with outward appearance, but are only barely accessible or completely inaccessible to visual art: deportment, gait, vocal timbre, changing facial expression; the changing expression of outward appearance as a whole at various historical moments of a human being's life; the expression of irreversible moments of the event of life in the historical sequence of a human being's progress; features of his gradual growth as it passes through outwardly expressed ages; images of youth, maturity, old age in their plastic-pictorial continuity. In other words, all those features that could be subsumed under the expression "the history of the outer man."

For self-consciousness, this integral image is dispersed in life and enters the field of seeing the external world only in the form of fortuitous fragments. And what is lacking, moreover, is precisely *external* unity and continuity; a human being experiencing life in the category of his own *I* is incapable of gathering himself by himself into an outward whole that would be even relatively finished. The point here is not the deficiency of material provided by outer vision (although the deficiency is in fact considerable); the point, rather, is the absence in principle of any unitary axiological approach from within a human being himself to his own outward expressedness in being. No mirror, photograph, special self-observation will help here. At best, we might get an aesthetically spurious product, created for one's own selfish purposes from the position of a possible other who lacks any standing of his own.

In this sense, one can speak of a human being's absolute need for the other, for the other's seeing, remembering, gathering, and unifying self-activity—the only self-activity capable of producing his outwardly finished personality. This outward personality could not exist, if the other did not create it: aesthetic memory is *productive*—it gives birth, for the first time, to the *outward* human being on a new plane of being.

3. [*Outward Boundaries of the Body*]

A special and extremely important feature in the outer plastic-pictorial seeing of a human being is the experience of the outward boundaries that encompass him. This feature is indissolubly associated with outward appearance and can be detached from it only in abstraction, inasmuch as it expresses the relationship of the outer, exterior man to the outside world that encompasses him—the *delimitation* of a human being in the world. This outward boundary is experienced in self-consciousness, i.e., in relation to myself, in an essentially different way from the way it is experienced in relation to another human being. It is only in the other human being, in fact, that a living, aesthetically (and ethically) convincing experience of human finitude is given to me, the experience of a human being as a delimited empirical object. The other is given to me entirely enclosed *in* a world that is external to me; he is given to me as a constituent in it that is totally delimited on all sides in space. Moreover, at each given moment, I experience distinctly all of his boundaries, encompass all of him visually and can encompass all of him tangibly. I see the line that delineates his head against the background of the outside world and see all of the lines that delimit his body in the outside world. The other, *all* of him, is laid out before me in the exhaustive completeness as a thing among other things *in* the world external to me, without exceeding in any way the bounds of that world, and without in any way violating its visible, tangible plastic-pictorial unity.

There can be no doubt that the entire stock of my perceptual experience will never be able to provide me with the same kind of seeing of *my own* total outer delimitedness. Not only actual perception, but even mental representations are incapable of constituting the kind of horizon within which all of me would be included, without any remainder, as a totally delimited being. As regards actual perception, no special demonstration is required: I am situated on the frontier of the horizon of my seeing; the visible world is disposed before me. By turning my head in all directions. I can succeed in seeing all of myself from all sides of the surrounding space in the center of which I am situated, but I shall never be able to see myself as actually surrounded by this space.

As regards mental representation, the situation is somewhat more complicated. We have already seen that, even though I do not ordinarily represent to myself an image of myself, I *could* do it with a certain amount of effort. In such a case, I could represent it to myself as delimited from all sides, of course, much as I see the other. This represented image, however, lacks any inner cogency, for I do not stop experiencing myself from within myself, and this self-experiencing remains with me or, rather, I myself remain *in* it and do not introduce it into the mentally represented image of myself. The consciousness that this is all of me, that outside of this totally delimited object I do not exist—this consciousness can never be convincing within myself, since a necessary coefficient of any perception and of any mental representation of my outward expressedness in being is consciousness of the fact that this is not *all* of me. While my mental representation of another human being corresponds quite adequately to the fullness of my actual seeing of him, my *self*-representation is contrived and does not correspond to any actual perception. The most essential part of my actual experience of myself is excluded from outward seeing.

This difference in the experiencing of myself and the experiencing of the other is overcome by cognition, or, rather, cognition ignores this difference, just as it ignores the uniqueness of the cognizing *subiectum*. In the unitary world of cognition, I cannot find a place for myself as a unique *I-for-myself* in distinction to all other human beings without exception—past, present, and future—as *others* for me. On the contrary, I know that I am just as limited a human being as all others, and that any other human being experiences himself essentially from within himself and is not embodied for himself in his own outward expressedness. Such cognition, however, does not provide those conditions which enable an actual seeing and experiencing of the once-occurrent concrete world of a once-occurrent *subiectum*. The correlation of the image-categories of *I* and the *other* is the form in which an actual human being is concretely experienced; this form of the *I* (the form in which I experience myself as the one-and-only me) is radically different from the form of the *other* (in which I experience all other human beings without exception). And the other person's *I* is also experienced by me in a manner which is completely different from the manner in which I experience my own *I:* the other person's *I* is also subsumed under the category of the *other* as a constituent feature of him.

This radical difference is of essential significance not only for aesthetics, but also for ethics. It should suffice to recall the inequality in principle between the *I* and the *other* with respect to value in Christian ethics: one must not love oneself, one must love the other; one must not be indulgent toward oneself, one must be indulgent toward the other; and in general, we must relieve the other of any burdens and take them upon ourselves.* 55 Or consider altruism, which evaluates the other's happiness and one's own happiness in completely different ways. As regards ethical solipsism, we shall have to come back to it below.

What is essential for the aesthetic standpoint is the following: I am—for myself—the *subiectum* of any self-activity whatsoever (seeing, hearing, touching, thinking, feeling, and so forth); in my lived experiences, I start out from within myself and I am directed forward, ahead of myself, upon the world, upon an object. The object stands over against me myself as *subiectum.* The point here is not the epistemological subject-object correlation, the point is the living correlation of me—the one-and-only *subiectum,* and the rest of the world as an object not only of my cognition and my outer senses, but also of my volition and feeling. The other human being exists for me entirely *in* the object and his *I* is only an object for me. I can remember myself, I can to some extent perceive myself through my outer sense, and thus render myself in part an object of my desiring and feeling—that is, I can make myself an object for myself. But in this act of self-objectification I shall never coincide with myself—*I-for-myself* shall continue to be in the *act* of this self-objectification, and not in its product, that is, in the *act* of seeing, feeling, thinking, and not in the *object* seen or felt. I am incapable of fitting all of myself into an object, for I exceed any object as the active *subiectum* of it.

We are not concerned here with the cognitive aspect of this state of affairs (which constitutes the foundation of idealism). Our concern is rather with the concrete lived experience of our subjectivity and the impossibility of its—of our—being exhaustively present in an object,[b] in contrast to the object-status of any other human being. Cognition introduces a certain rectification here, according to which even I myself—the unique, the one-and-only human being—am not an absolute *I* for myself or an epistemological *subiectum:* everything that enables me to be myself, that renders me a determinate human being, as opposed to all other human beings (a determinate place and time, a determinate destiny, and so forth), is an *object* of cognition as well, rather than a *subiectum* of cognition (cf. Rickert).[56] Nevertheless, what makes idealism intuitively convincing is the experience I have of myself, and not the experience I have of the other human being (the latter tends rather to make realism and materialism intuitively convincing). Solipsism, which places the entire world within my consciousness, may be intuitively convincing, or at any rate understandable. But it would be intuitively quite incomprehensible to place the entire world (including myself) in the consciousness of *another* human being who is so manifestly himself a mere particle of the macrocosm.

It is impossible for me to experience convincingly all of myself as enclosed within an externally delimited, totally visible and tangible object, that is, to experience myself as coinciding with it in every respect. Yet that is the only way in which I can represent the other to myself. Everything inward that I know and in part co-experience in him I put into the outward image of the other as into a vessel which contains his *I*, his will, his cognition. For me, the other is gathered and fitted as a whole into his outward image. My own consciousness, on the other hand, I experience as encompassing the world, as embracing it, rather than as fitted into it [indecipherable]. In other words, the outward image of a human being can be experienced as consummating and exhausting the *other*, but I do not experience it as consummating and exhausting *myself*.

To avoid misunderstanding, let me stress once more that we are not dealing here with moments of cognition, such as the relationship of body and soul, consciousness and matter, idealism and realism, and other problems associated with these moments. Our concern here is only concrete lived experience, its purely aes-

---

[b] This point was thoroughly understood and assimilated in the aesthetics of Romanticism (cf. Schlegel's theory of irony).* [57]

thetic convincingness. We could say that idealism is intuitively convincing from the standpoint of self-experience, whereas, from the standpoint of my experience of the other human being, materialism is intuitively convincing (omitting any consideration here of the philosophical, cognitive justification of these orientations).

The line as a boundary of the body is axiologically adequate for determining and consummating the *other*—moreover, all of the other, in all of his constituent features—but it is utterly inadequate for determining and consummating me for myself, because I experience myself essentially by encompassing any boundaries, any body—by extending myself beyond any bounds. My self-consciousness destroys the plastic convincingness that any image of me might have.

What follows from all this is that only the other human being is experienced by me as connatural with the outside world and thus can be woven into that world and rendered concordant with it in an aesthetically convincing manner. Man-as-nature is experienced in an intuitively convincing manner only in the other, not in myself. I am not—for myself—*entirely* connatural with the outside world, for there is always something essential in me that I can set over against that world, namely, my inner self-activity, my subjectivity, which confronts the outside world as object, and which is incapable of being contained in it. This inner self-activity of mine exceeds both nature and the world: I always have an outlet along the line of my experience of myself in the act [indecipherable] of the world—I always have a loophole,[58] as it were, through which I can save myself from being no more than a natural given.

The other [indecipherable] is intimately associated with the world; *I* am intimately associated with my inner, world-exceeding self-activity. When I possess myself in all my seriousness, everything in myself that has the character of an object[c] ceases to express me for myself, and I begin to withdraw myself as a whole into the very act of this thinking, seeing, and feeling. I am not contained altogether in any external state of affairs—none of them includes all of myself exhaustively; for myself, I am located

---

[c] E.g., fragments of my outward expressedness; anything already given, present-on-hand in myself; I myself as a determinate content of my thinking about myself, of how I feel.

on the tangent, as it were, to any given state of affairs. Everything in myself that is spatially given gravitates toward my own *nonspatial* inner center, whereas everything that is ideal in the other gravitates toward his givenness *in space.*

The distinctiveness with which I concretely experience the other sharply poses the aesthetic problem of how to provide a purely intensive justification for a *given* delimited finitude, without exceeding the bounds of a *given* external, spatial-sensuous world. It is only in relation to the other that one experiences immediately the insufficiency of cognitive comprehension as well as the insufficiency of ethical justification (which occurs purely in terms of meaning and is indifferent to the concrete uniqueness of an image). For both cognitive comprehension and ethical justification bypass the constituent feature of outward expressedness, which is so essential in my experiencing of the other, and unessential within myself.

My aesthetic self-activity[d] contains within itself syncretically the seed, as it were, of creative plastic images and finds expression in a number of irreversible actions that issue from within myself and affirm the other axiologically in respect to those features which constitute his outward consummatedness: such actions, for example, as embracing, kissing, or "overshadowing" him.[60]

The productiveness and irreversibility of these actions is particularly evident in my living experience of them. In these actions I actualize in an intuitably convincing manner the privilege of my position outside the other, and the axiological bodiedness of the other becomes tangibly real in this context. After all, it is only the other who can be embraced, clasped all around, it is only the other's boundaries that can all be touched and felt lovingly. The other's fragile finiteness, consummatedness, his here-and-now being—all are inwardly grasped by me and shaped, as it were, by my embrace; in this act, the other's outward existence begins to live in a new manner, acquires some sort of new meaning, is born on a new plane of being. Only the other's lips can be touched with our own, only on the other can we lay our hands, rise actively above the other and "overshadow" all of him totally, "overshadow" him

---

[d] Aesthetic self-activity *not* as it manifests itself in the special activity of an author-artist, but aesthetic self-activity in my once-occurrent *life,* where it is still internally undifferentiated and not disengaged from non-aesthetic elements.[59]

in every constituent feature of his existence, "overshadow" his body and within his body—his soul.

I am incapable of experiencing any of these actions in relation to myself. Not just because of the physical impossibility of doing so, but, rather, because of the emotional-volitional *untruth* involved in turning these acts upon myself. As an object of these acts of embracing, kissing, "overshadowing," the other's outward, delimited existence takes on the character of an axiologically resilient and heavy, inwardly weighty, material for shaping and sculpting the given human being—not as a physically closed and physically delimited space, but as an aesthetically closed and delimited space—as a *living* space that has the character of an aesthetic *event*.

It should be evident, of course, that we are abstracting here from the sexual features, which cloud the aesthetic purity of these irreversible actions. We take these actions as artistically symbolic lived-life reactions to the whole of a human being, where in embracing or "overshadowing" his body we also embrace or "overshadow" the soul enclosed in and expressed by that body.

4. [Outward Actions]

We now turn our attention to a third feature—a human being's actions or external deeds that take place in the spatial world. The questions to be examined in this section are these. How is an action and its space experienced in the action-performer's self-consciousness? How is the action of the other experienced by me? On what plane of consciousness is its aesthetic value located?

We noted earlier that fragments of my outward expressedness in being become part of me only through inner experiences that correspond to them. And indeed, when my own reality becomes doubtful for some reason, when I do not know whether I am dreaming or not, the mere visibility of my own body is not enough to convince me: either I must make a movement of one kind or another or I must pinch myself. That is, in order to verify my own reality, I must translate my exterior into the language of my internal sensations of myself. When, as the result of an illness, we lose control of one of our limbs—a leg, for example—this limb appears to us as if it did not belong to us, as if it was not "mine," although in the externally intuitable image of my body it is undoubtedly part of the whole of myself. Any fragment of my body given from outside must be experienced or "lived through" by me from within myself, and it is only through this experiencing-from-within that it can be rendered part of myself, part of my once-occurrent unity. And if, on the other hand, this translation into the language of my inner sensations of myself fails to succeed, I am quite prepared to reject a given fragment as not mine, as not part of my body, and its intimate association with me is broken off. This purely internal experiencing of the body and its limbs is especially important at the moment of performing an action which, after all, invariably establishes a connection between myself and another external object, invariably expands the sphere of my physical influence.

By way of introspective observation, it can easily be ascertained that I focus on my outward expressedness least of all when performing a physical action. Strictly speaking, I act, I grasp an object not with my hand as an externally complete image or configuration; rather, I grasp it with my internally experienced muscular feeling corresponding to my hand. And what I grasp is not the object as an externally complete image, but rather my tactile experience corresponding to the object, and my muscular feeling of the object's resistance, its heaviness, compactness, and so forth. What is seen merely complements what is internally experienced and is of secondary significance in the actualization of an action. And, in general, all that which is given, present-on-hand, already realized and available—recedes, as such, into the background of the action-performing consciousness. This consciousness is directed toward a goal, and the given course followed in performing the action as well as the means of achieving the goal are both experienced from within. The path followed in performing an action is a purely internal one, and the continuity of this path is internal as well (cf. Bergson).[61]

Suppose that I perform a certain movement with my hand—I take *this* book from the shelf, for example. I do not follow the external movement of my hand, the visible course it traverses, the positions it assumes during its movement in relation to the various objects in this room. All of this enters my consciousness only in the form of fortuitous bits and pieces that are of very little moment for the action; it is from within myself that I control and guide my hand.

Or, for example, when I walk along the street, I am internally directed forward, I calculate and evaluate all of my movements internally. In doing so, of course, I may occasionally need to see some things as distinctly as possible (at times even within myself). But this outer seeing during the performance of an action is always one-sided. That is, what I perceive in an object in such outer seeing is only that which is immediately relevant to a given action; as a result, such a way of seeing destroys the object's fullness as an intuitable given. What is present-on-hand, given, determined in the visual image or configuration of an object located in the area of action is eroded and decomposed during the performance of an action by what is yet-to-be, what is still in the future, what is still being actualized in relation to the given object by my action: I see an object from the standpoint of a future inner experience, and this is a standpoint which is most unjust in regard to the externally completed character of an object. Thus, to pursue our earlier example, when I was walking along the street and suddenly saw a person walking toward me from the opposite direction, I quickly shifted to the right to avoid colliding with him; what was in the foreground for me in my seeing of that person was the possible jolt I was anticipating—a jolt I would have experienced from within myself[e]—and my (internally directed) shift to the right followed directly from this.

An object located in the area of intense external action is experienced now as a possible impediment, pressure, or possible pain and now as a possible support for my hand, my foot, and so on. And all this, moreover, is experienced in the language of my inner self-sensation; it is this that breaks up the object as an externally completed given. Thus, inner sensation of self remains the foundation—the proper world of action—during intense external action: it dissolves within itself or subordinates to itself everything that is externally expressed, and it does not allow anything external to complete itself in a stable intuitable given either within or without myself.

Focusing on one's own exterior in performing an action may even prove to be fatal, a force that destroys the action. Thus, when one has to perform a difficult and risky jump, it is extremely dangerous to follow the movement of one's own feet: one has to col-

---

[e] This anticipation itself, moreover, is accomplished in the language of my inner sensation of myself.

lect oneself from within and to calculate one's own movements—again from within. The first rule of any sport: look directly *ahead* of yourself, not *at* yourself. During a difficult and dangerous action, I contract and concentrate all of myself to the point of becoming a pure inner unity, I stop seeing and hearing anything external, I reduce all of myself and my world to pure self-sensation.

The external image or configuration of an action and its external, intuitable relation to the objects of the outside world are never given to the performer of the action himself, and if they do irrupt into the action-performing consciousness, they inevitably turn into curbs or "dead points" of action.

Action experienced from within the action-performing consciousness negates in principle the axiological independence of anything given, already on hand, available, completed; it destroys the present of the object for the sake of its future—a future anticipated from within. The world of action is a world of the internally anticipated future. The prospective *goal* of an action breaks up the presently given makeup of the external world of objects, the *plan* of a future actualization breaks up the *body* of an object's present state. The anticipation of a future actualization permeates the entire horizon of the action-performing consciousness and dissolves its stability.

It follows from this that the artistic truth of an expressed and externally apprehended action, its organic wovenness into the outer fabric of what exists around it, its harmonious correlatedness with the background (as the totality of the presently stable world of objects)—all this is transgredient in principle to the consciousness of the person performing the action; all this is actualized only by a consciousness situated outside such a person, by a consciousness that takes no part in the action with respect to its purpose and meaning.

Only the other's action is capable of being artistically understood and formed by me, whereas from within myself my own action does not yield in principle to artistic forming and consummation. What we mean here is, of course, action in a purely plastic-pictorial sense.

The basic plastic-pictorial characterizations of an external action (such as epithets, metaphors, similes, and so on) are never actualized in the action-performer's consciousness, nor do they ever coincide with the inner truth of an action—its truth in respect to purpose and meaning. All artistic characterizations transpose the action to a different plane, a different axiological context, where the purpose and meaning of the action become immanent to the event of its performance—become merely a moment bestowing meaning upon the outward expressedness of the action. That is, they take the action out of the horizon of the person performing the action and place it within the horizon of a contemplator situated outside the performer of that action.

If, on the other hand, the plastic-pictorial characteristics of an action are present-on-hand in the action-performer's own consciousness, then his action instantly breaks away from the compelling seriousness of its purpose, breaks away from the needfulness, newness, and productiveness of what is being actualized, and turns into mere *play* or degenerates into mere *gesture*.

All one need do is analyze any artistic description of an action in order to see (1) that the artistic consummatedness and convincingness in the plastic-pictorial image or character of this description are located in an already dead meaning-context of life—a meaning-context that is transgredient to the action-performer's consciousness at the moment of his action—and (2) that we ourselves—the readers—are not internally interested in the purpose and meaning of the action,[f] that we expect nothing from the action, and hope for nothing in the real future. The real future has been replaced for us by an *artistic* future, and this artistic future is always predetermined in artistic terms. An action that has been given artistic form is experienced outside the fateful time of the ongoing event of my once-occurrent life. For in the fateful time of my ongoing life, no action ever presents itself to me in terms of its artistic aspect. All plastic-pictorial characterizations, especially similes, neutralize the real and fateful future; they are deployed entirely on the plane of the self-sufficing past and present, from which there is no access to the living and still risk-fraught future.

All features of the plastic-pictorial consummation of an action are transgredient in principle to the world of purposes and meaning in their ineluctable needfulness and consequence. An artistic action is consummated apart from purposes and meaning at the

---

[f] For otherwise the object-world of the action would be involved in our action-performing consciousness (as experienced from within), and its outward expressedness would thus be dissolved.

point where they cease to be the sole forces that impel my self-activity, and that is possible and internally justified only in relation to the other's action, where my own horizon complements and consummates the action-performing horizon of the other—a horizon disintegrated by the prospective, compellingly needful purpose.

5. [The Inner and the Outer Body]

We have delineated the distinctive character of experiencing (1) outward appearance, (2) the outward boundaries of the body, and (3) outward physical action, both in relation to oneself (in one's self-consciousness) and in relation to another human being. We must now synthesize these three abstractly isolated moments in the single axiological whole of the human body. That is, we have to pose the problem of the body as constituting a value.

It should be clear, of course, that, insofar as the problem relates specifically to value, it is definitely demarcated from the viewpoint of natural science—from the biological problem of the organism, from the psycho-physiological problem of relations between the bodily and the psychological, and from related problems in the philosophy of nature. The problem of the body as value can be located only on the ethical plane, on the aesthetic plane, and to some extent on the religious plane. . . .

What is extremely important for our problem is the unique place which the body as value occupies in the unique concrete world in relation to the *subiectum*. My own body is, at its very foundation, an inner body, while the other's body is, at its very foundation, an outward body.

The inner body—my body as a moment in my self-consciousness—represents the sum total of inner organic sensations, needs, and desires that are unified around an inner center. The outward aspect, as we saw, is fragmentary and fails to attain independence and completeness. And since it always has an inner equivalent, it belongs—through the mediation of that equivalent—to my inner unity. I cannot react to my own *outward* body in an unmediated way: all of the immediate emotional-volitional tones that are associated for me with my body relate to its inner states and possibilities, such as suffering, pleasure, passion, gratification, and so forth. One may love one's own body, one may feel a sort of tender-

ness toward it, but this means only one thing: the constant striving and desiring of those purely internal states and experiences
which are actualized through my body, on the one hand, and the
love of one's own body, on the other, have essentially nothing in
common with the love of another human being's individual exterior. The case of Narcissus is interesting precisely insofar as it is
an exception that characterizes and clarifies the rule. I may wish
to be loved, I may visualize and anticipate the other's love—but I
cannot love myself as I love the other, in an unmediated way.
That is, I may be solicitous for myself and I may be equally solicitous for someone I love, but this does not justify the conclusion
that my emotional-volitional relationship to myself and to the
other is similar in kind—or, in other words, that I love myself the
way I love the other. For the emotional-volitional tones that lead
in both cases to the same actions of solicitude are radically dissimilar. I cannot love my fellow being as myself or, rather, I cannot *love* myself as a fellow being. All I can do is transfer to him all
of those actions which I usually perform for my own sake.

Law and lawlike morality cannot extend the application of
their requirements to the inner emotional-volitional reaction. All
they require are certain external actions that one performs in relation to oneself and that must be performed for the sake of the
other. But it is out of the question to transpose one's inner (axiological) *self*-relationship to the *other*. For the point at issue is the
creation of a completely new emotional-volitional relationship to
the other *as other*—the relationship which we call "love" and
which we are quite incapable of experiencing in relation to *ourselves*. My suffering, my fear for myself, my joy are profoundly
different from my compassion or suffering *with* the other, rejoic-
ing *with* the other, and fearing *for* the other—whence the difference in principle in the way these feelings are ethically qualified.
The egoist acts *as if* he loved himself, but in reality he experiences nothing that resembles love or tenderness for himself; the
point is precisely that he does not know these feelings at all. Self-
preservation is an emotional-volitional attitude that is cold and
cruel: it is utterly devoid of any loving and cherishing elements,
any aesthetic elements whatsoever.

The value of my external personality as a whole (and, first and
foremost, the value of my external body—which is our exclusive
concern in the present context) has a borrowed character: it is

constructed by me, but is not experienced by me in any unmediated way.

I *can* strive in an unmediated way for self-preservation and well-being, defend my life with all the means at my disposal, and even strive for power and the subjection of others, but I can never experience within myself in any unmediated way that which constitutes me as a legal person,[62] because my legal personality is nothing else but my guaranteed certainty in being granted recognition by *other* people—a certainty that I experience as *their* obligation in relation to myself. For it is one thing to defend one's own life in fact against an attack in fact—animals act in exactly the same way in this case. It is an entirely different thing to experience one's *right* to life and safety and the obligation of others to respect this right.

And, similarly, there is an equally profound difference between my inner experience of my own body and the recognition of its outer value by *other* people—my right to the loving acceptance or recognition of my exterior by *others:* this recognition or acceptance descends upon me from others like a gift, like grace, which is incapable of being understood and founded from within myself. And it is only in this case that certainty in the outer value of my body is possible, whereas an immediately intuitable experience of that value is impossible—all I can do is have pretensions to it.

The plastic value of my outer body has been as it were sculpted for me by the manifoled acts of other people in relation to me, acts performed intermittently throughout my life: acts of concern for me, acts of love, acts that recognize my value. In fact, as soon as a human being begins to experience himself from within, he at once meets with acts of recognition and love that come to him from outside—from his mother, from others who are close to him. The child receives all initial determinations of himself and of his body from his mother's lips and from the lips of those who are close to him. It is from their lips, in the emotional-volitional tones of their love, that the child hears and begins to acknowledge his own *proper name* and the names of all the features pertaining to his body and to his inner states and experiences. The words of a loving human being are the first and the most authoritative words about him; they are the words that for the first time determine his personality *from outside,* the words that *come to meet* his indistinct inner sensation of himself, giving it a form and a name in which, for the first time, he finds himself and becomes aware of himself as a *something*. Words of love and acts of genuine concern come to meet the dark chaos of my inner sensation of myself: they name, direct, satisfy, and connect it with the outside world—as with a response that is interested in me and in my need. And as a result, they give plastic form, as it were, to this boundless, "darkly stirring chaos" * 63 of needs and dissatisfactions, wherein the future dyad of the child's personality and the outside world confronting it is still submerged and dissolved.

What helps to disclose this dyad are the loving words and actions of the child's mother: it is in her emotional-volitional tones that the child's personality is demarcated and upbuilt, and it is in her love that his first movement, his first posture in the world, is formed. The child begins to see himself for the first time as if through his mother's eyes, and begins to speak about himself in his mother's emotional-volitional tones—he caresses himself, as it were, with his first uttered self-expression. Thus, he uses affectionate-diminutive terms in the appropriate tone of voice in referring to himself and the limbs of his own body—"my footsies," "my tootsies," "my little head," "go night-night," "nightie-night." He determines himself and his states in this case through his mother, in his mother's love for him, as the object of his mother's cherishing, affection, her kisses; it is his mother's loving embraces that "give form" to him axiologically. From within himself, without any mediation by the loving other, a human being could have never begun to speak about himself in such affectionate-diminutive forms and in such affectionate-diminutive tones, or, at any rate, these forms and tones would not express properly the actual emotional-volitional tone of my self-experience, my immediate inner relationship to myself, and they would be aesthetically counterfeit. For what I experience from within myself is not in the least my "darling little head" or "darling little hand," but precisely my "head" and my "hand"—I act with my "hand," not my "darling little hand." It is only in relation to the other that I can speak about myself in an affectionate-diminutive form, in order to express the *other's* actual relationship toward me or the relationship I wish he would show toward me.

[indecipherable] I feel an absolute need for love that only the other is capable of internally actualizing from his own unique place *outside* of me. To be sure, this need shatters my self-sufficiency from within myself, but does not yet shape me affirmatively *from outside.* In relation to myself, I am profoundly *cold,* even in the act of self-preservation.

This love that shapes a human being from outside throughout his life—his mother's love and the love of others around him—this love gives body to his inner body, and, even though it does not provide him with an intuitable image of his inner body's *outer* value, it does make him the possessor of that body's potential value—a value capable of being actualized only by another human being.

The other's body is an *outer* body, and its value is actualized by me intuitionally and is given to me immediately. The outer body is unified and shaped by cognitive, ethical, and aesthetic categories, and by the sum total of external, visual, and tangible features that make up the plastic and pictorial values in it. My emotional-volitional reactions to the other's outer body are unmediated, and it is only in relation to the other that I experience the *beauty* of the human body in an immediate way—that is, the human body begins to live for me on an entirely different axiological plane, on an axiological plane inaccessible to my inner self-sensation and my fragmentary outer seeing. Only the other is *embodied* for me axiologically and aesthetically. In this respect, the body is not something self-sufficient: it needs the *other,* needs his recognition and his form-giving activity. Only the inner body (the body experienced as heavy) is *given* to a human being himself; the other's outer body is not given but *set as a task:* I must actively produce it.

A quite distinctive approach to the other's body is the sexual approach. By itself, it is incapable of developing form-giving plastic-pictorial energies, i.e., it is incapable of giving form to the body as a determinate external entity that is finished and self-contained. In the sexual approach, the other's outer body disintegrates and becomes merely a constituent in my own *inner* body, or, in other words, it becomes valuable only in connection with those intracorporeal possibilities (the possibilities of carnal desire, pleasure, gratification) which it promises me, and these inner possibilities submerge and dissolve its resilient outward completeness. In the sexual approach to the other's body, my own body and the other's merge into one flesh, but this unitary flesh can be only an *inner* flesh. To be sure, this merging into one *inner* flesh is an ultimate limit toward which my sexual attitude tends in its purest form; in reality, it is always complicated by aesthetic moments that derive from my loving admiration of the other's body, and, consequently, by form-giving, constructive energies as well. In this case, however, the formation of aesthetic value through these energies is only a means and does not attain autonomy and fullness.

Such, then, is the difference between the outer and the inner body (between the other's body and my own) within the concrete and closed context of a unique person's life, for whom the relationship of "*I* and the *other*" is absolutely irreversible and given once and for all.

Let us now turn our attention to the religious-ethical as well as the aesthetic problem of the value of the human body from the standpoint of its history, and let us try to clarify that history in terms of the distinction we have established.

[The Value of the Human Body in History]

In all of the historically significant, fully developed, and complete ethical-religious-aesthetic conceptions of the body, the body is usually represented in a generalized and internally undifferentiated way. Yet, at the same time, there is an inevitable preponderance in any given case now of the inner, now of the outer body, now of the subjective, now of the objective point of view; the living experience from which the "idea of man"[64] arises is founded either in *self*-experience or in the experience of the *other* human being.

In the first case, it will be the axiological category of the *I* (which also encompasses the other) that provides the foundation; in the second case, it will be the category of the *other* (which encompasses me as well). In one case, the process of constructing the "idea of man" (man as value) may be expressed in the following way: man is I myself, as I myself experience myself, and others are the same as I myself. In the second case, it may be expressed as follows: man is all other human beings surrounding me, as I experience them, and I am the same as the others.

Accordingly, either the distinctiveness of *self*-experience is reduced under the influence of experiencing other people, or the distinctiveness of experiencing the *other* is reduced under the influence of and in favor of *self*-experience. Of course, we are dealing here only with the preponderance of one or the other moment as the axiologically determinant moment; both, of course, are part of the whole of a human being.

It should be evident that, when the category of the *other* has a determining significance in constructing the "idea of man," then an aesthetic and positive valuation of the *body* will predominate: man is *embodied* and is plastically and pictorially significant. The inner body merely adjoins the outer body: it reflects the value of the outer body and is consecrated by the outer body.

Such was the character of man in antiquity at the time of its flowering. Everything corporeal was consecrated by the category of the *other* and was experienced as something immediately valuable and significant; inner axiological self-determination was subordinated to being determined externally through the other and for the other: the *I-for-myself* was dissolved in the *I-for-the-other*.* [65] The inner body was experienced as biological value. (The biological value of the healthy body is an empty and dependent value, a value incapable of engendering anything creatively productive and culturally significant out of itself. It can only reflect a value of another kind, mainly aesthetic value; in itself it is "precultural.") Epistemological reflection and pure idealism were absent (Husserl). Zielinski.[66] The sexual element was by no means predominant, for it is inimical to plasticity. It was only with the appearance of bacchantes * [67] that a different current (essentially Oriental in character) began to emerge. In the Dionysian cult, an inner *but not solitary* "living-out" of the body to its fullest predominates. Sexuality grows stronger. Plastic bounds begin to dissolve. The plastically consummated human being—the *other*—is submerged in faceless yet unified intracorporeal lived experience. But the *I-for-myself* does not yet separate and oppose itself to others as an essentially different category of experiencing a human being; as yet, only the ground is being prepared for that separation. But the boundaries are no longer consecrated and are beginning to be experienced as oppressive (the anguish of individuation). The *inward* has lost any authoritative *outward* form, but has not yet found a "form" for the spirit ("form" in the strict sense does not apply here, for it is no longer aesthetic: the spirit is not something given, but something present in itself as a task to be accomplished).

Epicureanism occupies a distinctively mediating position in this history. In Epicureanism, the body has become an organism: it is an inner body * [68] (a sum total of needs and satisfactions) but an inner body that has not yet isolated itself and still bears upon it a reflected gleam (even if a feeble one at this point) of the positive value of the other. All of the plastic and pictorial aspects, however, have already dimmed and gone out. The lenient *askesis* in Epicureanism signifies an anticipation of the heaviness of the solitary inner body in the "idea of man" conceived in the category of the *I-for-myself*, as spirit.

This idea begins to emerge and develop in *Stoicism*. The outer body dies, and a struggle begins with the inner body (within the self and for the self) as with something that is unreasonable. The Stoic embraces a statue in order to make himself cold.* [69] Self-experience is taken as the basis of the conception of man (the other is I myself), whence the inflexibility (rigorism) and cold lovelessness of Stoicism.* [70]

Finally, the highest point in the denial of the body—as *my* body—was reached in *Neoplatonism*.* [71] The aesthetic value of the body becomes almost extinct. The idea of a living birth (of the other) is replaced by the self-reflection of the *I-for-myself* in cosmogony, where I give birth to the other inside myself, without going beyond my own bounds and without ceasing to be alone. The distinctiveness of the category of the *other* fails to gain a foothold. The emanationist theory prevails: I *think* myself, *I* as the one *thought-of* (the product of self-reflection) detach from *I* as the one *thinking;* the one divides into two, a new person is created, and the latter, in turn, divides himself into two in the act of self-reflection, etc. All events are concentrated in the unitary *I-for-myself*, without introducing the new value of the *other*. The second member in the dyad of *I-for-myself* and *I-as-I-appear-for-the-other* is thought of as a vitiating limitation, a temptation, and as devoid of substantial reality. The pure relationship to oneself (a relationship that has no aesthetic constituents and can be only ethical and religious) becomes the sole creative principle of experiencing and justifying man and the world axiologically.

But within the relationship to oneself, certain reactions are incapable of becoming imperative—namely, tenderness, forbearance, mercifulness, loving admiration. That is, all those reactions which could be summed up in the one word "kindness." [72] For within the relationship to oneself it is impossible to understand and to justify kindness as a principle of comportment toward something given, because kindness constitutes a domain of that which is not given but imposed purely as a task, and, therefore, anything already given, anything already on hand, is surmounted as something unworthy or degraded, including all those reactions which structure and consecrate a given. (A ceaseless going beyond oneself on the basis of self-reflection.) Existence consecrates itself reflexively through the inevitable penitence of the body.

Neoplatonism is the purest and the most consistently prosecuted axiological comprehension of man and the world on the basis of pure *self*-experience: the universe, God, other people—all are no more than *I-for-myself*. Their own judgment about themselves is the most competent and the final judgment. The *other* has no voice here. As for the fact that they are also an *I-for-the-other*, it is fortuitous and unessential and engenders no valuation that is new in principle.

Hence, Neoplatonism also includes the most consistent denial of the body: for me myself, my body cannot be a value. Purely elemental self-preservation is incapable of engendering any value out of itself. In preserving myself, I do not evaluate myself, for self-preservation is accomplished outside any valuation and justification. An organism simply lives, without any justification *from within itself*, for the grace of justification can descend upon it only *from outside*. I myself cannot be the author of my own value, just as I cannot lift myself by my own hair. The biological life of an organism becomes a value only in *another*'s sympathy and compassion with that life (motherhood). It is the *other*'s sympathy and compassion that introduce biological life into a new value-context. With respect to value, my own hunger and the hunger of another are profoundly different: in myself desire is simply a "desiring," "wanting," whereas in the other desire is sacred for me, etc. Where the possibility and justification of an evaluation which is impossible and unjustified in relation to oneself is not admitted in relation to the other, and where the other as such has no privileges, the body as the bearer of bodily life for the *subiectum* himself must be categorically denied (that is, where the other does not produce any new point of view).

From the standpoint of our problem, *Christianity* presents itself as a complex and heterogeneous phenomenon.*[73] It took into its composition the following heterogeneous constituents. (1) The highly distinctive consecration by Judaism of inner human bodiliness—of bodily needs—on the basis of a collective experience of the body with the category of the *other* predominating; one perceived oneself in the category of the other. Ethical self-experience in relation to the body was almost absent (the unity of the people as an organism). The sexual moment of inner bodily unification was equally weak. The value of bodily well-being. But due to special conditions of religious life, the plastic-pictorial aspect could not attain any significant development (except in poetry): "Thou shalt not make unto thee any graven image." * [74]

(2) The idea of the deity becoming human (Zielinski)[75] and man becoming divine (Harnack)[76]—an idea that originates purely in antiquity.

(3) Gnostic dualism and *askesis*.

And finally, (4) the Christ of the Gospels. In Christ we find a synthesis of unique depth, the synthesis of *ethical solipsism* (man's infinite severity toward himself, i.e., an immaculately pure relationship to oneself) with *ethical-aesthetic kindness* toward the other. For the first time, there appeared an infinitely deepened *I-for-myself*—not a cold *I-for-myself*, but one of boundless kindness toward the other; an *I-for-myself* that renders full justice to the other as such, disclosing and affirming the other's axiological distinctiveness in all its fullness. All human beings divide for him into himself as the unique one—and all other human beings, into himself as the one bestowing loving mercy—and all others as receiving mercy, into himself as the savior—and all others as the saved, into himself as the one assuming the burden of sin and expiation—and all others as relieved of this burden and redeemed.

Hence, in all of Christ's norms the *I* and the *other* are contraposed: for myself—absolute sacrifice, for the other—loving mercy. But *I-for-myself* is the *other* for God. God is no longer defined essentially as the voice of my conscience, as purity of my relationship to myself (purity of my penitent self-denial of anything *given* within myself), as the one into whose hands it is a fearful thing to fall and to see whom means to die (immanent self-condemnation).* [77] God is now the heavenly father who is *over me* and can be merciful to me and justify me where I, from within myself, cannot be merciful to myself and cannot justify myself in principle, as long as I remain pure before myself. What I must be for the other, God is for me. What the other surmounts and repudiates within himself as an unworthy given, I accept in him and that with loving mercy as the other's cherished flesh.

These are the pertinent components of Christianity. From the standpoint of our problem, we can observe two trends in the evolution of Christianity. (1) Neoplatonic tendencies assume the foremost position: the *other* is first and foremost *I-for-myself*, and the flesh is in itself an evil—both in myself and in the other. (2) Both principles of axiological relationship find expression in all their distinctiveness—the relationship to oneself as well as the relationship to the other. Of course, neither of these trends exists in a form that is pure. Rather, they represent two abstract tendencies, and in any given concrete phenomenon only one of them may predominate.

It was the second trend that enabled and gave rise to the idea of transfiguration of the body in God as the transfiguration of that which is the other for God. The church as the body of Christ,* 78 the bride of Christ.* 79 cf. the commentaries of St. Bernard of Clairvaux on the Song of Songs.* 80 Finally, the idea of grace as the bestowal—from outside—of lovingly merciful acceptance and justification of the given, as of that which is in principle sinful and, therefore, cannot be surmounted from within itself. This includes the associated idea of confession (total and utter penitence) and absolution. From within my own penitence, there is negation of the whole of myself; from outside myself (God is the other), there is loving mercy and restoration. In himself, a human being can only repent; and only the other can give absolution.

This second tendency within Christianity finds its deepest expression in the phenomenon that is St. Francis of Assisi, Giotto, and Dante.* 81 In his conversation with Saint Bernard in Paradise, Dante suggests that our body shall be resurrected not for its own sake, but for the sake of those who love us—those who knew and loved our one-and-only countenance.[82]

The "rehabilitation of the flesh" in the Renaissance has a mixed and confused character. The purity and depth of St. Francis's, Giotto's, and Dante's acceptance of the body was lost, while the naive acceptance that had been characteristic of antiquity could not be restored. The body sought but could not find an authoritative author in whose name an artist might create. Hence the body's *solitariness* in the Renaissance.

Nevertheless, in the most noteworthy phenomena of this epoch (Leonardo, Raphael, Michelangelo) the St. Francis–Giotto–Dante current does break through, although not in its former purity. On the other hand, the sheer technique of representation achieved a very high degree of development, even if it often lacked a pure and

authoritative bearer. The naive acceptance of the body characteristic of antiquity[g] could not be restored after all the inward experience accumulated in the Middle Ages; one could not help but
read and understand St. Augustine along with the Classical authors (cf. Boccaccio, Petrarch).* [83] Furthermore, the disintegrative
sexual element was quite strong, and the Epicurean art of dying
had gained greater influence as well.

The individualist *Ego* in the "idea of man" in the Renaissance.
Only the soul can detach and isolate itself, but not the body. The
idea of *glory:* parasitical assimilation of the nonauthoritative
other.[84]

In the following two centuries, the position of authoritative
"outsidedness"[85] with respect to the body was definitely lost. In
the Enlightenment, the body degenerates at the end into an organism as the sum total of the needs of "natural man."

The "idea of man" continued to grow and gain in richness, but
it did so in ways different from those that are of concern to us.
Positive science reduced the *I* and the *other* definitively to a common denominator. Political philosophy. Rehabilitation of sexuality in Romanticism.* [86] The legal idea of man: man-as-the-other.[87]
This, in brief, is the history of the body in the "idea of man," presented here in its most general outlines and, therefore, inevitably
in an incomplete form.

However, the "idea of man" as such is always monistic. It always strives to overcome the dualism of the *I* and the *other*, even
if in doing so it advances one of these categories as fundamental.
A critique of such a generalized "idea of man," a critique of the
extent to which this monistic overcoming is legitimate,[h] exceeds
the bounds of our subject. We shall also have to leave open the
question of whether it is possible for me—as an *I* opposed to all
other human beings, past, present, and future—to abstract myself
from my unique place in being, in order to understand the world

---

[g]In antiquity, the body was not divorced from the bodily unity of the outside world of others, for the self-consciousness of one's own *I-for-myself*
had not yet secluded itself from others, and man had not yet attained the
pure relationship to himself which differs in principle from the relationship to others.

[h]In the majority of cases, it is not an overcoming at all but simply an
ignoring of the fundamental difference in ethical and aesthetic significance between the *I* and the *other*.

fully as an ongoing event and in order to orient myself in the world as in an open and once-occurrent event.

[THE INNER AND THE OUTER BODY IN SELF-EXPERIENCE]

There is one thing that, indubitably, has essential significance for us here: the actual, concrete axiological experiencing of another human being within the closed whole of my own unique life, within the actual horizon of my own life, has a *twofold* character, because *I* and the *others*—we move on different planes of *seeing* and *evaluating* (not abstract, but actual, concrete evaluating), and, in order to transpose us to a single unified plane, I must take a stand axiologically *outside* my own life and perceive myself as an *other* among others. This operation is easily accomplished by abstract thought when I subsume myself under a norm that I share with the other (in morality, in law) or under a common cognitive law (a physiological, psychological, social law, etc.). But this abstract operation is far removed from the concrete and axiologically intuitable experience of myself as another—it is far removed from seeing my own concrete life and myself, the hero of that life, on a par with other people and their lives, on one and the same plane with them. Such seeing presupposes an authoritative axiological position outside myself, for it is only in a life perceived in the category of the *other* that my body can become aesthetically valid,[88] and not in the context of my own life as lived for myself, that is, not in the context of my self-consciousness.

If, however, an authoritative position for such concrete axiological seeing—for perceiving myself as another—is absent, then my exterior—my being-for-others—strives to connect itself with my self-consciousness, and a return into myself occurs, a return for the purpose of selfishly exploiting my being-for-others for my own sake. In this case, the reflection of myself in the other, i.e., that which I am for the other, becomes a *double* of myself. This double irrupts into my self-consciousness, clouds its purity, and deflects my self-consciousness from its direct axiological relationship to itself. Fear of the double.

A man who has grown accustomed to dreaming about himself in concrete terms—a man who strives to visualize the external image of himself, who is morbidly sensitive about the outward impression he produces and yet is insecure about that impression and easily wounded in his pride—such a man loses the proper, purely inner stance in relation to his own body. He becomes awkward, "unwieldy," and does not know what to do with his hands and feet. This occurs because an indeterminate *other* intrudes upon his movements and gestures and a second principle of axiological comportment toward himself arises for him: the context of his *self*-consciousness is muddled by the context of the *other's* consciousness of him, and his inner body is confronted by an outer body that is divorced from him—an outer body living in the eyes of the *other*.

To understand this difference between the significance of bodily value in experiencing *myself* and in experiencing the *other*, I must try to evoke an image of my whole life that would be as full and concrete as possible and would be entirely permeated by a particular emotional-volitional tone. And I must try to do this, moreover, without any intention of communicating this image of my life to the other, of embodying it *for* the other. This life—my own life as recreated in my imagination—will be filled with finished and indelible images of other people in all their externally intuitable completeness (with images of others who are close and dear to me, and even with images of people I have only met in passing). The external image of *myself*, however, will not be present among them. *My own* face will be absent from among all these unique, inimitable faces. What will correspond here to my own *I* are the recollections, the re-experiencings of purely inner happiness, anguish, regret, desires, strivings, that pervade this intuited world of *others*. That is, I shall recall my own inner attitudes in particular circumstances of my life, but not my own outer image. All of the plastic and pictorial values (colors, tones, forms, lines, images, gestures, postures, faces, and so forth) will be distributed between the object-world and the world of other people, whereas I myself shall enter this world as an invisible bearer of those emotional-volitional tones which issue from the unique and active axiological position I have assumed in this world and which imbue this world with a particular coloration.

I actively produce the other's outer body as a value by virtue of assuming a determinate emotional-volitional attitude toward him, i.e., toward him as the *other*. This attitude is directed *forward* and cannot be turned back upon myself immediately.

The experience of the body from within oneself—the hero's inner body—is enclosed by his outer body for the other, for the author, and is aesthetically consolidated or "bodied" by the latter's axiological reaction. Every aspect of this outer body (the body enclosing the inner body) performs, as an aesthetic phenomenon, a double function: an "expressive" function and an "impressive" function.[89] And to these corresponds a twofold active position or attitude assumed by the author and by the contemplator.

6. The "Expressive" and "Impressive" Functions of the Outer Body as an Aesthetic Phenomenon

[EXPRESSIVE AESTHETICS]

In the aesthetics of the second half of the nineteenth century and the beginning of the twentieth, one theory exerted a particularly powerful influence and was probably more fully worked out than any other. I have in mind here the theory which conceives aesthetic activity as "empathizing" or "co-experiencing."[90] In the present context, we are not interested in the varieties of this theory, but only in its most basic idea and that, moreover, in its most general form. The idea is this: an object of aesthetic activity (works of art, phenomena of nature and of life) expresses a certain inner state, and aesthetic cognition of such an object is the act of co-experiencing that inner state. For our purposes, moreover, the difference between "co-experiencing" and "empathizing" is not material, for when we empathize or "in-feel" our own inner state into an object, we still experience this state not as immediately *our own*, but as a state of contemplating the *object*, i.e., we co-experience with the *object*.

"Co-experiencing" gives a clearer expression to the actual sense of the lived experience (phenomenology of lived experience), whereas "empathizing" seeks to explain the psychological genesis of this lived experience. An aesthetic theory, however, must be independent of specifically psychological theories (except for psychological description, phenomenology), and we can, therefore, leave all those questions open that have to do with the way in which co-experiencing is psychologically actualized, e.g., whether it is possible to have immediate experience of another person's psychological life (cf. N. O. Lossky);[91] whether it is necessary to become outwardly like the person contemplated (the immediate reproduction of the other's facial expressions); what particular role is played by associations and memory; whether it is possible to represent feelings to oneself (H. Gomperz denies it, S. Witasek affirms it);[92] and so forth. But there can be no doubt that, phenomenologically, co-experiencing of another being's inner life does occur, whatever the unconscious technique of its actualization might be.

The aesthetic theory under discussion defines the essence of aesthetic activity as a co-experiencing of the inner state of an object or of the inner activity of contemplating an object: a human being, an inanimate object, and even a color or a line. While geometry (cognition) defines a line in relation to another line, point, or plane as vertical, parallel, oblique, etc., aesthetic activity defines it from the standpoint of its inner state (or rather, in aesthetic activity the line is not defined but experienced) as striving upward, as falling, etc.

From the standpoint of this very general formulation of the fundamental principle of aesthetics, we must assign to the theory under discussion not only the "aesthetics of empathy" (*Einfühlungsästhetik*) in the strict sense (already Fr. Th. Vischer and Lotze to some extent, Robert Vischer, Johannes Volkelt, Wilhelm Wundt, and Theodor Lipps),[93] but also the aesthetics of "inner imitation" (Karl Groos),[94] and the aesthetics of "play" and "illusion" (Karl Groos and Konrad Lange),[95] Hermann Cohen's aesthetics,[96] in part the aesthetics of Schopenhauer and his followers (immersion in the object),[97] and, finally, Bergson's aesthetic views. Using an arbitrarily coined term, we shall call aesthetics of this orientation "expressive aesthetics," in contrast to those theoretical positions which shift the center of gravity to outward features, which we shall designate as "impressive aesthetics" (Konrad Fiedler, Adolf Hildebrand, Eduard Hanslick, Alois Reigl, and others; the aesthetics of Symbolism, etc.).[98]

For "expressive aesthetics," the aesthetic object is expressive as such, i.e., it is the outward expression of an inner state. And what is essential, moreover, is that *what* is actually expressed is not something objectively valid (an objective value), but, rather, the inner life of an object expressing itself from within, its emotional-volitional state and its directness from within itself; it is only to this extent that there can be any question of co-experiencing. If the aesthetic object expresses an idea or a certain objective state of affairs in an immediate manner, as it does for Symbolism and for "content aesthetics" (Hegel, Schelling),[99] then there is no room for co-experiencing here, and we have to do with a different theoretical position.

For "expressive" aesthetics, the aesthetic object is man, and everything else is animated ("ensouled") or made human (even colors and lines). In this sense, one could say that "expressive" aesthetics conceives of any spatial aesthetic value as a body that expresses a soul (an inner state); aesthetics is in effect the study of the expressive movements and expressive features that belong to an animate body ("frozen" expressive movements).

To perceive a body aesthetically is to co-experience its inner states (both physical and psychological) through the medium of their outward expressedness. Or, in other words, aesthetic value is actualized at the moment when the contemplator abides within the contemplated object; at the moment of experiencing the object's life from within the object itself, the contemplator and the object contemplated—ultimately—coincide. The aesthetic object is the *subiectum* of its own inner life, and it is on the plane of this inner life of the aesthetic-object-as-*subiectum* that aesthetic value gets actualized, i.e., on the plane of a single consciousness, on the plane of the *subiectum*'s co-experienced *self*-experiencing, in the category of the *I*.

This point of view, however, cannot be consistently maintained from beginning to end. Thus, in elucidating the nature of the tragic or the comic, it is quite difficult to limit oneself only to co-experiencing with the suffering hero or to "communing in folly" with the comic hero. Nevertheless, the basic tendency remains the same: it aims at achieving an actualization of aesthetic value that would be totally immanent to a single consciousness and refuses to admit the contraposition of the *I* and the *other*. Such feelings as compassion (with the tragic hero), the sense of one's own superiority (to the comic hero), the sense of one's own nullity or moral superiority (in face of the sublime)—all these feelings are excluded precisely because they relate to the *other* as such and, therefore, presuppose the axiological contraposition of the *I* (the contemplator) and the *other* (that which is contemplated), as well as their distinctness in principle.

The concepts of play and illusion are particularly characteristic in this connection. Indeed, in playing I experience another life without exceeding the bounds of my own self-experience and self-consciousness and without having anything to do with the other as such. And the same is true when I am conscious of an illusion, for once again I experience another life, while remaining myself. What is forgotten, however, is that in this case *contemplation* is absent (in playing, I contemplate my partner with the eyes of a participant, not a spectator). All the feelings that are possible in relation to the *other* as such are excluded here, yet what one actually experiences is *another* life.

To describe its position, "expressive" aesthetics often invokes the concepts of play and illusion for support: in one case, I suffer as the hero; in another, I am free of suffering as the contemplator. In every case, however, we have to do with a relationship to *oneself*, with an experience in the category of the *I*, and the values presented are invariably correlated with the *I*: my own death, not my own death. In other words, the position of "expressive" aesthetics is that of being located *inside* the experiencing person for the purpose of actualizing aesthetic value—a position of experiencing life in the category of the *I*, whether it is a fictitious or an actual *I*. (The categories pertaining to the structure of an aesthetic object, such as the beautiful, the sublime, the tragic, become possible forms of *self*-experiencing: self-sufficient beauty, etc.—without any reference to the *other* as such. A matter of unimpeded "living out" to the utmost of one's own self, of one's own life, according to Lipps.)

A CRITIQUE OF THE FOUNDATIONS
OF "EXPRESSIVE" AESTHETICS

"Expressive" aesthetics is in our view unsound at its very foundation.[100] In itself, the moment of co-experiencing (empathizing, "identifying" oneself with the inner life of the other) is, in essence, *extra-aesthetic*. Empathizing occurs in all dimensions of life, not just in aesthetic perception (cf. practical, ethical, psychological empathizing, etc.)—a fact which even the representatives of "expressive" aesthetics admit. And yet none of them has indicated those features which demarcate *aesthetic* co-experiencing from co-experiencing in general (cf. Lipps's purity of empathy, Cohen's intensity of empathy, Groos's sympathetic imitation, Volkelt's enhanced empathy).[101]

And, in fact, such a demarcation is impossible as long as we continue to adhere to co-experiencing as the fundamental principle. The inadequacy of the "expressive" theory may be validated by the following considerations.

(1) "Expressive" aesthetics cannot account for the *whole* of a work of art. Consider the following case: I have Leonardo da

Vinci's painting *The Last Supper* before me. To be able to understand the central figure of Christ and each one of the apostles, I must empathize myself into each one of the participants, co-experience the inner state of each one of them, by starting from their "expressive" outward expressedness. Passing from one figure to the other, I can, by co-experiencing, understand each figure taken separately. But in what possible way can I experience the aesthetic *whole* of the work? After all, the work cannot simply be equivalent to the sum of my co-experiences of the various participants.

Perhaps what I must do is empathize myself into the unitary inner movement of the entire group of participants? But such a unitary inner movement is simply not there: what I have before me is not an elementally unified mass movement that could be understood as constituting a single *subiectum*. On the contrary, the emotional-volitional attitude of each participant is intensely individual, and they are all in a state of active contraposition to each other. What I have before me is a unitary yet complex event, in which every participant occupies his own unique position within the whole of it, and this whole event cannot be understood by way of co-experiencing with its participants, but, rather, presupposes a position outside each one of them as well as outside all of them taken together.

In cases of this kind, the *author* is invoked for help: we gain possession of the *whole* of a work by co-experiencing with its author. While each hero expresses only himself, the whole of a work is said to be the expression of the author. But the result of involving the author in this way is that he is placed on a par with his own heroes (although this does take place at times, it is not the normal case, and it does not take place in our example from Leonardo). Furthermore, what exactly is the relationship of the author's experience to the experiences of the heroes or of the author's emotional-volitional position to the emotional-volitional positions of the heroes?

The introduction of the author subverts the "expressive" theory at its very root. Co-experiencing with the author, insofar as he has expressed himself in a given work, is not a co-experiencing of his inner life (his joy, anguish, desires, and strivings) in the same sense as our co-experiencing with the hero is. Co-experiencing with the author is a sharing of the actively creative position he has assumed in relation to what is presented, i.e., it is not co-experiencing any longer, but *co-creation*. It is precisely this co-experienced creative relationship of the author that constitutes the specifically *aesthetic* relationship which needs to be explained. And, of course, this relationship cannot be interpreted simply as a co-experiencing. But if that is the case, then it follows that contemplation is also not susceptible of being interpreted as co-experiencing.

The root error of "expressive" aesthetics derives from its representatives having elaborated their fundamental principle by proceeding from an analysis of aesthetic *elements* or of particular (usually natural) images or configurations, and not from the *whole* of a work. A partiality for elements is a fault common to all contemporary aesthetics. An element or an isolated natural configuration or image has no author, and the aesthetic contemplation of them is hybrid and passive in character.

When I am in the presence of a simple figure, color, or combination of two colors—in the presence of *this* actual cliff or *this* surf on this particular seashore—and I attempt to find an aesthetic approach to them, the first thing I must do is vivify them, make them into potential heroes—the bearers of a destiny. That is, I must endow them with a determinate emotional-volitional attitude, make them human. By doing all this, I gain for the first time the *possibility* of approaching them aesthetically, i.e., I actualize the fundamental condition for aesthetic vision. But active aesthetic activity proper has not even begun yet, inasmuch as I remain at the stage of simple co-experiencing with the vivified image (my activity, moreover, may also proceed in a different direction: I may be frightened by the menacing aspect of the animated sea, I may come to feel pity for the constrained cliff, etc.). What I must do is paint a picture or produce a poem or compose a myth (even if only in imagination) where the given phenomenon will become the hero of the event consummated around the hero. So long as I remain inside the given image or configuration (co-experiencing with it), this is impossible to do, for it presupposes a stable position outside that image or configuration.

What I shall have created—a painting, a poem—will constitute an artistic *whole* comprising all the necessary aesthetic *elements*. The analysis of it will be quite productive. The external image of the *imaged* cliff will not only express its soul (its possible inner states: stubbornness, pride, steadfastness, self-sufficiency, yearning, loneliness), but will also consummate this soul with values transgredient to its possible self-experience: aesthetic grace will be bestowed upon it—a lovingly merciful justification of its being that is impossible from within the soul itself. Beside this soul will appear a series of object-related aesthetic values that possess artistic validity but lack any inner position of their own, since in an aesthetic whole there is only one aesthetically valid constituent that has an inner life and is accessible to co-experiencing: the participating heroes. The aesthetic *whole* is not something co-experienced, but something actively produced, both by the author and by the contemplator (in this sense, by stretching the point, one could speak about the beholder's experiencing the creative activity of the author). Co-experiencing is required only in relation to the heroes. But even that is not yet the aesthetic moment proper; what constitutes this specifically aesthetic moment is *consummation*.

(2) "Expressive" aesthetics is unable to provide a valid foundation of *form*. In point of fact, the most consistent foundation and validation of form in "expressive" aesthetics consists in its reduction to purity of expression (Lipps, Cohen, Volkelt). The function of form is to aid co-experiencing, to give expression as clearly, fully, and purely as possible to an interiority (whose?—the hero's or the author's?). This is a purely expressive understanding of form: form does not *consummate* content (in the sense of the sum total of what has been internally co-experienced, empathized), but merely *expresses* it. Form may deepen, clarify the inner life that is being expressed, but it introduces nothing that is in principle new, i.e., nothing that is in principle transgredient to the inner life being expressed. Form expresses only the interiority of the one who is invested in this form: it is pure *self*-expression (self-utterance). The form of the hero expresses only the hero himself, his soul, and not the author's relationship to him; the form of the hero must be founded from within the hero—the hero, as it were, engenders his own form out of himself as an expression adequate to himself.

This line of reasoning cannot be applied to an artist. The form of the *Sistine Madonna* expresses the madonna, the mother of God. If, on the other hand, we say that the *Sistine Madonna* expresses Raphael, expresses his understanding of the madonna, then expression is understood here in an entirely different sense, in a sense that is alien to "expressive" aesthetics, for in this case expression does not express Raphael-as-a-man at all, does not express his inner life, just as a felicitous theoretical formula that I may have discovered in no way represents an expression of my own inner life.

The attention of "expressive" aesthetics is everywhere fixed in a fatal way upon the hero and upon the author *as* hero or upon the author insofar as he coincides with the hero. Form is physiognomic and "gestural" in character: [102] it expresses a single *subiectum*. It does so, to be sure, for the other who is the auditor-contemplator, but this other is passive, merely receptive, and if he exerts any influence on the form at all, it is only insofar as the one who is expressing himself takes his auditor into account himself (thus, for example, when I express myself—through expressive movements or in words—I adapt my utterance to the peculiarities of my auditor). Form does not descend *upon* an object, but issues *from* the object as its own expression and, ultimately, as its self-determination. Form must accomplish only one thing—it must enable us to experience an object internally, i.e., it affords us no more than an ideal co-experience with the object's self-experience. The form of *this* particular cliff, for instance, expresses only its inner solitariness, its self-sufficiency, its emotional-volitional posture in the world, and the only thing left for us to do is to co-experience that posture. Even if we described this by saying that we express *ourselves, our own* inner life, through the form of that cliff, or that we empathize *our own I* into the cliff, the form would still remain the self-expression of a single soul, the pure exteriorization of an interiority.

"Expressive" aesthetics rarely manages to maintain this kind of consistent interpretation of form. The evident inadequacy of this interpretation compels "expressive" aesthetics to bring in, as a supplement to such an interpretation, other ways to ground form and, consequently, other formal principles as well. But these are not connected—nor can they be connected—with the principle of expressiveness, and they exist alongside it like a mechanically attached addendum, like a peculiar accompaniment of expression that has no inner connection with expression itself. It is impracticable to explain the form of the *whole* as an expression of the hero's inner posture (where the author, moreover, expresses himself only through the hero, while striving to render form an adequate expression of the hero, and where at best the author adds no more than the subjective element of his own *understanding* of the hero).

Negative definitions of form: as "isolation,"[103] etc. The formal principle proposed by Lipps (the Pythagoreans—Aristotle)[104]—"unity in variety"—is a mere addendum to the "expressive" significance of expression. This accessory function of form inevitably assumes a hedonic coloration and divorces itself from its interconnectedness in principle with that which is being expressed. Thus, in elucidating tragedy, the pleasure we derive from co-experiencing with the hero's suffering is explained not only by the enhancement of the sense of *ego*-value (Lipps), but also by the effect of form on us, by the pleasure felt in the very *process* (formally conceived) of co-experiencing, regardless of its content. Rephrasing the well-known proverb, we could say: "a spoonful of honey in a barrelful of pitch."[105]

The fundamental fault of "expressive" aesthetics consists in placing content (the sum total of inner experiences) and formal constituents on one and the same plane, in a single consciousness, or, in other words, in striving to derive form from content. Content itself—as inner life—creates a form *for* itself as the expression *of* itself. This could be put in the following way: inner life, the inner attitude in lived life, is in itself capable of becoming the author of its own outward aesthetic form. . . . But is it capable of engendering *aesthetic* form, *artistic* expression, directly out of itself? And, conversely: does artistic form lead *only* to this inner attitude? Is it the expression *only* of that attitude? The answer to this question must be negative. A *subiectum* who experiences his own directed life objectively can and does express his life in performed actions or deeds, he can and does give utterance to his life from within himself in a confessional self-accounting (an act of self-determination), and, finally, he can express his own cognitive directedness, his world view, in the categories of a cognitive utterance (as a theoretically valid utterance). Performed action and confessional self-accounting—these are the forms in which I can give immediate expression to my emotional-volitional attitude in the world, to my life's directedness from within myself, without the addition of any values that are in principle transgredient to that directedness (the hero acts, repents, and cognizes—from within himself). From within itself, a life cannot give birth to an aesthetically valid form without going beyond its own bounds, without, in other words, ceasing to *be* what it *is* in itself.

Consider Oedipus. As long as he experiences his own life himself, every constituent of his life possesses the validity of an object for him within the value-and-meaning context of his own life. At every given moment, his inner emotional-volitional attitude finds its expression in a performed action (action-as-doing and action-as-speech) and reflects itself in confession and penitence. From within himself, he is *not tragic* (where the word "tragic" is understood in a *strictly aesthetic sense*): suffering, experienced as an object from within the sufferer, is not tragic for the sufferer himself; a lived life is incapable of expressing and shaping itself as a tragedy from within itself. If we were to coincide internally with Oedipus, we would immediately lose the purely aesthetic category of the tragic, for within the value-and-meaning context in which Oedipus himself objectively experiences his own life, there is nothing that could constitute the form of tragedy.

From within lived experience, life is neither tragic nor comic, neither beautiful nor sublime, for the one who objectively experiences it himself and for anyone who purely co-experiences with him. A soul living and experiencing its own life will light up for me with a tragic light or will assume a comical expression or will become beautiful and sublime—only insofar as I step beyond the bounds of that soul, assume a definite position outside it, actively clothe it in externally valid bodiliness, and surround it with values that are transgredient to its own object-directedness (i.e., provide it with a background or setting as its *environment* and not with a field of action—as its *horizon*). If we simply co-experience with Oedipus (let us grant the possibility of such pure co-experiencing), if we see through his eyes and hear through his ears, then his outward expressedness in being, his body, and the entire series of plastic-pictorial values clothing and consummating his life for us will immediately disintegrate: having served as the means to co-experiencing, they cannot enter into the one with whom we are co-experiencing, inasmuch as Oedipus's world, as he experiences it himself, does not include his own outward body, does not include his individual-pictorial countenance as a value, does not include those plastically significant positions [106] which his body assumes at various moments of his life. In Oedipus's own world, only the *other* participants of his life are invested in outward corporeity, and these other persons and objects do not surround him, do not constitute his aesthetically valid *environment,* but are part of his *horizon*—the horizon of an action-performer. And yet it is in this Oedipus's own, world that aesthetic value must actualize itself, according to the "expressive" theory, [indecipherable] the constitution or construction of him within ourselves is the ultimate goal of aesthetic activity, in which the purely expressive form serves only as a means.

In other words, aesthetic contemplation must bring us to a reproduction of the world of my lived life, the world of my fantasies about myself or the dream world, as I myself experience these worlds, and in which I, as their hero, am not expressed outwardly (see above). But the world of my lived life is constituted and structured only through cognitive-aesthetic categories, and the structure of tragedy, comedy, etc., is, therefore, profoundly alien to its structure (although the elements of tragedy, comedy, etc., may be self-interestedly imported from the consciousness of others; see above concerning doubles). Having merged with Oedipus, having lost our own position outside him (this is, according to "expressive" aesthetics, the ultimate limit toward which aesthetic activity strives), we immediately lose the tragic: my being-outside[107] will cease to be for me—as Oedipus—an adequate expression and form of the life I experience. And although it will express itself in those words and actions which Oedipus himself performs, these words and actions will be experienced by me only from within *myself*, only from the standpoint of that real meaning which they possess in the events of *my own* life—and not in the least from the standpoint of their aesthetic validity, i.e., not as a constitutive moment in the artistic whole of a tragedy. Having merged with Oedipus, having lost my own place *outside* him, I cease to enrich the event of his life by providing a new, creative standpoint, a standpoint inaccessible to Oedipus himself from his own unique place. In other words, I cease to enrich the event of his life as an author/contemplator.

As a result, tragedy is nullified, inasmuch as tragedy was precisely the result of the *enrichment*, an enrichment *in principle*, which was introduced into the event of Oedipus's own life by the author/contemplator. For the event of tragedy as an artistic (and religious) performance does not coincide with the event of Oedipus's life, and its participants include not only Oedipus, Jocasta, and the other dramatis personae, but the author/contemplator as well. In the whole of a tragedy as an artistic event, it is the author/contemplator who is active, whereas the heroes are passive; *they* are the ones who are saved and redeemed through aesthetic salvation. If the author/contemplator were to lose his firm and active position outside each of the dramatis personae, if he were to merge with them, the artistic event and the artistic whole as such, i.e., the whole in which he, as a creatively independent person, is an indispensable constituent, would disintegrate. Oedipus would be left alone with himself, unsaved and unredeemed aesthetically; life would not be consummated and justified on an axiological plane that is different from the one on which it actually unfolded for the one who lived it. . . . What aesthetic creation strives to achieve, however, is hardly this ever-renewed repetition of an actually experienced life or of a possible life, along with the same participants and in the same category in which it was actually experienced or could have been experienced.

It should be noted that we are not objecting here to realism or naturalism, and we are not defending an idealist transfiguration of reality in art, although this might seem to be the case. Our argument is on a plane which is entirely different from the one on which the dispute between realism and idealism unfolds. A work that transfigures life idealistically can be equally well interpreted from the standpoint of "expressive" theory, for this transfiguration can be conceived in the category of the *I*; on the other hand, the most exact naturalistic reproduction of life can be perceived in the axiological category of the *other*—as the life of *another* human being.

Our concern is the problem of the relationship between the hero and the author/beholder. And more specifically—whether (1) the author/beholder's aesthetic activity is a co-experiencing with the hero that tends ultimately toward both of them coinciding, and (2) whether form can be understood from within the hero, as an expression of his life—an expression that tends ultimately toward an adequate *self*-expression of that life. And what we have established is that, according to "expressive" theory, the structure of the world we reach through the "expressively" conceived work of art (the aesthetic object proper)[108] is similar not just to the structure of the world of lived life (as I actually experience that life), where the main hero (I myself) is *not* expressed plastically and pictorially; it is similar as well to the structure of the world of my most unrestrained daydreaming about myself, where the hero is, likewise, not expressed in plastic-pictorial terms and where there is also no pure *environment* but only a *horizon*. We shall see later that the "expressive" conception is justified most of all precisely in relation to Romanticism.

The radical error in "expressive" theory that leads ultimately to the destruction of the specifically aesthetic whole becomes particularly evident in the example of a theatrical presentation (a stage performance). "Expressive" theory would have to interpret the event of a drama in its specifically aesthetic constituents (i.e., the aesthetic object proper) as follows: the spectator loses his place *outside* and *over against* the imaged life event of the dramatic personae; at each given moment, the spectator experiences the life of one of the characters inside and from inside that character—seeing the stage through his eyes, nearing other dramatis personae through his ears, co-experiencing all his actions from within him. There is no spectator, but neither is there an author as an independent and effective participant in the event. The spectator has nothing to do with the author at the moment of co-experiencing, for he is wholly inside the heroes, inside those with whom he is co-experiencing. Nor is there a stage director; the director did no more than prepare the "expressive" form of the actors, thus making it easier for the spectator to get inside them. The director coincides with the actors; beyond that, there is no place for him. What, then, are we left with?

Empirically, the spectators are still there, of course, sitting in their seats in the pit and in the boxes; the actors, too, remain onstage, and the director, excited and intent, remains in the wings. And perhaps the author-as-person is also there in one of the boxes. But none of these is a constitutive moment in a drama as an *artistic* event. What remains, then, in the *aesthetic object* proper?

What remains is life experienced from within, and not just *one* life so experienced, but several—as many, in fact, as there are participants in the drama. Unfortunately, "expressive" theory fails to tell us whether one should co-experience with the main hero alone or with all the others equally. It is unlikely that the latter requirement could be fully actualized in reality. In any case, all these co-experienced lives cannot be added up to form one whole event unless a principled and noncontingent position outside each one of them is present as well. This position, however, is excluded in "expressive" theory.

There is no drama, then; there is no artistic event. Such would be the ultimate result if "expressive" theory were consistently prosecuted to its ultimate conclusion (although this is never done in fact). But since a complete coincidence of the spectator with the hero never takes place, nor of the actor with the person he is enacting, we end up with a mere *playing* at life, which "expressive" aestheticians affirm, in fact, as right and proper.

At this point, it would not be amiss to take up briefly the question of the actual relationship of play to art (excluding, of course, the genetic standpoint entirely). "Expressive" aesthetics, as we saw, tends ultimately to exclude the author as a constitutive moment that is in principle independent of the hero, by restricting the author's functions merely to techniques of "expressiveness." "Expressive" aesthetics shows greatest theoretical consistency, in my opinion, when it defends some version of the play theory. And if the most eminent representatives of "expressiveness" (Lipps, Volkelt) fail actually to do this, then this inconsistency is precisely what constitutes the price they must pay for salvaging the verisimilitude and scope of their theory. For what radically distinguishes play from art is the absence in principle of spectator and author.

Playing, from the standpoint of the players themselves, does not presuppose any spectator (situated outside their playing) *for whom* the whole of the event of a life imaged through play would be actually performed; in fact, play *images* nothing—it merely *imagines*. The boy who plays a robber chieftain experiences his own life (the life of a robber chieftain) from within himself: he looks through the eyes of a robber chieftain at another boy who is playing a passing traveler; his horizon is that of the robber chieftain he is playing. And the same is true of his fellow players. The relationship of each of the players to the event of life they have decided to enact (the attack of robbers on a group of travelers) is no more than the desire to take part in that event, to experience that life as one of its participants: one boy wants to be a robber, another—a traveler, a third—a policeman, and so forth. But his relationship to life as a desire to experience it himself is not an *aesthetic* relationship to life.

Playing, in this sense, is similar to daydreaming about oneself as well as to "artless" reading of novels, where we "identify" with the main character in order to experience—in the category of the *I*—his existence and his fascinating life, i.e., when we simply daydream under the guidance of the author. But there is no similarity at all between playing and the artistic event.

Playing begins really to approach art—namely, dramatic action—only when a new, nonparticipating participant makes his appearance, namely, a spectator who begins to admire the children's playing from the standpoint of the whole event of a life represented by their playing, a spectator who contemplates this life event in an aesthetically active manner and, in part, *creates* it (as an aesthetically valid whole, by transposing it to a new plane—the aesthetic plane). It should be evident, however, that, in doing so, he alters the event as it is initially given: the event becomes enriched with a new moment, new in principle—an author/beholder, and, as a result, all other moments of the event are transformed as well, inasmuch as they become part of a new whole: the children playing become *heroes*, and what we have before us is no longer the event of *playing*, but the artistic event of drama in its embryonic form. But this event will once again be transformed into play when the nonparticipating participant gives up his aesthetic position and, captivated by the play as a fascinating way to live, himself joins in this life as another traveler or robber. But even so much is not necessary in order to abolish the event as an artistic event; it is enough if the spectator, while empirically remaining in his own place, starts "identifying" himself with one of the participants and starts experiencing the participant's imagined life along with him and from within him.

Thus, there is no aesthetic constituent that is immanent to play in itself; such a constituent may be *introduced* into playing by an actively contemplating spectator. But play itself and the playing children who actualize it have nothing to do with this, for at the moment of playing this specifically aesthetic value is alien to them. If they happened to find themselves in the role of "heroes," they might react like Makar Devushkin, who was deeply offended and mortified when he imagined that Gogol' had portrayed him, Makar Devushkin,[109] in *The Overcoat*—that is, when he suddenly saw *himself* in the hero of a work of satire. What, then, does play have in common with art?

No more than a negative feature: what occurs in play as well as in art is not actual life, but only an imaging of life. And even that is saying too much, for it is only in art that life is *imaged forth*, whereas in play it is *imagined*, as we noted earlier; this imagined life becomes an imaged life only in the active and creatve contemplation of a spectator. Nor does the fact that this life can be made an object of aesthetic activity provide it with any special advantage, for we can contemplate actual life as well in an aesthetically active manner. Inner imitation of life (Groos) strives toward the ultimate end of an actual experience of life, or to put it crudely: it is a surrogate of life (such is the nature of play and to a large extent—that of wishful dreams); it is not an active aesthetic relationship to life. The latter also loves life, but loves it differently: first of all, it loves life more actively, and therefore wants to remain *outside* it in order to be able to help it where from within itself life is *in principle* powerless.

Such, then, is the nature of play. It is only by adding unconsciously the position of an author/contemplator (especially by association with the theater) that one manages to impart some verisimilitude to the theory of play in aesthetics.

At this point, it is appropriate to say a few words about the creative work of the actor. His position is highly complex from the standpoint of the author-and-hero relationship. When and to what extent is the actor aesthetically *creative?* It is not when he "lives" the part of the hero and expresses himself from within the hero in appropriate words and actions whose value and meaning are determined again from within; not when he experiences this or that action, this or that position of his body, only from within and determines its meaning in the context of his own life—the life of the hero—again from within. That is, the actor is not creative when he has *"reincarnated"* himself[110] and now, in imagination, experiences the hero's life as his *own* life, whose horizon includes all the other dramatis personae, the scenery, the various objects on stage, etc.; he is not creative when his consciousness includes nothing that would be transgredient to the consciousness of the hero he is playing.

The actor is aesthetically creative only when he produces and shapes *from outside* the image of the hero into whom he will later "reincarnate" himself, that is, when he creates the hero as a distinct whole and creates this whole not in isolation, but as a constituent in the whole of a drama. In other words, the actor is aesthetically creative only when he is an author—or to be exact: a co-author, a stage director, and an active spectator of the portrayed hero and of the whole play (we could use an "equals" sign here, after discounting certain mechanical factors: the author = the director = the actor). For, just as much as the author and the director, the actor creates a particular hero in association with the artistic whole of a play, as a constituent in that whole. It should be evident that, when he does so, the whole of the play is no longer perceived from within the hero himself as the ongoing event of his life, i.e., it is no longer perceived as the *horizon* of his life. Rather, it is perceived as the *environment* of the hero's life from the standpoint of an aesthetically active author/contemplator situated outside the hero, and this environment includes features that are transgredient to the hero's consciousness.

The artistic image of the hero is created by the actor before a mirror, before a director, on the basis of his own stock of experience. This process of creation involves makeup (even if the actor is made up by someone else, he still takes makeup into account as an aesthetically significant constituent of the image of the hero); costume (that is, the creation of a plastic-pictorial axiological image of the hero); demeanor; the form given to various movements and positions of the body in relation to other objects and to the background; training of the voice as heard and evaluated from outside; and, finally, the creation of character (character as an artistic constituent is transgredient to the consciousness of the one who is characterized, as we shall soon see).[111] And all this is done by the actor in association with the artistic whole of the play (and not the event of the hero's life); in this context, the actor *is* an artist. In this context, the actor's aesthetic self-activity is directed to giving form to a human being as hero and to giving form to his life. When, on the other hand, the actor, in playing his role, "reincarnates" *himself* in the hero, then all these constituents of forming the hero from outside become transgredient to the actor's consciousness and experiencing *as* the hero (let us assume that the "reincarnation" is accomplished in its purest form). The form of the body as shaped from outside, its movements and positions, etc.—all these constituents will have artistic validity only for the consciousness of a contemplator—*within the artistic whole* of the play, not within the experienced life of the hero.

Of course, in the actual work of an actor, all these abstractly isolated constituents intertwine, and in this sense his playacting represents a concrete and living aesthetic event. The actor is an artist in the full sense of the term: all the constituents of an artistic whole are represented in his work, except that at the moment of playacting the center of gravity is displaced into the inner experiences of the hero as a human being, as the *subiectum* of lived life. That is, the center of gravity is displaced into that extra-aesthetic matter which had been actively shaped earlier by the actor himself *qua* author and stage director. At the moment of "reincarnation," he becomes passive material (passive in relation to aesthetic self-activity)—he becomes a life in that artistic whole which he had himself earlier created and which is now being actualized by the spectator; in relation to this aesthetic self-activity of the spectator, the actor's entire activity of living and experiencing *as* the hero is passive.

The actor both *imagines* a life and *images* it in his playacting. If he did no more than imagine it, if he played merely for the sake of experiencing this life from within—the way children play—and did not shape it through an activity that approaches it from outside, he would not be an artist. At best, he would be a sound but passive instrument in the hands of an artist (the director, the author, and the active spectator).

But let us return to "expressive" aesthetics. (In the present context, we are dealing, of course, only with the spatial constituent of aesthetic value and, hence, we gave prominence to the plastic-pictorial aspect of the hero in the actor's specifically aesthetic creativity, whereas the most important part of his work is actually the creation of character and of inner rhythm. Later on, we shall see that character and rhythm[112] are also transgredient to the internally experienced life of the hero himself and that they are created by the actor not at the moment of his "reincarnating" himself *in* the hero, not at the moment of his coinciding with the hero, but are created by him *from outside*, in his capacity as author-director-spectator. Sometimes the actor both experiences himself and aesthetically co-experiences with himself—as the author of a lyrical hero; this constitutes the specifically lyrical element of the actor's creative activity.) From the standpoint of "expressive" aesthetics, all the constituents which from *our* standpoint are specifically aesthetic—i.e., the actor's work in the capacity of an author-director-spectator—can be reduced to nothing more than production of a purely "expressive" form as a pathway for the fullest and purest possible actualization of empathetic co-experiencing. Specifically *aesthetic* value is actualized only after the actor has "reincarnated" himself in the hero—in the experience of the hero's life as his own, and it is at this point that the spectator as well must merge, by means of the "expressive" form, with the actor.

An attitude which, in our view, is much closer to the actual aesthetic position of a spectator is the naive attitude of the simple man who warned the hero of a play about an ambush laid for him and who was ready to rush to the hero's aid when he was attacked.

In this attitude, the naive spectator assumed a stable position *outside* the hero, took into account those features which were transgredient to the hero's consciousness, and was prepared to utilize the privilege of his own *outside* position by coming to the aid of the hero where the hero himself, from *his* place, was powerless. The attitude he assumed toward the hero is quite correct. His mistake consists in his failing to find an equally firm position *outside* the enacted life event[113] as a whole, for only that would have compelled his self-activity to develop in an aesthetic rather than ethical direction. He entered the enacted life in the capacity of a new participant in it and wanted to help it from within its own bounds, i.e., on its own cognitive-ethical plane. He stepped across the footlights and took up a position *beside* the hero on one and the same plane of life lived as a unitary and open ethical event, and, in so doing, he ceased to be an author/spectator and abolished the aesthetic event. For the event of lived life as a *whole* is without any ultimate issue out of itself. From within itself, a lived life can express itself in the form of an action, a confession-as-penitence, an outcry; absolution and grace descend upon it from the Author. An ultimate issue out of itself is not *immanent* to a lived life: it descends upon a life-lived-from-within as a gift from the self-activity of another—from a self-activity that *comes to meet* my life from *outside* its bounds.

In order to explain the special character of co-experiencing with an empathizing into another's inner life, some "expressive" aestheticians (cf. Eduard von Hartmann's "Schopenhauerian" aesthetics) introduce the notion of "ideal" or "illusory" feelings[114] in distinction to the real feelings of actual life and to the feelings roused by aesthetic form. Aesthetic pleasure is a real feeling, whereas co-experiencing the hero's feelings is only an "ideal" feeling. "Ideal" feelings are those which do not prompt the will to action. But this sort of distinction does not stand up to criticism. What we actually experience are not particular feelings of the hero (nor do such particular feelings really exist), but, rather, the whole of the hero's soul or inner life. That is, our *horizons* coincide, and this is the reason why we perform inwardly, along with the hero, all of his actions as necessary constituents of his, the hero's, life—the life we are co-experiencing: in co-experiencing his suffering, we also co-experience inwardly his cry of pain; in co-experiencing his hatred, we also co-experience inwardly his act of revenge, and so on. As long as we only co-experience with the hero, as long as we only coincide with him, any intervention in his life on our part is excluded, because such intervention presupposes our being situated *outside* the hero—as in the case of the naive spectator in our earlier example.

If we consider other explanations of what distinguishes a co-experienced life aesthetically, we find everywhere the same *closed* circle of a *single* consciousness, of *self*-experience, and of a relationship to *oneself.*[i] That is, the axiological category of the *other* continues to be excluded. Within the bounds of a consistently prosecuted "expressive" theory, co-experiencing with or empathizing into a life is simply another experiencing or a *repetition* of that life without its having been enriched by any values transgredient to it, i.e., an experiencing of another life in the same categories in which a *subiectum* actually experiences his *own* life. Art gives me the possibility of experiencing not just one but several lives, and this enables me to enrich the accumulated experience of my own actual life. It gives me the possibility, that is, of partaking, from within, in a different life for the sake of that life in itself, for the sake of its remarkable significance *qua* life (its "outstanding human significance," according to Lipps and Volkelt).

Our critique of the fundamental principle of "expressive" aesthetics has dealt with this principle in its purest form and in its most consistent application. But neither this purity nor this consistency is to be found in the actual works of "expressive" aestheticians. We already indicated that it is only by deviating from its own principle and through inconsistency that "expressive" theory is able to avoid severing its ties with art altogether and to remain an *aesthetic* theory. These deviations from its own principle are imported by "expressive" aesthetics from a stock of actual aesthetic experience, for "expressive" aesthetics does rely, of course, upon a stock of actual aesthetic experience, although the "expressive" interpretation of such experience is erroneous. And it is these importations of real aesthetic experience that obscure from us the erroneousness of the fundamental principle (when taken in its purest form)—obscure it from us as well as from the "expressive" aestheticians themselves.

---

[i] Consider, for example, such explanations as the following: in "reincarnating" ourselves, we extend the value of our own *I* or—we partake, from within, in what is humanly of great significance, etc.[115]

The most important deviation from the fundamental principle committed by the majority of "expressive" aestheticians—and the deviation that brings us closer to a proper understanding of aesthetic activity—is the characterization of co-experiencing as sympathetic and compassionate (this is either expressed directly— as in Cohen and in Groos, or unconsciously implied). The notion of *sympathetic* co-experiencing developed to its ultimate conclusion would destroy the "expressive" principle at its very root and would bring us to the idea of aesthetic *love* and thus to a proper understanding of the author's position in relation to the hero.[116]

[SYMPATHETIC CO-EXPERIENCING]

What, then, is sympathetic co-experiencing? Sympathetic co-experiencing, "akin to love" (Cohen), is no longer pure co-experiencing, or an empathizing of oneself into an object or into a hero. In the sufferings of Oedipus which we co-experience, that is, in Oedipus's own inner world, there is nothing akin to *love* of himself. His self-love of egoism is something entirely different (as we already have mentioned), and it is not this amour propre and this self-love, of course, that one has in mind when speaking of sympathetic empathizing, but the creation of a *new* emotional relationship to all of his inner life as a whole. This lovelike sympathy radically alters the entire emotional-volitional structure of the hero's inward experience, imparting an entirely different coloring or tonality to it.

Do we involve or weave this sympathy into the lived experiences of the hero, and, if so, how do we do it? One might think that we empathize this lovelike sympathy of ours into an aesthetically contemplated object in exactly the same way that we empathize into other inner states, such as anguish, tranquillity, joy, tension, etc. We call an object or a person "nice," "pleasant," "sympathetic"—we ascribe, that is, those qualities which express our own attitude toward the object *to* that object itself as its own qualities. And it is true that the feeling of love penetrates, as it were, into an object and alters its whole aspect for us. Nevertheless, this penetrating is entirely different in character from "introjecting" or empathizing another experience into an object as *its own* inner state, as we do, for example, in the case of empathizing joy into a happily smiling man or inner serenity into a motionless and calm sea, etc. These empathized or "introjected" experiences vivify an *external* object from within by creating an inner life that gives meaning to its exterior, whereas love permeates, as it were, *both* its outer *and* its empathized inner life; that is, it colors and transforms for us the *full* object, the object as already alive, already consisting of a body and a soul.

One could try to give lovelike sympathy a purely "expressive" interpretation. As a matter of fact, one could say that sympathy is a precondition of co-experiencing. In order that we should start co-experiencing with someone, he must first become sympathetic for us, for we do not co-experience with an unsympathetic object, we do not enter into it, but, on the contrary, we push it away, we draw away from it. To be really "expressive," to be capable of introducing us into the inner world of the agent of expression, a purely "expressive" expression must be sympathetic.

But while it is true that sympathy can be one of the conditions for co-experiencing (although not the only condition, nor a necessary one), this fact does not, of course, exhaust its role in aesthetic co-experiencing. Far from it. Lovelike sympathy accompanies and permeates aesthetic co-experiencing throughout the entire duration of the act of aesthetic contemplation of an object, transfiguring the entire material of what is contemplated and co-experienced. Sympathetic co-experiencing of the hero's life means to experience that life in a form completely different from the form in which it was, or could have been, experienced by the *subiectum* of that life himself. Co-experiencing in this form does not in the least strive toward the ultimate point of totally coinciding, merging with the co-experienced life, because such merging would be equivalent to a falling away of the coefficient of sympathy, of love, and, consequently, of the form they produced as well. A sympathetically co-experienced life is given form not in the category of the *I*, but in the category of the *other*, as the life of *another* human being, another *I*. In other words, a sympathetically co-experienced life is the life of another human being (his outer as well as his *inner* life) that is essentially experienced *from outside*. (On experiencing *inner* life *from* outside, see the next section.)

Only sympathetic co-experiencing has the power to conjoin or unite harmoniously the inward and the outward on one and the same plane. From within a co-experienced life itself, there is no access to the aesthetic value of what is outward in that same life (the body). It is only love (as an active approach to another human being) that unites an inner life (a *subiectum*'s own object-directedness in living his life) as experienced from outside with the value of the body as experienced from outside and, in so doing, constitutes a unitary and unique human being as an aesthetic phenomenon. That is, only love unites one's own *directedness* with a *direction* and one's own *horizon* with an *environment*. A whole, integral human being[117] is the product of the aesthetic, creative point of view and of that point of view alone. Cognition is indifferent to value and does not provide us with a concrete unique human being, while the ethical *subiectum* is in principle nonunitary (the specifically ethical obligation or "ought" is experienced in the category of the *I*). A whole, integral human being presupposes an aesthetically active *subiectum* situated outside him (we are abstracting from man's religious experience in the present context).

From the very outset, sympathetic co-experiencing introduces values into the co-experienced life that are transgredient to this life; it transposes this life from the very outset into a new value-and-meaning context and can from the very outset rhythmicize this life temporally and give it form spatially (cf. *bilden, ge-stalten*).[118] Pure co-experiencing of a life lacks all viewpoints except for those which are possible from within that co-experienced life itself, and among these there are no aesthetically productive viewpoints. It is not from within the co-experienced life itself that aesthetic form is produced and justified as the adequate expression of that life, i.e., as an expression which strives ultimately toward the point of pure *self*-utterance (the utterance by a solitary consciousness of its own immanent relationship to itself). Aesthetic form is pronounced and justified by an aesthetically productive sympathy or love that *comes to meet* the co-experienced life from *outside*. And, in this sense, aesthetic form does express that life, except that the creator of this expression, the active agent in it, is not the expressed life itself, but the *other* who is situated *outside* that life—the author; the expressed life itself is *passive* in the act that gives it aesthetic expression. But if aesthetic form is conceived in this way, then the word "expression" is misleading and should be abandoned as being more appropriate for the purely "expressive" conception of aesthetic form (especially the German word *Ausdruck*).[119] A word that comes closer to expressing the actual aesthetic event adequately is the term used in "impressive" aesthetics (with reference to the spatial as well as the temporal arts): *izobrazhenie* in Russian, or *imaging forth.*[120] This term shifts the center of gravity from the hero to the aesthetically active *subiectum*—the author.

Form expresses the *author*'s self-activity in relation to a hero— in relation to another human being. In this sense, we could say that form is the result of the interaction between hero and author. The hero, however, is passive in this interaction: he is not someone who *expresses*, but someone who *is expressed*. Yet even as such, he still has a determining effect on the form, inasmuch as the form must answer to *him* specifically, must consummate from outside *his own* inner object-directedness in his lived life, and in this respect, therefore, the form must be adequate to *him*, although not in the least as *his* possible *self*-expression.

This passivity of the hero in relation to form, however, is not something given from the outset, but is imposed as a task[121] and must be achieved, actively achieved. That is, it must be fought for and won by conquest within the work of art by both the author and the beholder, neither of whom invariably comes out of the struggle as the winner. This conquest can be achieved only if the author/contemplator maintains his intent and loving position outside the hero. The hero's inner directedness from within his own lived life possesses its own immanent necessity, its own autonomy; as such, it is capable of compelling us at times to become involved in its own sphere, in its own becoming (the becoming of a lived life, devoid of any issue aesthetically), and, as a result, we lose our stable position outside the hero and express the hero from within the hero himself, along *with* the hero. Where the author merges with the hero, the form we get is, indeed, no more than pure expression in the sense of "expressive" aesthetics, i.e., it is the result of the self-activity of the hero in relation to whom we failed to find an exterior position. The hero's self-activity, however, is incapable of being an *aesthetic* self-activity: it may comprise (give voice to) need, repentance, petition, and even pretensions to recognition by a possible author, but in itself it is incapable of engendering an aesthetically consummated form.

This inner, immanent necessity of the hero's own object-directed life must be understood and lived through by us in all its compelling force and significance; on this point, "expressive" theory is in the right. But it must be understood and lived through in a form which is *transgredient* to that life, i.e., in an aesthetically valid form, which relates to that life not as its *expression*, but as its *consummation*. The immanent necessity (not psychological,

of course, but meaning-related necessity) of a living consciousness (or the consciousness of lived life itself) must be met by a
justifying and consummating self-activity proceeding from outside; moreover, the gifts which this self-activity bestows must
have their place on the plane where life-experienced-from-within,
while remaining self-identical, is in principle powerless, and *not*
on the plane of that life's own sphere—as an enrichment of that
life with material (with content) of the very same category (this is
the way wishful dreaming or fantasizing actually operates, and in
real life a performed action—an act of assistance, for example—
operates in this way).

Aesthetic self-activity always operates on the boundaries (form
is a boundary) of a life-experienced-from-within—operates at
those points where this life is turned *outward*, where it comes to
an end (in space, time, and meaning) and *another* life begins, that
is, where it comes up against a sphere of self-activity beyond its
reach—the sphere of *another's* self-activity. A life's self-experience and self-awareness (and, consequently, its "expressive" self-
expression as well), as something unitary, have their own immovable bounds. And these bounds pertain, first of all, to one's own
external body: as an aesthetically intuitable value that may harmoniously combine with a lived life's inner directedness, my external body lies beyond the bounds of my unitary *self*-experience.

In my experiencing of my own life, my external body cannot
take up the place which an external body occupies for me in my
sympathetic co-experiencing of another's life—in the other's life
as a *whole* for me. The outward beauty of my body may be for
myself as well a highly important constituent in my own life, but
this is in principle different from experiencing the whole of my
body intuitively on one and the same axiological plane *with* my
own inner life *as the form* of my own inner life; it is different,
that is, from the intuitive experience of the whole of myself as
embodied in my own external body, the way I experience another's embodiedness in *his* external body.

I myself exist entirely *inside* my own lived life, and if I myself
were in some way to see the *exterior* of my own life, then this
seen exterior would turn at once into a constituent in my life-as-
experienced-from-within and would enrich that life only immanently. That is, it would cease to be a true exterior that actually
consummates my life from outside; it would cease to be an aesthetically formable boundary that consummates me from outside.

Let us suppose, for the moment, that I *could* physically stand outside myself, that I am given the possibility, the physical possibility, of giving form to myself from outside. Nevertheless, if I fail to take a stand *outside* my entire life as a whole, if I fail to perceive it as the life of *another*, I shall still find that I lack any *inwardly* convincing principle for giving form to myself from outside, for sculpting my own outward appearance, for consummating myself aesthetically. In order to obtain such a principle, I must succeed in finding a firm and convincing position (convincing not only outwardly, but also inwardly, i.e., with respect to meaning) *outside* my entire life with all its directedness to objects and to meaning, with all its desires, strivings, and achievements, and I must succeed in perceiving all these in the category of another. Not an expression or utterance *of* my own life, but an utterance *about* my own life through the lips of another is indispensable for producing an artistic whole, even that of a lyric. . . .

We can see, then, that the tacit addition of a sympathetic or loving relationship toward co-experienced life, or, in other words, the notion of *sympathetic* co-experiencing or empathizing, when consistently explicated and understood, totally destroys the purely "expressive" principle: the artistic event of a work of art assumes an entirely different aspect, develops in an entirely different direction, and pure co-experiencing or empathizing—as an abstract moment in the artistic event—proves to be merely *one* of its moments and, what is more, an *extra-aesthetic* moment.

Aesthetic activity *proper* comes into effect with the moment of *creative love* for the content (the life) which has been co-experienced, i.e., of that love which brings forth an aesthetic form for the co-experienced life that is transgredient to that life. Aesthetic creation cannot be explained or made intelligible as something immanent to a *single* consciousness. An aesthetic event cannot have merely one participant who would both experience his own life and express his own experiencing in an artistically valid form, because the *subiectum* of lived life and the *subiectum* of the aesthetic activity which gives form to that life are in principle incapable of coinciding with one another.

There are events which are in principle incapable of unfolding on the plane of one and the same consciousness and which presuppose *two* consciousnesses that never merge. Or, in other words, what is *constitutive* for such events is the relationship of one consciousness to *another* consciousness precisely as an *other*. Events of this kind include all of the *creatively* productive events—the once-occurrent and inconvertible events that bring forth something new.

[*"IMPOVERISHING" THEORIES*]

"Expressive" aesthetic theory is but one of many philosophical theories (ethical, philosophico-historical, metaphysical, religious) that we could call "impoverishing" theories, because they seek to explain the creatively productive event by reducing its full amplitude. And they do so, first of all, by reducing the number of its participants: for purposes of explanation, the event is transposed in all its constituents to the unitary plane of a single consciousness, and it is within the unity of this single consciousness that the event is to be understood and deduced in all its constituents. What one gains in this way is a purely theoretical transcription of an already accomplished event. But this gain is achieved at the cost of losing those actual creative forces which generated the event at the moment it was still being accomplished (when it was still open), i.e., at the cost of losing the living and in principle nonmerging participants in the event.

What one still fails to understand, then, is the idea of *formal enrichment*, in distinction to "material" enrichment or enrichment in content. And yet this idea is the fundamental, the motive idea of cultural creation. Cultural creation (in all cultural domains) does not in the least strive to enrich the object with material immanent to that object. Rather, it transposes the object to another axiological plane, bestows the gift of *form* upon it, transmutes it formally. And this formal enrichment is impossible if a *merging* with the object so treated occurs. In what way would it enrich the event if I merged with the other, and instead of *two* there would now be only *one?* And what would I myself gain by the other's merging with me? If he did, he would see and know no more than what I see and know myself; he would merely repeat in himself that want of any issue out of itself which characterizes my own life. Let him rather remain outside of me, for in that position he can see and know what I myself do not see and do not know from my own place, and he can essentially enrich the event of my own life. If *all* I do is merge with the other's life, I only intensify the want of any issue from within itself that characterizes his own life, and I only duplicate his life numerically. When there are two of us, then what is important from the standpoint of the productiveness of the event of my life is not the fact that, besides myself, there is *one more* person of essentially the *same* kind (*two* persons), but the fact that the other is for me a *different* person. And in this sense his ordinary sympathizing with my life is not a merging of the two of us into a single being and is not a numerical duplication of my life, but constitutes an essential enrichment of the event of my life, because my life is co-experienced by him in a new form, in a new axiological category—as the life of another, a different human being. That is, it is co-experienced as a life which, axiologically, is toned or colored differently from his own life and is received differently, justified differently, than his own life. The productiveness of the event of a life does not consist in the merging of all into one. On the contrary, it consists in the intensification of one's own *outsideness* with respect to others,[122] one's own *distinctness* from others: it consists in fully exploiting the privilege of one's own unique place outside other human beings.

"Impoverishing" theories assume cultural creation to be founded on the renunciation of one's own unique place, one's own position over against others—founded, in other words, on *participation in one unitary consciousness*, on solidarity or even complete merging. What accounts for all these theories and, in particular, for the "expressive" theory in aesthetics is the "epistemologism" pervading all nineteenth-century and twentieth-century philosophy. Theory of knowledge has become the model for theories in all other domains of culture. In place of ethics, or the theory of action, one substitutes an epistemology of actions already performed. In place of aesthetics, or the theory of aesthetic activity as already completed, that is, the object chosen for consideration is not directly the actual fact of aesthetic performance, but the possible theoretical transcription of it, the cognizance of it. As a result, the unity of the event's performance is displaced by the unity of one's consciousness, one's understanding of the event, and the *subiectum* who was a participant in the event itself is transformed into the *subiectum* of a nonparticipant, purely theoretical cognition of the work.

Epistemological consciousness, the consciousness of science, is a unitary and unique consciousness, or, to be exact—a single consciousness. Everything this consciousness deals with must be determined by itself alone: any determinateness must be derived from itself and any determination of an object must be performed by itself. In this sense, epistemological consciousness cannot have another consciousness outside itself, cannot enter into relation with another consciousness, one that is autonomous and distinct from it. Any unity is its *own* unity; it cannot admit next to itself any other unity that would be different from it and independent of it (the unity of nature, the unity of another consciousness), that is, any sovereign unity that would stand over against it with its *own* fate, one *not* determined by epistemological consciousness. This unitary consciousness creates and forms any matter it deals with solely as an object and not as a *subiectum*, and even a *subiectum* is no more than an object for it. The *subiectum* is known and understood only as an object, for only valuation could render him a *subiectum*—the bearer of his *own* autonomous life, experiencing his *own* fate.

Aesthetic consciousness, on the other hand, as a loving and value-positing consciousness, is a consciousness of a consciousness: the author's (the *I*'s) consciousness of the hero's (the *other*'s) consciousness. In the aesthetic event, we have to do with a *meeting* of two consciousnesses which are in principle distinct from each other, and where the author's consciousness, moreover, relates to the hero's consciousness not from the standpoint of its objective makeup, its validity as an object, but from the standpoint of its subjectively *lived* unity; and it is this, the hero's own consciousness, that is concretely localized and *embodied* (the degree of concreteness is variable, of course) and lovingly *consummated*. The *author's* consciousness, on the other hand, just like epistemological consciousness, is incapable of being consummated. . . .

[AESTHETIC FORM]

Thus, spatial form is not *sensu stricto* the form of a work as an object, but the form of a hero and his world—the form of a *subiectum*; on this point "expressive" aesthetics is substantially correct.[j] Contrary to "expressive" aesthetics, however, form is not *pure* expression of the hero and his life, but an expression which,

---

[j] Granting a certain imprecision, we could, of course, say that the form of the *life* represented in a novel is the form of the *novel*, except that the novel (including the constituent of isolation,[123] i.e., of fiction) is precisely a form for mastering life.

in giving expression to the hero, also expresses the author's relationship to the hero, and it is this relationship that constitutes the specifically *aesthetic* moment of form. Aesthetic form cannot be founded and validated from within the hero, out of his own directedness to objects and meaning, i.e., on the basis of that which has validity only for his own lived life. Aesthetic form is founded and validated from within the *other*—the author, as the author's *creative* reaction to the hero and his life. As a reaction, that is, which produces values that are transgredient in principle to the hero and his life and yet are essentially related to the latter.

This creative reaction is aesthetic love. The relationship of transgredient aesthetic form to the hero and his life (where both are taken from within) is the relationship *sui generis* of the one who loves to the one who is loved (with the sexual moment entirely removed, of course). Similar to the aesthetic relationship of the author to the hero, or of form to the hero and his life, are such relationships as the following: the relationship of an unmotivated valuation to the object of such valuation ("I love him, whatever he may be," and only after this act of valuation comes the active idealization, the gift of form); the relationship of a confirmative acceptance to the one accepted and confirmed; the relationship of a gift to a need; of an act of freely granted forgiveness * [124] to a transgression; of an act of grace to a sinner. The essential constituent common to all these relationships is, on the one hand, the transgredient gift bestowed upon a recipient of the gift, and, on the other, the profound relation which this gift bears to the recipient: not he, but *for him*. Hence, the enrichment in this case is formal, transfigurative in character—it transposes the recipient of the gift to a new plane of existence. And what is transposed to a new plane, moreover, is not the material, not an object, but a *sub-iectum*—the hero. It is only in relation to the hero that aesthetic obligation (the aesthetic "ought") as well as aesthetic love and the gift bestowed by such love are possible.

Form must utilize a moment or constituent feature which is transgredient to the hero's consciousness (transgredient to his possible self-experience and concrete self-valuation) and yet is essentially related to him, determining him from outside *as a whole:* the moment of the hero's "advertedness" outward, his *boundaries, and his boundaries, moreover, as boundaries of the whole that he is. Form is a boundary* that has been wrought aesthetically. . . . The boundary in question, moreover, is a boundary of the body as well as a boundary of the soul and a boundary of the spirit (one's directedness to meaning). Boundaries experienced from within, in one's self-consciousness, are experienced in a manner essentially different from boundaries experienced from without, in one's aesthetic experience of the other. In every act (inner as well as outer) of my own object-directed life, I start out from within myself; I do not encounter any *axiologically valid* boundaries, any boundaries that consummate me *positively*; I go forward ahead of myself and cross over my own boundaries. From within myself, I can perceive my own boundaries as an impediment, but not at all as a consummation, while, on the contrary, the aesthetically experienced boundary of the other does consummate him, contracting and concentrating all of him, all of his self-activity, and closing off this self-activity. The object-directedness of the hero living his life is fitted in and enclosed in its entirety within his body *qua* aesthetically valid boundary or, in other words, it is *embodied*. (This twofold significance of the boundary will become clearer in what follows below.) We open the boundaries when we "identify" ourselves with the hero and experience his life from within; and we close them again when we consummate him aesthetically from without. If in the initial movement from within we are passive, then in the answering movement from without we are active—we create something absolutely new, something "excessive." And it is this meeting of *two* movements on the surface of a human being that consolidates or gives body to his axiological boundaries—produces the fire of aesthetic value (much as fire is struck from a flint).

Hence, any aesthetic existence, i.e., a whole, integral human being, is not founded and validated from within—from a possible self-consciousness. And that is why beauty, insofar as we abstract from the author/contemplator's self-activity, appears to be passive, naive, and elemental. Beauty does not know itself; it cannot found and validate itself—it simply *is*. Beauty is a gift, a gift taken in abstraction from the bestower of the gift and his internally founded self-activity (for it is from within the gift-bestowing activity that this gift is founded and validated). . . .

THE "IMPRESSIVE" THEORY IN AESTHETICS

To this theory we assign all those theoretical positions in aesthetics for which the center of gravity is located in the formally productive self-activity of the artist.*[125] Such are the positions of Fiedler, Hildebrand, Hanslick, Riegl, Witasek,[126] and the so-called Formalists. (Kant occupies an ambivalent position in this context.)

In contrast to "expressive" aesthetics, "impressive" aesthetics loses not the author, but the hero as an independent, even if passive, moment in the artistic event. Indeed, the artistic event as a living relationship of two consciousnesses does not exist for "impressive" aesthetics. Once again, the artist's act of creation is conceived as a one-sided act confronted not by another *subiectum*, but only by an object, only by material to be worked. Form is deduced from the peculiarities of the material—visual, auditory, etc.

In terms of this approach, form cannot be founded and validated in any depth, and ultimately finds no more than a (more or less refined) hedonic explanation. Aesthetic love becomes objectless— it becomes a pure, contentless process of loving, it is love at play. The extremes converge: "impressive" aesthetics as well must ultimately end up in play, except that it is play of a different kind. This is no longer a playing at life for the sake of a life as such—the way children play; rather, this is a playing with nothing but the contentless reception of a possible life, with nothing but the bare moment of aesthetic justification and consummation of a life that is merely possible. For "impressive" aesthetics, only the author exists—an author without a hero; his self-activity, directed only to the material, becomes a purely instrumental activity.

Our elucidation of the significance of the "expressive" and "impressive" aspects of the outer body in the artistic event constituted by a work of art should be sufficient to provide a basis for understanding the proposition that the center of value in spatial form is precisely the *outer body*. What we need to do now is develop this proposition in more detail in relation to *verbal* art.

7. The Spatial Whole of the Hero and His World in Verbal Art: The Theory of Horizon and Environment

To what extent does verbal art have to do with the spatial form of the hero and his world? There can be no doubt, of course, that verbal art deals with the hero's exterior and with the spatial world in which the event of his life unfolds. What gives rise to considerable doubts, however, is the question of whether verbal art has to do with the *spatial form* of the hero as an *artistic form;* in most cases, the problem is resolved in a negative sense. To resolve the problem correctly, it is necessary to take into account the twofold sense of aesthetic form.

[INNER AND OUTER FORM]

As we have already indicated, aesthetic form may be both an inner and an outer, or empirical, form. Or, in other words, it may be the form of the aesthetic object, i.e., the form of the world which is constructed on the basis of a given work of art but does not coincide with that work; or it may be the form of the work of art itself, i.e., a material form.[127]

On the basis of this distinction, one cannot claim, of course, that the aesthetic objects in the different arts (painting, poetry, music, etc.) are all the same and that the difference between the arts consists, therefore, only in the different means used for the actualization or construction of the aesthetic object (that is, the difference is reduced solely to the technical or instrumental moment). This is not at all the case. On the contrary, the material form, the form that determines whether a given work is a pictorial or a poetic or a musical work of art, also determines, in an essential way, the structure of the appropriate aesthetic object, rendering that object somewhat one-sided by accentuating some particular aspect of it. But in spite of that, the aesthetic object is many-sided and *concrete* nevertheless—as many-sided and concrete as that cognitive-ethical reality (the "lived" or experienced world) which is justified and consummated in it artistically. This world, moreover—the world consummated in the aesthetic object—achieves the highest degree of concreteness and many-sidedness in *verbal* creation (it is least concrete and many-sided in music).

To be sure, verbal creation does not produce an *external* spatial form, for it does not operate with spatial material the way painting, drawing, or sculpture does; the material it works with—language—is in its essence nonspatial (sound in music is even less spatial).[k] The aesthetic object itself, however—the object imaged

---

[k] The spatial form of the disposition of a text (stanzas, chapters, the *figurae* of scholastic poetry, etc.) has only a minimal significance.

through the words—consists not of words alone, of course, even if it includes a great deal that is purely verbal. And *this object of aesthetic vision* has an artistically valid *inner spatial form* which is imaged through the words of a given work (whereas in painting it is imaged through colors, and in drawing—through lines, and, once again, it does not follow that the aesthetic object consists here of nothing but lines or colors; the whole point is that a concrete object is to be produced out of such lines and colors).

There can be no doubt, then, about the existence of a spatial form within an aesthetic object which is expressed verbally in a given work. A different question is *how* this inner spatial form gets actualized: whether it has to be reproduced in a purely *visual* representation[128] (a visually full and distinct representation), or whether the only thing that gets actualized is an emotional-volitional *equivalent* of it, i.e., a feeling-tone,[129] an emotional coloring corresponding to that form (visual representation can be intermittent and fleeting in this case, or it may even be entirely absent, being replaced by words).[1] A thorough elaboration of the question so posed exceeds the bounds of the present inquiry and has its proper place in the aesthetics of verbal creation. As far as our problem is concerned, a few brief remarks on this question should suffice.

Even in the visual arts, inner spatial form is never actualized as a *visually* full and complete form (just as the temporal form, for that matter, is never actualized as a phonically full and complete form). *Visual* fullness and completeness are proper only to the external or material form of a work, and the qualities of this external form are, as it were, transposed upon the inner form (even in the visual arts, the visual image of inner form is to a considerable extent subjective). The visual inner form is experienced emotionally and volitionally *as if* it were visually full and complete, but this fullness and completeness can never be a really actualized representation. Of course, the degree to which inner form

---

[1]Even though the emotional-volitional tone is conjoined with words (is attached, as it were, to the intonated sound-image of words), it relates, of course, not to words, but to the object expressed in words, even if such an object is not actualized in consciousness as a visual image; the sense of the emotional-volitional tone is determined solely by the object, even if this tone develops jointly with the sound of words.

is actualized in visual representation varies in different kinds of verbal creation and in different individual works.

In narrative literature, this degree of visual actualization is higher: the description of the hero's exterior in the novel, for example, must necessarily be recreated visually, even if the image produced on the basis of verbal material will be visually subjective with different readers. In lyric poetry, the degree of actualization is lowest of all, especially in the Romantic lyric. In lyric poetry, the frequently heightened degree of visual actualization (a habit inculcated by the novel) destroys the aesthetic impression. In all lyric poetry, however, we meet everywhere with the emotional-volitional equivalent of an object's exterior, i.e., with an emotional-volitional directedness upon this possible, although not visualized, exterior—with a directedness that produces this exterior as an artistic value. That is why we must recognize and must understand the *plastic-pictorial* moment or constituent in verbal creation.

Man's outer body is *given*; his outer boundaries and those of his world are *given* (given in the extra-aesthetic givenness of life). This is a necessary and inalienable moment of being as a given. Consequently, they need to be aesthetically received, recreated, fashioned, and justified. And this is precisely what is accomplished by art with all the means at its disposal—with colors, lines, masses, words, sounds. Inasmuch as the artist has to do with man's existence and with his world, he has also to do with the givenness of man in space as a necessary constituent of human existence. And in transposing this existence of man to the aesthetic plane, the artist must transpose to this plane man's exterior as well, within the bounds which are determined by the type of material he utilizes (e.g., colors, sounds, etc.).

A poet creates the hero's exterior, the spatial form of the hero and his world, by means of verbal material; the meaninglessness of this exterior from within and its cognitional factuality from without are rendered meaningful and justified by the poet aesthetically, i.e., rendered valid artistically.

The external image of the hero and his world, expressed in words—regardless of whether it is visualized (as it is to some extent in the novel, for example) or whether it is experienced only in emotional-volitional terms—has the significance of a consummating form, i.e., the external image is not only "expressive," but is "impressive" artistically as well. All of the propositions we have advanced above are applicable here as well—the verbal portrait is subject to them just as much as the pictorial portrait. Here as well, it is only the position of being situated outside the hero that enables the author to produce the aesthetic value of the hero's exterior: the spatial form *of* the hero expresses the author's relationship *to* the hero. Here as well, the author must assume a firm stand outside the hero and his world and utilize all the transgredient features of the hero's exterior.

The verbal work of art is created from outside each one of its heroes, and, in reading, we must follow the heroes from outside, not from within. Yet it is precisely in the case of verbal creation (and in the case of music even more so, of course) that the purely "expressive" interpretation of the exterior appears to be especially seductive and convincing, inasmuch as the author/beholder's situatedness outside the hero lacks here the spatial distinctness it has in the visual arts (visual representation being replaced here by an emotional-volitional equivalent "affixed" to words). On the other hand, language as a material is not sufficiently neutral in relation to the cognitive-ethical sphere, where it is used as both self-expression and communication, i.e., is used expressively. And these expressive habits of using language (giving utterance to oneself and designating objects) are transposed by us into our apprehension of works of verbal art. Coupled with this, moreover, is our spatial and visual passivity during such apprehension: the words image, as it were, an already finished spatial given, and what is not evident is the *creation* of the spatial form from outside through lines and colors, that is, the action of constituting and producing the form from outside through a movement of the hand and of the whole body that conquers the merely imitative movement-gesture. The manner of utterance as well as gestures and the play of features, inasmuch as they occur in lived life, just as language does, possess a much stronger expressive tendency (the manner of utterance and gestures either express or imitate); the creative emotional-volitional tones of the author/contemplator can easily be absorbed in the tones proper to the hero as he lives his own life.

That is why it is necessary to emphasize especially that both content (i.e., what is put *into* the hero—his life from within) and form are unjustified and unexplainable on the plane of a single consciousness; that it is only on the boundaries of two consciousnesses, on the boundaries of the body, that an encounter is actually realized and the artistic gift of form is bestowed. Without this essentially necessary[130] reference to the *other*, i.e., as a gift to the other that justifies and consummates him (through an immanent-aesthetic justification), form fails to find any inner foundation and validation from within the author/contemplator's self-activity and inevitably degenerates into something that simply affords pleasure, into something "pretty," something I find immediately agreeable, the way I find myself feeling immediately cold or warm. By using a certain technique, the author produces an object of pleasure, and the contemplator passively affords himself this pleasure.

Without the application of the mediating value-category of the *other*, the author's emotional-volitional tones that actively constitute and produce the hero's exterior as an artistic value cannot be brought into immediate accord with the hero's own directedness from within his own lived life. It is only thanks to this category of the other that it becomes possible to transform the hero's exterior into an exterior that encompasses and consummates him totally, that is: to fit the hero's own directedness to meaning in living his life into his exterior as into a form; to fill his exterior with content and give it life; to create a whole human being as a unitary value.

[HORIZON AND ENVIRONMENT]

How are objects of the outside world imaged with relation to the hero in works of verbal creation? What place do they occupy in verbal creation?

There are two possible ways of combining the outside world with a human being: from within a human being—as his *horizon*, and from outside him—as his *environment*. From within me myself, within the meaning-and-value context of my own life, an object *stands over against* me as the object of my own (cognitive-ethical and practical) directedness in living my life; in this context, the object is a constituent of the unitary and unique *open* event of being, in which I partake as a participant who has an urgent interest in the outcome of that event. From within my actual participation in the event of being,[131] the outside world is the *horizon* of my active, act-performing consciousness. It is only in cognitive, ethical, and practico-instrumental categories[m] that I can (so long as I remain within myself) orient myself in this world as in an event and introduce a certain order into its composition with respect to objects; this is what determines the outward aspect, the "face," of each object for me—determines its emotional-volitional tonality, its value, its significance. From within my own consciousness—as a consciousness participating in being—the world is the object of my acts: acts of thinking, acts of feeling, acts of speaking, acts of doing. The center of gravity in this world is located in the future, in what is desired, in what ought to be, and *not* in the self-sufficient givenness of an object, in its being-on-hand, *not* in its present, its wholeness, its being-already-realized. My relationship to each object within my horizon is never a consummated relationship; rather, it is a relationship which is imposed on me as a task-to-be-accomplished, for the event of being, taken as a whole, is an open event; my situation must change at every moment—I cannot tarry and come to rest. The object's standing over against me, in space and in time, is what constitutes the principle of the *horizon:* objects do not *surround* me (my outer body) in their presently given makeup and their presently given value, but rather—*stand over against* me as the objects of my own cognitive-ethical directedness in living my life within the open, still risk-fraught event of being, whose unity, meaning, and value are not *given* but imposed as a *task* still to be accomplished.

If we turn our attention to the world of objects in a work of art, we should have no difficulty in ascertaining that the unity and structure of this object-world is *not* the unity and structure of the hero's lived *horizon,* and that the fundamental principle of its organization and ordering is transgredient to the hero's own actual and possible consciousness. A verbal landscape, a description of surroundings, a representation of everyday communal life, that is, nature, city, communal life-style, etc.—all these are not constituent features within the horizon of a human being's active, act-performing consciousness (his ethically and cognitionally acting consciousness). There can be no doubt that all the objects presented in a work bear and must bear an essential relation to the hero, for otherwise they would be mere *hors d'oeuvres;* but this

---

[m] The categories of the true, the good, and the practically effective.

relation in its essential aesthetic principle is not a relation that is given from within the hero's lived-life consciousness. What constitutes the center of the spatial disposition and axiological interpretation of all objects presented in a work is man's *outer* body and his *outer* soul. All of the objects are correlated with the hero's exterior, with his boundaries—his outer as well as inner boundaries (the boundaries of his body and the boundaries of his soul).

The object-world within a work of art is understood and is correlated with the hero as his *environment*. The distinctiveness of the environment expresses itself first of all in an outward formal combination of plastic and pictorial features: in the harmony of colors and lines, in symmetry, and in other purely aesthetic combinations that are independent of meaning.[132] In verbal creation, this plastic-pictorial aspect does not attain, of course, any externally intuitable fullness and completeness (in the form of a representation); what we get here are emotional-volitional equivalents of possible visual representations that correspond in the aesthetic object to the meaning-independent plastic and pictorial whole (in the present context, we shall not deal with the combination of painting, drawing, and sculpture). As a combination of colors, lines, and masses, the object has an independent status: it acts upon us alongside of the hero and around him. That is to say, it does not stand over against the hero within the hero's own horizon; it is perceived as an integral object and, as such, allows us to walk around it, as it were. It should be evident that this purely plastic and pictorial principle of ordering and giving form to the external world of objects is completely transgredient to the hero's living consciousness, inasmuch as colors, lines, and masses (treated aesthetically) constitute the utmost bounds of an object or of a living body, i.e., the point where an object is turned outward, where it exists axiologically only in and for the other, where it is part of the outside world, and where, from within itself, it does not exist. . . .

The Temporal Whole of the Hero
(The Problem of the Inner Man—the Soul)

1. [*The Soul*]

Man, as he exists in art, is man in his totality. In the preceding section, we determined that man's outer body constitutes an aesthetically significant moment and that the object-world is the environment of his outer body. We ascertained that the outer man (the exterior human being) as a plastic-pictorial value and the outside world correlated and aesthetically combined with that outward person are both transgredient to a human being's possible and actual *self*-consciousness, to his *I-for-myself*, to his consciousness as living and experiencing a life of its own; that is, both are in principle incapable of being located on the line of a human being's axiological *self*-relationship. The aesthetic interpretation[133] and organization of the outer body and its correlative world is a *gift* bestowed upon the hero from another consciousness—from the author/contemplator; it is not an expression of the hero from within the hero himself, but represents the author-*other*'s creative, constructive relationship *to* the hero.

What we need to demonstrate in the present section is that the same is valid in relation to the inner man, in relation to the inner whole of the hero's soul as an aesthetic phenomenon. As the *given*, artistically experienced *whole* of the hero's inner life, the soul as well is transgredient to the hero's *self*-consciousness, to his directedness to meaning in living his own life. We shall see that the soul, as an inner whole that comes to be *in time*, the soul as a *given*, *presently existing* whole, is constituted in terms of aesthetic categories; the soul is spirit the way it looks *from outside*, in the other.

The problem of the soul, from a methodological standpoint, is a problem in aesthetics. It cannot be a problem in psychology—a science that is nonvaluational and causal, for even though the soul evolves and becomes in time, it is a whole that is individual, valuational, and free. Nor can the soul be a problem in ethics, for the ethical *subiectum* is present to itself as a task—the task of actualizing itself as a value, and it is in principle incapable of being given, of being present-on-hand, of being contemplated: it is *I-for-myself*. The spirit in Idealism (constructed on the basis of self-experience and a solitary self-relationship) is, likewise, something posited purely as a task. The transcendental *ego* in epistemology (constructed, once again, on the basis of self-experience) has a purely formal character. We shall not deal here with the religious-metaphysical problem of the soul (metaphysics can only be religious), but there is no doubt that the problem of immortality concerns the soul, not the spirit. That is to say, it concerns that individual and valuational whole of inner life proceeding in time

which we experience in the *other*, and which is described and imaged in art with words, colors, and sounds; it concerns the soul as
situated on one and the same plane with the other's outer body
and as indissociable from it in the moment of death and immortality (resurrection in the flesh).

From within myself, the soul does not exist for me as an axiological whole that is given or already present-on-hand in me. In
my relationship to myself, I have nothing to do with the soul. My
self-reflection, insofar as it is mine, is incapable of engendering a
soul; all it can engender is a spurious and disjected subjectivity—
something that ought not to be. My own inner life, proceeding in
time, is incapable of consolidating[134] for me into something valuable or precious, into something that should be preserved and
should abide eternally (the only thing I find intuitively understandable from within myself, within my solitary and pure self-
relationship, is the eternal condemnation of the soul, and it is
only with this condemnation that I can be solidary from within
myself). The soul descends upon me—like grace upon the sinner,
like a gift that is unmerited and unexpected. In the spirit I can and
must do nothing but lose my own soul; the soul may be saved and
preserved, but *not through my own* powers.

What, then, are the principles of ordering, organizing, and forming the soul (the principles of rendering it *whole*) in active artistic vision?

2. The Active Emotional-Volitional Relationship to the Inner Determinateness of a Human Being: The Problem of Death (Death from Within and Death from Without)

The principles of giving a form to the soul are the principles of
giving a form to inner life *from outside*, from *another* consciousness; the artist's work proceeds here, once again, *on the boundaries*—the boundaries of *inner life*, i.e., at the point where the soul
is inwardly turned ("adverted") *to the outside* of itself. The other
human being is situated outside me and over against me not only
outwardly, but also inwardly. By using an oxymoron, we could
speak here of the other's *inward* outsideness and over-against-
ness. The other's inner experiences (his joy, anguish, desire, striv-

ing, and, finally, his directedness to meaning), even if they are not manifested in anything external (are not uttered, are not reflected in his face or in the expression of his eyes, but are only surmised or guessed by me from the context of his life)—all these experiences are found by me *outside* my own inner world, outside my *I-for-myself* (even where I experience them in some way, they do not relate—axiologically—to me, they are not imputed to me as mine); *for me,* they are located in *being*—they are constituents of the *other*'s axiological existence.

Lived experiences, when experienced outside myself in the other, possess an inner exterior, an inner countenance adverted toward me, and this inner exterior or countenance can be and should be lovingly contemplated, it can be and should be remembered the way we remember a person's face (and not the way we remember some past experience of our own), it can be and should be made secure, given a form, regarded with loving-mercy, cherished with our inner eyes, and not our physical, outward eyes. It is this exterior of another's soul (an inner flesh of the subtlest kind, as it were) that constitutes an intuitively palpable artistic individuality (character, type, personal situation, etc.), that is, a particular realization of meaning in being, an *individual* realization and embodiment of meaning, a clothing of meaning with inner flesh— that which can be idealized, heroicized, rhythmicized, etc.

This self-activity of mine in relation to another's inner world (from outside this world) is usually called "sympathetic understanding." What should be emphasized is the absolutely incremental, excessive, productive, and enriching character of sympathetic understanding. The word "understanding," in its usual, naively realistic, interpretation, is always misleading. For the point here is not the exact, passive mirroring or duplication of another's experience within myself (nor is such duplication really possible); the point is a transposition of another's experience to an entirely *different* axiological plane, into an entirely *new* category of valuation and forming. Thus, the *other*'s suffering as co-experienced by me is in principle different (different, moreover, in the most important and essential sense) from the other's suffering as *he* experiences it for himself and from my *own* suffering as I experience it in myself. The only thing these experiences of suffering have in common is the logically self-identical concept of suffering—an abstract moment that is never and nowhere realized in its pure form, for even the word "suffering" is, after all, characteristically intonated in our thinking within lived life. The other's co-experienced suffering is a completely new *ontic* formation that I alone actualize *inwardly* from my unique place *outside* the other. Sympathetic understanding is not a mirroring, but a fundamentally and essentially [135] new valuation, a utilization of my own architectonic position in being outside another's inner life. Sympathetic understanding recreates the whole inner person in aesthetically loving categories for a new existence in a new dimension of the world.

First of all, we need to determine the character of the emotional-volitional relationship to my own inner determinateness and to the inner determinateness of another human being. Above all, we need to determine the character of this relationship to the very being or existence of these determinate entities. That is to say, in relation to the *soul* as a given we also need the kind of phenomenological description of self-experiencing and of experiencing the other that we provided in relation to the *body* as a value.

A human being's inner life, just like his outward givenness— his body—is not something indifferent to form. Inner life—the soul—is given a form either in my self-consciousness or in my consciousness of the other, and what is surmounted in both cases is the properly empirical reality of inner life. The soul as an empirical reality that is neutral toward these forms represents an abstract construction produced by the thought of psychology. The soul is something that is essentially formed or shaped. In what direction and in which categories is this forming or shaping of inner life accomplished in my *self*-consciousness (my own inner life) and in my consciousness of the *other* (the other's inner life)?

Just like the spatial form of a human being's outward existence, the aesthetically valid *temporal* form of his inner life develops from the *excess* inherent in my temporal seeing of another soul— from an excess which contains within itself all the moments that enter into the transgredient consummation of the whole of another's inner life. What constitutes these transgredient moments, i.e., moments that exceed self-consciousness and consummate it, are the outer *boundaries* of inner life—the point where inner life is turned *outward* and ceases to be active out of itself. These boundaries are first and foremost *temporal* boundaries: the beginning and the end of a life, which are not given to a concrete self-consciousness and for the possession of which self-consciousness lacks any active axiological approach (any emotional-volitional position that would give them meaning with respect to value)—birth and death in their axiologically consummating significance (their characterological, lyrical significance, their storyline significance,[136] etc.).

In the life I live and experience from within myself, my own birth and death are events which I am in principle incapable of experiencing; birth and death as *mine* are incapable of becoming events of my own life. Just as in the case of outward appearance, the point here is not merely the impossibility of experiencing these events in fact; the point is first of all that I lack any essential axiological approach to them. My being afraid of my own death and my attraction to life-as-an-abiding are essentially different in character from my being afraid of the death of another person, a person dear to me, and from my striving to safeguard that other person's life. The most essential moment for the second case is absent in the first—namely: the loss of the other as a qualitatively determinate, unique personality, the impoverishment of the world of my life, in which that other was present and now is absent—absent as *this* determinate and unique other (this loss, moreover, is not just an egoistically experienced loss, of course, for my whole life may lose its value as well after the other has departed from it).

But even apart from this fundamental moment of loss or bereavement, the moral coefficients of being afraid of one's own death and of the death of another are profoundly different (just as self-preservation is profoundly different from safeguarding another person's life), and this difference is ineradicable. The loss of myself is not a parting from myself—a parting from a qualitatively determinate and beloved human being, inasmuch as my own life-as-an-abiding is not a matter of joyously abiding with myself as with a qualitatively determinate and beloved human being. Moreover, it is impossible for me to *experience* the axiological picture of the world in which I used to live and in which I am no longer present. I can, of course, *think* the world as it would be after my death, but I cannot experience it, from within myself, as a world that is emotionally toned by the fact of my death, the fact of my nonexistence. To be able to do that, I must project myself into the life of another or others, for whom my death, my absence, will be an event of *their* lives. And in making the attempt to perceive emotionally (axiologically) the event of my own death in the world, I come to be swayed, possessed by the soul of a possible other; I am no longer alone, when I attempt to contemplate the whole of my own life in the mirror of history, just as I am not alone when I contemplate my own exterior in a mirror. The *whole* of my life has no validity within the axiological context of my own lived life. My birth, my axiological abiding in the world, and, finally, my death are events that occur neither *in* me nor *for* me. The emotional weight of my own life *taken as a whole* does not exist for me myself.

The values that pertain to the existence of a qualitatively determinate person are characteristic only of the other. It is only with the other that I have the possibility of experiencing the joy of meeting and abiding with him, the sorrow of parting and the grief of bereavement; it is only with him that I can meet in the dimension of time as well as part in the dimension of time; only he can *be* as well as *not be* for me. I am always with myself—there can be no life for me without myself.

All these emotional-volitional tones, which are possible only in relation to the existence of another, create that special weight—the weight of an event—which his life possesses for me, and which my own life does not possess. The point here is the qualitative character of value, not the degree of value. These tones consolidate the other, as it were, and create the distinctive character of my lived experience of the whole of his life, that is, they tone or color this whole with respect to value. In my own life, people are born, pass by, and die, and their life/death is often the most important event of my own life—an event that determines the content of my life (cf. the essential constituents that determine the stories or plots of world literature). The terminal points of my own life cannot have this plot-determining significance; my own life is that which temporally encompasses the existence of others.

When the existence of the other has incontrovertibly and conclusively determined the fundamental plot or storyline of my own life; when the boundaries of the other's valuable existence/ nonexistence have been wholly encompassed by my own boundaries, which are never given to me myself and which are in principle incapable of being experienced by me; when the other has been experienced (temporally encompassed) by me from his *natus est anno Domini* to his *mortuus est anno Domini*—it becomes

unmistakably evident[n] that my own life sounds altogether different to me myself than does the life of another; it becomes distinctly evident that my own life, within its own context, lacks
any aesthetic weight with respect to plot or storyline and that its
value and meaning are located on a completely different axiological plane. I am in myself the condition of possibility for my
own life, but I am not its valuable hero. I am not capable of experiencing the emotionally consolidated time that encompasses me,
just as I am not capable of experiencing the space that encompasses me. My time and my space are the time and space of an
author, and not those of a hero. In such time and space, I can be
aesthetically active, but not aesthetically passive, in relation to
the other whom they encompass; I can aesthetically justify and
consummate the other in such time and space, but not myself.

This does not in the least diminish, of course, the significance
of the moral awareness of one's own mortality, nor the biological
function performed by the fear of death and the avoidance of death.
But this anticipated mortality, anticipated from within, is radically different from my experiencing—from outside—the death of
another and the world in which he is no longer present as a qualitatively determinate and unique individuality, as well as from my
active valuational attitude or position in relation to that event. It
is only this active position that is aesthetically productive.

My self-activity in relation to the other also continues after his
death, and now aesthetic constituents begin to predominate in it
(in comparison to ethical and practical ones): the whole of his life
lies directly before me, freed of such constituents as future time,
goals, and obligation (the ought-to-be). Interment and putting up a
memorial are followed by *memory*. I have the other's *entire* life
outside myself, and it is at this point that the aesthetization of
his personality begins: the securing and consummating of his personality in an aesthetically valid image. The aesthetic categories
of giving a form to the inner person (as well as to the outer, for
that matter) are generated, in essentials, from the emotional-

---

[n] Inasmuch as these *natus* and *mortuus* are in principle incapable of
being experienced in relation to my own existence in all their concreteness and force, and thus my own life cannot become an event for me the
way another's life does.

volitional attitude assumed in commemorating the dead ("remembering the dead in one's prayers"). For only this attitude in relation to the other provides a valuational approach to the temporal and already completed whole of a human being's outer and inner life. And we must repeat, once again, that the point here is not the availability of the entire material of a person's life (all the facts of his biography), but, first and foremost, the availability of an axiological approach capable of aesthetically forming the given material (the material constituted by a given person's life as an event, as a plot or storyline).

My *memory* of the other and of the other's life differs radically from my contemplating and remembering my own life. Memory sees a life and its content in a different way formally: only memory is aesthetically productive (the constituent of content can, of course, be supplied by the observation and recollection of one's own life, but these cannot provide the forming and consummating activity). Memory of someone else's finished life (although anticipation of its end is possible as well) provides the golden key to the aesthetic consummation of a person. An aesthetic approach to a *living* person forestalls his death, as it were—predetermines his future and renders his future redundant, as it were; immanent to any determinateness of inner life is fate. Memory is an approach to the other from the standpoint of his axiological consummatedness. In a certain sense, memory is hopeless; but on the other hand, only memory knows how to value—independently of purpose and meaning[137]—an already finished life, a life that is totally present-on-hand.

The givenness of the temporal limits of another's life, even if only potentially; the givenness of an axiological approach to another's *finished* life, that is, the perception of the other under the token of death, of his potential absence, even if the determinate other outlives me in fact—this is what provides the enabling conditions for the consolidation and formal modification of a life—of its entire course within these temporal limits. (The moral and biological anticipation of such limits from within does not have the same formally transformative significance; and this applies even more to theoretical knowledge of one's own temporal limitedness.) When these limits are given, then a life can be arranged and formed in a completely different way, just as an exposition of the train of our thought, when a conclusion has already been reached and is given (the dogma is given), can be framed in a way which is completely different from the way it would be framed when a conclusion is still being sought.

A *determined* life, a life freed from the claws of what-is-yet-to-be, of the future, of purpose and meaning—such a life becomes emotionally measurable, musically expressive, and self-sufficient (sufficient to itself as totally present-on-hand); its being-already-determined becomes a *valuable* determinateness. Meaning is not born, nor does it die; the meaning-governed sequence or progression of one's life, that is, the cognitive-ethical tension of a lived life from within itself, can be neither started nor consummated. Death cannot be the consummation of this meaning-governed progression—that is, death cannot assume here the significance of a *positive* consummation; from within itself, such a progression knows no positive consummation and is incapable of turning back upon itself, in order to coincide contentedly with its own already existent makeup; a consummation—a consummating acceptance—can descend upon it only where it is turned to the outside of itself, where, for itself, it does not exist.

The temporal limits of my own life, just like its spatial boundaries, do not have, for myself, the *formally* organizing significance which they have for another's life. I live—think, feel, act—in the meaning-governed sequence or progression of my own life, and not in the potentially consummated *whole* of what constitutes my present-on-hand life. Such a temporal whole is not capable of determining and organizing my thoughts and my acts from within me myself, for these thoughts and acts possess cognitional and ethical validity—they are extratemporal. One could say: I myself do not know how my soul looks from outside—in the world, in being; and even if I knew, its image would not be capable of founding and organizing a single act of my own life from within myself, for the axiological validity (aesthetic validity) which such an image possesses is transgredient to myself (recourse to feigning is possible here, but feigning, too, exceeds the bounds of such an image, is not founded by it, and destroys it). Any consummation represents a *deus ex machina* for a life-sequence which, from within itself, is directed toward meaning (toward the validity of meaning).

An almost complete analogy exists between the significance of temporal limits and the significance of spatial boundaries in my consciousness of another and in my consciousness of myself. A phenomenological examination and description of my self-experience and my experience of the other makes evident° the fundamental and essential difference in the significance of time in organizing these experiences. The other is more intimately associated with time (this is not, of course, the "processed" time of mathematics and the natural sciences, for that would presuppose a corresponding generalization of man as well). The other, all of him, is totally *in* time, just as he is altogether in space; there is nothing in my experience of him that interrupts the continuous temporality of his existence. I myself am not, for myself, altogether in time—not *all* of myself: "a mighty part of me"[138] is intuitionally, evidently experienced by me outside time, for I possess an immediately given point of support in meaning. This point of support is not given to me *immediately* in the other; the other I place totally *in* time, whereas myself I experience *in the act* that encompasses time. As the *subiectum* of the act that postulates time, I am extratemporal.

The other always stands over against me as an object: the exterior image of him stands over against me in space and his inner life stands over against me in time. I myself as *subiectum* never coincide with me myself: I—the *subiectum* of the act of self-consciousness—exceed the bounds of this act's content. And this is not a matter of abstract discernment, but a matter rather of securely possessing an intuitionally experienced *loophole* out of time, out of everything given, everything finitely present-on-hand: I do not, evidently, experience the *whole* of myself in time. It should be clear, furthermore, that I do not arrange and do not organize my own life, my own thoughts and acts, *in time* (into a certain temporal whole)—a daily timetable does not, of course, organize my life; rather, I organize my life more in the form of a system and, in any event, the organization is governed by meaning (we are abstracting here from the psychology of the cognition of inner life and from the psychology of self-observation, or introspection; inner life as an object of theoretical cognition is what Kant had in view). I do not live my life in its temporal dimension, and it is not the temporal side of my life that constitutes the guiding principle even in the simplest practical act; time is instru-

---

°So long as the purity of this description is not clouded by the importation of theoretical generalizations and regularities (e.g., man-in-general, the equation of the *I* and the *other*, the exclusion of the validity of values).

mental for me, just as space is (I master the instruments of time and space).

The life of a concrete, determinate *other* is organized by me essentially in time (in those cases, of course, where I do not abstract his actions or his thoughts from his personality)—not in chronological time, nor in mathematical time, but in the emotionally and axiologically ponderable time of lived life that is capable of becoming a musical-rhythmic time. My own unity is a unity of meaning (transcendency is given in my intellectual experience), whereas the unity of the other is a spatial-temporal unity. And here as well we could say, once again, that idealism is intuitionally convincing in my experience of myself. Idealism is a phenomenology of my experience of myself, but not of my experience of the other; the naturalistic conception of consciousness and of man in the world is a phenomenology of the other. We are not concerned, of course, with the philosophical validity of these conceptions. Our only concern here is the stock of phenomenological experience that underlies them; in themselves, these conceptions are the result of a theoretical processing of that stock of experience.

I experience the inner life of another as his *soul;* within myself, I live in the *spirit.* The soul is an image of the totality of everything that has been actually experienced—of everything that is present-on-hand in the soul in the dimension of time; the spirit is the totality of everything that has the validity of meaning—a totality of all the forms of my life's directedness from within itself, of all my acts of proceeding from within myself (without detachment from the *I*). What is intuitionally convincing from the standpoint of my *self*-experiencing is the spirit's immortality as an immortality of meaning; what becomes convincing from the standpoint of my experience of another is the postulate of the immortality of the soul, that is, of the inner determinateness of the other—of his inner countenance (memory)—which is loved independently of meaning (and what becomes equally convincing from this standpoint is the postulate of the immortality of the beloved body—cf. Dante).[139]

The soul experienced from within is spirit, and the spirit is extra-aesthetic (just as the body experienced from within is extra-aesthetic). The spirit cannot be the bearer of a plot or storyline, for the spirit is not present, it does not exist—at every given moment, it is set as a task, it is yet-to-be. Repose from within itself is impossible for the spirit: there is no stopping point, no limit, no period of time; there is no support for rhythm and measuring—for absolute, emotionally positive measuring. Hence, the spirit is also incapable of being the bearer of rhythm (or of being the bearer of an account or exposition, and in general—of any aesthetic order at all). The soul is spirit-that-has-not-actualized-itself as it is reflected in the loving consciousness of another (another human being, God); it is that which I myself can do nothing with, that in which I am passive or receptive (from within itself, the soul can only be ashamed of itself; from without, it can be beautiful and naive).

Inner determinateness—the embodiment of meaning in mortal flesh—is born and dies *in* the world and *for* the world; it is given totally in the world and can be totally consummated in the world; the whole of it is gathered and consolidated into a finite object. As such, inner determinateness *can* have the significance of a plot or story, it *can* be a hero.

Just as the plot or story of my own personal life is created by other people—the heroes of my life,[p] so the aesthetic vision of the world, its image, is created only by the consummated or consummatable lives of other people who are the heroes of this world. The first and foremost condition for an aesthetic approach to this world is to understand it as the world of other people who have accomplished their lives in it—that is, to understand it as the world of Christ, of Socrates, of Napoleon, of Pushkin, etc. One must come to feel at home in the world of other people, in order to be able to go on from confession—to objective aesthetic contemplation, from questions about meaning and searchings for meaning—to the world as a beautiful given. One must come to understand that it is the *other*, as an other capable of being justifiably consummated, who constitutes the hero of all the positively valuable determinations of the world as a given, of all the intrinsically valuable "fixations" of the world's existent makeup: it is about the other that all the stories have been composed, all the books have been written, all the tears have been shed; it is to him that all the monuments have been erected; it is only with others that all the cemeteries are filled; it is only others who are known, remembered, and recreated by productive memory, so

---

[p] It is only when my life is set forth for another that I myself become its hero—in the eyes of the other and in his emotional-volitional tones.

that my own memory of objects, of the world, and of life could also become an artistic memory. It is only in the world of others that an aesthetic, plot-bearing, intrinsically valuable movement is possible—a movement *in the past* which has value regardless of the future and in which all obligations and debts are forgiven and all hopes are abandoned. To be artistically interested is to be interested, independently of meaning, in a life that is in principle consummated. I have to withdraw from myself, in order to free the hero for unconstrained plot movement in the world.

3. [Rhythm]

We have examined, from the standpoint of the character of value, the very fact of the existence/nonexistence of a human being's inner determinateness, and we have established that my own existence is devoid of aesthetic value, devoid of plot-bearing significance, just as my physical existence is devoid of plastic-pictorial significance. I am not the hero of my own life.

We must now investigate the conditions for giving an aesthetic form to inner determinateness, that is, to a particular lived experience, to an inner situation, and, finally, to the whole of inner life. In the present chapter, we are interested merely in the general conditions for such forming of inner life into a "soul," and specifically—we are interested in the conditions (meaning-governed conditions) of *rhythm* as a purely temporal ordering. The special forms of giving expression to the soul that occur in verbal art (confession, autobiography, biography, character, type, personal situation, *personnage*) we shall examine in the next section (the whole as a whole governed by meaning).

Just like the inwardly experienced outward physical movement, inner movement, inner directedness, and inner experiencing are, likewise, devoid of any valid determinateness, already-givenness, and do not live by their presently existing makeup. A lived experience as something determinate is not experienced by the one who is experiencing: a lived experience is directed upon a certain meaning, object, state of affairs; but it is directed not upon itself, not upon the determinateness and fullness of its own present-on-hand existence in the soul. I experience the object of my fear as fearful, the object of my love as lovable, the object of my suffering as oppressive (the degree of cognitive determinateness is not essential, of course, in this case), but I do not experience my own fearing, loving, suffering. My lived experience is an axiological position or attitude assumed by the *whole* of myself in relation to some object; my own "posture" in this position is not given to me.

To be able to experience my own acts of experiencing, I have to make them a special object of my own self-activity. To be able to experience my own experiencing as something determinate and present-on-hand, I have to detach myself from those objects, goals, and values to which my living experience was directed and which gave it meaning and filled it. I must stop fearing, in order to experience my own fear in its inwardly given determinateness (and not its object-related determinateness); I must stop loving, in order to experience my own love in all the constituents of its present existence within myself.

The point here is not psychological impossibility, not "narrowness of consciousness,"[140] but impossibility with respect to value and meaning: I must go beyond the bounds of the axiological context in which my lived experience had actually proceeded, in order to be able to make the very act of experiencing—the incarnate being of my inner life—an *object* for myself; I must assume a different position within a different axiological horizon, where the resulting axiological rearrangement, moreover, is of the most essential kind. I must become *another* in relation to myself—to myself as living *this*, my own, life in *this* axiological world—and this *other* must take up an essentially founded axiological position outside myself (the position of a psychologist, of an artist, etc.). We could put it this way: it is not in the axiological context of my own life that my act of experiencing, as a determinate entity of my inner life, acquires its validity. In my own life, my experiencing is not present for me. What is necessary is an essential point of support in meaning *outside* the context of my own life—a living and creative and, hence, *rightful* point of support—in order to be able to remove the act of experiencing from the unitary and unique event of my own life[q] and to apprehend its present-on-hand determinateness as a characteristic, as a trait of the *whole* of inner life, as a lineament of my inner countenance

---

[q] And, hence, to remove it from the unique event of being as well, for being *qua* event is given to me only from within myself.

(no matter whether of the whole of a character or of a type or only of an inner situation).

To be sure, there is the possibility of moral reflection upon one-self that does not exceed the bounds of the context of one's own lived life. Moral self-reflection does not abstract from the object and meaning which keep a lived experience in motion; it is precisely from the standpoint of this object to-be-attained that moral reflection images any givenness of lived experience as spurious. Moral self-reflection knows no given that is positive, no present-on-hand being that is intrinsically valuable, inasmuch as—from the standpoint of that which is yet to be attained (the task to be accomplished)—any given is always something unworthy, something that ought not to be. *That-which-is-mine* in a lived experience is illegitimate subjectivity from the standpoint of the valid object toward which that experience is directed. Hence, a lived experience as an inward given can be perceived in moral self-reflection only in penitent tones. But a penitent reaction does not produce a whole and aesthetically valid image of inner life. From the standpoint of the constraining validity of the meaning to-be-attained, as it confronts me in all its seriousness—inwardly given existence does not embody such meaning, but rather deforms (subjectivizes) it (in the face of meaning, a lived experience cannot justifiably come to rest and suffice unto itself).

Lived experience as a positive individual given is unknown to epistemological reflection as well—and, as a matter of fact, to philosophical reflection in general (cf. the "philosophy of culture").[141] Epistemological reflection has nothing to do with the individual form of experiencing an object—a constituent of the given individual inner whole of a soul; it has to do with the transcendent forms of the object (and not of the experience) and their ideal unity (a unity to-be-attained).

What-is-mine in the experiencing of an object is studied by psychology, but it is studied here in complete abstraction from the axiological weight of the *I* and the *other*—in abstraction from their uniqueness; psychology knows only a "hypothetical individuality" (cf. Ebbinghaus).[142] The inward given is not something contemplated, but something investigated, without any value judgment, within the prescribed (to-be-attained) unity of a psychological regularity conforming to psychological laws.

What-is-mine in lived experience becomes a positive given—a positive given that is contemplated—only when approached aesthetically. Not, however, *what-is-mine* in myself and for myself, but—in the *other*. For in myself it is illuminated immediately by the object and meaning to-be-attained, and, as such, it cannot freeze and solidify into something contentedly present-on-hand, it cannot constitute the axiological center of receiving contemplation *not* in the capacity of a purpose (in the system of practical purposes), but in the capacity of an inner *purposelessness*. Inner determinateness possesses this character only when it is illuminated *not* by meaning, but by love regardless of any meaning whatsoever. Aesthetic contemplation must abstract from the constraining validity of meaning and purpose. Object, meaning, and purpose cease to govern axiologically and turn into mere characteristics of a lived experience as an intrinsically valuable given.

A lived experience is a trace of meaning in what exists, a gleam of meaning reflected by what exists. From within itself, a lived experience maintains its life not through its own resources, but through that meaning beyond its own bounds which it seeks to capture, for when it fails to capture any meaning, it has no existence at all. A lived experience is a relationship *to* meaning and *to* an object, and beyond this relationship it does not exist for itself. It is born, as an embodiment in flesh (inner flesh), involuntarily and naively and, consequently, not for itself, but for the *other*, for whom it becomes a value that is contemplated independently of the validity of meaning—it becomes a valued form, whereas meaning becomes content. Meaning is subordinated to the value of individual existence, to the mortal flesh of a lived experience. A lived experience retains, of course, a reflected gleam of the meaning it sought to attain, for without this gleam of reflected meaning it would be empty; but the positive consummation of it is accomplished independently of that meaning in all its constraining nonrealizedness (its being in principle nonactualized in existence).

To consolidate aesthetically, to become positively determinate, a lived experience must be purged of all undissolvable admixtures of meaning—of all that gives it meaning *not* in the axiological context of a determinate person and a life capable of being consummated, but in the objective and always to-be-attained context of the world and of culture: all these moments must be rendered immanent to the lived experience, must be gathered into a soul that is in principle finite and definitively completed, that is, must be concentrated and enclosed within this soul, within its individual, inwardly intuitable unity. Only this kind of soul can be placed within the given, present-on-hand world and conjoined with it; only this kind of concentrated soul is capable of becoming an aesthetically valid hero in the world.

But this essential exemption from what is imposed as a task, as something still to be achieved, is impossible in relation to any experiencing, striving, action that is my own. The anticipated inner future of my experiencing and action, their purpose and meaning, undermine and break up the inner determinateness of the path followed by my striving; no experience on this path is capable of becoming for me an independent and determinate experience that could be adequately described and expressed in words or even in sounds of a certain tonality (from within myself, this tonality could be only petitionary and penitent—the tonality of prayer). Moreover, this indeterminateness and this noncontentedness have an essentially necessary[143] character: the loving lingering over an experience which my inner striving requires in order to be able to illuminate and determine that experience, and the emotional-volitional forces themselves needed for such illuminating and determining—all this would constitute a betrayal of the constraining seriousness of the meaning/purpose of my striving, a falling away *from* the act of living in relation to what is imposed as a task and *into* what is given. I must go beyond the bounds of my striving, must take up a position outside it, in order to be able to see it in the flesh, i.e., embodied in valid inner flesh.

To do this, it is not enough to go beyond the bounds of just a given experience that is temporally demarcated from other experiences;[r] that is a possibility I have when an experience recedes for me into the *temporal past*—whereupon I come to stand *outside* of it *in time.* But such temporal outsideness with respect to an experience is not enough to accomplish an aesthetically cherishing determination and forming of that experience; to accomplish that, it is necessary to go beyond the bounds of the whole given experience, beyond the bounds of the whole that gives meaning to particular experiences, that is, beyond the bounds of the given experiencing soul. The experience must recede into the absolute past, into the *past of meaning,* along with the entire con-

---

[r] Meaning-governed demarcation would either be systematic in character or would constitute an aesthetic "immanentization" of meaning that has been divested of its specific validity.

text of meaning into which it was inseparably woven and in which it received its meaning. It is only on this condition that the lived experience of striving can acquire a certain extension, a certain content that is contemplated almost palpably. It is only on this condition that the inward course of action can be secured, determined, lovingly consolidated and measured by a *rhythm*, and that is accomplished only by the self-activity of another soul, within the encompassing meaning-and-value context of this other soul.

For myself, none of my lived experiences and strivings can recede into the absolute past, into the past of meaning, which is detached and sheltered from the future, i.e., justified and consummated independently of the future. For, insofar as I find precisely *myself* in a given lived experience, insofar as I do not renounce it as *my own* within the unique unity of my own life, I connect it with the future—the future of meaning, I render it unindifferent to this future, I transpose its definitive justification and accomplishment into what-is-yet-to-be (that is, it has not yet become closed with respect to its outcome); as long as I am the one living in it, it does not yet exist in full. This brings us up directly to the problem of *rhythm.*

Rhythm is the axiological ordering of what is inwardly given or present-on-hand. Rhythm is not expressive in the strict sense of the term; that is, it does not express a lived experience, is not founded from within that experience; it is not an emotional-volitional reaction to an object and to meaning, but a reaction *to* that reaction. Rhythm is objectless in the sense that it has to do with the reaction to an object, with the experience of an object, and not directly with an object. As a result, rhythm tends to reduce the objective validity of the elements that compose a rhythmic sequence.

Rhythm presupposes an "immanentization" of meaning to lived experience itself, an "immanentization" of purpose to striving itself; meaning and purpose must become no more than a moment in an experience/striving that is intrinsically valuable. Rhythm presupposes a certain *predeterminedness* of striving, experiencing, action (a certain hopelessness with respect to meaning). The actual, fateful, risk-fraught absolute future is surmounted by rhythm—the very boundary between the past and the future (as well as the present, of course) is surmounted in favor of the past; the future as the future of meaning is dissolved, as it were, in the past and the present—is artistically predetermined by them (for the author-contemplator always encompasses the whole temporally, that is, he is always *later*, and not just temporally later, but later *in meaning*). But the very moment of transition, of movement from the past and the present into the future,[s] constitutes a moment in me that has the character purely of an event, where I, from within myself, participate in the unitary and unique event of being. It is in this moment that the issue of the event, the "either/or" of the event, is perilously and absolutely unpredetermined (unpredetermined with respect to meaning, and not with respect to *fabula* or plot; the fabula, just like rhythm, just like all aesthetic moments in general, is organic and internally predetermined—it can be and must be encompassed at a single inner glance in its entirety, from beginning to end, in all its constituents, for only the whole, even if only a potential whole, can have aesthetic validity). It is precisely in this moment that rhythm has its absolute limit, for this moment does not submit to rhythm—it is in principle extrarhythmic, nonadequate to rhythm; here rhythm becomes a distortion and a lie. It is a moment where that which *is* in me must overcome itself for the sake of that which *ought to be*; where being and obligation meet in conflict within me; where *is* and *ought* mutually exclude each other. It is a moment of fundamental and essential dissonance, inasmuch as what-is and what-ought-to-be, what-is-given and what-is-imposed-as-a-task, are incapable of being rhythmically bound *within me myself* from within myself, i.e., they are incapable of being perceived on one and the same plane, incapable of becoming a moment in the development of a single positively valuable sequence (of becoming the *arsis* and the *thesis* of rhythm,[144] its dissonance and cadence, inasmuch as both of these

---

[s] Into the absolute future, the future of meaning. That is, not into the future which will leave everything in its place, but into the future which must finally fulfill, accomplish everything, the future which we *oppose* to the present and the past as a salvation, transfiguration, and redemption. That is, the future not as a bare temporal category, but as a category of meaning—as that which axiologically does not yet exist; that which is still unpredetermined; that which is not yet *discredited* by existence, not sullied by existence-as-a-given, free from it; that which is incorruptible and unrestrictedly ideal—not epistemologically and theoretically, however, but practically, i.e., as an ought or obligation.

moments are located on an equally positive axiological plane; dissonance in rhythm is always conditional).

And yet it is precisely this moment, where the ought-to-be (obligation) in principle confronts me within myself as another world—it is precisely this moment that constitutes the highest point of my creative seriousness, of my pure productiveness. Hence, the creative act (experience, striving, action)—as an act that enriches the event of being,[t] brings something new into being—is in principle extrarhythmic (in the course of its performance, of course; once it has been performed, it falls away into what-is: within me myself—in penitent tones, and in the other—in heroic tones).

Free will and self-activity are incompatible with rhythm. A life (lived experience, striving, performed action, thought) that is lived and experienced in the categories of moral freedom and of self-activity cannot be rhythmicized. Freedom and self-activity create rhythm for an existence that is (ethically) unfree and passive. The creator is free and active, whereas that which is created is unfree and passive. To be sure, the unfreedom, the necessity of a life shaped by rhythm is not a *cruel* necessity, not a necessity that is indifferent to value (cognitive necessity); rather, it is a necessity bestowed as a gift, bestowed by love: it is a beautiful necessity. A rhythmicized existence is "purposive without purpose."[145] A purpose is neither chosen nor deliberated, and there is no responsibility for a purpose; the place occupied by an aesthetically apprehended whole in the open event of unitary and unique being is not deliberated, does not come into play, i.e., the whole is axiologically independent of the perilous future within the event of being—it is justified independently of this future. Yet it is precisely the choice of purpose, the place within the event of being, for which *moral* self-activity is answerable, and in this respect it is free.

In this sense, ethical freedom ("freedom of the will") is not only freedom from cognitive necessity (causal necessity), but also freedom from aesthetic necessity—the freedom of my performed action from the *being* in me (both the axiologically nonaffirmed, nonvalidated being and the axiologically affirmed and validated

---

[t] Only a qualitative, formal enrichment of the event is possible, and not a quantitative, "material" enrichment, if it does not change into a qualitative one.

being, i.e., the being which is contemplated in artistic vision). Wherever I am present as I myself, I am free and cannot free myself from obligation, from the ought-to-be. To be actively aware of me myself is to illuminate myself with the yet-to-be meaning confronting me; outside this meaning, I do not exist for myself. My relationship to myself is incapable of being rhythmical; to find me myself in rhythm is impossible. The life which I recognize as *mine*, the life in which I *actively* find myself, is incapable of being expressed in rhythm—is ashamed of rhythm: any rhythm must break off here, for the sphere of such life constitutes a domain of sobriety and quiet (starting from the practical lowlands and reaching up to the ethical-religious heights). Rhythm can only possess or sway me; in rhythm, as under narcosis, I am not conscious of myself. (Being ashamed of rhythm and of form is the root of *"playing a fool"*:[146] proud solitude and resistance to the other; a self-consciousness that has passed all bounds and wants to draw an unbreakable circle around itself.)

In the interior being of another person, when I experience that being actively in the category of *otherness*, "is" and "ought" (being and obligation) are not severed and are not hostile to each other, but are organically interconnected and exist on one and the same axiological plane; the *other* grows organically *in* meaning. His self-activity is heroic for me and is graciously cherished by rhythm (for the whole of him may be in the past for me, and I can justifiably free him from the ought-to-be, which confronts only myself, within me myself, as a categorical imperative). Rhythm is possible as a form of relating to the other, but it is impossible as a form of relating to myself (moreover, the impossibility in question here is the impossibility of an axiological position or attitude). Rhythm is an embrace and a kiss bestowed upon the axiologically consolidated or "bodied" time of another's mortal life. Where there is rhythm, there are two souls (or, rather, a soul and a spirit)—two self-activities; one of these lives and experiences its own life and has become passive for the other, which actively shapes and sings the first.

Sometimes I become justifiably alienated from myself axiologically—I live in the other and for the other. And in that case I may become a participant in rhythm, although, for myself, I remain ethically passive in rhythm. In my lived life, I participate in a communal mode of existence, in an established social order, in a nation, in a state, in mankind, in God's world. In all these cases, I live my life, axiologically, in the other and for others, i.e., I am clothed in the axiological flesh of the other. In all these cases, my life can submit rightfully to the sway of rhythm (although the very moment of submission or subordination is characterized by sobriety); I experience, strive, and speak here in the *chorus* of others. But *in a chorus* I do not sing for myself; I am active only in relation to the other and I am passive in the other's relationship to me; I exchange gifts, but I do so disinterestedly; I feel in myself the body and the soul of another. (Wherever the purpose of a movement or an action is incarnated into the other or is coordinated with the action of the other—as in the case of joint labor— my own action enters into rhythm as well. But I do not *create* rhythm for myself: I *join* in it for the sake of the other.) Not my own nature but the human nature in me can be beautiful, and not my own soul but the human soul can be harmonious.

We can now develop in greater detail the thesis we proposed earlier concerning the essential difference between my own time and the time of the other. In relation to myself, I experience time extra-aesthetically. The immediate givenness to me *of everything that has the validity of meaning*[147] (outside which I cannot become actively conscious of anything as *mine*) renders impossible any positive axiological consummation of my temporality. In my living self-experience, the ideal extratemporal meaning is not indifferent to time, but is set over against it as the future of meaning—as that which *ought to be* in contrast to that which already *is*. All of temporality or duration is set over against meaning as that which is *not yet fulfilled*, as something *not yet final*, as that which is *not all yet:* this is the only way in which I can actually experience within myself the temporality, the givenness of my being in the face of meaning.

The consciousness of being fully consummated in time (the consciousness that what *is* constitutes *all* there is) is a consciousness with which one can do nothing or with which it is impossible to live; in relation to my own, already finished life, any active axiological position is impossible. Of course, this consciousness—the consciousness of being finished—may be present in the soul, but it is not the one that organizes lived life. On the contrary, the act of experiencing it (the illuminatedness, the axiological weight of such experiencing) derives its activeness, its weight, from that which confronts it compellingly as a task (something-to-be-achieved), and it is only the latter that organizes a life's actualization-from-within (transforms possibility into actuality). This absolute future, the future of meaning that stands axiologically over against me, over against my whole temporality (everything that is already present in me), is not a future in the sense of being a temporal continuation of *the same life*, but in the sense of being a constant possibility, a constant need to transform my life *formally*, to put new meaning into my life (the last word of consciousness).

The future as the future of meaning is hostile to the present and the past as to that which is devoid of meaning; hostile in the way a task is hostile to not-being-fulfilled-yet, or what-ought-to-be is hostile to what-is, or atonement is hostile to sin. Not a single constituent of what is already on hand for me myself can become self-contented, already justified. My justification is always in the future, and this prospective justification, perpetually set over against me, abolishes my past and my present (my past and present for myself), insofar as they claim to be something already on hand in a lasting way, claim to be stilled in the given, to be self-sufficient, to be the true reality of being, and claim to be the essential me and the whole of me or to determine me exhaustively in being (my givenness pretending here to be the whole of me, to be me in truth—my givenness acting in the capacity of an impostor). The future realization is not, for myself, an organic continuation or growth of my own past and present—not a crowning fulfillment of them. Rather, it is an essential abolition or annulment of my own past and present, just as bestowed grace is not the result of an organic growth of man's sinful nature. A gradual coming to perfection (an aesthetic category) occurs *in the other*; in myself, only new birth is possible. Within myself, I always live in the face of the absolute demand/task that is presented to me, and this demand/task is inaccessible by way of a merely gradual, partial, relative approach.

The demand is: live in such a way that every given moment of your life would be both the consummating, final moment and, at the same time, the initial moment of a new life. As such, this demand is in principle incapable of being fulfilled by me, for it includes an aesthetic category (a relationship *to the other*) which, although attenuated, is still alive in it. For me myself, no given moment of my life is capable of becoming so self-sufficing that it could be axiologically apprehended as constituting a justified consummation of my whole life and a worthy beginning of a new life. Moreover, on what possible plane of value could such consummation and beginning be located?

The demand itself, as soon as it has been acknowledged by me, becomes an unattainable task—in principle unattainable, in the light of which I shall always be in a state of indigence. For me myself, only a history of my fall is possible, whereas a history of my gradual ascent is in principle impossible. The world of my future, as the future of meaning, is wholly different in nature from the world of my past and present. In every act, in every deed that I perform, both outer and inner (in the act of feeling, in the act of cognition), my future confronts me as pure valid meaning and impels my act, but is never realized, for me myself, in any given act, always remaining a pure demand for my own temporality, historicity, finitude.

So long as the point at issue is not the value of life for me, but my own value for myself rather than for others—I place this value in the future, the future governed by meaning. At no point in time is my reflection upon myself realistic, for in relation to myself I do not know any form of givenness: the form of a given radically distorts the picture of my interior being. I am—in my meaning and value for me myself—thrust back into the world of endlessly demanding meaning. As soon as I attempt to determine my self *for myself* (and not for and from the other), I find my self only in that world, the world of what is yet to be achieved, *outside* my own temporal being-already-on-hand; that is, I find my self as something-yet-to-be with respect to meaning and value. In the dimension of time, on the other hand (if we abstract completely from that which is imposed as a task), I find only my own dispersed directedness, my unrealized desire and striving—the *membra disiecta* of my potential wholeness; whereas that which could assemble these *membra disiecta*, vivify them, and give them a form—namely, their soul, my authentic *I-for-myself*— that is not yet present in being, but is set as a task and is yet-to-be. My determination of myself is given to me (given as a task—as something yet to be achieved) not in the categories of temporal being, but in the categories of *not-yet-being*, in the categories of purpose and meaning—in the meaning-governed future, which is hostile to any factual existence of myself in the past and the present. To *be* for me myself means—to be present to myself as someone-yet-to-be (and *to cease being present to myself as some-one-yet-to-be*, to turn out *to be all I can be already here and now*, means—*to die as an intelligent being*).[148]

There can be nothing of value in the determinateness of my lived experience for me myself (the determinateness of my feeling, desire, striving, thought), except for that to-be-achieved meaning and object which was being actualized in my experience and through which my experience sustained its life. The determinateness of my interior being with respect to content is, after all, only a reflected gleam or a trace of the object and meaning set over against me. Any anticipation of meaning from within myself, even the fullest and most complete (the determination for and in the other), is always subjective, and its determinateness and consolidatedness (so long as we do not bring in from outside any justifying and consummating categories, that is, any forms of the other) constitutes a spurious consolidatedness—something like a consolidation of the temporal and spatial distance separating my interior being from the meaning and object to-be-achieved. Now, if my interior being detached itself from the yet-to-be meaning confronting it (the meaning which had brought the whole of it into being and rendered it meaningful in all its constituents), and if it opposes itself to that meaning as an independent value (becomes self-sufficient and self-contented in the face of meaning), then, in so doing, my interior being falls into a profound contradiction with itself, into a negation of itself. That is, it negates the content of its own being through the being of its factual givenness: it becomes a falsehood—the being of falsehood and the falsehood of being. We could say that this constitutes a fall (a lapse into sin) that is immanent to being and is experienced from within being: it is inherent in the tendency of being to become sufficient unto itself; it is an inner self-contradiction of being—insofar as being pretends here to self-contented abiding, in its presently given makeup, in the face of meaning; it is a self-consolidated self-affirmation on the part of being in defiance of the meaning that engendered it (a breaking off from the source); it is a movement that has suddenly come to a stop and is discontinued without justification—a movement that has turned its back on the goal that had brought it into being (like matter which has suddenly hardened into a rock of determinate form). It is an incongruous and perplexed completedness that feels ashamed of its own form.

In the *other*, however, the determinateness of interior and exterior being is experienced as a pitiful, indigent passivity, as a defenseless movement toward being and eternal abiding that is naive in its hunger at any cost to *be*. The being which lies outside me is, as such, only naive and femininely passive even in its most outrageous pretensions, and my aesthetic self-activity gives meaning to its boundaries, illuminates them, gives them a form—from outside, and thus consummates it axiologically. (When I myself fall away altogether into being, I extinguish the clarity which the *event of being* has for myself—I become a blind and elementally passive participant in the event of being.)

Within myself, a living experience, in which I am actively active, can never come to rest in itself, can never stop, end, and become consummated; it cannot drop out of my self-activity, cannot freeze suddenly into self-sufficiently finished being, with which my self-activity has nothing to do. For if something is actually experienced by me, then what always stands out as immediately compelling in my experiencing is that which is set as a task—as something to-be-achieved. From within, my experiencing is infinite and cannot justifiably stop being experienced, that is, cannot free itself of all obligations in relation to its object and meaning. I cannot stop being active in it, for that would be equivalent to abolishing myself in my own meaning, equivalent to transforming myself into a mere mask of my own being, transforming myself through my own inaction into a lie for me myself. I may forget it, but then it does not exist for me; I can remember it axiologically only insofar as it is set as a task (by renewing the task), but not insofar as it is already present-on-hand. Memory is for me the memory of the future; for the other—it is the memory of the past.

The activity of my self-consciousness is always in effect and proceeds uninterruptedly through all lived experiences that are *mine*. It releases nothing from itself and it renews the life of those experiences which tend to fall away and become consummated—that is what constitutes my responsibility, my fidelity to myself with respect to my own future, my ultimate direction.

I remember my own lived experience in an axiologically active manner not from the aspect of its factually existing content (taken in isolation), but from the aspect of its to-be-attained meaning and object, that is, from the aspect of that which had given meaning to its appearance within me. And in so doing, I renew the still-to-be-achieved character of every one of my experiences, I collect all of my experiences, collect all of myself *not* in the past, but in the future that confronts me eternally as a future yet-to-be. My own unity, for myself, is one that confronts me eternally as a unity-yet-to-be. It is a unity that is both given and not given to me, a unity that is incessantly conquered by me at the sharpest point of my self-activity. It is not the unity of my having and possessing, but the unity of not-having and not-possessing; not the unity of my already-being, but the unity of my not-yet-being. Everything positive in this unity belongs solely to that which is set as a task, whereas that which is already given comprises everything negative. It is a unity which is given to me only when any value confronts me as a task—as a value to *be* achieved.

It is only when I do not bar myself off from to-be-attained meaning that I possess myself intensely in the absolute future, maintain myself as the-one-who-is-yet-to-be-achieved, govern myself actually from the infinite prospect of my absolute future. I can linger over my factually given being, but I can do so only in penitent tones, inasmuch as such lingering takes place in the light of what is yet-to-be-achieved. But as soon as I release myself as the-one-who-is-yet-to-be-achieved from the axiological field of my vision and stop being intensely with myself in the future, my own givenness loses its yet-to-be unity for me and disintegrates into factually existent, senseless fragments of being. The only thing left for me to do is to find a refuge in the *other* and to assemble—out of the *other*—the scattered pieces of my own givenness, in order to produce from them a parasitically consummated unity in the *other's* soul using the *other's* resources. Thus, the spirit breaks up the soul from within myself.

This, then, is the character of time in a *self*-experience which has attained complete purity of *self*-relationship—has attained the axiological standpoint of the spirit. But even in a more naive consciousness, where the *I-for-myself* has not yet fully differentiated itself (on the plane of culture—the consciousness of antiquity), I still determine myself in terms of the future.

What is the basis of my inner confidence? What straightens my back, lifts my head, and directs my gaze forward? Is it really pure givenness—uncomplemented and unextended by what is desired and what is still to be accomplished? Once again, it is my being present to myself as someone yet-to-be—that is what supports my pride and self-satisfaction; once again, the axiological center of my self-determination is displaced into the future. It is not only that I want to appear to be more than I am in reality, but that I am really unable to see my own pure givenness—I really never believe completely that I am only that which I actually am here and now; I render myself complete out of what is yet-to-be, what ought to be, what is desired. That is, the real center of gravity of my own self-determination is located solely in the future. However fortuitous and naive may be the form assumed by what is desired and what ought to be, the important thing is that it is *not* here, *not* in the past and present. And whatever I may be able to achieve in the future—even if it be everything I had anticipated— the center of gravity of my self-determination will continue to shift forward, into the future, and I shall rely for support on myself as someone yet-to-be. Even my pride and self-satisfaction about the present are rendered complete at the expense of the future (let it but begin to express itself—and it will immediately show its tendency to proceed forward, ahead of itself).

What constitutes the organizing principle of my life from within myself (in my relationship to me myself) is solely my consciousness of the fact that in respect to all that is most essential I do not exist yet. The form of my life-from-within is conditioned by my rightful folly or insanity[149] of *not coinciding*—of not coinciding *in principle*—with me myself as a given. I do not accept my factually given being; I believe insanely and inexpressibly in my own noncoincidence with this inner givenness of myself. I cannot count and add up all of myself, saying: this is *all* of me— there is *nothing more* anywhere else or in anything else; I already exist *in full*.

The point here is not the fact of death (I *shall* die), but ultimate meaning. In the deepest part of myself, I live by eternal faith and hope in the constant possibility of the inner miracle of a new birth. I cannot, axiologically, fit my whole life into time—I cannot justify it and consummate it in full within the dimension of time. A temporally consummated life is a life without hope from the standpoint of the meaning that keeps it in motion. From within itself, such a life is hopeless; it is only from outside that a cherishing justification may be bestowed upon it—regardless of unattained meaning. So long as a life is not cut off in the dimension of time (for itself, a life is cut off, and not consummated), it lives from within itself by hope and faith in its own noncoinci-

dence with itself, in its own unrealizedness with respect to meaning (that is, its being present to itself as a life yet-to-be with respect to meaning). And, in this respect, life is insane from the
standpoint of its factual existence, inasmuch as both that faith
and that hope are totally unfounded from the standpoint of their
present-on-hand existence (in being, there are no guarantees of
the ought-to-be, "no sureties from heaven").[150] Hence, both have a
supplicatory or prayerlike character (from within lived life itself
there can be only supplicatory and penitent tones).

And within myself, as well, this insanity of faith and hope remains the last word of my life: from within myself in relation to
my own givenness—only prayer and penitence are possible, that
is, my givenness ends in a state of indigence (the last thing it can
do is—supplicate and repent; God's last word descending upon us
is—salvation or condemnation). My own last word is devoid of
any consummating, any positively founding energies; it is aesthetically unproductive. In my last word, I turn to the outside of
myself and surrender myself to the mercy of *the other* (the ultimate sense of deathbed confession). I know that in the other as
well there is the same insanity of not coinciding (in principle)
with himself, the same unconsummatedness of life. Yet for me
that is not his last word—it is not for me that it sounds: I am situated outside him, and the last, consummating word belongs to
me. This last word is conditioned and required by my being situated concretely and completely outside the other—by my spatial,
temporal, and meaning-related outsideness in relation to the other's life as a whole, in relation to the other's axiological posture
and responsibility. This position of outsideness makes possible
(not only physically, but also morally) what is impossible for me
in myself, namely: the axiological affirmation and acceptance of
the whole present-on-hand givenness of another's interior being.
The other's very noncoincidence with himself, his tending to be
beyond himself as a given, his deepest point of contact with the
spirit—constitutes for me no more than a characteristic of his interior being, a moment in his given and present-on-hand soul, that
is, it consolidates for me into something like a subtle body totally
encompassed by my admiring and cherishing contemplation.

In this outside position, *I* and the *other* find ourselves in a relationship of absolute mutual contradiction that has the character
of an event: at the point where the *other*, from within himself,
negates himself, negates his own being-as-a-given, at that point *I*,

from my own unique place in the event of being, affirm and validate axiologically the givenness of his being that he himself negates, and his very act of negation is, for me, no more than a moment in that givenness of his being. What the other rightfully
negates in himself, I rightfully affirm and preserve in him, and, in
so doing, I give birth to his soul on a new axiological plane of
being. The axiological center of his own vision of his life and the
axiological center of my vision of his life do not coincide. In the
event of being, this mutual axiological contradiction cannot be
annihilated.

No one can assume a position toward the *I* and the *other* that is
neutral. The abstract cognitive standpoint lacks any axiological
approach, since the axiological attitude requires that one should
occupy a unique place in the unitary event of being—that one
should be embodied. Any valuation is an act of assuming an individual position in being; even God had to incarnate himself in
order to bestow mercy, to suffer, and to *forgive*—had to descend,
as it were, from the abstract standpoint of justice. Being is, as it
were, once and for all, irrevocably, between myself as the unique
one and everyone else as others for me; once a position has been
assumed in being, any act and any valuation can proceed only
from that position—they presuppose that position. I am the only
one in all of being who is an *I-for-myself* and for whom all others
are *others-for-me*—this is the situation beyond which there is
and there can be nothing axiological for me: no approach to the
event of being is possible for me outside that situation; it is from
here that any event began and forever begins for me. The abstract
standpoint does not know and does not see the movement of
being as an ongoing event, does not know and does not see being
as a still open process of axiological accomplishment. One cannot
be neutral within the unitary and unique event of being. It is only
from my own unique place that the meaning of the ongoing event
can become clearer, and the more intensely I become rooted in
that place, the clearer that meaning becomes.

For me, the other coincides with himself, and, through this integrating coincidence that consummates him positively, I enrich
the other from outside, and he becomes aesthetically significant [151]
—becomes a hero. Hence, from the aspect of his form, considered
as a whole, the hero is always naive and immediate, however divided and deep he might be inside himself. Naiveté and immediacy are constituent moments of the aesthetic form as such.

Where they fail to be achieved, there the hero is not yet fully objectified aesthetically: the author has not yet succeeded in taking up a firm position outside the hero—the hero is still inwardly authoritative for the author from the standpoint of his validity with respect to meaning. The aesthetically valid form does not seek revelations of meaning in the hero; its last word is a consummation accomplished in being *qua* the past—the past in principle. To perceive the deepest contradiction *in being*—that is, to embrace the contradiction at a single glance as a constituent in being, instead of becoming a part of the contradiction—means to render this contradiction immediate and naive.

Where the *other* and his meaning-directed tension are inwardly authoritative for us, where we co-participate in the other's directedness to meaning, aesthetic mastering and consummating of the other becomes difficult: the authoritative meaning decomposes the other's outer and inner corporeality, destroys the valid, naive-immediate form of the other. (It is difficult to transpose the other into the category of being, for I am *in* him.)

Of essential significance for accomplishing the aesthetic consummation of a human being is the anticipation of his death. Indeed, this anticipation of death constitutes a necessary moment in the aesthetically valid form of the other's interior being, in the form of his soul. We anticipate the other's death as the inevitable nonrealization or failure of his entire life in respect to meaning, and we seek to create forms of justification for his life, forms of justification that he is in principle incapable of finding from his own place. At every given moment of an aesthetic approach to the other (from the very outset), the other must coincide positively with himself, at every given moment we must see *all* of him, even if only potentially. The artistic approach to another's interior being predetermines the other: a soul is always predetermined (in contrast to spirit). To be able to see one's interior portrait is the same as to see one's exterior portrait: it is a looking-in from outside into a world in which I am in principle absent and in which there is nothing I can do as long as I remain myself. That is to say, my aesthetically valid inner countenance is a kind of horoscope, with which, once again, there is nothing I can do. If someone really knew his horoscope, he would find himself in an inwardly contradictory and incongruous situation: the seriousness and the risk of living would be impossible; the proper position for performing an action would be impossible.

The aesthetic approach to another's interior being requires first of all that we should not put our faith and hope in that other, but that we should accept and receive him axiologically apart from this faith and hope, i.e., that we should be outside of him, and not *with* him and *in* him (for there can be no axiological movement in him from within himself outside the sphere of his faith and hope). Memory begins to act as a gathering and completing force from the very first moment of the hero's appearance; the hero is born in this memory (of his death), and the process of giving form to him is a process of commemoration (commemoration of the departed). The aesthetic embodiment of the inner man anticipates from the very outset the hero's hopelessness with respect to meaning. Artistic vision presents us with the *whole* hero, measured in full and added up in every detail; there must be no secrets for us in the hero with respect to meaning; our faith and hope must be silent. From the very outset, we must experience all of him, deal with the whole of him: in respect to meaning, he must be dead for us, formally dead.

In this sense, we could say that death is the form of the aesthetic consummation of an individual. Death as a want of success and justification with respect to meaning settles the accounts as regards meaning, sets a task, and provides the methods for an *aesthetic* justification, i.e., a justification independent of meaning. The deeper and the more perfect the embodiment, the more distinctly do we hear in it the definitive completion of death and at the same time the aesthetic victory over death—the contention of memory against death (memory in the sense of a certain value-related act of exerting, fixating, and accepting independently of meaning). Throughout the entire course of an embodied hero's life, one can hear the tones of a requiem. Hence that distinctive hopelessness of rhythm as well as its sorrowfully joyful lightness, that is, its relievedness of the pressure exerted by the irresolvable seriousness of meaning. Rhythm takes possession of a life that *has been lived:* the requiem tones at the end were already heard in the cradlesong at the beginning. In art, however, this lived-out life is saved, justified, and consummated in eternal memory; [152] hence the kind, cherishing hopelessness of rhythm.

If, however, the meaning that impels the hero's life fascinates and absorbs us *as* meaning, i.e., if we are fascinated with its being imposed as a task to be accomplished, and not with its individual givenness in the interior being of the hero, then the achievement of form and rhythm is rendered difficult. For in that case the hero's life strives to break through form and rhythm; it strives to acquire the significance of authoritative meaning, and from the standpoint of this authoritative meanin any *individual* realization of meaning, any factual existence of *embodied* meaning, must appear as a distortion of meaning. An artistically convincing consummation becomes impossible: the hero's soul is transposed from the category of the *other* into the category of the *I*, and as a result it disintegrates and loses itself in the spirit.

4. [The Soul's Surrounding World]

Such is the aesthetically valid whole of a human being's inner life—his soul. The soul is actively produced and positively shaped and consummated only in the category of the *other*—in the category which enables us to affirm present-on-hand being positively independent of meaning or the ought-to-be. The soul is the self-coincident, self-equivalent, and self-contained whole of inner life that postulates another's loving activity from outside its own bounds. The soul is a gift that my spirit bestows upon the *other*.

In art the object-world in which the hero's soul lives and moves has the aesthetic validity of a surrounding world or environment of that soul. In art the world is not the *horizon* of an act-performing spirit, but the *environment* of a departed or departing soul. The relationship of the world to the soul (the aesthetically valid relation and union of the world with the soul) is analogous to the relationship of the world's visual image to the body: the world does not stand over against the soul, but environs and encompasses the soul, joining with its bounds. The world as a given conjoins with the soul as a given.

What is already present-on-hand in all of being or the *countenance* of being *that has already determined itself* in respect to its content (i.e., the *"thisness"* of being) needs a justification outside the realm of meaning. For in relation to the yet-to-be-attained fullness of meaning of the *event* of being, the "thisness" of being is only *factual* (obstinately present-on-hand). Even where meaning and obligation (the ought-to-be) are anticipated as determinate with respect to their content (in the form of images or concepts), such *determinateness* of anticipation passes immediately and of itself into the domain of being, the domain of what is present-on-hand. Any embodiment of the yet-to-be meaning of the *event* of being is only factual in its *determinateness* (i.e., in the finished expressedness of its countenance) and, as such, is unjustified precisely in respect to that which is *already* present-on-hand in it. Everything that *already exists* exists without justification: it has dared, as it were, to become already determinate and to abide (obstinately) in this determinateness within a world, the whole of which is *yet-to-be* in respect of its meaning and justification—*like a word that seeks to become totally determined within a sentence we have not yet finished saying and thinking through to the end.* The entire world, insofar as it is already actual, already present-on-hand,[u] fails to stand up to a meaning-directed criticism immanent to the very same world.

"An uttered thought is a lie"[153]—the *actual* world (in abstraction from the yet-to-be and yet-to-be-achieved meaning—the meaning that has not yet been uttered) is an already uttered, already pronounced meaning of the event of being; the world in its presently existing makeup is a world that *has* achieved expression—it is an already uttered word, a word that *has* already sounded. A word that has been uttered is ashamed in the unitary light of the meaning which had to be uttered (if, with respect to value, there is nothing but this to-be-uttered meaning). So long as the word remained unsaid, it was possible to believe and to hope, for one could still look forward to the compelling fullness of meaning. But when the word *is* pronounced, it is completely *here* in all its ontically obstinate concreteness—*all* of it is here, and there is nothing else. The word that *has* been pronounced sounds hopeless in its already-pronouncedness; the uttered word is an embodiment of meaning in mortal flesh. All being that is already present-on-hand in the past and the present is only a mortal incarnation of the yet-to-be meaning of the event of being, the meaning of the absolute future; such being is without hope (outside the sphere of future accomplishment).

The other human being, however, is wholly *in* this world; he is the hero of this world, and his life is accomplished totally *in* this world. He is flesh and bone from the flesh and the bone of the

---

[u] That is, insofar as it pretends to coincide with itself, with its own given-ness, contentedly and independently of what is yet-to-be or, in other words, insofar as being suffices unto itself.

present-on-hand world: outside this world, he does not exist. It is *around* the other—as the other's world—that present-on-hand being finds its affirmation and positive consummation independently of meaning. The soul is fused and intertwined with the world's givenness and it consecrates that givenness. To me, the world presents itself in the aspect of a world still-to-be-achieved, a not-yet-fulfilled world. It constitutes the *horizon* of my act-performing (forward-looking) consciousness: the light of the future decomposes the stability and intrinsic value of the corporeity of the past and the present. With respect to its total givenness, the world gains positive validity for me only as the surrounding world or *environment* of another.

In art and in aestheticized philosophy, all axiologically consummating determinations and characterizations of the world are oriented with reference to the *other*—the hero of that world. Insofar as they are positively affirmed in their value regardless of meaning and are gathered and rendered complete in eternal memory, *this* world, *this* nature, *this* particular history, *this* particular culture, and *this* historically determinate world view constitute the world, the nature, the history, and the culture of man-as-the-*other*. All characterizations and determination of present-on-hand being that set it into dramatic motion[v] blaze with the borrowed axiological light of *otherness*. Birth and death and all the stages of life between them: this is the scale of any valuational statement about present-on-hand being. The world's mortal flesh has validity with respect to value only when it has been vivified by the mortal soul of the *other*; in the realm of spirit, the world's mortal body disintegrates (the spirit does not vivify it, but judges it).

From what has been said of the soul, and of all forms of the aesthetic embodiment of inner life (rhythm), as well as of forms of the given world aesthetically correlated with the soul, it follows that all these forms are in principle incapable of being forms of pure *self*-expression (the expression of *myself* and what is *mine*). Rather, they are forms of my relationship to the *other* and to the *other's* self-expression. All determinations that possess aesthetic

---

[v] From the naive anthropomorphism of myth (cosmogony, theogony) and all the way to the devices of modern art and the categories of aestheticizing intuitive philosophy: beginning and end, birth and annihilation, being and becoming, life, etc.

validity are transgredient to lived life itself and to the world's givenness as experienced from within lived life, and it is only this transgrediency that produces their power and validity;[w] without transgrediency, they would be spurious and empty.

The necessary condition for giving an aesthetic form to present-on-hand being is the author's self-activity as an activity *above* present-on-hand being. *I* must be active, in order that being may be trustfully passive; *I* must see more than being (I gain this essential axiological excess of seeing only if I assume a position outside the being that I am forming aesthetically), in order that being may be naive for me. I must place my creatively active act outside any pretensions to beauty, in order that being may present itself to me as beautiful. A pure creative activity, proceeding from within myself, begins at the point where anything present-on-hand in me axiologically ends, where in me all being as such ends. To the extent that I actively find and become aware of something as given and present-on-hand or determinate, I am already above it in my act of determining (and to this extent the determination of what has value is above it with respect to value). Therein consists my architectonic privilege: in proceeding from within myself, I find a world outside myself—myself as the one proceeding in the act.

Hence, only I, while situated outside given being, can receive and consummate that being independently of meaning. This is an absolutely productive or "gainful" act of my self-activity. But in order to be really productive, in order to enrich being, this act must be totally above given being. I must withdraw all of myself axiologically from being, so that nothing of *myself* and of what is *mine* that has value for me myself would remain in the being which is subjected to the act of aesthetic reception and consummation. I must clear the entire field of given, immediately present being *for the other*—that is, I must direct all of my self-activity forward and ahead of myself (so that it would not deviate back upon itself in striving to place itself as well within the field of vision, encompass itself as well with the same gaze). And only then

---

[w] Just as the power and validity of forgiving and absolving from sins is produced by the fact that it is the *other* who performs the act of forgiving and absolving: I myself cannot forgive and absolve myself from my own sins—such forgiving and absolving would be devoid of any validity with respect to value.

will being present itself as indigent, as weak and fragile, as a forlorn and defenseless child, as passive and naive (naive in the sense of *sancta simplicitas*). *Already-to-be* is to be in a state of need: to be in need of affirmation from outside, in need of affection and safeguarding from outside; to be *present-on-hand* (from outside) means to be feminine for the pure and affirming self-activity of the *I*. But in order that being should open up before me in its feminine passivity, I must take a stand totally outside it and must become totally active.

Being as present-on-hand being, as fully expressed, fully uttered being, is given to my pure self-activity in an atmosphere of need and emptiness which is in principle incapable of being made replete from that being itself with its own resources: all of its self-activity that I come upon is passive for my own self-activity (issuing from within myself); all of its meaning-governed boundaries are given to me manifestly and palpably; its entire present-on-hand being implores, desires, and demands that I should be situated intently *outside* it. And this self-activity from the position of being-outside must actualize itself in the fullest affirmation of given being independently of meaning, i.e., for the sake of being as such, and it is in this act that the feminine passivity and the naiveté of present-on-hand being are transformed into that which is beautiful. If, however, I myself, along with my self-activity, fall away into being, then the expressed beauty of given being is immediately destroyed.

What is possible, of course, is that I come to partake passively in the justified givenness of being, in the *joyful* givenness of being. Joy knows no active relationship to being; I must become naive in order to rejoice. From within myself, in my own self-activity, I cannot become naive, and, hence, I cannot rejoice. Only being, and not my self-activity, can be naive and joyful; my self-activity is inescapably and irresolvably serious. Joy is the most passive, the most defenselessly pitiful condition of being. Even the wisest smile is pitiful and feminine (or is the imposture of a smile, if it is self-satisfied). Joy is possible for me only in God or in the world, that is, only where I partake in being in a justified manner *through* the other and *for* the other, where I am passive and receive a bestowed gift. It is my otherness that rejoices in me, not I for myself. Celebration, too, is possible only for the naive and passive force of being; jubilant celebration is always elemental; I can celebrate and jubilate in the world and in God, but not within myself. I can only reflect the joy of the affirmed being of others. The spirit's smile is a *reflected* smile, a smile not from within oneself (cf. the reflected joy and smile in hagiography and in icon painting).

Insofar as I participate in the world of otherness in a justified manner, I may become passively active in that world. A luminous image of such passive activity is the dance. In dancing, my exterior, visible only to others and existing only for others, coalesces with my inner, self-feeling, organic activity. In dancing, everything inward in me strives to come to the outside, strives to coincide with my exterior. In dancing, I become "bodied" in being to the highest degree; I come to participate in the being of others. What dances in me is my *present-on-hand* being (that has been affirmed from outside)—my *sophianic* being[154] dances in me, the *other* dances in me. The moment of being-swayed, of being-possessed by being is manifestly experienced in dancing. Whence the cultic significance of dancing in the "religions of being." Dancing represents the ultimate limit of my passive self-activity, but the latter occurs everywhere in life. I am passively active whenever my action is not conditioned by the purely meaning-directed activity of my *I-for-myself*, but rather is justified from present-on-hand being itself, from nature; that is, whenever this present-on-hand being is elementally active in me rather than the spirit (i.e., that which does not exist yet and is not predetermined or— that which is insane from the standpoint of present-on-hand being). Passive self-activity is conditioned by the already given, available resources: it is predetermined by given being; it does not enrich being with what is in principle unattainable; it does not alter the meaning-governed countenance of being. Passive self-activity does not transform anything formally.

What has been said marks even more firmly the boundary between the author and the hero, that is, between the bearer of the meaning-governed content of lived life and the bearer of the aesthetic consummation of the former.

Our earlier proposition concerning the aesthetic union of body and soul thus finds its final validation here. There can be a conflict between the spirit and the inner body, but there can be no conflict between the soul and the body, for these are constructed in identical value-categories and express a unitary and creatively active relationship to man as a given.

The Whole of the Hero as a Whole of Meaning

The architectonic of the world in artistic vision organizes not only spatial and temporal features,[155] but also features that relate purely to meaning; there is not only spatial and temporal form, but meaning-governed form as well. Thus far, we have examined the conditions under which the space and time of a human being and his life assume aesthetic validity. But what also assumes aesthetic validity is the hero's meaning-governed attitude in being— that interior place which he occupies in the unitary and unique event of being,[156] his axiological position in the event. It is this position that is isolated[157] out of the event of being and consummated aesthetically; the selection of particular meaning-features of that event conditions the selection of the transgredient features corresponding to the meaning-features selected, and this expresses itself in the diversity of forms which the meaning-governed whole of the hero assumes. The present section will be devoted to an examination of these forms. What should be noted is that the spatial, temporal, and meaning-governed wholes do not exist discretely: just as the body, in art, is always animated by a soul (even if it is a soul that has died, as in the representation of someone deceased), so the soul is never apprehended independently of the position it assumes with respect to value and meaning, independently of its being specified as "character," "type," "inner situation," etc.

1. Performed Action and Confessional Self-Accounting

From within himself, a living human being positions himself in the world actively; his consciously lived life is a process of performing actions at every moment of it. I act through deed, word, thought, and feeling; I live, I come-to-be through my acts. However, I neither express myself nor determine myself through my acts; I actualize through them something that has validity with respect to objects and meaning, but I do not actualize *myself* as something that is determinate or that is being determined: only objects and meaning stand over against an act I perform. What is absent in a performed act is the feature of self-reflection on the part of the act-performing person. The act performed proceeds in an objectively valid context: in the world of narrowly practical

ends (ends that relate to living one's daily life), in the world of social and political values, the world of cognitive validities (the act
of cognition), in the world of aesthetic values (the act of artistic
creation or apprehension), and, finally, in the ethical domain
proper (in the world of narrowly ethical values—in an *immediate*
relation to good and evil). And all these object-worlds determine
the value of the act totally for the act-performer himself.

For the acting consciousness itself, its act needs no hero (that
is, a determinate person); it needs only goals and values that regu-
late it and determine its sense. My act-performing consciousness
as such poses questions only of the following type: what for? to
what end? how? is it correct or not? is it necessary or not? is it
required or not? is it good or not? It never asks such questions as
the following: who am I? what am I? what kind am I?

My own determinateness (I am such as I am) is not, for me myself, part of the motivation of my act; the determinateness of the
act-performer's personality is not present in the context which
determines the sense of an act for the acting consciousness itself.
(In Classicism, a performed act is always motivated by the determinateness of the hero's character; the hero acts not only because
he is obliged to act and needs to act, but also because he is such as
he is. That is, the act is determined by his position or situation as
well as by his character; it expresses the situation of his character, although not for the acting hero himself, of course, but rather
for the author-contemplator situated outside the hero. This occurs
in any work of art that aims to produce character or type.)

There should be no doubt about the absence of a determinate
personality (I am such as I am) within the motivational context of
an act in those cases where acts of cultural creation are involved.
Thus, when I act through cognition, the act of my thought is determined and motivated solely by what has the validity of an object
toward which that thought is directed. I can, of course, explain
the success of a given act as being due to my giftedness and its failure as being due to my lack of ability; indeed, I can operate with
such determinations of myself generally. But they cannot become
part of the motivational context of an act as its determinants:
they are unknown to the cognitionally acting consciousness.

The act of artistic creation, likewise, has to do solely with what
has the validity of an object to which artistic activity is directed.
Even if an artist strives to put his own individuality into his creation, this individuality is not *given* to him as determinative of his

act, but is set as a *task* to be fulfilled in the object. That is, his individuality is a value which is still to be actualized in the object, a value that is not the bearer of the act, but its object: it is only in the object that it becomes part of the motivational context of the act of creation. It should be evident that social, political, and narrowly instrumental acts are in the same situation.

The matter is somewhat more complicated in the activity of living one's own life, where, it would seem, a performed act is often motivated by the determinateness of its performer or bearer. However, in this case, too *everything that is mine* is part of the object which constitutes a task to be accomplished by my act: everything that is mine stands over against my act as a particular end to which it is directed. Hence, in this case as well, the motivational context of the act itself lacks a hero.

In the final analysis, therefore, an act expressed or uttered in all its purity, i.e., without introducing any transgredient features and values alien to the act itself, will prove to be without a hero as an essentially determinate entity. If we were to restore exactly the world in which a performed act became axiologically conscious of itself and determined itself or in which it oriented itself in a responsible manner, and if we were to describe that world, we would not find a hero in it (the hero's value with respect to a *fabula*, his characterological value, his typological value, etc., would not be present in that world).

A performed act needs the determinateness of the end to which it is directed and the determinateness of the means for achieving that end, but it has no need for the determinateness of its performer—it does not need a hero. The performed act itself tells us nothing about the performer; it tells us only about the objective state of affairs in which it is performed: it is axiologically generated only by this state of affairs, and not by a hero. The account of an act is utterly objective. Whence the idea of the ethical freedom of the performed act: it is determined by what does not exist yet, by what is objectively, teleologically set as a task; its source lies ahead, not behind, not in what exists, but in what does not exist yet. That is why any reflection upon an already accomplished act does not illuminate the author (in regard to who he is, what sort of person he is), but represents a merely immanent critique of the act from the standpoint of its own ends and its own "ought." And even if this critique may at times go beyond the bounds of the acting consciousness, it does so by no means in order to introduce features that are in principle transgredient to the acting consciousness, but rather in order to bring in those features which were factually absent and were not taken into account, but which *could* have been taken into account (so long as one does not introduce a value alien to the act, namely, how my act looks to the other).

In an acting consciousness, even where it gives an account of itself, where it gives utterance to itself, there is no hero in the sense of an effective, determining factor; the acting consciousness is object-directed, but is not psychological or aesthetic (it is regulated neither by causes nor by aesthetic laws, such as the laws of a *fabula*, the characterological laws, etc.). When my act is regulated by the ought-to-be as such, when it evaluates its own objects immediately in the categories of good and evil (excluding, for purely technical reasons, the cultural series of evaluations), that is, when my act is a specifically ethical act, then my reflection upon it and my account of it start determining me as well and involve my own determinateness.

Remorse is translated from the psychological plane (chagrin) to the creative-formal plane (repentance, self-condemnation),[158] thus becoming a principle that organizes and gives form to inner life— a principle of seeing and fixating oneself axiologically. Wherever there is an attempt to fixate oneself in repentant tones in the light of the ethical ought-to-be, the first essential form of verbal objectification of life and personality (a verbal objectification of *personal* life, that is, without abstraction from the *bearer* of that life) arises: confession as an accounting rendered to oneself for one's own life.

The essential, *constitutive* moment of this form is the fact that it is a *self*-objectivation, that the *other* with his special, *privileged* approach is excluded; the only principle that organizes the utterance here is the pure relationship of the *I* to itself. Confession as a self-accounting comprises only that which I myself can say about myself (in principle, of course, and not in fact); it is immanent to the morally acting consciousness—it does not exceed the essentially necessary bounds of that consciousness; all moments transgredient to *self*-consciousness are excluded. In relation to these transgredient moments, that is, to the possible axiological consciousness of the other, confessional self-accounting[159] assumes a negative attitude and contends against them for purity of self-consciousness—for the purity of one's solitary relationship to oneself. For the other's aesthetic approach and justification is capable of penetrating into my axiological relationship to myself and clouding its purity (cf. my repute among other people, the opinion of other people, fear of shame before other people, the favor of other people, etc.).

A pure, axiologically solitary relationship to myself—this is what constitutes the ultimate limit toward which confessional self-accounting strives by overcoming all the transgredient moments of justification and valuation that are possible in the consciousness of other people. And on the way toward this ultimate limit, the *other* may be needed as a judge who must judge me the way I judge myself, without aestheticizing me; he may be needed in order to destroy his possible influence upon my self-evaluation, that is, in order to enable me, by way of self-abasement before him, to liberate myself from that possible influence exerted by his valuating position outside me and the possibilities associated with this position (to be unafraid of the opinion of others, to overcome my fear of shame). In this respect, any quiescence in my self-condemnation, any positive evaluation of myself (I am becoming better) is perceived as a falling away from the purity of my self-relationship, as a possession by the possible valuating *other* (cf. Tolstoy's qualifications and amendments in his diaries).[160]

This contention against the possible valuational position of the other poses, in a distinctive way, the problem of outward form in confession as a self-accounting. Conflict with form and with the very language of expression is inevitable here, for, on the one hand, both of them are indispensable, yet, on the other, both are in principle inadequate, inasmuch as they contain aesthetic moments which are grounded in the valuational consciousness of the other ("playing a fool,"[161] as a form of negating in principle the validity of the form of expression, has its roots in this conflict). Confessional self-accounting is in principle incapable of being consummated, for it does not admit any consummating transgredient constituents. Even if such constituents enter the plane of consciousness in a self-accounting, they are devoid of their positive axiological validity, that is, devoid of their powers to consummate and appease; everything that has already gained determinateness and has come to be is badly determined and has come to be unworthily; any value-related, aesthetically valid stop is precluded. No act of reflection upon myself is capable of consummating me fully, for, inasmuch as it is immanent to my sole answerable consciousness, it becomes a value-and-meaning factor in the subsequent development of that consciousness. My own word about myself is in principle incapable of being the last word, the word that consummates me. For me myself, my own word is an act that I perform, and my performed act is alive only in the unitary and unique event of being. Hence, no act performed by me is capable of consummating my own life, for it connects my life with the open infinitude of the event of being. Confessional self-accounting does not isolate itself from this unitary event of being; hence, it is potentially infinite.

Confessional self-accounting is precisely the act of noncoinciding with oneself in principle and in actuality (there is no power situated outside myself that could realize such self-coinciding—the axiological position of the *other* is absent), the act of pure axiological passing-beyond-oneself that knows no justified ending from within itself (a justified ending is alien to it). This act consecutively overcomes all those axiological forces which could compel me to coincide with myself, and that overcoming itself is incapable of being realized, of being justifiably ended and brought to rest. However, this restlessness and unconsummatedness of confessional self-accounting in itself is only one of its aspects, only one of the ultimate limits toward which it tends in its concrete development. The negation of any justification in *this* world is transformed into a need for *religious* justification: confessional self-accounting is filled with the need for forgiveness and redemption as an absolutely *pure gift* (an unmerited gift), with the need for a mercy and grace that are totally otherworldly in respect to their value. Such justification is not immanent to self-accounting, but lies beyond its bounds, in the unpredetermined, risk-fraught future of the actual event of being, just as the actual fulfillment of a petition and a supplication that depends on another's will lies beyond the bounds of the petition itself, the supplication itself, i.e., is transcendent to them. The petition and the supplication themselves remain open, unconsummated: they break off, as it were, into the unpredetermined future of the event. This constitutes the specifically confessional moment within a confessional self-accounting. Pure self-accounting—that is, addressing oneself axiologically only to oneself in absolute solitariness—is impossible; pure self-accounting is an ultimate limit which is balanced by another ultimate limit—by confession, that is, the petition-ary advertedness outward from oneself, toward God. Petitionary

tones, the tones of prayer, intertwine with repentant or penitential tones.

Pure, solitary self-accounting is impossible; the nearer a self-
accounting comes to this ultimate limit, the clearer becomes the
other ultimate limit, the action of the other ultimate limit; the
deeper the solitude (value-related solitude) with oneself, and, consequently, the deeper the repentance and the passing-beyond-
oneself, the clearer and more essential is one's referredness to God.
In an absolute axiological void, no utterance is possible, nor is consciousness itself possible. Outside God, outside the bounds of trust
in absolute otherness, self-consciousness and self-utterance are
impossible, and they are impossible not because they would be
senseless practically, but because trust in God is an immanent constitutive moment of pure self-consciousness and self-expression.
(Where I overcome in myself the axiological self-contentment of
present-on-hand being, I overcome precisely that which concealed
God, and where I absolutely do not coincide with myself, a place
for God is opened up.) A certain degree of warmth is needed in the
value-related atmosphere that surrounds me, in order that my
self-consciousness and my self-utterance could actualize themselves in it, in order that life could commence. The mere fact that
I attach any significance at all to my own determinateness (even if
it is an infinitely negative significance), the mere fact that I bring
it up at all for discussion, that is, the very fact of becoming conscious of myself in being, testifies in itself that I am not alone in
my self-accounting, that someone is interested in me, that someone wants me to be good.

But this moment of otherness is axiologically transcendent to
self-consciousness and is *in principle not guaranteed*, for a *guarantee* would reduce it to the level of present-on-hand being (at
best, aestheticized being, as in metaphysics). One can live and
gain consciousness of oneself neither *under a guarantee* nor *in a
void* (an axiological guarantee and an axiological void), but only
in faith. Life (and consciousness), from within itself, is nothing
else but the actualization of faith; the process of life's gaining self-
consciousness is a process of gaining consciousness of faith (that
is, of need and hope, of non-self-contentment and of possibility).
The life which has no knowledge of the air it breathes is a naive
life. Thus, entirely new tones, the tones of faith and hope, irrupt
into the penitent and petitionary tones of confessional self-ac-

counting, and these new tones make possible the order or concord that is intrinsic to prayer. Pure and profound examples of confessional self-accounting with all the constitutive moments and tones we have examined may be found, in an ideally condensed form, in the prayers of the Publican and the Canaanite woman ("I believe—help my unbelief").* [162] But these prayers do not end, they can be eternally repeated; from within themselves, they are incapable of being consummated—they constitute movement as such (repetition of prayers).

The more the moment of *trust* and the tones of faith and hope gain immediate actuality, the more certain aesthetic moments begin to penetrate into self-accounting. When the organizing role passes from repentance to trust, an aesthetic form, a *concord*, becomes possible. Anticipating through faith my justification in God, I change little by little from an *I-for-myself* into the *other* for God—I become naive in God. It is at this stage of *religious naïveté* that the psalms (as well as many Christian hymns and prayers) have their place; rhythm becomes possible, a rhythm that cherishes and elevates the image, etc.; in anticipation of beauty in God, tranquillity, concord, and measure become possible. An especially profound example of a confessional self-accounting, in which the organizing role passes from repentance to trust and hope (naive confession), may be found in the penitential psalm of David (the purely *petitionary* tones generate here an aestheticized imagery: "create in me a clean heart, O God," "thou shalt wash me, and I shall be made whiter than snow").* [163] An example of constructing a system on the basis of certain constituents of confessional self-accounting is St. Augustine: incapacity for good, unfreedom in good, grace, predestination. Bernard de Clairvaux, on the other hand, provides an example (in his commentary to the Song of Songs) [164] of an aesthetic conception: beauty in God, the bridehood of the soul in Christ. However, prayer, too, is not a produced *work*, but a performed *act*. (The organizing force of the *I* is replaced by the organizing force of God; my earthly determinateness, my earthly name, is surmounted, and I gain a clear understanding of the name written in heaven in the Book of Life [165]—the *memory* of the future.)

This correlation of value-and-meaning features in confessional self-accounting that we have examined may sometimes undergo an essential modification, and the basic type becomes more complex. An element of theomachy and anthropomachy[166] is possible in confessional self-accounting, that is, the refusal to accept a possible judgment by God or by man, and as a result tones of resentment, distrust, cynicism, irony, defiance appear. ("Playing a fool"[167] is almost invariably characterized by an element of anthropomachy. Cf. the cynically capricious twists and contortions, the provocatively defiant, perversely teasing frankness of "playing a fool.")

We find such confession and frankness in relation to a human being one despises in Dostoevsky's works (almost all instances of confession and outspokenness on the part of his heroes are, on the whole, of this kind). In Romanticism, the positioning of otherness (of the possible other, of the auditor or the reader) is anthropomachic in character (Ippolit's attitude in Dostoevsky's *Idiot* is completely distinctive in its character, and so is the attitude of "the man from the underground"). Anthropomachic and theomachic elements (the result of despair) preclude aesthetic concord, preclude the concord intrinsic to prayer (sometimes parody provides the means of succor).

What is also possible is the infinite self-revocation of repentance. This constituent in confessional self-accounting is analogous to the hatred one may feel toward possession by the mirrored image of oneself; one's soul could look exactly the way one's face looks. We shall examine all these variations in the basic form of confessional self-accounting when we consider the problem of author and hero in Dostoevsky's works.

A distinctive perversion of the form of confessional self-accounting is represented by invective in its deepest and, therefore, its worst manifestations. This is confessional self-accounting turned inside out. The tendency of this worst kind of invective or abuse is to tell the other what he alone can and *must* say about himself—to "cut him to the quick." The worst kind of invective is the just invective, which expresses in tones of malice and mockery what the other himself could say about himself in penitential-petitionary tones, that is, where one utilizes one's privileged place outside the other for purposes that are diametrically opposed to what ought to be the case ("stay in your solitude—for you, there *is* no other"). Thus, a particular passage of the penitential psalm may turn into the worst kind of invective.[168]

To sum up, let us draw the conclusions that follow from everything we have said. In confessional self-accounting, there is no hero and there is no author, for there is no position for actualizing their interrelationship, no position of being axiologically situated outside it. Author and hero are fused into one: it is the spirit prevailing over the soul in process of its own becoming, and finding itself unable to achieve its own completion or consummation, except for a certain degree of consolidation that it gains, through anticipation, in God (the spirit that has become naive). In confessional self-accounting, there is not a single constituent that is self-sufficient and disengaged from the unitary and unique event of being—the event that is in process of issueless becoming; there is no constituent that is free from the absolute meaning-governed future.

It should be clear that a *fabula*,[169] as an aesthetically valid constituent, is impossible in confessional self-accounting (*fabula* in the sense of a self-sufficient and delimited, self-contained body of the event—an isolated body with its own positive, justified beginning and end). Nor can there be any object-world as an aesthetically valid surrounding world or environment—that is, confessional self-accounting excludes the constituent of artistic description (landscape, setting, communal existence, etc.). The biographical whole that a life constitutes with all its events is not a self-sufficient whole and does not represent a value in confessional self-accounting (this value of life can be only an artistic value); confessional self-accounting simply does not know the task of constructing a biographically valuable whole out of a life that has been (potentially) lived. The form of one's self-relationship makes all these axiological constituents impossible.

How does the reader perceive a confessional self-accounting? Through whose eyes does he read it? Our perception of a self-accounting will inevitably tend toward aestheticizing it. When approached in this way, a confession will present itself to us as raw material for possible aesthetic treatment—as a possible content of a possible work of art (in its most immediate form, a biographical artifact). In reading a confession with our own eyes, we introduce thereby our axiological position of being situated outside the *subiectum* of confessional self-accounting; along with all the possibilities associated with that position, we introduce, that is, a whole series of transgredient moments: we impart a consummating significance to its ending as well as to other constituents (for we are temporally outside); we provide it with a background (we perceive it in the context of a determinate historical period and a determinate historical setting, if these are known to us, or we simply perceive it against the background of what is more familiar to us); we situate certain moments of its accomplishment within an encompassing space; and so forth. All these features of "excess" introduced by our perception provide a basis for constituting the aesthetically finished form of a work. The contemplator begins to gravitate toward authorship, and the *subiectum* of self-accounting becomes a hero (of course, the beholder does not co-create here with the author, as he does in the perception of a work of art, but performs a primary act of creation—a primitive one).

Such an approach to confessional self-accounting diverges radically from its own purpose,[170] which is from the outset consciously nonartistic. It is possible, of course, to make any human document the object of artistic perception, and this is particularly easy to do in the case of documents from a life that is already over (indeed, the consummation of it in our aesthetic memory is often our obligation). But artistic perception is not always the fundamental perception, the perception determined by the document's own purpose, and even more: the completeness and depth of aesthetization presuppose that one has already understood the document's immanent and extra-aesthetic purpose in its integrity and self-regulatedness[171] (something that "fictionalizing" does not do).

Who, then, should the reader of a confessional self-accounting be? And *how* should he perceive it in order to actualize the extra-aesthetic purpose that is immanent to it? What is essential here is that there is no author before us with whom we could *co*-create, nor is there a hero whom we could, together with the author, consummate in purely aesthetic terms. The *subiectum* of a confessional self-accounting stands over against me in the event of being as the performer of his own act, and I must neither reproduce this act (imitatively) nor contemplate it artistically, but must react to it by performing an answering act of my own (just as in the case of a request addressed to me, I must neither reproduce it—imitate, co-experience it—nor apprehend it artistically, but react to it with an answering act: either fulfill it or refuse to do so; this act is not immanent to the request, whereas aesthetic contemplation—

co-creation—*is* immanent to a work of art, although not to the empirically given work of art).[172]

I stand over against the *subiectum* of a confessional self-accounting in the unitary and unique event of being that encompasses *both* of us, and my answering act must not isolate him in that event; the yet-to-be future of the event conjoins both of us and determines our mutual relationship (both of us stand over against one another in God's world). The position of being situated outside him remains, of course, and it becomes even more intense (otherwise it would not be creatively productive), except that in this case it is not utilized aesthetically, but is put to moral-religious use. Besides aesthetic memory and the memory of history, there is, after all, also eternal memory, proclaimed by the church:[173] the memory that does not consummate the individual person (on the phenomenal plane), the petitionary commemoration of the dead ("the departed servant of God so-and-so") and the commemoration in prayers for the repose of the soul of the departed. The *first* performed act which is determined by the intrinsic purpose of the confessional self-accounting is *praying* on behalf of the departed for the forgiveness and remission of his sins (this is an *essential* prayer, that is, one which presupposes a corresponding or answering inner state of forgiveness in my own soul). Any immanent secular-cultural act will be inadequate and vapid in this context. However, the analysis of this constituent exceeds the bounds of our inquiry, which is strictly secular.

There is also a *second* constituent that is part of the intrinsic purpose of confessional self-accounting: *edification* (purely practical ethical-religious cognition). In actualizing the edificatory purpose of confessional self-accounting, I project myself into the *subiectum* and reproduce within myself the *subiectum*'s inner event, but I do so not for purposes of consummating and liberating him, but for purposes of my own spiritual growth, my own enrichment through accumulated spiritual experience. Confessional self-accounting informs and teaches about God, for, as we see, by way of solitary self-accounting one gains cognizance of God and becomes aware of the faith that is already living within life itself (life-as-lived-faith). (Cf. the purely edificatory significance in the parable of the Publican,[174] and partly in the psalms.) Such is, basically, the intrinsic purpose of confessional self-accounting for the reader. This does not exclude, of course, the possibility of approaching it in aesthetic terms or in terms of theoretical cognition, except that both of these approaches fail to actualize the purpose of confessional self-accounting with respect to its essence.

2. [*Autobiography*]

We must now consider *autobiography*, and examine the hero and the author of autobiography.

Toward the end of the Middle Ages, which knew no biographical values, and in the early Renaissance we can observe the appearance of distinctive and internally contradictory forms that are in transition from confessional self-accounting to autobiography. Peter Abelard's *Historia Calamitatum Mearum*[175] already represents this kind of mixed form, where the first biographical values appear on the basis of confession (marked by a somewhat anthropomachic[176] overtone), and the soul begins to gain body, although not in God. The biographical position in relation to one's own life, i.e., the position governed by biographical value, prevails over the confessional position in Petrarch, even if it does so against some resistance. Confession or biography, posterity or God, St. Augustine or Plutarch, hero or monk: this dilemma (with an inclination toward the second alternative) continues to be present throughout Petrarch's life as well as his works, and it finds its clearest expression (a somewhat primitive one) in his *Secretum*.*[177] (The same dilemma is present in the second half of Boccaccio's life.) The confessional tone often irrupts into the biographical self-containedness of a life and its expression during the time of the early Renaissance. But the ultimate victory belongs to biographical value. (We can observe the same kind of collision and contention, the same compromises or the victory of one of the principles, in modern diaries. Diaries may be at times confessional, at times biographical: all of Tolstoy's last diaries are confessional, insofar as one can judge from those available to us;[178] Pushkin's diary[179] is completely autobiographical; on the whole, all classic diaries are autobiographical—they are unclouded by a single penitent tone.)

There is no clear-cut, essentially necessary dividing line between autobiography and biography, and this is a matter of fundamental importance. There *is* a difference, of course, and it may even be considerable, but it is not located on the plane of the fundamental attitude that consciousness assumes with respect to values. Neither in biography nor in autobiography does the *I-for-myself* (my relationship to myself) represent the organizing, constitutive moment of form.

By biography or autobiography (the account of a person's life), we understand the most immediate transgredient form in which I can objectify myself and my own life artistically. We shall consider the form of biography solely in those respects in which it may serve the purpose of self-objectification, that is, may constitute an autobiography. Or, in other words, we shall consider it from the standpoint of a possible coincidence within it of the hero and the author or, to be exact—from the standpoint of the special character of the author in his relationship to the hero. For the coincidence of author and hero is, after all, a *contradictio in adiecto:* the author is a constitutive moment of the artistic whole, and as such he cannot coincide, within this whole, with the hero, who represents another constitutive moment of that whole. The personal coincidence "in life" of the person *spoken of* and the person *speaking* does not nullify the distinctness of these constituents within the artistic whole. After all, it is still possible to ask "how do I image myself?" as opposed to the question "who am I?"

In the present context, we are not interested in autobiography as a form of communicating information about oneself that may be ordered into the outwardly coherent whole of a story, but that does not actualize artistic-biographical values and instead pursues objective or practical ends of some kind. And since a purely scholarly biography of some culturally significant figure does not set any artistic-biographical aims for itself, we are also not interested in the present context in the purely scholarly-historical purpose of such biography. As regards the so-called autobiographical elements in any given work, it should be noted that such elements may be extremely diverse: they may be confessional in character; they may have the character of a purely objective, matter-of-fact account of some performed act (a cognitive act of thinking, a political act, a practical act, etc.); or, finally, they may have the character of lyric. Such elements can be of interest to us only where they are specifically biographical in character, that is, where they actualize biographical value.

Of all artistic values, biographical value is the one least transgredient to self-consciousness. Hence, in a biography the author is closest to the hero—they can change places, as it were. This is also the reason why it is possible for author and hero to coincide in person outside the bounds of an artistic whole. Biographical value is capable of organizing not only the story of another person's life, but also the experiencing of life itself and the story of one's own life; it can be the form in which one gains consciousness of one's own life, the form in which one sees and gives utterance to one's own life.

Biographical form is the most "realistic" of forms, for it contains the least amount of constituents that isolate [180] and consummate. The author's self-activity is least transformative in this form; he utilizes his axiological position outside the hero in the least principled manner, confining himself almost exclusively to being outside the hero only externally—only spatially and temporally. There are no clear-cut boundaries of character, no clear-cut isolation, and no finished and intense *fabula*.

Biographical values are values that are shared in common by life and by art, that is, they are capable of determining practical acts in the capacity of ends these acts strive to attain; we have to do here with the form and the values of an *aesthetic of lived life*. The author of biography is that possible other by whom we are most likely to be possessed in lived life; the possible other who is with us when we look at ourselves in the mirror, when we dream of glory, when we make plans for our life; the possible other who has permeated our consciousness and who often guides our acts, our value judgments, and our vision of ourselves side by side with our own *I-for-myself*; the other in our consciousness with whom our external life can still be sufficiently active (whereas an intense inner life, when we are possessed by another, is impossible, of course, and it is here that a conflict arises and a struggle begins with the other for the liberation of my *I-for-myself* in all its purity: confession as an account rendered to myself for my own life). This other, however—the other in our consciousness—may also turn into a usurping double, if we give him free rein and suffer defeat, but a usurping double with whom, in return, we can live a life that is immediate (naively immediate), intense, and happy (to be sure, it is this same other who delivers us into the power of fate: other-possessed life can always turn into fated life).

In our ordinary recollections about our past, it is often this other who is active, and it is in his value-tones that we remember ourselves (in remembering our childhood, this bodied other within ourselves is our mother). The mode of tranquil recollection of our distant past is distinctly aestheticized in its character and, formally, it comes close to being a story (recollections in the light of the meaning-governed future are penitent recollections). Any memory of the past will be somewhat aestheticized; memory of the future is always ethical.

The other who possesses me does not come into conflict with my *I-for-myself*, so long as I do not sever myself axiologically from the world of others, so long as I perceive myself within a collective (a family, a nation, civilized mankind). In this case, the axiological position of the other within me is *authoritative* for me; he can narrate the story of my life and I shall be in full inner agreement with him. So long as my life proceeds in indissoluble unity with the collective of others, it is interpreted,[181] constructed, and organized (with respect to all the constituents it shares with the world of others) on the plane of another's possible consciousness of my life; my life is perceived and constructed as a possible story that might be told about it by the other to still others (to descendants). My consciousness of a possible narrator, the axiological context of a possible narrator, organizes my acts, thoughts, and feelings where, with respect to their value, they are involved in the world of others. Each one of these constituents of my life may be perceived within the whole of a narrative—a narrative that is the story of my life; each one may be found on everyone's lips. My contemplation of my own life is no more than the anticipation of others' recollections about my life—of recollections by descendants or simply by family members and close relatives (the amplitude of any life's biographicalness may be variable); the values that organize life itself as well as the recollection of life are one and the same.

What renders the other an *authoritative* and inwardly intelligible author of my life is the fact that this other is not *fabricated* by me for self-serving purposes, but represents an axiological force which I confirm in reality and which actually determines my life (like the axiological force of my mother that determines me in childhood). This other is not I myself as produced through the agency of the other, but the valued other himself in me, another human being in me. The one who governs me internally is the lovingly authoritative other within me, and not I myself, by way of reducing the other to a means (it is not the world of others that is within me, but I am myself within that world as a participant in it); there is no parasitism here.

The hero and the narrator can easily change places in this case: whether it is I who tell of another, of someone close to me (someone with whom I live one and the same axiological life in a family, in a nation, in mankind, in the world), or whether it is the other who tells of me, in either case I am still woven into the narrative in the same tones and in the same form as he is. Without detaching myself from the life in which *others* are the heroes and the world is *their* surrounding world, I—as narrator of this life—become assimilated, as it were, to its heroes. When I narrate my own life, in which the heroes are those who are others for me, I am step by step woven into its formal structure (I participate in my own life, but I am not the hero in it); I put myself in the hero's place, I captivate myself through my own narration. Wherever I am in solidarity with others, the forms in which others are axiologically perceived are transposed upon myself. It is thus that the narrator becomes the hero.

If the world of others is axiologically authoritative for me, then it assimilates me-as-the-other to itself (it does so, of course, in those respects in which it is authoritative for me). I come to know a considerable portion of my own biography from what is said by others, by people close to me, as well as in the emotional tonality of these others: my birth and my descent, the events of family life and national life in my early childhood (that is, everything that could not have been understood or simply could not even have been perceived by a child). All these moments are indispensable for reconstructing an even minimally intelligible and coherent picture of my life and its world; I—as narrator of my own life—come to know all of them from the lips of others who are its heroes.

Without these stories told by others, my life would not only lack fullness and clarity in its content, but would also remain internally dispersed, divested of any value-related *biographical unity*. The *fragments* of my life as I experienced them from within myself ("fragments" from the standpoint of the biographical whole) are, after all, capable of gaining only the inner unity of my *I-for-myself* (the future unity of a task), or the unity of confessional self-accounting, and *not* the unity of biography. For only the yet-to-be-achieved unity of the *I-for-myself* is immanent to the life that is lived and experienced from within. The inner principle of unity is not suited to biographical narration: my *I-for-myself* is incapable of *narrating* anything. But the axiological position of the other, which is so indispensable for biography, is the position closest to me: I immediately become involved in it through the others who are the heroes of my life and *through the narrators of my life*. Thus, the hero of a life may become the narrator of it.

Consequently, it is only an intimate, organic axiological participation in the world of others that renders the biographical self-objectification of a life authoritative and productive; only such participation strengthens and renders nonfortuitous the position of the other in me—the possible author of my life (that is, makes firm the position in which I am situated outside myself, the position that finds its support in the loved world of others—the others from whom I do not detach myself and the world to which I do not oppose myself; the position that finds its support in the strength and power of the axiological existence of otherness in me, of human *nature* in me, although not raw and indifferent nature, but the nature which I myself have axiologically confirmed and shaped; still, even such nature is not without a certain degree of elemental spontaneity).

From the standpoint of biographical value, there are two basic types of biographical consciousness of a life and of giving a form to that life, depending on the amplitude of the biographical world (on the scope of the value-context that bestows meaning), and depending on the character of authoritative otherness. Let us call the first type the *adventurous-heroic* (the Renaissance, "Storm and Stress,"[182] Nietzscheanism), and the second—the *social-quotidian* (Sentimentalism and, in part, Realism). Let us first of all examine the distinctive features of the first type of biographical value.

Adventurous-heroic biographical value is grounded in the will or drive to be a hero—to have significance in the world of others; in the will to be loved; and, finally, in the will to live life's "fabular" possibilities,[183] the manifoldness of inner and outer life, to the full. These three values, organizing the life and actions of the biographical hero for that hero himself, are to a considerable degree aesthetic, and may constitute the values which organize the artistic representation of that hero's life by an author. All three values are individualistic, but this individualism is an unmediated, naive individualism that is still not cut off from the world of others, still participating in the being of otherness—needing this otherness and sustaining its strength through the authoritativeness of this otherness (in this instance, there is no contraposition of one's own solitary *I-for-myself* to the other—a contraposition which is characteristic of the anthropomachic type of confessional self-accounting). This naive individualism is tied up with a naive, unmediated parasitism. Let us examine the first of these three values: the striving to live a heroic life, to achieve significance in the world of others, to win fame and glory.

Striving for glory organizes the life of the naive hero, and it is glory that also organizes the *story* of that life—its glorification. To strive for glory is to gain consciousness of oneself within the civilized mankind of history (or within a nation); it means to found and build one's own life in the possible consciousness of this civilized mankind; to grow in and for others, and not in and for oneself; to assume a place in the proximate world of one's contemporaries and descendants. Of course, the future in this case as well has an organizing significance for the individual person, who sees himself, with respect to value, in the future and is guided out of this future. This future, however, is not the absolute, meaning-governed future; rather, it is the temporal, historical future (the tomorrow) that does not negate the present, but organically continues it. It is not the future of the *I-for-myself*, but the future of others—of descendants (when the individual person is directed by the meaning-governed future, all aesthetic moments in his life fall away, lose their significance for the individual himself, and, consequently, biographical value also ceases to exist for him). In rendering others heroic, in establishing a pantheon of heroes, I seek to become a participant in such a pantheon, to place myself in it, and to be guided from within it by the longed-for future image of myself that was created in the likeness of others. The heroic constituent in biographical value is characterized by this organic sense of oneself within the heroicized mankind of history; by the organic sense of being a participant in it, of experiencing one's essential growth within it, of taking root in it and gaining full consciousness and understanding of one's own works and days within it. (Parasitism may be more or less powerful in this case, depending on the weight which the purely objective meaning-values have for the individual person. The striving for glory and the sense of participation in historical-heroic existence can be no more than a warmth-infusing accompaniment; what will

actually govern one's works and days is that which has the validity of meaning. That is to say, the *temporal* future will cloud
the *meaning*-governed future like a slight shadow, while at the
same time biography will start disintegrating as its place is taken
by an objective, matter-of-fact report or by a confessional self-
accounting.)

The second constituent in the first type of biographical value is
love. The thirst to be loved; the consciousness of oneself, the
seeing of oneself, and the forming of oneself in the possible loving
consciousness of another; the striving to turn the longed-for love
of another into a force that impels and organizes my life in many
of its constituents: all this, too, constitutes growth in the atmosphere of another's loving consciousness. The heroic value determines the basic constituents and events of personal-social,
personal-cultural, and personal-historical life (*gesta*), the basic
volitional directedness of a life; love, on the other hand, determines its emotional excitedness and tension, giving meaning and
body to all of its inner and outer particulars from the standpoint
of value.

My body, my exterior, my dress; various inner-outer particulars
of my soul; certain details and particulars of my life that cannot
have axiological significance and cannot be axiologically reflected
in the historical-heroic context—in mankind or in a nation (everything that is inessential historically, yet is present in the context
of my life): all this assumes axiological weight and gains meaning
and form in the loving consciousness of another. All narrowly
personal moments are organized and regulated by what I would
wish myself to be in the other's loving consciousness—by the anticipated image of myself, which must be axiologically created
in that consciousness (discounting, of course, everything that is
axiologically determined and predetermined in my exterior, my
comportment, my way of life, etc., by the communal mode of
existence, by social etiquette, that is, once again, by the bodied
value-consciousness of others; love introduces individual and
more emotionally intense forms into these extrahistorical aspects
of life).

In love a human being strives—while in a state of intense emotional possession by another's loving consciousness—to outgrow
himself, as it were, in a certain axiological direction (cf. the role of
the beloved that formally organizes one's inner and outer life, and
the lyrical expression of this life, in the *dolce stil nuovo:* in the

Bolognese school of Guido Guinicelli, in Dante, in Petrarch).[184] For the hero himself, his own life seeks to become beautiful and even feels its own beauty within itself, given that state of intense possession by the longed-for loving consciousness of the other. But love may spill over into the historical-heroic sphere of the hero's life as well: the name of Laura intertwines with the laurel (*Laura/lauro*),* [185] and the anticipation of his own image in posterity intertwines with his image in the soul of the beloved; the form-giving axiological power of the descendants intertwines with the axiological power of the beloved—they reinforce each other mutually in his life and merge into a single motif in his biography (and especially in lyrical poetry); this is what happens in Petrarch's poetic autobiography.

Let us now turn our attention to the third constituent in biographical value: the hero's affirmative acceptance of life's "fabular" possibilities. This is the thirst to live life's "fabular" possibilities to the full—not a definite and distinctly completed *fabula*, but the manifold *fabulas* inherent in life; the thirst to live and experience the ontic particularity of life's situations, their variability, their diversity, although this is a diversity that neither determines nor consummates the hero; life's manifold *fabulas* that complete nothing and leave everything open. This "fabular" joy of life is not equivalent, of course, to purely biological vitality: a simple desire, a need, a biological attraction can engender only the *factuality* of an act, but not the axiological consciousness of that act (and even less so the forming of it).

Only when the process of life becomes a matter of axiological awareness and is filled with content, only then do we have to do with life's "fabular" possibilities as an axiologically founded series of deeds accomplished in the process of living, as a series in which life presents itself as a given with respect to its content. On this axiological plane of consciousness, even the struggle for life (the biological self-preservation and adaptation of an organism) becomes, in the determinate conditions of an axiologically founded world (*this* world with *this* sun, etc.), an adventure-value (as such it is almost completely free of anything that has objective and meaning-related validity—it is a *playing* with life as a "fabular" value, freed of any answerability within the unitary and unique event of being). The adventurer's individualism is unmediated and naive; adventure-value presupposes an established world of others, in which the adventure-hero is rooted and by the valued being of which he is possessed. The moment you deprive him of this soil and this atmosphere of otherness (of *this* earth, *this* sun, *these* human beings), adventure-value dies (for it has no air to breathe). Being adventurous and *critical* is impossible: what has the validity of meaning undermines adventurousness and breaks it up, or, alternatively, it becomes a desperate adventurousness (a matter of capricious contortions and excruciating strain).

Adventure-value is also impossible, of course, in God's world, on God's earth, and under God's sky, where a saint's life is accomplished. The valued "fabular" manifoldness of life has the character of an unconscious oxymoron: joy and suffering, truth and falsehood, good and evil—all are indissolubly merged in the unity of the continuous stream of life's manifold *fabulas*, for my acts are determined here not by the context of meaning that urgently confronts my *I-for-myself*, but by the *other* who has possessed me— by the valued being of otherness in me (of course, this is not the elemental force of nature, a force that is completely indifferent to value, but rather the axiologically founded and formed *nature in man*; in this sense, the good has axiological weight precisely as the good, and evil—as evil, joy—as joy, suffering—as suffering, except that they are counterbalanced by the heaviest axiological weight of life itself as something given with respect to its content, by the weight of human existence itself as an otherness in me; hence, their validity with respect to meaning does not become an inescapably compelling force—the sole force that decides and determines life, because it is not based on gaining full consciousness of the uniqueness of one's own place in the unitary and unique event of being in the face of the future as the future of meaning).

This valued manifoldness of life with respect to *fabulas* organizes not only the hero's life and his performed act-adventures, but also the narrative of his life, the endless and thoughtless *fabula* of the pure form of adventure: the naive author/reader's interest in *fabulas* and adventures is not transgredient to the naive hero's interest in living his life.

These are the three fundamental constituents in the "adventurous-heroic" biographical value. Of course, any one of them may predominate in a given, concrete form, but all three are present in biography of the first type. This form comes closest to dreaming about one's own life. Except that the dreamer (of the type we meet in the hero of Dostoevsky's *White Nights*) is a biographical hero who has lost his immediacy, his naiveté, and has started to reflect.

The biographical hero of the first type is distinguished by his own specific standards of value, his own biographical virtues: bravery, honor, magnanimity, generosity, etc. This is a naive morality, a morality consolidated to the point of becoming a given: its virtues are the virtues of overcoming neutral and elemental natural being (biological self-preservation, etc.) for the sake of being, once again, except that this being is affirmed as value (the being of otherness), it is cultural being, historical being (the frozen trace of meaning in being that has value in the world of others; the organic growth of meaning in being).

Biographical life of the first type is like a dance in slow tempo (lyric is like a dance in rapid tempo); everything inward and everything outward strives here to coincide in the other's axiological consciousness—the inward strives to become the outward and the outward the inward. An example of a philosophical conception that arose on the basis of the essential moments of the first type of biography is the aestheticized philosophy of Nietzsche; in part, F. H. Jacobi's philosophy (except that Jacobi's conception includes a religious moment—faith); [186] contemporary biologically oriented "philosophy of life" [187] is also sustained by the added biographical values of the first type.

We turn now to the analysis of the second type of biography: the "social-quotidian" type. In this second type of biography, history is not present as a life-organizing force. The humanity of others, in which the hero participates and in which he lives, is not given historically (historical humanity), but is given socially (social humanity); this is a humanity of the living (those who are living *now*), and not the humanity of deceased heroes and of descendants who have yet to live (the humanity in which those who are living now, with all their relationships, constitute merely a transitory moment).

In the historical conception of humanity, the axiological center is occupied by *historical* cultural values which organize the form of the hero and of heroic life (not happiness and prosperity, not purity and honesty, but greatness, strength, historical significance, exploits, glory, etc.). In the social conception, the axiological center is occupied by *social* values, and first and foremost—by familial values (not historical renown in posterity, but a "good name" among one's contemporaries, the "good and upright human being"); these values organize the private form of life, quotidian life (familial or personal), with all its everyday details (not

events, but workaday existence), that is, a life whose most important events do not exceed in their significance the axiological
context of familial or personal life, fulfilling themselves exhaustively within that context from the standpoint of my own happiness or unhappiness or from that of the happiness or unhappiness of those who are close to me (the number of these, within
the bounds of social humanity, may be as great as one likes). Nor
does this type of biography include the constituent of adventure;
what predominates in it is the descriptive constituent—love for
ordinary things and ordinary persons. It is these that produce the
positively valuable uniformity of life with respect to its content
(in biography of the first type we have to do with great contemporaries, with historically significant figures and great events).

Love of life in biography of this type is a love for the prolonged
abiding of loved persons, things, situations, and relations (the
point is not—to *be* in the world and to have significance in it,
but—to be *with* the world, to observe it and to experience it again
and again). In the axiological context of social biography, love undergoes, of course, an appropriate modification in kind, by asso-
ciating *not* with the "laurel,"[188] but with other values, appropriate to that context. Nevertheless, the function of ordering and
forming the details and meaning-exempt particulars of life on the
plane of another's axiological consciousness continues to be performed by love (for, on the plane of self-consciousness, these details and particulars are incapable of being ordered and rendered
meaningful).

In the second type of biography, the manner of narrating is usually more individualized, but the activity of the main hero—the
narrator—is confined to loving and observing: for the most part,
he does not act at all (does not have a character appropriate to a
fabula); he lives and experiences "every day," and his self-activity
is absorbed in observing and narrating.

In biography of the second type, one can often distinguish two
planes. (1) The narrator-hero himself, represented from within, in
the way we experience ourselves in the hero of our own fantasies
and recollections. He is weakly assimilated to the surrounding
others; in distinction to them, he is displaced to the interior plane,
although the difference in planes is usually not perceived in a
clear-cut way. He is located on the boundary of narrative, as it
were: sometimes he enters the narrative as a biographical hero;
sometimes he tends toward coinciding with the author—the

bearer of form; and sometimes he draws closer to the *subiectum* of confessional self-accounting. (This is what we find in Tolstoy's trilogy *Childhood, Boyhood,* and *Youth:* in *Childhood* the difference in planes is almost unnoticeable, whereas in *Boyhood,* and especially in *Youth,* it becomes much more pronounced—the hero is self-reflective and psychically "unwieldy"; author and hero draw closer to each other.)

(2) The other dramatis personae. The representation of them includes many transgredient features; they may function not only as *characters,* but even as *types* (the features transgredient to them are given in the consciousness of the main hero—the narrator, who is the biographical hero proper, thus moving him closer to the author's position). Their life may often have a finished *fabula,* as long as the latter is not too intimately intertwined with the life of the biographical hero—the narrator.

The presence of two planes in the construction of biography is an indication of the incipient disintegration of the biographical world: the author becomes critical, his situatedness outside any other becomes essential; his axiological involvement in the world of others diminishes, and the authoritativeness of the other's axiological position decreases. The biographical hero becomes someone who only sees and loves, and not someone who *lives;* the others who stand over against him, and who had begun to detach themselves axiologically from him, are now invested in an essentially transgredient form. (There are some supplementary features in the constitution of biographical value that should be mentioned: kin, family, nation; the justification of national determinateness, of meaning-exempt national typicality; the social estates; the historical period and its meaning-exempt typicality or distinctive "color." The idea of fatherhood, motherhood, and sonship in the biographical world. The "social-quotidian" type of biography and Realism: to fulfill oneself and one's life exhaustively within the context of contemporary life; the effort to isolate the value-context of contemporary life out of the past and the future. "Life" is something one draws from the value-context of newspapers, periodicals, official records, popularized science, contemporary conversations, etc. Biographical value of the "social-quotidian" type and the crisis in the domain of authoritative, transgredient forms and their unity—in the domain of authorship and style.)

Such, then, is biographical form in its basic variants. We shall now formulate as clearly as possible the relationship of author and hero in biography.

In creating the hero and his world, the author is guided by the same values as those that the hero follows in living his life. The author is in principle not richer than the hero; he does not have any additional, transgredient moments for his creative work that the hero could not have in living his life; the author, in his creative work, simply continues that which was inherent in the hero's life itself. There is no contraposition here, no contraposition in principle, of the aesthetic point of view and the point of view of lived life; there is no differentiation: biography is syncretic. The author sees and wants in the hero and for the hero only that which the hero saw and wanted in himself and for himself in his own life. The hero, interested in adventure, goes through his adventurous encounters, and the author, in his representation of them, is guided by the same interest in adventures; the hero acts with deliberate heroism, and the author heroicizes him from the same point of view. The values that guide the author in his representation of the hero and the inner possibilities of the author are the same as those which guide the life of the hero, for his life is immediately and naively aesthetic (the guiding values are aesthetic or, to be exact, syncretic), just as the author's creative work is immediately and naively syncretic (the author's values are not purely aesthetic values, they are not contraposed to the values of lived life, that is, to cognitive-ethical values); the author is not a pure artist, just as the hero is not a pure ethical *subiectum*. What the hero believes in, the author as artist believes in as well; what the hero regards as good, the author also regards as good, without opposing to the hero his own purely aesthetic goodness. For the author, the hero does not suffer any fundamental and essential failure with respect to meaning and, consequently, he does not have to be saved by way of an entirely different axiological course of action, an axiological course of action that is transgredient to his own life. The death of the hero *is* taken into account, but it does not render the hero's life meaningless, since it does not constitute an essentially necessary support for a meaning-independent justification of his life; his life, in spite of his death, does not require any new value; all one need do is to remember and record it the way it was lived. Thus, in biography, the author not only agrees with the hero in regard to faith, convictions, and love, but is guided in his (syncretic) artistic work as well by the same values as those which guide the hero in his lived life. Biography is an organic product of organic historical periods.

In biography, the author is naive; he is connected with the hero by kinship: they can change places (whence the possibility that they may personally coincide in life). Of course, the author as a constituent moment of a given work of art can never coincide with the hero; there are *two of them*, except that they are not contraposed to each other in principle. Their axiological contexts are the same in kind: the bearer of the unity of lived life—the hero—and the bearer of the unity of form—the author—belong to one and the same axiological world. The author—the bearer of the consummating unity of form—does not have to overcome the *resistance* of the hero's meaning-governed (cognitive-ethical) life; and, on the other hand, the hero himself, in his lived life, is possessed by the (axiologically) possible author-*other*. Both of them— hero and author—are *others* and belong to one and the same authoritative axiological world of *others*.

In biography, we do not go outside the bounds of the world of *others*. Even the creative activity of the author does not take us outside these bounds—his creative activity is wholly enclosed by the being of otherness, is solidary with the hero in his naive passivity. The author's creative activity is not an act, but—being, and hence, it is itself insecure and in need. The act of biography is somewhat one-sided: there are two consciousnesses, but they do not represent two different positions with respect to value; there are two human beings, except that they are not the *I* and the *other*, but—two others. The fundamental and essential character of the hero's otherness is not expressed; the task of saving the past independently of meaning has not imposed itself in all its imperative clarity. Here, too, there is a meeting of two consciousnesses, except that they are in agreement, and their axiological worlds are almost coincident; there is no "excess" in principle in the author's world, and there is no self-determination in principle of two consciousnesses against each other (one of them—on the plane of lived life—being passive, and the other—on the aesthetic plane— being active).

Of course, deep inside himself the author of a biography lives by noncoinciding with himself and with his hero; he does not surrender all of himself to the biography, but rather leaves an inner loophole for himself through which he can escape beyond the bounds of the given. And, of course, he stays alive through this "excess" of his above and beyond existence-as-a-given, except that this "excess" fails to find a positive expression inside the biography itself. Nevertheless, it does find a certain negative expression: the author's "excess" is transposed into the hero and his world, and it prevents them from being closed and definitively completed.

The world of biography is not a closed and definitively completed world; it is not isolated out of the unitary and unique event of being by any firm and essentially necessary boundaries. To be sure, this continued participation of biography in the unitary event of being is indirect, for what it participates in directly or immediately is the proximate world (kin, nation, state, culture), and this proximate world, to which both the author and the hero belong—the world of otherness—is somewhat consolidated or bodied with respect to value, and, consequently, is somewhat isolated. This isolation, however, is a natural-naive isolation, a relative isolation, and not an isolation in principle, not an aesthetic isolation.

Biography is not a produced *work*, but an aestheticized, organic, and naive *act* performed in a proximate, axiologically authoritative world that is in principle open and yet organically sufficient unto itself. Biographical life and biographical utterance about a life are always enveloped by a naive faith—by that faith's atmosphere of warmth. Biography is deeply trustful, but trustful naively (without any crises); it presupposes a benign or kind self-activity which proceeds from outside its bounds and encompasses it as a whole. This is not the *author*'s self-activity, however, for the author himself is in need of it along with the hero (they are both passive, after all, and both exist in one and the same world); this is a self-activity that must be situated beyond the bounds of a work as a whole (for the work is not, after all, consummated to the full and not isolated). Biography, just like confessional self-accounting, points beyond its own bounds. (Biographical value, as a value that is possessed by otherness, is highly insecure or precarious; the biographically valuable life hangs by a thread, for it is incapable of being definitively founded and validated from within itself; once the spirit awakens, such a life can persist only by way of being insincere with itself.)

What biography aims to accomplish is meant to be relevant for a kindred reader, a reader who participates in the same world of otherness, and this reader assumes the position of the author. The critical reader perceives biography to a certain extent as raw material for artistic forming and consummating. His perception usually completes the author's position to the point where he is situated (axiologically) altogether outside, and it introduces more essential and consummating transgredient moments.

It should be clear that biography so conceived and formulated represents an ideal form, an ultimate limit which concrete works of a biographical character (or only the biographical parts of concrete nonbiographical works) strive to attain. There is, of course, the possibility where the biographical form is stylized by a critical author.

Where the author ceases to be naive and totally rooted in the world of otherness; where the *kinship* between author and hero *is not severed*; where the author is skeptical toward the hero's life: there the author can become a pure *artist*. As such, he will constantly oppose the transgredient *values of consummation* in the *values of the hero's lived life*; he will seek to consummate the hero's life from a point of view which is in principle different from the way that life was lived and experienced by the hero himself from within himself. Every line written, every step taken by the narrator, will strive, in that case, to utilize the narrator's *fundamental and essential excess of seeing*, for the hero is *in need* of a transgredient justification; the author's gaze and self-activity will *encompass* and shape essentially what constitutes *in principle* the hero's *limits with respect to meaning* at the point where the hero's life is turned outside itself; and thus, a demarcation in principle will be set between the hero and the author. It should be clear that biography does not present us with the whole hero; the hero is incapable of being consummated within the bounds of biographical value.

Biography is bestowed as a gift: I receive it as a gift from others and for others, yet I possess it naively and calmly (whence the somewhat fateful character of a biographically valuable life). Of course, the boundary between horizon and surrounding world or environment is unstable in biography and has no significance in principle; empathy has maximal significance. Such, then, is the character of biography.

3. Lyrical Hero and Author

Lyrical objectification of the inner man may become a self-objectification. Here, as well, the hero and the author are close to each other. The author, however, has more transgredient moments at his disposal, and they are more essential in character.

In the preceding section, we ascertained that rhythm is in principle transgredient to the experiencing soul. From within itself, inner life is not rhythmic and—we can put it even more broadly—it is not lyrical. Lyrical form is introduced from outside and it expresses the axiological relationship of the other as such to the experiencing soul, and not the relationship of the experiencing soul to itself. This renders the author's position of axiological outsideness in lyrical objectification essentially necessary and axiologically intense; the author must utilize his privilege of being outside the hero to the fullest extent. Nevertheless, the closeness of author and hero in a lyrical work is no less evident than it is in biography. But if in biography, as we saw, the world of others, the heroes of my life, has assimilated me—the author—and as a result the author has nothing to set over against his strong and authoritative hero, besides agreement with him (the author is poorer, as it were, than the hero), then in a lyrical work we observe a converse phenomenon: the hero has almost nothing to set over against the author; the author permeates, as it were, all of him thoroughly, leaving only a potential possibility of self-dependence in him, in his very depths. The author's victory over the hero is too complete: the hero is totally deprived of strength (this victory is even more complete in music—music is an almost pure form of otherness, behind which one can almost no longer feel the presence of a possible hero living his own distinct life). Everything interior in the hero is, as it were, turned totally outward, toward the author, and is shaped by the author. Almost all object-related and meaning-related moments in the hero's lived experience that could have persisted against the fullness of aesthetic consummation are absent from the lyrical work—whence the ease with which the *hero's self-coincidence, self-equivalence* is accomplished. (Even in the philosophical lyric, meaning and object are rendered totally immanent to lived experience, are contracted into lived experience, and as a result leave no room for noncoinciding with oneself and for going out into the open event of being;

the thought here is thought that *has been lived through*, thought that believes only in its own factual existence and neither supposes nor sees anything outside itself.)

What gives the author such full power over the hero? What renders the hero so weak internally (so unserious, one might say)? What makes the isolation of lived experience out of the event of being so complete? In other words: what makes the author and the author's axiological creative position in the lyrical work so *authoritative* for the hero that lyrical self-objectification becomes possible (i.e., the coincidence in person of hero and author outside the bounds of a work)? (One might get the impression that in the lyrical work there is only one unity, not two; the author's sphere and the hero's sphere have merged, and their centers coincide.) This authoritativeness of the author's position is founded and validated by two constitutive moments.

(1) The lyrical work excludes all those moments which constitute a human being's spatial expressedness, his being exhaustively present in space; it does not localize and does not delimit the whole of the hero totally in the outside world, and, consequently, it provides no clear-cut impression of a human being's finiteness in the world (Romantic phraseology concerning the infinity of the spirit is highly compatible with the constituents of lyrical form).

Furthermore, the lyrical work does not determine, does not delimit the movement of its hero's lived life by means of a finished and clear-cut *fabula*.

Finally, the lyrical work does not seek to produce a finished character for the hero, does not draw a clear-cut boundary around the entire whole of the hero's soul and all of his inner life (it deals only with a *constituent* of that whole, with an *episode* from his inner life).

This first moment of the two constitutive moments under consideration produces the illusion that the hero preserves himself and preserves his own inner position—the accumulated stock of pure self-experience; it produces the illusion that in a lyrical work the hero has to do only with himself and for himself, the illusion that he is *solitary*, and *not possessed*. This illusion makes it easier for the author to penetrate into the innermost depth of the hero and take complete possession of him. It enables the author to permeate all of the hero with his own, i.e., the author's, self-activity: the hero is pliant, yielding, and surrenders all of himself to the author's self-activity of his own accord. But in order to take possession of the hero in this intimate, inward position, the author, in his turn, must refine himself to the point of achieving a purely *inward* position outside the hero: the author must refrain from using his position of being outside the hero in space and external time (externally temporal outsideness is necessary for a clear-cut conception of a finished *fabula*), and from using the *excess* of seeing and knowing which is tied up with that position. The author must refine himself to the point of assuming a purely axiological position *outside the line of the hero's own directedness from within himself* (and not outside the whole human being), that is, outside his forward-striving *I*, outside the line of his possible pure relationship to himself. And then the outwardly solitary hero turns out not to be solitary inwardly, from the standpoint of inward values: the *other*, penetrating inside him, deflects him from his axiological self-relationship and does not allow this relationship to become the sole power (to repent, implore, and go beyond himself) that orders and shapes his inner life, the power that delivers him up to the constraining task constituted by the unitary and unique event of being, in which his life can express itself only in the form of a performed act, an objective self-accounting, and in prayer. (In the lyrical work, even confession and prayer turn back upon themselves, as it were, and begin to suffice contentedly unto themselves, to coincide joyously with their present-on-hand-being, unaware of anything outside themselves—in the yet-to-be event of being. Repentance is no longer contemplated and cherished in penitent tones, but in tones of affirmation; supplication and need are cherished without needing an actual satisfaction.) Thus, the first constitutive moment reveals, so far as the hero is concerned, his *inner* possessedness by another's *inner* axiological position.

(2) The authority of the author is the authority of a *chorus*. Lyrical possessedness is, fundamentally, *possessedness by a chorus*. It is an existence that has found its confirmation and support in a chorus. What sings in me is not indifferent nature, for nature is capable of engendering only the fact of a desire, the fact of an action, but not the expression of the value of that desire or that action, regardless of how immediate they might be. This expression of value becomes strong and powerful (not naturally and physically, but axiologically strong and powerful, axiologically victorious and conquering) only in the chorus of others. In this con-

text, it is translated from the plane of being purely factual, of being physically present-on-hand, to another plane, to the axiological plane of an emotionally sanctioned existence, an existence that is confirmed from outside.

Lyrical self-objectification is a seeing and hearing of myself from within with the emotional eyes of the other and in the emotional *voice* of the other: I *hear* myself in the other, with others, and for others. Lyrical self-objectification is a being possessed by the *spirit of music* (a being permeated and saturated by it). The spirit of music, the possible chorus—this is what constitutes here the firm and authoritative position of being the inner author, outside myself, of my own inner life. I seek and find myself in another's emotional-excited voice; I embody myself in the voice of the other who sings of me; I find in that voice an authoritative approach to my own inner emotion or excitement; I sing of myself through the lips of a possible loving soul. This other voice which is heard from outside and which organizes my inner life in lyric is the possible chorus or a voice that is in accord with a chorus, a voice that feels a possible choral support outside itself. (In an atmosphere of absolute silence and emptiness, this voice would be incapable of sounding in such a way. An individual and totally solitary violation of absolute silence has a frightening and sinful character; it degenerates into a scream which startles and frightens itself and finds itself hard to bear—finds it hard to bear its own intrusive and bare givenness. A solitary and totally arbitrary breaking of silence imposes an infinite responsibility or it is cynical without justification. The voice can *sing* only in a *warm* atmosphere, only in the atmosphere of possible choral support, where *solitariness* of sound is in principle excluded.)

One's own fantasy about oneself may also be lyrical, but only when it has mastered the music of otherness and, hence, has become creatively productive. Lyrical self-objectification, too, is full of deep trust that has been rendered immanent to its powerful, authoritative, and lovingly affirming form, i.e., immanent to the author—the bearer of the consummating unity of form. In order to make my lived experience sound lyrically, I need to feel in it not my solitary answerability, but my own naturalness as value; I need to feel the other in myself, my own passiveness in the possible chorus of others—in the chorus which has closed around me on all sides and has screened off, as it were, the *immediate* and urgent task constituted by the unitary and unique event of being. In a lyrical work, I have not yet stepped forward out of the chorus in the capacity of its hero-protagonist,[189] that is, a hero who still retains the chorally determined axiological bodiedness of his soul or otherness, but who already feels his own solitariness—in the capacity of a tragic hero (the solitary other). In a lyrical work, I am still wholly within a chorus and I speak from within a chorus.

The organizing power of love is, of course, especially great in lyric, much greater than in the case of any other formal artistic value. This is a love which is divested of almost all objective (meaning-related and object-related) constituents and which organizes the pure self-sufficiency of the process of inner life: the *love of woman*, which screens off human beings and the human race, both social and historical (church and God). A passionate, sultry atmosphere of love is needed to give body to the purely internal, almost objectless, and at times capricious movements of one's soul (I can be capricious only in another's love; this is desire at play in the heavy and heady atmosphere of love; sin is often a matter of being perversely capricious in God). Even the lyric of hopeless love moves and lives only in the atmosphere of possible love, by the anticipation of love. (Cf. the typical and paradigmatic character of the lyric of love and death; immortality as a postulate of love.)[190]

Lyric is susceptible of a distinctive form of disintegration, conditioned by the weakening of the authoritativeness of the other's axiological position outside me, by the weakening of *trust* in the possible support of a chorus, and this produces a distinctively lyrical state of being *ashamed* of oneself, ashamed of *lyrical exaltation*, ashamed of lyrical frankness (resulting in *lyrical mannerism*, in irony, and in *lyrical cynicism*). One could describe this as breaks or failures of a voice that suddenly feels itself to be outside any chorus. This occurs in Decadence,[191] and also in so-called Realistic lyric (Heinrich Heine). Examples may be found in Baudelaire, Verlaine, Laforgue; in Russian poetry, Sluchevsky and Annensky[192] especially are—*voices outside a chorus*. (From our point of view, there is no sharp divide between "choral" and "individual" lyric. Any form of lyric lives only through the trust it has in a possible choral support, and the only possible difference consists in the particularity of certain stylistic features and formal-technical peculiarities. An essential difference arises only where trust in a chorus grows weaker; at that point, the lyrical mode begins to disintegrate. Individualism can determine itself positively and feel no shame about its own determinateness only in an atmosphere of trust, love, and possible choral support. The individual does not exist outside the bounds of otherness.)

Distinctive forms of "playing a fool"[193] are also possible in the lyrical mode. In all cases where the hero begins to free himself from possession by the other—the author (i.e., the author ceases to be authoritative); where meaning-related and object-related moments gain *immediate validity* for the hero, that is to say, where he suddenly finds himself to be in the event of being, in the light of to-be-attained meaning—in all these cases, the ends of the lyrical circle no longer meet, and the hero can no longer coincide with himself: he begins to see his own nakedness and to be ashamed, and paradise is lost. (There is a certain admixture of "playing a fool" in some of Andrei Bely's prose lyric.[194] Examples of prose lyric in which being-ashamed-of-oneself constitutes the organizing force may be found in Dostoevsky. This form is close to the anthropomachic type of confessional self-accounting.)

Such, then, is the essential character of lyric and of the author-hero relationship in it. The position of the author is strong and authoritative, whereas the independence of the hero and of his directedness in living his own life is minimal: he does not really *live* a life of his own, but only *reflects* himself in the soul of the active author—the other by whom he is possessed. There is almost no inner resistance on the part of the hero that the author must overcome: one more step—and the lyrical work is on the verge of becoming a pure, objectless form of the possible cherishing of a possible hero (for only the hero can be the bearer of content, i.e., of the prosaic value-context). Isolation[195] out of the event of being is full and complete in lyric, but there is no need to underline it. In the present context, the difference between "declamatory" and "cantatory" lyric is not essential for us—it is a difference in the degree of the hero's independence with respect to meaning and objects, and not a difference in principle.

4. Character as a Form of the Interrelationship of Hero and Author

We must now turn our attention to character and examine it solely from the standpoint of the interrelationship of hero and author within it. We shall forego the analysis of aesthetic constituents in the structure of character, inasmuch as they have no direct bearing on the problem we are considering. Hence we are not going to present here an even relatively complete aesthetic of character.

Character is sharply and essentially differentiated from all forms of expression of the hero that we have examined up to now. Neither in confessional self-accounting, nor in biography, nor in lyric does the *whole* of the hero constitute the fundamental artistic task, the axiological center in artistic vision. (The hero is always the center of artistic vision, but not the *whole* that he is, not the fullness and completeness of his determinateness.)

Confessional self-accounting does not set itself any artistic task at all, and hence, it excludes the purely aesthetic value of a whole—the given, present-on-hand whole.

In biography, the fundamental task is a *life* as biographical value, that is, the *life* of a hero is the fundamental goal, and not the inner and outer determinateness of the hero, not a finished image of his personality. What is important is not who he is, but what he has lived through and what he has done. Of course, biography, too, knows those constituents which determine the image of a personality (heroization), but none of them closes and consummates that personality: the hero is important as the bearer of a determinate life, a rich and full life, a life that is historically significant. It is this life that occupies the center of vision, and not the *whole* of the hero, in which even his life in all its determinateness would constitute only a characteristic of him.

The task of producing the *whole* of a hero is absent from lyric as well: what is in the axiological center of vision here is an inner state or event, which is by no means just a characteristic of the experiencing hero himself; the hero is only the bearer of a lived experience, but this lived experience neither closes nor consummates him as a determinate whole.

That is why the hero and the author could be so close to each other (and could coincide in person outside the bounds of a work) in all of the forms of the hero-author relationship that we have examined up to now; for in all these forms the author's self-activity was *not* directed to the creation and forming of clear-cut and essential *boundaries of the hero.* Consequently, it was not directed to the creation of fundamental and essential *boundaries between author and hero.* (What is important is the *world* that encompasses both hero and author, the constituents and situations of that world.)

Character is the name we give to that form of the author-hero interrelationship which actualizes the task of producing the *whole* of a hero as a determinate personality, where, moreover, this task constitutes the fundamental task: the hero is given us, from the very outset, as a determinate whole, and the author's self-activity proceeds, from the very outset, along the essential boundaries of the hero. Everything is perceived here as a constituent in the characterization of the hero, i.e., fulfills a characterological function; everything reduces to and serves the answer to the question: *who* is he?

It should be clear that we have to do here with two planes of axiological perception, with two meaning-bestowing axiological contexts (one context of which encompasses and overcomes the other with respect to value): (1) the horizon of the hero and the cognitive-ethical (lived-life) significance of every constituent (every act, every object) within that horizon for the hero himself; and (2) the context of the author-contemplator, in which all these constituents become characteristics of the whole of the hero, i.e., take on a determining and delimiting significance in relation to the hero (a life turns out to be the image of a life). The author is quite *critical* here (as an author, of course): at each moment of his creative activity, he uses all the privileges of his all-round position outside the hero. At the same time, the hero in this form of interrelationship is, in his turn, most independent, alive, aware, and persistent in the cognitive and ethical (value-oriented) position he maintains in living his own life. The author stands totally over against this activity of the hero, the activity of living his life, and translates it into aesthetic language, i.e., produces a transgredient artistic determination for every constituent moment in the hero's activity of living. The relationship between author and hero in this case is intense, essential, and principled in character at every point.

Character construction may proceed in two basic directions. The first one we shall call "Classical character construction"; the second we shall call "Romantic character construction." The foundation for the first type of character construction is provided by the artistic value of *fate* (we are using this term here in a very specific, restricted sense which should become clear from what follows).

Fate is the all-round determinateness of a person's existence that necessarily predetermines all the events of that person's life; hence, life is merely the actualization (and fulfillment) of what was inherent from the very outset in the determinateness of the person's existence. From within himself, the person builds up his life (thinks, feels, acts) in accordance with particular goals, by actualizing various forms of that which has validity with respect to meaning and objects, upon which his life is directed: he acts in a particular way because he feels he ought to act that way, considers it proper, necessary, desirable to act that way, wants to act that way, etc. And yet, in reality, he merely actualizes the necessity inherent in his own fate, the determinateness of his own existence, his own countenance in being. Fate is the artistic transcription of the trace in being which is left by a life that is regulated from within itself by purposes; it is the artistic expression of the *deposit* in being laid down by a life that is understood or interpreted totally from within itself.

This deposit in being must also have a logic of its own, except that this logic is not the *goal-directed logic* of lived life itself, but the purely artistic logic which governs and directs the unity and inner necessity of the formed image. Fate is individuality, that is, the essential determinateness of a person's existence that determines his entire life, all his acts. In this respect, even the act of thinking is determined not from the standpoint of its theoretical-objective validity, but from the standpoint of individuality—as characteristic precisely for the given determinate person, as predetermined by that person's existence; and all other possible acts are, likewise, predetermined by individuality or actualize the individuality. The very course of a person's life, all of its events, and, ultimately, its termination are perceived as necessary and as predetermined by that person's determinate individuality—by his fate. And, on this plane of character-as-fate, the death of the hero is not a termination, but a consummation; indeed, every constituent moment of his life assumes artistic significance, becomes artistically necessary.

It should be clear that our understanding of fate differs from the usual, very broad, understanding of it. Thus, fate, experienced from within as an external irrational force which determines our life regardless of its goals, meaning, and desires, is not the artistic value of fate in our sense, for this fate does not, after all, order our life, for ourselves, into a necessary and artistic whole. Rather, it has the purely negative function of disarranging our life, which is ordered or, rather, strives to be ordered by purposes and by various forms of that which has validity with respect to meaning and objects. It is possible, of course, to feel deep faith in that external force, and, through this faith or trust, to perceive it as the providence of God; God's providence is accepted and received by me, but it cannot, of course, become a form which orders my life for me myself. (It is possible to love one's fate *in absentia*, or without actually seeing it, but we cannot contemplate our fate as a necessary, internally unified, and fully consummated artistic whole, the way we contemplate the fate of a hero.)

We do not understand, we only believe in the logic of God's providence. The logic of the hero's fate, on the other hand, we understand quite well and we do not, by any means, accept it on faith (of course, the point here is not the cognitive but the artistic understanding and the artistic convincingness of fate). Fate as an artistic value is transgredient to self-consciousness. Fate is the fundamental value which regulates, orders, and reduces to unity all of the moments that are transgredient to the hero; we use our situatedness outside the hero, in order to comprehend and to see the whole that his fate constitutes. Fate is not the *I-for-myself* of the hero, but the existence of the hero, i.e., that which is *given* to him, that which he turned out to *be*; it is the form he has as a given, and not the form he has as a task-to-be-fulfilled.

The Classical character is constructed or constituted precisely as a fate. The Classical hero occupies a determinate place in the world; with respect to what is most essential, the Classical hero has already become totally determinate and, hence, has perished. Furthermore, his *entire* life is given, given in the sense of what it might ultimately achieve. Everything the hero does is artistically motivated not by his moral free will, but by his determinate being: he acts the way he does because he is such as he is. There must be nothing indeterminate in him for us; everything that is done, everything that happens, unfolds within pregiven and predetermined limits, without going beyond them; what is accomplished is that which *must* be accomplished and cannot *but* be accomplished. Fate is the form of ordering the past as the past of meaning; we contemplate the Classical hero, from the very outset, in the past, in which there can be no discoveries and no revelations.

It should be noted that in order to construct the Classical character as a fate, the author must not exalt himself excessively above the hero and must not use the purely temporal and fortuitous privileges of his situatedness outside the hero. The Classical author uses the external moments of his position outside the hero, and, hence, the past of the Classical hero is the *eternal* past of man. The position of being situated outside the hero must not be exceptional, self-confident, and original.

(Kinship is not yet severed, the world is perfectly clear, and there is no belief in miracles.)

In relation to the world view of the Classical hero, the author is dogmatic. His cognitive-ethical position must be indisputable or, to be exact, it is simply not brought up for discussion at all. For to do so would be to introduce the moment of *guilt* and *responsibility*, and the artistic unity and pervasiveness of fate would be destroyed. The hero would turn out to be free, he could be put on trial morally; there would be no necessity in him, he *could* be other than he is. In those cases where moral guilt and responsibility have been introduced into the hero (and, hence, also moral freedom, freedom from natural and from aesthetic necessity), the hero ceases to coincide with himself, and the author loses what is most essential in his position of being outside the hero (namely, the liberation of the other from guilt and responsibility, the contemplation of the other *outside meaning*);[196] any artistic, transgredient consummation of the hero becomes impossible.

Of course, guilt *does* occur in the Classical character (the hero of tragedy is almost invariably guilty), except that this is not moral guilt, but the guilt of being: the guilt must have the *force of being*, and not the *force of meaning* that distinguishes moral *self*-condemnation (offense against the person of the deity, rather than against meaning; offense against the cult, etc.). The conflicts within the Classical character are conflicts between contending *forces of being* (between the value-bearing natural forces of the being of otherness, of course, and not between physical or psychological magnitudes), and not conflicts between various forms of that which has the validity of meaning (both duty and obligation are value-bearing natural forces in this context). This contention of forces is an internally *dramatic* process, which nowhere exceeds the bounds of being-as-a-given; it is not a dialectical, meaning-related process in moral consciousness.

Tragic guilt is located totally on the axiological plane of being-as-a-given and is immanent to the fate of the hero. That is why guilt can be placed completely *outside* the bounds of the hero's consciousness and knowledge[x] *into* the past of his kin or kind (the kin or kind is a value-bearing natural category of the being of otherness); the hero could commit an offense without being aware of the significance of what he had done. In any case, the guilt is in *being*, as a force, and is not born for the first time in the free moral consciousness of the hero. The hero is not a totally free initiator of guilt; there is no way out for him from within the bounds imposed by the category of axiological *being*.

What constitutes the axiological soil in which the Classical character grows and develops? In what value-bearing cultural context is *fate* possible (in the sense of a positively valuable force that organizes and consummates another's life artistically)? The soil in which fate as a value can grow and develop is constituted by *the value of one's kin*, conceived as a category of the validating being of otherness, which involves me as well in the axiological sphere of its accomplishment. *I do not initiate life*, i.e., I am not the one who is axiologically responsible for beginning it; indeed, I have no axiological access at all to being the *active initiator of a responsibly lived life whose sequence is determined by meaning and values*. I can act and evaluate on the basis of an already given and evaluated life; the *sequence of performed acts does not begin out of myself*—I only *continue* that sequence (the acts of thinking as well as the acts of feeling and the acts that constitute deeds). I am bound by an indissoluble *relation of sonship* to the fatherhood and motherhood of my kin or kind (kin or kind in the restricted sense of a people or of humankind). In the question "who am I?" one can hear the question "who are my parents, from what kind am I descended?" I can be no more than what I am already in essentials; I cannot reject my essential *already-being*, for it is not *mine*, but belongs to my mother, father, kin, people, mankind.

My kin (or my father, mother) have value not because they are *mine*, that is, it is not *I* who make my kin valuable (it is not my kin who become a moment of my valuable being). My kin have value because I am *theirs*, because I am of my mother's or my father's kind. From the standpoint of value, I do not belong to my-

---

[x] Moral guilt must be immanent to self-consciousness—I must be conscious of myself in it as "I."

self; from the standpoint of value, I am nonexistent in contraposition to my kind. (I can reject and overcome in myself, from the standpoint of value, only that which is unquestionably mine, only that in which I alone am present, in which I violate what has been handed down to me from my kind.) The determinateness of my being in the value-category of my kin is unquestionable; this determinateness is given within myself, and within myself I cannot stand over against it; from the standpoint of value, I do not exist yet, for myself, outside that determinateness. The moral *I-for-myself* is kinless (the Christian felt himself to be kinless: the immediacy of heavenly fatherhood destroys the authoritativeness of earthly fatherhood).

It is in this soil that the axiological force of fate is born for the author. Author and hero still belong to one and the same world, in which the value of one's kin or kind is still dominant (in its various forms: nation, tradition, etc.). It is in this constitutive moment that the author's position of being outside the hero finds its limitation: it does not extend to the point of being outside the bounds of the hero's world view and sense of the world. Author and hero have nothing to dispute about, although, on the other hand, the author's position outside the hero is particularly firm and stable in this case (disputes render it unstable). The value constituted by one's kin transforms fate into a positively valuable category in the aesthetic vision and consummation of a human being (he is not required to show moral initiative). Where a human being initiates, from within himself, a sequence of acts determined by meaning and value; where he is morally culpable and answerable for himself, for his own determinateness, the category of fate as value is inapplicable to him and is incapable of consummating him (cf. Blok's poem "Retribution").[197] (On the basis of this value, repentance is incapable of penetrating and permeating all of myself, and, hence, pure confession as self-accounting cannot arise; only kinless human beings appear to know repentance in its fullest form.) Such, then, is the essential nature of the Classical character.

We turn now to the second type of character construction—the "Romantic character." In distinction to Classical character, the Romantic type of character is arbitrarily self-active and full of initiative with respect to value. What is of the utmost importance, moreover, is that the hero *responsibly initiates* the sequence of his life as determined by meaning and values. It is precisely this

solitary and utterly active position or attitude of the hero with respect to meaning and values, i.e., his cognitive-ethical position in
the world, that the author must overcome and consummate aesthetically. The value of fate, which presupposes kin and tradition,
is useless here for accomplishing artistic consummation.

What is it, then, that imparts artistic unity and wholeness, imparts inner artistic necessity, to all transgredient determinations
of the Romantic hero? The term that would fit best here is a term
we find in Romantic aesthetics itself: the *value* constituted by
"the idea".[198] The hero's individuality reveals itself here not as
fate, but as idea, or, rather, as an embodiment of the idea. Acting
from within himself in accordance with various purposes, the
hero actualizes that which has validity from the standpoint of
meaning and objects, and, in doing so, he actualizes, in reality, a
certain idea, a certain necessary truth of his life, a certain arche-
type of himself, the design God has conceived for him. The result
is that the course of his life, its various events and constituents,
and often its objective surroundings as well are somewhat *symbolized*. The hero is a homeless wanderer, a sojourner, a seeker
(cf. Byron's and Chateaubriand's heroes, Faust, Werther, Heinrich
von Ofterdingen, and others), and all of the moments that constitute his quest for meaning and value (he wants, he loves, he considers something to be true, etc.) find their transgredient determination as the symbolic stages of a single artistic course, the
course of actualizing a certain idea. It is inevitable that lyrical
moments occupy a prominent place in the Romantic hero (the
love of woman, just as in lyric). The attitude or position with respect to meaning that is deposited in the Romantic character has
ceased to be authoritative and is only re-experienced, lyrically re-
experienced.

The author's position outside the Romantic hero is undoubtedly less stable than it was in the case of the Classical type of
hero. The weakening of this position leads to the disintegration of
character; the boundaries begin to be effaced, the center of value
is transposed from the boundaries into the very life of the hero
(into his cognitive-ethical directedness from within himself). Romanticism is a form of the *infinite hero:* the author's reflection
upon the hero is introduced inside the hero and restructures him;
the hero takes away from the author all of his transgredient determinations and uses them in his own self-development and
self-determination, with the result that his self-determination be-

comes infinite. Parallel to this occurs a destruction of the boundaries that demarcate cultural domains (the idea of the whole or integral human being). In this context, we find seeds of irony and of "playing a fool."[199] The unity of a work often coincides here with the unity of the hero; the transgredient moments become fortuitous and dispersed, losing their unity. Or the unity of the author becomes emphatically conventional, *stylized*. The author begins to expect revelations from the hero. There is an attempt to force an admission from within self-consciousness, which is possible only through the other; an attempt to do without God, without listeners, without an author.

The products of the disintegration of Classical character are the "Sentimental" and the "Realistic" character. In this case, the transgredient moments begin to weaken the hero's independence everywhere. This is accomplished by way of an increase in the strength of either the moral element of the author's position outside the hero or the element of cognition (i.e., the author begins to examine his erring hero from the height of new ideas and theories).

In Sentimentalism, the author's position of being-outside is used not only artistically, but also morally (to the detriment of the artistic quality, of course). Pity, tender emotion, indignation, etc.—all these ethical value-reactions, which place the hero outside the bounds of a work, destroy the artistic consummation of the hero; we begin to react to the hero the way we react to a living human being (the reaction of readers to the first Sentimental heroes, such as Clarissa, Grandison, poor Liza,[200] etc., and to some extent Werther, is impossible in relation to the Classical hero), in spite of the fact that artistically he is much less alive than the Classical hero. The hero's misfortunes are no longer a matter of his fate; his misfortunes are simply caused, inflicted upon him by wicked people. The hero is passive, he merely undergoes life; he does not even perish, but is brought to ruin by others. The Sentimental hero is most suitable for tendentious works—for arousing extra-aesthetic social sympathy or social hostility. The author's position of being-outside is almost completely divested of its essential artistic constituents and approaches the position of being-outside which the ethical human being assumes in relation to his *fellow beings* (in the present context, we are omitting any consideration of humor[201]—a powerful and purely artistic force in Sentimentalism).

In Realism, the author's cognitional excess reduces character to the status of a simple illustration of the author's social theory or some other of the author's theories; by using his heroes and their life conflicts as examples (the heroes themselves have no time for theory), the author seeks to resolve his own cognitive problems (at best the author merely poses the problem apropos of the heroes). The problem side is not incarnated here in the hero and constitutes the active cognitional excess of the author's own knowledge, an excess that is transgredient to the hero. All these constituents weaken the independence of the hero.

The *form* assumed by a *situation* occupies a very special place, although it does sometimes appear as a product of the disintegration of character. Insofar as we have to do with the situation purely as a situation, that is, insofar as the center of artistic vision is occupied solely by the determinateness of an object-related and meaning-related set of affairs, in abstraction from the determinateness of the bearer of that set of affairs—the situation exceeds the bounds of our analysis. Where, on the other hand, it is merely a product of the disintegration of character, it represents nothing essentially new. These are, then, the basic features of character as a form of the interrelationship between author and hero.

5. The Problem of Type as a Form of the Author-Hero Interrelationship

If character, in all of its variants, is plastic, then type is pictorial (the Classical character is, of course, especially plastic). Character is established in relation to the ultimate values of a world view; it is immediately correlated with these ultimate values. That is, it expresses a human being's cognitive-ethical stance in the world and is placed into direct contact, as it were, with the very limits of being. Type, on the other hand, is remote from the world's limits and expresses a human being's stance in relation to values that have been concretized and delimited by an epoch and a milieu, or in relation to "goods," that is, in relation to meaning that has already become being (in an act performed by character, meaning is still in process of becoming alive for the first time). Character is in the past, type is in the present; the environment of character is somewhat symbolized, whereas the object-world surrounding the type has the nature of an inventory, or stock of goods. Type is the *passive* position of a collective personality.

What is fundamental in this form of the interrelationship between hero and author is the following: the cognitive element is of essential significance in the excess which the author possesses by virtue of his situatedness outside the hero, even if this element is not scientifically cognitive or is not discursive (although it may sometimes undergo even a discursive development). We shall designate this utilization of the author's cognitive excess as "intuitive generalization," on the one hand, and as "intuitive functional dependency," on the other. In fact, it is in these two directions that the cognitive element of the author's outside position actually develops when he constructs a type.

It should be evident that the intuitive generalization, which produces the typicality of a human being's image, presupposes a firm, calm, confident, and authoritative position of being outside with respect to the hero. How is this firmness and authoritativeness of the type-creating author's position achieved? It is achieved through his profound inward nonparticipation in or aloofness from the world he is imaging: axiologically, this world is, as it were, dead for him. That is to say, for the author himself, this imaged world is, from the very outset, totally contained in being: it simply *is* and *means nothing*. It is utterly clear in every respect and, consequently, it is completely unauthoritative; it is incapable of setting anything axiologically weighty over against the author; the cognitive-ethical position of its heroes is completely unacceptable. That is why the tranquillity, strength, and assurance of the author are analogous to the tranquillity and strength of the *subiectum* of cognition, where the hero—the object of aesthetic activity (another *subiectum*)—begins to approach the status of an *object* of cognition. Of course, this ultimate limit is never actually reached in the form of the type, and, hence, the type remains an artistic form; for the author's self-activity continues to be directed upon a human being as a human being, and, consequently, the event remains an aesthetic event.

The moment constituted by typological generalization is, of course, distinctly transgredient. What is least of all possible is rendering *oneself* typical; typicality that is referred to oneself is perceived axiologically as an affront. In this respect, typicality is even more transgredient than fate. I am not only unable to perceive my own typicality as value, but even more: I cannot allow that my deeds, actions, words (directed upon that which has the validity of goals and objects, even if only upon the most proximate ones, namely, "goods") should actualize nothing more than a certain type, that they should necessarily be predetermined by this typicality of mine. The almost insulting character of typal transgredience makes the form of the type quite acceptable for accomplishing the task of satire, which generally looks for trenchant and offensive transgredient deposits in the existence of a goal-directed and internally meaningful human life that lays claim to objective validity. Satire, however, presupposes a higher degree of obstinacy on the part of the hero (one is compelled to contend with him) than the one required in calm and confident type-producing contemplation.

Besides the moment constituted by intuitive generalization, there is also a moment constituted by intuitively apprehended functional dependency. The type is not only distinctly intertwined with the world surrounding it (with its object-environment), but it is also imaged as conditioned in all of its constituents by that surrounding world: it is a necessary constituent of a certain environment (it is not a whole, but only a part of a whole). The cognitive element in the author's position outside the hero may attain considerable power here, to the point where the author can disclose the factors which determine the hero's acts (his thoughts, feelings, etc.) causally: economic, social, psychological factors, and even physiological factors (the artist is a physician, and the human being who is the hero—is a sick animal). Of course, these are extremes of typological treatment. In all cases, however, the type is imaged as inseparable from a particular objective unity (a social system, an established order of collective life, a communal mode of daily life, etc.) and as necessarily conditioned by that unity, i.e., as engendered by it. Type presupposes the author's superiority to the hero and the author's complete aloofness, with respect to value, from the world of the hero; hence, the author may often be completely critical. In the type, the hero's independence is considerably reduced. All of the problem-related elements are transposed from the context of the hero into the context of the author; they develop with reference to the hero and in connection with the hero, but not in the hero, and their unity is provided by the author, and not by the hero, who is the bearer of the cognitive-ethical unity of a lived life—a unity which is reduced to the utmost in the type. It is, of course, completely impossible to introduce any lyrical elements into the type. Such, then, is the form of the type, as seen from the standpoint of the author-hero interrelationship in it.

6. Lives of the Saints

We cannot deal with this form in detail, for this would exceed the bounds of our theme. The *vita* of a saint is accomplished immediately in God's world. Every moment of the *vita* is imaged as possessing validity precisely in God's world; the *vita* of a saint is a life that has significance *in God*.

This significant life in God must be invested in traditional forms; the author's sense of reverence leaves no room for individual initiative, for individual choice of expression: the author renounces himself here, renounces his own individually answerable activity. Hence, the form assumes a traditional and conventional character. (What is conventional in a positive sense is that which is in principle inadequate to the object treated and which, in the awareness of that inadequateness, renounces adequation. But this premeditated renunciation of adequation is far removed from "playing a fool,"[202] for the latter is *individual* in character and is marked by an inherent element of anthropomachy. The form of a *vita* is conventional traditionally, is sanctioned by incontestable authority, and lovingly accepts the *given being of expression*, even if it is inadequate and, hence, merely receptive.)

Thus, the unity of the transgredient moments of a saint is not the individual unity of an author who actively utilizes his position outside the saint; the author's position outside the saint is assumed and maintained in humility—it is a position which renounces all initiative (since, in fact, there are no essentially transgredient moments for accomplishing a consummation) and which falls back upon forms consecrated by tradition. An examination of the traditional forms of hagiography would exceed, of course, the scope of our investigation. We shall restrict ourselves to just one general observation: hagiography, just like icon painting, avoids any transgredient moments which delimit a human being and render him overly concrete, because they invariably diminish authoritativeness. What must be excluded is anything typical for a given epoch, for a given nationality (for example, the national typicality of Christ in icon painting), for a given social position or a given age in the life of a human being; anything concrete in a person's appearance, anything concrete in his life (its details and particulars, precise indications of the place and time of action). That is, anything that reinforces a given person's *determinateness in being* (the typical and the characteristic, and even biographical concreteness) and thus reduces the authoritativeness of that person (the life of a saint proceeds from the very outset in eternity, as it were). It should be noted that the traditional and conventional character of the transgredient moments which enable a consummation contributes decisively to the reduction of their delimitative power.

A symbolic tradition in the treatment of the *vita* is also possible. (The problem of imaging a miracle and the supreme religious event; here the humble renunciation of adequacy and individuality and submission to strict tradition are especially important.) Where the task is to image and express a valid achievement of ultimate meaning, humility to the point of submission to traditional conventionality is indispensable (the Romantics either broke off a work or ended it by means of the traditional forms of a *vita* or a mystery play). Thus, *renunciation* of his position outside the saint as constituting an *essential* position and humbling himself to the point of submission to pure traditionality (medieval "realism")[203] are highly characteristic of the author of a saint's life (cf. the idea of *blago-obrazie* in Dostoevsky).[204]

Such are the forms of the whole which the hero constitutes as a whole of meaning. These forms do not coincide, of course, with the concrete forms of particular works; we have formulated them here as abstract-ideal forms or utmost limits toward which the concrete moments of a work tend. For it is difficult to find pure biography, pure lyric, pure character, and pure type. What we usually have is the union of several ideal forms, the action of several ultimate limits, with the predominance now of one, now of another (of course, concrescence is not possible among all of these forms). In this sense, we can say that the event of the author's and the hero's interrelationship within a particular, concrete work is often composed of several acts: the author and the hero contend with each other; now they approach and join each other, now they abruptly dissociate themselves from each other. But the precondition for the fullest consummation of a work consists in their dissociating themselves decisively from each other and in the author's being victorious.

The Problem of the Author

In the present section, we must first recapitulate some of the final results of our inquiry, and then determine in a more detailed way the author as participant in the artistic event.

1. [Recapitulation]

At the beginning of our inquiry we ascertained that *man* is the organizing form-and-content center of artistic vision and, moreover, man as a *given human being* in his axiological present-on-hand existence in the world. The world of artistic vision is a world which is organized, ordered, and consummated—independently of what-is-yet-to-be-achieved and independently of meaning[205]—*around* a given human being as *his* axiological surroundings or environment: we can see the way various objects and all relations (spatial and temporal relations, and relations of meaning) gain the validity of artistic objects and relations *around* that human being. This axiological orientation and consolidation of the world *around* a given human being creates its aesthetic reality, which is distinct from its cognitional and ethical reality (the reality of performed actions, the ethical reality of the unitary and unique event of being), without being indifferent to them, of course.

Furthermore, we ascertained that there is a fundamental and essential difference in value between the *I* and the *other*, a difference that has the character of an event: outside the bounds of this difference, no axiologically ponderable act is possible. The *I* and the *other* are the fundamental *value-categories* that for the first time make possible any *actual valuation*, and the moment of valuation, or, rather, that of the valuational attitude of consciousness, is present not only in an act proper, but also in every lived experience and even in the simplest sensation: to live means to

take an axiological stand in every moment of one's life or to position oneself with respect to values.

Furthermore, we gave a phenomenological description of the
axiological consciousness of oneself and of one's consciousness of
the other in the event of being[y] and we ascertained that only the
other as such is capable of constituting the axiological center of
artistic vision and, consequently, the hero of a work of art. Only
the other is capable of being formed and consummated *essentially*, for all the constituents of an axiological consummation
(spatial, temporal, and those of meaning) are axiologically transgredient to an active self-consciousness, that is, are not located
along the line of one's own axiological relationship to oneself. As
long as I remain *myself* for myself, I cannot be active in the aesthetically valid and consolidated space and time; I am not present
for myself axiologically in that space and time, I am not upbuilt,
shaped, and determined in them. The aesthetically significant
value of my own *body* and my own *soul* as well as their organic
artistic unity in a *whole* human being do not exist in the world of
my own self-consciousness, for they are not constructed within
my own horizon by my own self-activity and, consequently, my
own horizon cannot close contentedly and surround me as my
axiological environment: I *do not yet exist* in my own axiological
world as a contented and self-equivalent positive *given*. My own
axiological relationship to myself is completely unproductive
aesthetically: for myself, I am aesthetically unreal. I can be only
the bearer of the task of artistic forming and consummating, not
its object—not the hero.

Aesthetic vision finds expression in art—*verbal* art, in the
given case. In art, aesthetic vision is complemented by strict isolation (the possibilities of which were already inherent in aesthetic vision, as we demonstrated) and by a determinate, limited
formal task which is fulfilled by means of determinate material—
verbal material, in the given case. The fundamental artistic task
is actualized on the basis of word-material (which becomes artistic, insofar as it is governed by that task) in the particular forms of

---

[y] The *event* of being is a phenomenological concept, for being presents
itself to a living consciousness as an event, and a living consciousness
actively orients itself and lives in it as in an event.

a verbal work of art and with the particular devices that depend not only on the fundamental artistic task, but also on the nature of the given material—words (which have to be adapted for artistic purposes). (This is how the transition from aesthetic vision to art is accomplished.)[206] It is at this point that special aesthetics— the aesthetics that accounts for the distinctive qualities of the material used in a given art—comes into its own. Special aesthetics must not, of course, detach itself from the fundamental aesthetic task, detach itself from the fundamental creative relationship of the author to the hero that determines, in fact, the artistic task in all of its essentials. We have seen that I myself as a *determinatum* may become the *subiectum* (but not the hero) of only one type of utterance—the confessional self-accounting, in which one's own axiological relationship to oneself constitutes the organizing power, and which is, therefore, completely extra-aesthetic.

The organizing power in all aesthetic forms is the axiological category of the *other*, the relationship to the other, enriched by an axiological "excess" of seeing for the purpose of achieving a transgredient consummation. The author becomes close to the hero only where there is no purity of axiological self-consciousness, where self-consciousness is possessed by the consciousness of another (where it becomes axiologically conscious of itself in an authoritative other—in the latter's love and interest), and where the "excess" (the sum total of transgredient moments) is reduced to a minimum and is not principled and intense in character. In this case, the artistic event is actualized between two souls (almost within the bounds of a single possible axiological consciousness), and not between a soul and a spirit.

All this determines the work of art as a living artistic event— an effective moment in the unitary and unique event of being, and not as a thing—an object of purely theoretical cognition devoid of the validity or force of an event, devoid of any weight with respect to value. And it is precisely as such an event that we must understand and know the work of art—we must understand and know it in the very principles of its value-governed *life*, in its *living* participants, and not as something that has been first put to death and reduced to the bare empirical givenness of a verbal whole (it is not the author's relationship to the material that constitutes an event and has the validity or force of an event, but—the author's relationship to the hero). And this determines the author's position as well—the position of the bearer of the act of artistic vision and creation in the event of being—for it is only in the event of being that any kind of creation whatsoever can have weight, can be serious, significant, and responsible. The author assumes an answerable position in the event of being, deals with the constituents of this event, and, hence, the work he produces is also a constituent of that event.

The hero and the author/beholder—these are the fundamental constituents, the fundamental participants in the event of a work of art: [207] they alone can be answerable, and they alone are capable of giving it the unity of an event and of bringing it into an essential communion with the unitary and unique event of being. We have provided a sufficient determination of the hero and of the form of him: of his axiological otherness, of his body and his soul, of his wholeness. In the present context, we need to examine the *author* more closely.

All of the world's values enter into the aesthetic object, but they do so with a particular aesthetic coefficient, and the author's position as well as the artistic task he has set himself must be understood in the world in conjunction with all these values. What is consummated or formed into an integral whole is not the material (words), but the comprehensively lived and experienced makeup of being. The artistic task organizes the concrete world: the spatial world with its own axiological center—the living body, the temporal world with its own center—the soul, and, finally, the world of meaning—all in their concrete interpenetrating unity.

The aesthetically creative relationship to the hero and his world is a relationship to him as one who is going to die (*moriturus*): it is the act of setting a saving consummation of him over against his own directedness to meaning. To accomplish this, one must clearly see in a human being and his world that which he himself is in principle incapable of seeing in himself, and do so while remaining in oneself and living one's own life in earnest; one must be able to approach him not from the standpoint of a lived life, but from a different standpoint—from a standpoint that is active outside a lived life.

The artist is, in fact, someone who knows how to be active outside lived life, someone who not only partakes in life from within (practical, social, political, moral, religious life) and understands

it from within, but someone who also loves it from without—
loves life where it does not exist for itself, where it is turned outside itself and is in need of a self-activity that is located outside it
and is active independently of meaning. The divinity of the artist
consists in his partaking of the supreme outsideness. But this situatedness of the artist outside the event of other people's life and
outside the world of this life is, of course, a special and justified
kind of participation in the event of being. To find an essential
approach to life from outside—this is the task an artist must accomplish. In doing this, the artist and art as a whole create a completely new vision of the world, a new image of the world, a new
reality of the world's mortal flesh, unknown to any of the other
culturally creative activities. And this external (and internally external) determinateness of the world that finds its highest expression and preservation in art always accompanies our emotional
thinking about the world and about life.

Aesthetic activity collects the world scattered in meaning and
condenses it into a finished and self-contained image. Aesthetic
activity finds an emotional equivalent for what is transient in the
world (for its past and present, for its present-on-hand being), an
emotional equivalent that gives life to this transient being and
safeguards it; that is, it finds an axiological position from which
the transient in the world acquires the axiological weight of an
event, acquires validity and stable determinateness. The aesthetic
act gives birth to being on a new axiological plane of the world: a
new human being is born and a new axiological context—a new
plane of thinking about the human world.

The author must be situated on the boundary of the world he is
bringing into being as the active creator of this world, for his in-
trusion into that world destroys its aesthetic stability. We can
always determine the author's position in relation to the world represented from the way in which outward appearance is represented: whether or not a whole, transgredient image of outward
appearance is presented; to what extent the boundaries are alive,
essential, and persistent; to what extent the hero is woven into
the surrounding world; to what extent the resolution and consummation are full, sincere, and emotionally intense; to what extent the action is calm and plastic; to what extent the souls of the
heroes are alive (as opposed to being no more than the misguided
exertions of the spirit to convert itself into a soul through its own

resources). Only when all of these conditions are observed is the aesthetic world stable and self-contained and coincides with itself in our active artistic seeing of it.

2. Content, Form, Material

The author's activity is directed upon content (upon the hero's own tension in living his life, i.e., his cognitive-ethical directedness): the author gives form to this content and consummates it by using a particular material for this purpose (verbal material, in our case) and by subordinating this material to his artistic task, i.e., the task of consummating a given cognitive-ethical tension. Proceeding from this, we can distinguish three constituents in a work of art or, rather, in a given artistic task: content, material, and form.

Form cannot be understood independently of content, but neither can it be independent of the nature of the material used and the devices determined by the latter. Form is conditioned by the given content, on the one hand, and, on the other, by the particular nature of the material and the methods of working that material. A purely *material* artistic task would constitute a technical experiment. An artistic device cannot be solely a device of working the verbal material (words as a linguistic datum); it must be first and foremost a device of working a particular content, except that it must do so by means of a particular material. It would be naive to think that the only thing the artist needs is language, along with the knowledge of the devices of working with language, and that he receives this language as nothing more than language, receives it, that is, from the linguist (for only the linguist has to do with language as language); it is this language, supposedly, that inspires the artist, and the artist performs all kinds of tasks on its basis without exceeding its bounds *as language only* (such as a phonetic task, a syntactic task, a semantic task, etc.).

And, in fact, the artist does work on language, but not on language as language. Language as language is something he surmounts, for language must cease to be perceived as language in its linguistic determinateness (its morphological, syntactic, lexico-

logical determinateness, etc.), and must be perceivable only insofar as it becomes a means of artistic expression. (Words must
cease to be palpable as words.) It is not in the world of language
that the poet creates; language is something he merely uses. In
relation to material, the artist's task (based in the fundamental artistic task) could be described as the *surmounting of material*.
This surmounting, however, is positive in character and does not
tend at all toward illusion. What is surmounted in the material
is its extra-aesthetic determination: marble must cease to persist
as marble, i.e., as a particular physical phenomenon; it must
give plastic expression to the forms of the body, but without
in any way producing an illusion of the body, for everything physical in the material is surmounted precisely as that which is
physical.

Do we have to feel the words in a work of art precisely as words,
i.e., in respect to their linguistic determinateness? That is, do we
have to feel the morphological form as specifically morphological, the syntactic form as syntactic, the semantic order as semantic? Of course, the work must also be studied as a *verbal* whole,
and this lies within the linguist's competency. But this *verbal*
whole, by the very fact that it is perceived as verbal, is not the
artistic whole. The surmounting of language, however, as a surmounting of physical material is completely immanent in character: it is surmounted not by way of negation, but by way of *immanent perfecting* in a prticular, required direction. (Language *per se*
is axiologically indifferent: it is always a servant, it is never a
goal; it *serves* cognition, art, practical communication, etc.)

People who have studied science for the first time may naively
assume that the world of creative activity as well consists of scientifically abstract elements: it turns out that we have been speaking
in prose all the time without even suspecting it. Naive positivism
assumes that what we have to do with in the world—that is, in
the *event* of the world,[208] since, after all, we live and act and create
in it—is matter, psyche, mathematical numbers, and that these
have a bearing on the meaning and purpose of our acts and are capable of explaining our acts, our creative activity, precisely as *acts*
and as *creative* activity (cf. the example concerning Socrates in
Plato). Meanwhile, the only thing these concepts explain is the
material of the world, the technical apparatus of the event of the
world. This material of the world is immanently surmounted by

our acts and our creative activity. At the present time, naive positivism has spilled over into the human sciences as well (the naive conception of what constitutes scientific knowledge). What needs to be understood, however, is not the technical apparatus, but the *immanent logic of creative activity*, and what needs to be understood first of all is the value-and-meaning structure in which creative activity comes to pass and in which it gains an axiological awareness of itself—that is, the context in which the act of creation becomes meaningful.

The author-artist's creative consciousness is never *coincident* with language-consciousness: language-consciousness is no more than a constituent, a material that is totally governed by the purely artistic task. What I may have represented to myself as a way, as a course to follow in the world, turns out to be merely a semantic series (of course, the latter has its place as well, but the question is: what place exactly?). It constitutes a semantic series outside the bounds of the artistic task, outside the bounds of a work of art—otherwise, we would have to claim that semantics is not and cannot be a department of linguistics in any conception of linguistic science (so long as it *is* a science of language). To compose a semantic dictionary according to subjects does not yet mean at all that we have come into the presence of creative art. The fundamental problem is to determine first of all the artistic task and its actual context, i.e., that axiological world in which the artistic task is set and actualized.

Of what does the world in which we live, act, and create consist? Of matter and psyche? And of what does the work of art consist? Of words, sentences, chapters, and perhaps of pages and paper? In the artist's axiological context of active creation, all these constituents are secondary, and by no means primary: it is not these constituents that axiologically determine the artist's creative context, but, rather, they are themselves determined by that context. This is not meant to deny the legitimacy of studying these constituents, but only to indicate the place appropriate to such study in a real understanding of creative activity as creative activity.

Thus, the author's creative consciousness is not a language-consciousness (in the broadest sense of the word); language-consciousness is merely a passive constituent in creative activity—an immanently surmounted material.

3. The Substitution of the Material-Literary Context for the Author's Axiological Context

We have established, then, that the artist's relationship to words as words is a secondary, derivative moment, which depends on his primary relationship to context, i.e., to the immediate givenness of a lived life and the world of that life (the cognitive-ethical tension of that life). One could say that the artist fashions the world by means of words, and to this end words mut be immanently surmounted as words and must become an expression of the world of others and of the author's relationship to that world. *Verbal* style (the author's relationship to language and the methods of operating with language as determined by that relationship) is a reflection in the given nature of the material of the author's *artistic* style (of his relationship to a life and the world of that life, and of the method of shaping a human being and his world as determined by that relationship). Artistic style works not with words, but with constituent features of the world, with the values of the world and of life; it could be defined as the sum total of the devices for giving form to and consummating a human being and his world. And it is this style that also determines the relationship to the given material (words), whose nature we must know, of course, in order to be able to understand that relationship. The artist's relationship to an object is an immediate relationship to it as a constituent of the event of the world, and it is this that thereupon determines (not in the sense of chronological order, of course, but in that of an axiological hierarchy) his relationship to the object-referring signification of words as constituents of a purely verbal context—that is, determines the utilization of phonetic features (the acoustic image), emotional features, pictorial features, and so on.[z]

The substitution of material for content (or even the mere tendency toward such a substitution) annihilates the artistic task by reducing it to a secondary and wholly dependent constituent—

---

[z] Emotion itself relates axiologically to an object, is directed upon an object, and not upon a word, even if the object is not given apart from the word.

the relationship to words (in doing so, however, the primary constituent—the relationship to the world—is always added, of course, even if in an uncritical form, for without this addition there would simply be nothing to say).

What is also possible, however, is a substitution in which the author's actual axiological context is displaced not by the verbal context (the linguistically conceived language context), but by the literary context—the verbal-art context—that is to say, by language that has been already fashioned for the purposes of some primary artistic task (we have to grant, of course, that somewhere in the absolute past there *was* a primary act of creation that did not proceed in a literary context, since the latter did not exist yet).

According to this conception,[209] the author's act of creation is accomplished totally within the purely literary value-context (without in any respect exceeding its bounds) and is rendered meaningful in all of its constituents solely by that context: it is born (with respect to value) in this context, is consummated in this context, and dies in this context. What the author finds is literary language and literary forms—the world of literature and nothing else—and it is in this literary world that his inspiration is born, i.e., his creative impulse to produce new form-combinations within that literary world, without in any way exceeding its bounds.[aa] In his creative activity, the author overcomes the purely literary resistance of old, purely literary, forms, practices, and traditions (that the author actually does this is unquestionable), without ever encountering a different kind of resistance (the cognitive-ethical resistance of the hero and his world). And he does this, moreover, in order to produce a new *literary* combination out of purely *literary* elements. The reader, in his turn, must also "feel" the author's act of creation solely against the background of the usual literary manner, i.e., he, too, must not exceed the bounds of the value-and-meaning context of literature materially conceived.

In reality, the author's creative value-and-meaning context (the context that renders the work he produces meaningful) does not

---

[aa] It is true that there may be works which were conceived, nurtured, and born in the purely literary world, but these works are very rarely discussed, in view of their complete artistic nullity (although personally, I would not venture to assert categorically that such works are really possible).

in the least coincide with the purely literary context (moreover, a materially conceived literary context). The latter, along with its values, enters, of course, as a constituent part into the former context, except that here it is not a determining but an entirely determined context. The creative act also has to determine itself in the material-literary context, has to assume an axiological position in that context as well, and, undoubtedly, an essential one. But this position is determined by the more fundamental position of the author in the event of being, in the values of the world. The author's axiological position is established first and foremost in relation to the hero and his world (the world of his life), and it is this artistic position of the author that also determines his material-literary position.

One could say that the forms of an artistic vision and consummation of the world determine the external literary devices, and not vice versa; that the architectonic of the artistic world determines the composition of a work (the order, the disposition, the concatenation, and the consummation of verbal masses), and not vice versa. The author is compelled to contend with old or with more recent literary forms, compelled to overcome their resistance or to find support in them, yet what underlies this movement is the most essential, the determining, the *primary artistic contention*—the contention with the cognitive-ethical directedness of a life and its valid persistence as a distinct life. This is where the act of creation (for which everything else is but a means) attains the point of highest tension, where every artist attains the point of highest tension in his creative activity, if he is significantly and seriously a *primary artist*, that is, if he is an artist who collides and contends immediately with the raw cognitive-ethical element of a lived life, with the chaos of a lived life (element and chaos from the aesthetic standpoint), and it is only this collision that ignites the purely artistic spark. Every artist in every one of his works is each time compelled to conquer artistically [indecipherable]; is compelled again and again to justify, and justify essentially, the aesthetic standpoint as such. An author enters into immediate contact with the hero and his world, and it is only through this unmediated axiological relationship to the hero that the author determines his own position as artistic; it is only through this axiological relationship to the hero that the formal literary devices for the first time acquire their validity, meaning, and axiological weight (prove to be necessary and important as events), and that the movement of an event is also introduced into the *material* literary sphere. (Cf. the context constituted by periodicals: the struggle among periodicals, the life of periodicals, and the theory of periodicals.) * 210

Not a single complex of concrete, material-literary (formal) devices (and all the more so, a complex of linguistic, verbal elements, such as words, sentences, verbal symbols, semantic series, and the like) can be understood as style and composition solely from the standpoint of a narrowly aesthetic, literary system of regularities or laws (which is always reflected, secondary, derivative in character)—except for the deliberate artistic experiment. That is, it cannot be understood solely from the author and his purely aesthetic energy (this also applies to lyric and music), but necessarily requires that we also take into account the meaning-governed sequence of life, the meaning-governed cognitive-ethical autonomy of the hero's life, the meaning-governed laws or regularities of his *act-performing consciousness*, for everything that is aesthetically valid encompasses not a void, but the persistent and self-regulated (aesthetically inexplicable) directedness to meaning on the part of an *act-performing life*.

A work does not break down into a number of purely aesthetic compositional constituents joined according to purely aesthetic compositional laws (and even less into linguistic constituents: into verbal symbols with an emotional "nimbus" that are joined according to the laws of verbal-symbolic association). On the contrary, an artistic whole represents the overcoming (*essential* overcoming) of a certain necessary whole of meaning (the whole of a possible life that possesses validity for lived life). In the artistic whole, we have to do with two powers and with two interdependent systems of laws established by those powers; every constituent in the artistic whole is determined in terms of two value-systems, and in every constituent these two systems are in a state of intense and essential axiological interaction—they are the two paired powers that endow every constituent of the whole and the entire whole itself with the axiological weight of an event.

The artist never begins from the very outset purely as an artist, i.e., he cannot deal from the very outset with nothing but aesthetic elements. The work of art is regulated by two systems of laws: the hero's and the author's, i.e., the laws of content and the laws of form. Where the artist deals from the very outset with nothing but aesthetic quantities, the result is a contrived and empty work that does not overcome anything and, in effect, does not produce anything that has axiological weight. A hero cannot be created from start to finish out of nothing but purely aesthetic elements, a hero cannot be "made": he would not be alive, and one would not "feel" his purely aesthetic validity. The author cannot *think up* a hero, devoid of any independent status in relation to the author's creative act that affirms him and gives him a form. The author-*artist finds* the hero as already given *prior* to and apart from his own purely artistic act: he cannot engender the hero out of himself—such a hero would be unconvincing.

Of course, the hero we mean is the *possible* hero, that is, the one that has not yet become a hero, has not yet been shaped aesthetically, for the hero of a *work* is already invested in an artistically valid form, that is, we mean the givenness of a human being as *another*. It is this givenness of the *other* that the author-artist finds prior to his own artistic act[bb] and it is only in relation to this givenness that his act of aesthetic consummation acquires axiological weight. The author's artistic act encounters a certain persistent (resilient, impermeable) reality which it cannot ignore and which it cannot totally absorb into itself. It is this extra-aesthetic reality of the hero that will enter as a shaped reality into the work produced. And it is this reality of the hero—the reality of another consciousness—that constitutes the *object* of aesthetic vision which imparts *aesthetic objectivity* to that vision. This reality of the hero is not the reality (the actuality and possibility, regardless of whether physical or psychic) of natural science, the reality confronted by the author's free creative imagination, but rather the inward reality of a life's own directedness to values and meaning. What we require from the author in this respect is axiological verisimilitude—we require that his images or figures should have the axiological weight of an event. We require, that is, not cognitive and empirical-practical reality, but the *reality of an event* (not a physically possible movement, but a movement that is possible as an event): this may be the event of a life *in the sense of axiological weightiness,* even if it is impossible and improbable physically and psychologically (psychologically understood here in accordance with its method as a branch of natural science).

[bb] We do not mean, of course, the hero's prior givenness empirically—his being on hand in a particular place and at a particular time.

That is the way we measure artistic verisimilitude, artistic objectivity (i.e., faithfulness to the artistic object—the cognitive-ethical directedness of a human being's lived life): the verisimilitude of plot, character, situation, lyrical motif, and so forth. We must be able to feel in a work the resistance of the reality of being *qua* event; where this resistance is absent and where there is no opening into the axiological event of a world,²¹¹ the given work is an excogitation and lacks any artistic convincingness.

There can be, of course, no objective, universally valid, criteria for identifying aesthetic objectivity: this is inherently a matter of intuitive cogency alone. Behind the transgredient moments that constitute artistic form and artistic consummation, we must vividly feel the presence of that possible human consciousness to which these moments are transgredient and which they cherish and bring to consummation; besides our own creative or co-creative consciousness, we must vividly feel *another* consciousness—the consciousness upon which our creative self-activity is directed as upon an *other* consciousness. To feel this means to feel the form, to feel its saving power, its axiological weight—to feel its beauty. (I said "to feel," for in feeling it, we do not necessarily have to be conscious of it in a theoretical, cognitively distinct, manner.)

Form cannot be referred to *oneself*, for when we try to refer it to ourselves we become other than what we were for ourselves, we cease to be ourselves, we cease to live from within ourselves: we become possessed. And, in any case, the attempt to do so results in the destruction of the significance and axiological weight of form in all domains of art, except for certain kinds of lyric and music. When we attempt to do so, it becomes impossible to deepen and expand artistic contemplation: the spuriousness of it is instantly exposed, while perception becomes passive and unsteady. There are two participants in the artistic event: one is passively real, the other is active (the author/contemplator). The withdrawal of one of the participants destroys the artistic event, and we are left with nothing but a misleading illusion of an artistic event—with a counterfeit (an artistic deception of oneself): the artistic event is unreal, it has not really taken place.

Artistic objectivity is artistic *kindness*, and kindness cannot be objectless, cannot have weight in a void: there must be an *other* who axiologically stands over against it. Certain kinds of art are called objectless (ornament, arabesque, music), and this is correct, in the sense that there is no *determinate* (internally differentiated and delimited) object-content in these arts. But they are not objectless in our sense, of course; there *is* an object in them that imparts aesthetic objectivity to them. In music, we can feel the resistance, the persistent presence of a possible consciousness, a lived-life consciousness, a consciousness incapable of being consummated from within itself, and it is only insofar as we feel it that we perceive the power, the axiological weight of music, and that we perceive every new step it takes as an act of overcoming and a victory. In feeling this possible cognitive-ethical tension or directedness, which is incapable of being consummated from within itself yet is mortal,[cc] we also feel the great privilege *qua* event of being another, of being situated *outside* the bounds of another possible consciousness; we feel our own gift-bestowing, resolving, and consummating possibility, our own aesthetically actualized formal power; *we create musical form not in an axiological void* and *not amidst other musical forms (music in the midst of music)*, but *in the event* of lived life. And it is only this that renders musical form *serious*, renders it valid and momentous *qua* event. (The arabesque of pure style: behind style we always feel a possible soul.) Thus, objectless art does have a content (i.e., a possible life's persistent tension or directedness *qua* event), but this content is not determined and internally differentiated as an *object*.

Thus, in the world of forms alone, form has no validity or force. The value-context in which a work of literature is actualized and in which it is rendered meaningful is not just a literary context. A work of art must feel its way toward and find an axiological reality, the reality of the hero as an event. (Psychology is an equally technical moment that lacks the character of an event.)

4. Tradition and Style

Style is the *unity* of two kinds of devices: the devices of giving form to and consummating the hero and his world, and the

---

[cc] In feeling, that is, this *penitent and petitionary infinitude*, this possibility of an everlasting discontentedness, an essentially necessary and rightful discontentedness.

devices determined by the former, the devices of working and adapting (immanently overcoming) the material. What is the relationship that obtains between style and the author as an individuality? What is the relationship of style to content, i.e., to the world of others that is being consummated? What significance does tradition have in the value-context of the author-contemplator?

A confident unity of style (the great and powerful style) is possible only where a life's cognitive-ethical tension or directedness constitutes a unity, where the task-to-be-achieved that governs its directedness is incontestable. That is the first condition. The second condition consists in the incontestability and confidence of the position of being situated outside that life,[dd] in the firmness and incontestability of the place of art in the whole of culture. A fortuitous position of outsideness cannot have any confidence in itself; style cannot be fortuitous. These two conditions are intimately connected with each other and mutually interdependent. The great style encompasses all domains of art or it does not exist at all. For it is first and foremost a style of seeing the world, and only after that—a style of working the material.

It should be evident that style excludes innovation in the creation of new content, resting as it does on the stable unity of life's cognitive-ethical value-context. Thus, Classicism does not seek to produce new cognitive-ethical values, a new directedness of lived life as such, but, rather, it applies all its strength to the moments constituting aesthetic consummation and to the immanent deepening of life's traditional directedness from within itself. (The novelty of content in Romanticism; the contemporaneity of content in Realism.) Tension and innovation in the creation of content are, in the majority of cases, already a sign of a crisis in the domain of aesthetic creation.

The crisis of authorship: the very place of art in the whole of culture, in the event of being, is reevaluated; any traditional place of art appears to be unjustified; the artist is *something determinate*—it is impossible to be an artist, it is impossible to become totally part of this limited sphere; the point is not to surpass others in art, but to surpass art itself; the immanent criteria of a

---

[dd] Ultimately, as we shall see, a religious confidence or faith in the fact that life is not solitary, that it is intent and does not proceed from within itself in an axiological void.

given domain of culture are not accepted any longer, nor are the domains of culture as determinate cultural domains. Romanticism and its idea of integral or "total" creation and of "total" man. One strives to act and create directly in the unitary event of being as its sole participant; one is unable to humble oneself to the status of a toiler, unable to determine one's own place in the event of being through others, to place oneself on a par with others.

But the crisis of authorship may also take a different direction. The very position of the author's outsideness is shaken and is no longer considered essential: one contests the author's right to be situated outside lived life and to consummate it. All stable transgredient forms begin to disintegrate (first of all in prose—from Dostoevsky to Bely; the crisis of authorship is always of lesser significance in lyric—Annensky,[212] and so forth). Lived life becomes intelligible and obtains the weight of an event only from within itself, only where I live and experience it as an *I*, in the form of my relationship to myself, in the value-categories of my *I-for-myself*: to understand means to project myself into an object and experience it from within, look at it with its own eyes, give up my own situatedness outside its bounds as unessential. All those forces which consolidate or give body to a life from outside are seen as unessential and fortuitous, and a deep distrust of any outsideness develops (in religion this is associated with the "immanentization" of God, the "psychologization" of both God and religion, with the inability to understand the church as an outward institution, and with the general reevaluation of everything that is inward-from-within). Lived life tends to recoil and hide deep inside itself, tends to withdraw into its own inner infinitude, *is afraid of boundaries*, strives to dissolve them, for it has no faith in the essentialness and kindness of the power that gives form from outside; any viewpoint from outside is refused. And, in the process, the *culture of boundaries* (the necessary condition for a confident and deep style) becomes impossible, of course; boundaries are just what life has nothing to do with; all creative energies withdraw from the boundaries, leaving them to the mercy of fate.

Aesthetic culture is a culture of boundaries and hence presupposes that life is enveloped by a warm atmosphere of deepest trust. A confident and founded act of constituting and shaping the *boundaries* of man and his world (outer as well as *inner* boundaries) presupposes the existence of a firm and secure position outside of him, presupposes a position in which the spirit can abide for a long time, can be master of its own powers, and can act without constraint. It should be evident that this presupposes an essential axiological consolidatedness of the enveloping atmosphere. Where this axiologically "bodied" atmosphere is absent, where the position of outsideness is fortuitous and unstable, and where the living axiological understanding is totally immanent to a life experienced from within (practical-egoistic life, social life, moral life, etc.)ᵉᵉ—any axiologically prolonged and creative dwelling on the boundaries of man and his life is impossible, and the only thing one can do is to mimic or simulate a likeness to man and his life (that is, to utilize the transgredient moments in a negative way).

The negative utilization of transgredient constituents (of the "excess" of seeing, knowing, and valuation), which occurs in satire and in the comical (but not in humor,[213] of course), depends to a considerable extent on the exceptional weight of the life that is experienced axiologically from within (moral life, social life, etc.) and on the lowered weight (or even complete devaluation) of the axiological position of outsideness—on the loss, that is, of everything that founded and strengthened the position of outsideness and, consequently, also on the loss of that exterior of life which exists outside the bounds of meaning. This exterior (the exterior independent of meaning) becomes meaningless, i.e., it is defined negatively in relation to the nonaesthetically possible meaning and turns into an exposing or unmasking potency (whereas in a positive consummation this meaning-"exempted" exterior becomes an aesthetically valued exterior). In life, the moment of transgredience is established and organized by a tradition (outward appearance, the exterior, manners of comportment, etc.; the communal way of everyday life, etiquette, etc.), and the collapse of the tradition exposes their meaninglessness; life breaks up all forms from within. The category of "the ugly" is utilized. In Romanticism, we observe an "oxymoronic" construction of images or figures: the contradiction between the inner and outer, between social status and essence, between infinitude of content

---

ᵉᵉThat is, where a life's axiological weight is actually experienced only when we put ourselves inside that life (empathize ourselves into it), assume its own point of view, experience it in the category of the *I*.

and finitude of embodiment, is forcefully accentuated. There is no place where one could put the exterior of man and his life, and there is no founded position for providing it with a place. (Style as the unitary and finished picture of the world's exterior: the conjunction of exterior man—his costume, his deportment—with a setting. A *world view* organizes and unifies the performed acts [and anything can be understood from within as a performed act]; it imparts unity to a life's act-performing directedness to meaning—the unity of a life's answerability, the unity of its going beyond itself, of surmounting itself. *Style* imparts unity to the world's transgredient exterior, its reflection to the outside, its advertedness to the outside, its boundaries [the shaping and combining of boundaries]. A world view organizes and unifies man's *horizon;* style organizes and unifies his *environment.*) A more detailed examination of the negative utilization of the transgredient or "excessive" moments in satire and in the comical (ridiculing by way of given being), and also of the distinctive position of humor, exceeds the bounds of our inquiry.

But the crisis of authorship may also proceed in still another direction: the position of outsideness may begin to incline toward the ethical position, and thus lose its purely aesthetic distinctiveness. The interest in the pure phenomenality of life, its pure "viewability"[214]—the interest, that is, in the contented consummation of it in the present and the past—begins to slacken; not the absolute future, but the proximate, social (and even political) future—the proximate morally imperative plan of the future— undermines the stable boundaries of man and his world. The position of outsideness becomes excruciatingly ethical (the insulted and injured as such become the heroes for the act of seeing— which is no longer purely artistic, of course). There is no confident, calm, immovable, and rich position of outsideness. There is no inner *axiological tranquillity* required for such a position (that is, there is no inwardly wise awareness of the mortality of cognitive-ethical directedness, or its hopelessness—a hopelessness mitigated by trust, or faith). By tranquillity, we do not mean the psychological notion of tranquillity (as a state of the psyche); we do not mean simply a factually present tranquillity. We mean a tranquillity as a founded axiological posture of consciousness that constitutes a precondition for aesthetic creativity; tranquillity as an expression of trust, or faith, during the event of being; an answerable, calm tranquillity.

We must say a few words about the difference between aesthetic outsideness and ethical outsideness (moral, social, political, practical-life outsideness). Aesthetic outsideness and the constituent of isolation; situatedness outside being, whence being assumes the character of pure phenomenality; liberation or release from the future.

Inner infinitude breaks into the open and finds no repose; life is intensely principled. Aestheticism, covering a void, is the second site of crises. The hero is lost; a playing with purely aesthetic elements. Stylization of a possible essential aesthetic directedness. Outside the bounds of style, the creator's individuality loses its assurance and is perceived as irresponsible. Responsibility for individual creativity is possible only in a style, when this responsibility is founded and sustained by a tradition.

The crisis of life, in distinction to the crisis of authorship (although the former often accompanies the latter), consists in populating life with literary heroes, in life's falling away from its absolute future, in the transformation of life into a tragedy without a chorus and without an author.

These, then, are the conditions for the author's participation in the event of being, for the strength and foundedness of his creative position. It is impossible to prove one's *alibi* in the event of being. Nothing answerable, serious, and significant can exist where that *alibi* becomes a presupposition for creation and utterance. Special answerability is indispensable (in an autonomous domain of culture)—one cannot create directly in God's world. This specialization of answerability, however, can be founded only upon a deep trust in the highest level of authority that blesses a culture—upon trust, that is, in the fact that there is another—the highest other—who answers for my own special answerability, and trust in the fact that I do not act in an axiological void. Outside this trust, only empty pretensions are possible.

The author's actual creative act (and, in point of fact, any performed act) always proceeds along the boundaries (the axiological boundaries) of the aesthetic world, along the boundaries of the reality of the given (the reality of the given is an aesthetic reality), along the boundary of the body and the boundary of the soul; and it proceeds in the spirit. The spirit, however, does not exist yet; everything is yet-to-be for the spirit, whereas everything that already exists is, for the spirit, something that *has* already existed.

All that remains to be done is to deal briefly with the problem of the beholder's relationship to the author (we already touched upon this problem in the preceding sections). The author is authoritative and indispensable for the reader, whose relationship to the author is not a relationship to him as an individual, as another human being, as a hero, as a determinate entity in being, but rather a relationship to him as a *principle* that needs to be followed (only the biographical approach to the author turns him into a hero), into a determinate, existent human being, who can be contemplated).

The author's individuality as a creator is a creative individuality of a special, nonaesthetic, order; it is the active individuality of seeing and forming, and not the individuality that is seen and formed. The author becomes an individuality proper only where we assign to him the individual world of the heroes that he created and shaped or where he is partially objectified as a narrator. The author cannot and must not assume for us the determinateness of a person, for we are *in* him, we enter into and adapt to his active seeing. It is only upon finishing artistic contemplation, i.e., only when the author no longer actively guides our seeing—it is only then that we objectify our author-guided self-activity (our self-activity is his self-activity) in the form of a certain person, in the form of an individualized countenance of the author, which we often place into the world of the heroes that he created. But this objectified author (the author who has ceased to be a principle of seeing and has become an object that is seen) is quite distinct from the author as the hero of biography (a rather unprincipled form from the standpoint of scholarly discipline). The attempt to explain the determinateness of his creations from the individuality of his "face," to explain his creative self-activity from his existence: insofar as this is possible. This determines the position and method of biography as a form of scholarship.

The author must be understood first of all from the event of a work as a participant in that event and as an authoritative guide for the reader in that event. To understand the author in the historical world of his time, to understand his place in a social collective, his class position: here we go outside the bounds of an analysis of the event of a work and enter the domain of history; a purely historical study cannot but take into account all of these moments. The methodology of literary history exceeds the bounds of our inquiry.

For the reader, the author inside a work is the sum total of the creative principles that have to be actualized; he is the unity of the transgredient moments of seeing that are actively referred to the hero and his world. The individuation of the author as a human being is no longer a primary but a secondary creative act performed by the reader, the critic, the historian, independently of the author as an active principle of seeing—an act in which the author himself is rendered passive.

Supplementary Section

. . . is conditioned by the time of the researcher's life, as well as by the purely fortuitous condition of the materials, and this moment—the moment that introduces a certain degree of architectonic stability—is purely aesthetic in character. This is what characterizes Dante's map of the world, with its coinciding geographical, astronomical, and historical centers—centers of value as well as of events: the earth, Jerusalem, the event of redemption. Strictly speaking, geography knows no far or near, here and there; it is devoid of any absolute axiological standard of measurement within its chosen totality (the earth). And history, likewise, knows no past, present, and future; it knows no long or short time, no "long ago" or "recently"—as absolutely unique and nonconvertible moments. The time of history is itself nonreversible, of course, but within it all relations are fortuitous and relative (and reversible), for there is no absolute center of value. History and geography are invariably aestheticized to a certain degree.

From the physico-mathematical standpoint, the space and time of a human being's life constitute no more than negligible[215] segments[ff] of one infinite space and time, and it is only this, of course, that guarantees their univocity and determinateness with respect to meaning in any theoretical judgment. But, from within a human life, they acquire a unique center of value, in relation to which they gain body, [indecipherable]. In correlation with the "bodied" or consolidated time of human life, artistic time and space, nonconvertible and stably architectonic, acquire an emotional-volitional tonality and include [?] eternity and extra-

---

[ff] The word "negligible" is distinctively intonated and already possesses an aesthetic meaning.

temporality, [indecipherable] and infinitude, the whole and the part—as such.

It should be clear that we are speaking here of the *formal* ordering of a temporal and spatial whole, and not of its ordering with respect to content; we are speaking not only of the moment constituted by a plot [*fabula*], but also of the moment constituted by empirical form. Both the internal time of a plot and the external time of its transmission, both internal spatial vision and external spatial representation, possess axiological weight—as the environment and the horizon of a mortal human being's life, and as the course or progression of that life. If man were *not* mortal, the emotional-volitional tone of this progression—of this "before" and "after," this "not yet" and "already," this "now" and "then," this "always" and "never"—the gravity and significance of its sounding rhythm—would be extinguished. Once you annihilate the moment constituted by the life of a mortal human being, the axiological light of all rhythmic and formal moments will be extinguished. The point here is not, of course, the mathematically determinate duration of a human life, for that duration could be shorter or longer; the only important thing is that a life and its horizon have terminal limits—birth and death. It is only the presence of these terminal points, along with everything conditioned by them, that creates the emotional-volitional tonality of time's passage in a circumscribed life and [indecipherable] space—the reflection of the effort and directedness of a mortal human being; even eternity and limitlessness acquire their axiological meaning only in correlation with a life that is determined.

Let us now turn our attention to the ordering of meaning. Architectonics—as the intuitionally necessary, nonfortuitous disposition and integration of concrete, unique parts and moments into a consummated whole—can exist only around a given human being as a hero. A thought, a problem, and a theme are in themselves incapable of providing the foundation of architectonics, for they are themselves in need of a concrete architectonic whole in order to become consummated in any degree at all. A thought as such contains, inherently, the energy of extraspatial and extratemporal infinitude, in relation to which anything concrete is merely fortuitous; a thought can provide no more than the direction for seeing something concrete, but a direction that is infinite, a direction incapable of *consummating* a whole.

Even a prosaic, discursive whole constituted by a scientific or scholarly study is conditioned not by the essence of its fundamental thought, but by moments that are completely fortuitous in relation to that essence, and, among these moments, first and foremost by the consciously or unconsciously limited horizon of its author. Even a philosophical system is closed and consummated only externally, whereas internally it is open and infinite, for the unity of cognition is always a yet-to-be-achieved unity. It would be interesting from this point of view to examine the architectonics of such a work as Kant's *Critique of Pure Reason*, and to determine the origin of those moments in it which bring about its consummation. One would fairly readily see that these moments are aesthetic and even anthropomorphic in character, inasmuch as Kant believed in the possibility of a closed system, a closed table of categories.

The temporal and spatial articulation and disposition of the parts of a discursive whole, even of such an elementary one as a syllogism (antecedents, consequents, etc.), reflect not the moment itself[?], but the temporal process of the progression of human thinking, although not the fortuitous, psychological process, to be sure, but the aestheticized, rhythmic process of thinking. The architectonic of a prosaic, discursive whole is closest to musical architectonics, for a whole that is poetic includes too many moments that are spatial and visual. In order to become consummated, i.e., to assume the form of a finished work, prose must utilize the aestheticized process of the creative individual who is its author, that is, it must reflect within itself an image of the finished *event* of his act of creation, inasmuch as from within its own meaning, abstracted from the author, prose is incapable of finding any consummating and architectonically integrating moments. No special explanation is necessary for the fact that the *sensuous material*, which fills up the spatial-temporal order, fills up the schema of the internal event constituted by the plot [*fabula*] as well as the schema of the external composition of a work—the inner and outer rhythm, the inner and outer form—is also exclusively ordered around the axiological center constituted by a human being, i.e., the sensuous material *clothes* this human being himself as well as his world.

As for ethical meaning, we shall elucidate it in general terms when speaking of the difference between an event that is ethical and an event that is aesthetic (to concretize the moment constituted by ethical meaning at this point would be to anticipate). An ethical event with its invariably open, yet-to-be-realized meaning, may be given closure and may be ordered architectonically only by transposing the center of value from what-is-yet-to-be-achieved into what-is-given, i.e., into a given human being as a participant in that event.

Let us clarify everything we have said about the architectonic function of the axiological center constituted by a given human being within an artistic whole by analyzing a concrete example. Our analysis will isolate only those moments of the whole which are pertinent in the present context; it will not deal with other moments, even if they may be highly essential for a total artistic impression, in order to avoid anticipating, as far as possible, what will be dealt with later. This specialized character of our analysis, i.e., the fact that it does not approximate, even at times, an exhaustive treatment of the artistic whole, should be kept in mind throughout.

I shall analyze Pushkin's lyrical poem "Parting,"[216] written in 1830. Here is the poem:

Bound for the shores of your distant homeland
You were leaving this foreign land.
In that unforgettable hour, in that hour of sadness,
I wept before you for a long time.
My hands, growing ever colder,
Strained to hold you back.
My moans implored you not to break off
The terrible anguish of parting.

But you tore away your lips
From our bitter kiss;
From a land of gloomy exile
You called me to another land.
You said: "On the day of our meeting
In the shade of olive trees
Beneath an eternally blue sky,
We shall once more, my beloved, unite our kisses of love."

But there—alas!—where the sky's vault
Shines with blue radiance,
Where the waters slumber beneath the cliffs,
You have fallen asleep forever.
Your beauty and your sufferings
Have vanished in the grave—

And the kiss of our meeting has vanished as well . . .
But I am waiting for that kiss—you owe it to me . . .[217]

There are two heroes in this poem: the "lyrical hero" proper (in the given case—the objectified author) and "she" (probably Riznich), and, consequently, there are also two emotional-volitional attitudes toward objects, two axiological contexts, two unique points of reference for ordering the axiological moments or constituents of being. The unity of the lyrical whole is reestablished by the fact that the axiological context of the heroine is encompassed and affirmed, as a whole, by the hero's context—is integrated into the hero's context as a constituent moment of it; and both of these contexts are, in their turn, encompassed by the unitary—properly aesthetic—axiologically founding *active* context of author and reader.

By somewhat anticipating what will be dealt with later, we could say: the position occupied by the aesthetic *subiectum*, i.e., by the author and the reader—the *creators of form*—the position from which their artistic, form-giving self-activity proceeds, may be defined as situated—temporally, spatially, and with respect to meaning—*outside* all constituents, without exception, of the inner architectonic field of artistic vision. It is this outside position that makes it possible for the first time to encompass the entire architectonic—the axiological, temporal, spatial, and meaning-governed architectonic—through a unitary, equally founding, self-activity. Aesthetic empathizing (*Einfühlung*)—the seeing of objects and heroes from within—is actively accomplished from this *outside* standpoint, the standpoint where material obtained through empathizing, along with the matter of outer seeing and hearing, is integrated and shaped into one concrete, architectonic whole. The outside standpoint of the aesthetic *subiectum* constitutes the necessary condition for integrating the contexts that form around several heroes into a single formal-aesthetic, axiological context (this is especially the case in epic genres).

In our poem, all of the concrete moments that constitute the architectonic whole are concentrated into two centers of value—the hero and the heroine. The first circle, moreover, encompasses the second, is wider than the second, and both of them are equally encompassed—as a single event—by the form-giving activity of the author/reader. Thus, we are dealing with three interpenetrating contexts of value, and, consequently, the intonation of almost every word in the poem must be performed likewise in three directions: the real-life intonation of the heroine, the equally real-life intonation of the hero, and the formal intonation of the author/reader (in an actual recitation of the poem, the performer has the task of finding the "resultant" of these three directions of intonating). Let us examine, then, the disposition of the unique and concrete moments in this [indecipherable] architectonic:

Bound for the shores of your distant homeland
You were leaving this foreign land . . .

The "distant homeland" is located in the axiological spatial-temporal context of the heroine's life. It is for her, in her emotional-volitional tone, that the possible spatial horizon becomes a *homeland:* it is a moment in the event of her life. And it is also in correlation with the heroine that a certain spatial whole—as a constituent of her fate—becomes a *foreign land.* Her movement to her homeland ("you were leaving . . .") is toned more in the direction of the hero, in the context of his fate: in her direction it would have been better to say "you were returning," for she is going home, after all. In her fate as well as his, distance becomes axiologically consolidated (the epithet "distant")—they will be far from each other.

In a variant reading of the opening lines (cited by Annenkov),[218] it is the value-context of the hero that predominates:

Bound for the shores of a distant foreign land
You were leaving your homeland . . .

In these lines, the foreign land (Italy) and the homeland (Russia) are axiologically determined in relation to the hero.

In that unforgettable hour, in that hour of sadness,
I wept before you for a long time . . .

The hour with its [indecipherable] and temporal extension is toned by distance and has taken on axiological weight in the unique temporal sequences of the determined mortal lives of each—as the hour of their parting. The hero's axiological context predominates in the choice of words and central images.

My hands, growing ever colder,
Strained to hold you back.
My moans implored you not to break off
The terrible anguish of parting.
. . . .
You said: "On the day of our meeting
In the shade of olive trees
Beneath an eternally blue sky,
We shall once more, my beloved, unite our kisses of love."

But there—alas!—where the sky's vault
Shines with blue radiance,
Where the waters slumber beneath the cliffs,
You have fallen asleep forever.
Your beauty and your sufferings
Have vanished in the grave—
And the kiss of our meeting has vanished as well . . .
But I am waiting for that kiss—you owe it to me.

I shall not continue to dwell on this basically understandable poem: it should be evident that all the moments of this whole (the moments expressed directly as well as those that are unexpressed) become *values* and are ordered in correlation with one of the heroes or a human being in general—as his fate. Let us turn our attention to other, more essential moments of this whole.

Nature as well participates in this whole, participates in the *event* that this whole constitutes. Nature is animated here and brought into communion with the world of human givenness in two directions. First, as the environment and background of the event constituted by the promised and longed-for meeting of the hero and the heroine (the kiss beneath an eternally blue sky) and as the environment of the event of her actual death ("where the sky's vault shines . . . / you have fallen asleep forever"); in the first case, moreover, the background reinforces the joy of their meeting, it is in concord with that joy, whereas in the second case, it contrasts with the grief over her death. That is, here nature is animated and brought into communion with a human fate at the level of the plot [*fabula*]. Second, human movement and human life *qua* event are introduced inside nature: "the sky's *vault*"; the metaphors "the sky's vault *shines*" and "the waters *slumber* beneath the cliffs"—the cliffs shelter the sleep of waters; the eternally blue sky—the sky's eternity is correlated in terms of value with a human life that is determined (delimited). Some of the metaphors, moreover, are anthropomorphic in character ("shines," "slumber"), while others bring nature into communion with a human fate ("the sky's vault," "eternally blue"). This second direction of animating nature does not depend on the unmediated vivifying of nature at the level of the plot [fabula].

Now we must consider the following moments of the whole: the inner spatial form, the inner rhythm of the event's unfolding (inner artistic time), the external rhythm, the intonative structure, and, finally, the theme.

In the given poem, we find three sculptural-pictorial-dramatic images: the image of parting ("my hands, growing ever colder, strained to hold you back . . . ," "you said . . ."), the image of the promised meeting (their lips will join in a kiss beneath a sky forever blue), and, finally, the image of death (nature and the grave in which her beauty and her sufferings have vanished). These three images strive toward a certain purely representational completeness.

The inner temporal rhythm of the event is as follows: parting and the promised meeting, death and the actual meeting in the future. A continuous interconnection is established on the plane of events between the past and the future of the heroes through the present of remembering: the parting is the arsis, the promised meeting is the thesis;[219] death is the arsis, yet there will be a meeting, nevertheless—the thesis.

Let us now consider the intonative structure. Every word not only designates an object, not only calls forth a certain image, not only sounds in a particular way, but also expresses a certain emotional-volitional reaction to the object designated, and this reaction finds its expression in the intonation of the word when it is actually pronounced. The sound-image of a word is not only the bearer of rhythm, but is also thoroughly permeated by intonation, and in the actual reading of a work conflicts may arise between intonation and rhythm. Of course, rhythm and intonation are not elements that are alien to each other in kind: rhythm, too, expresses the emotional-volitional coloration of the whole, but it is less objective. The main thing, however, is that rhythm represents, almost exclusively, a purely formal reaction of the author to the event as a whole, whereas intonation is for the most part the intonational reaction of the hero to an object within the whole and, in conforming to the distinctive traits of each object, it is internally more differentiated and diversified. Nonetheless, the abstract separation of intonation and rhythm does not coincide with the other, equally abstract, separation—the separation of the hero's reaction and the reaction of the author: both intonation and rhythm are capable of expressing simultaneously the reaction of the hero as well as the reaction of the author. For the most part, the author's emotional-volitional reaction finds its expression in rhythm, the hero's—in intonation. The hero's reaction, i.e., the expression of the *evaluation* of an object in the hero's axiological context, we shall call realistic; the intonation and rhythm corresponding to it will be a realistic intonation and a realistic rhythm. The author's reaction, i.e., the evaluation of an object in the author's context, we shall call formal; the intonation and rhythm corresponding to it will be a formal intonation and a formal rhythm. Formal intonation and realistic rhythm are met with less often than realistic intonation and formal rhythm. As we shall see, an emotional-volitional reaction and evaluation can be expressed not only by intonation and rhythm, but also by all the constituents of an artistic whole and all aspects of a single word—by images and objects, as well as by concepts.

Let us clarify the distinction we have drawn. In drama, intonation usually has a purely realistic character. Dramatic dialogue as such represents a struggle between the axiological contexts of the dramatis personae; it is an expression of the collision between different emotional-volitional positions assumed by the dramatis personae in one and the same event—an expression of the struggle between different valuations. Every participant in a dramatic dialogue expresses in direct speech and with every word both an object and his active reaction to that object—the intonation is realistic (it is a lived-life intonation); the author, on the other hand, finds no immediate expression. But all these contending expressions of the characters' reactions are encompassed by a single rhythm (in tragedy, by iambic trimeter)[220] which imparts a certain unity of tone to all the utterances, that is, reduces all of them to a single emotional-volitional denominator, as it were. The rhythm expresses a reaction to another reaction—the author's unitary and uniform, purely formal-aesthetic reaction to all of the contending realistic reactions of the heroes, to the whole tragic event in its entirety—and thus aestheticizes that event, i.e., extracts it out of reality (cognitive-ethical reality) and frames it artistically.

The iambic trimeter does not express, of course, the author's individual reaction to the equally individual event constituted by a given tragedy. But the general character of the attitude it expresses in relation to what is happening, namely, its aesthetic character (the entire tragedy, with exception of almost the choruses alone, is written in trimeter), in itself performs the function of footlights, as it were: it separates the aesthetic event from lived life. As we know, certain rhythmic variations (deviations) are possible within a particular metrical structure of the iambic trimeter. Usually, these variations perform a realistic function—they underscore and reinforce the lived-life intonations of the heroes; but sometimes they [indecipherable] convey the rhythm of a speaker's inner life (the tension, the acceleration of tempo, etc.). We shall not deal in the present context with other constituents of a tragedy that express the author and his formal reaction (and sometimes his nonformal reaction as well), such as the choruses of ancient tragedy (to some extent), the disposition of parts, the selection of images or figures, the orchestration of sound, and other purely formal constituents. Nor shall we deal here with the fact that the sound-image of words may perform not only rhythmic and intonational functions, but also purely representational functions (onomatopoeia).

In narrative literature (epos), the direct speech of the heroes is intonated realistically, as in drama. The realistic reaction may be predominant in the indirect speech of the heroes quoted by the author, but what may also predominate is the formal reaction of the author. After all, the author can transmit the words of the hero that express his axiological position by expressing, in the tone of the transmission, his own relationship to the words of the hero, his own position in relation to the hero, e.g., ironically, with surprise, enthusiastically, in a profoundly calm epic tone, etc. The description of objects and the recounting of events in narrative literature are sometimes accomplished predominantly from the standpoint of their value (the value of objects and events) for the heroes, in the tone of the heroes' possible attitude toward these objects and events; sometimes, however, the axiological context of the author is totally predominant, i.e., the words describing the world of the heroes express the author's reaction to the heroes and their world. But regardless of which reaction is predominant, the word in narrative literature is always the author's word and, consequently, it also expresses the reaction of the author, even if cer-

tain words of a whole complex of words may be placed *almost* totally at the disposal of the heroes. In this sense, we could say that
every word in narrative literature expresses a reaction to another
reaction, the author's reaction to the reaction of the hero; that is,
every concept, image, and object lives on two planes, is rendered
meaningful in two value-contexts—in the context of the hero and
in that of the author. We shall see later that these axiological reactions are located in different cultural worlds: after all, the hero's
reaction and evaluation, his emotional-volitional attitude, have a
cognitive-ethical and realistic (lived-life) character; the author reacts to the reaction of the hero and consummates it aesthetically.
The essential life of a work is constituted by this event of the dynamic, living relationship of author and hero. When reading a
work aloud, one's voice can convey both intonations distinctly
enough (where it is necessary, of course, and not in relation to
every single word); a purely realistic reading is, in any case, inadmissible, for the author's active, aesthetically formative energy
must be audible in one's voice all the time.

In lyric, the author is most formalistic, i.e., he dissolves in the
outward, sounding form and in the inner, pictorial-sculptural and
rhythmic form, whence it seems that he is absent, that he merges
with the hero or, conversely, that there is no hero and only the
author is present. In reality, however, a hero and an author stand
over against each other here as well, and in every word one can
hear a reaction to another reaction. At this point, we cannot discuss the distinctive character of lyric in this respect, nor its objectivity. Rather, we shall now return to the intonative structure of
our poem. Here a twofold reaction can be heard in every word.
What must be kept in mind once and for all is that the reaction to
an object, the evaluation of an object, and the evaluated object itself are not given to us as different moments of a work and a
word—it is we who distinguish them abstractly. In reality, an
evaluation permeates the object evaluated, and, even more, it *creates* the image of the object evaluated, for it is precisely the formal-aesthetic reaction that condenses a concept into the image of
an object.

Does the tone of sorrow, the tone of parting, realistically experienced, really exhaust our poem in its first part? These realistically
sorrowing tones are there, but they are encompassed and enveloped by tones that sing or celebrate them—by tones that are not
the tones of sorrow at all: the rhythm and the intonation—"in

that unforgettable hour, in that hour of sadness / I wept before you for a long time"—convey not only the oppressiveness of that hour and that weeping but also the simultaneous *overcoming* of that oppressiveness and that weeping, i.e., the singing or celebration of them. Furthermore, the pictorial-plastic image of the agonizing parting ("my hands, growing ever colder . . . ," "my moans implored you not to break off . . .") does not convey solely the agony of that parting: the emotional-volitional reaction of a real agonizing parting could never engender from within itself any plastic-pictorial image. To be able to do that, the real agonizing reaction must itself become the object of a reaction that is not an agonizing reaction at all: it must become the object of an aesthetically cherishing reaction. That is, the image of agonizing parting is constructed in a value-context that is not the value-context of someone who is parting in reality. Finally, the tones of the hero's real expectation and faith in the future kiss ("and the kiss of our meeting has vanished as well . . .") are, likewise, encompassed by tones that expect nothing in the future and are fully consummated and stilled in the present; the hero's real future becomes an artistic future for the author—the creator of form. In addition, as we already noted, the hero's reaction itself encompasses at certain moments the reaction of the heroine, but the value-context of the hero, nevertheless, does not achieve full self-sufficiency in our poem.

We must now turn our attention to the theme of our poem.

(What must be constantly kept in mind is that the intonations we have distinguished—the realistic intonation and the formal intonation—are nowhere given to us in their pure form. Even in life, where every word is intonated by us, this intonation is never purely realistic, but always includes an admixture of aesthetic intonation. An actual cognitive-ethical reaction is pure, but the utterance of it for another inevitably absorbs into itself an element that is aesthetic; any expression as such is aesthetic from the outset. However, the aesthetic element plays a merely supporting role here, and the actual direction of such a reaction is realistic. What has been said applies to the formal reaction as well.)

And so, we turn now to the theme. As a consequence of the distinctive trait of pure lyric that we have already indicated above, it is extremely difficult to isolate and formulate that theme as a determinate, prosaically valid situation or narrative state of affairs. The content of lyric, just like that of music, is usually not concretized: it is a trace, as it were, of a cognitive-ethical tension or directedness, a global expression (not yet differentiated internally) of a possible[?] thought and act. That is why the theme must be formulated with extreme caution, and any actual formulation will be conditional, will not express the real prosaic context adequately. Here we do not intend to try establishing that context, for, in order to do so, we would have to take into account the following: (1) the biographical event (ethical event) of Pushkin's Odessa love and its subsequent echoes in his oeuvre; (2) the pertinent elegies of 1823 and 1824,[221] as well as other works written in 1830, and among these, the poem "Conjuration"[222] first of all; (3) the literary sources for the treatment of the "love and death" theme (in its broad formulation) that served as a condition for writing the thematically related poem "Conjuration," along with a number of other works written about the same time, and among these literary sources, Barry Cornwall's works first of all;[223] and, finally, (4) the entire biographical and intellectual setting of 1830 (Pushkin's forthcoming marriage, etc.). There can be no doubt that the ethical idea of "faithfulness" assumed, in connection with the biographical setting, one of the central places in the cognitive-ethical life of Pushkin in Boldino[224] (cf. "The Poor Knight," "Farewell," "The Stone Guest").[225] The author's nonlyrical works, moreover, are of essential significance for illuminating the prosaic context of lyrical poetry, inasmuch as the prosaic idea is always distinctly expressed in them. Such a study lies outside the task we have set ourselves. What is important for us is only the general moment constituted by the incarnation of a lyrical theme in an artistic whole, and hence our formulation cannot pretend to being strictly substantiated in all its constituents.

Thus, the "love and death" theme is rendered more complex and is concretized by a particular theme—the theme of "promise and fulfillment": the promise of meeting again with the beloved will be fulfilled in eternity, even if death has barred the way. This particular theme is incarnated[?] through the image of "the kiss of our meeting": the promised kiss of their meeting ("we shall once more join our lips in a passionate kiss"),[226] the kiss that has died ("the kiss of our meeting has vanished as well"), and the resurrected kiss ("I am waiting for that kiss—you owe it to me"). That is, the theme is concretized synecdochically. The theme is a purely ethical theme, except that it is deprived of its ethical sting—it is *closed* by the image of the kiss, which is the central thematic image of the poem. Otherwise, the consummatedness of the whole with respect to image and rhythm would have been decomposed by the yet-to-be-realized moments of the ethical event of love and of meeting again with the beloved beyond the grave, along with the various ethical acts connected with them,^{gg} that is, it would have been decomposed by the actual, absolute, *yet-to-be* event in the actual future. The actual *faith* and *hope* in the yet-to-be meeting,^{hh} if only they alone existed (i.e., if the author coincided absolutely with his hero), could not have engendered from within themselves anything that would be consummated and self-sufficient, regardless of the actual future—*in spite of* the meaning-governed future. The moment or constituent that brought about the consummation was introduced from a different emotional-volitional position in relation to the event as a whole—from a position which related this event to its given participants and made the experiencing and striving itself the center of value from the standpoint of the one experiencing and striving, rather than the *object* toward which that experiencing and striving is directed (the actual meeting beyond the grave). We do not need to know whether Pushkin actually received a kiss on the other side of the grave; we do not need a philosophical, religious, or ethical validation of the possibility and the necessity of meeting beyond the grave and of resurrection (immortality as a postulate of authentic love); the event is wholly consummated and resolved for us. To be sure, a prosaic analysis could and should deepen this theme philosophically and religiously in the appropriate direction: after all, the postulation of immortality by love, the ontological power of eternal memory ("he who has not forgotten gives up nothing," "the gift which God takes back is not lost by the stubborn heart")²²⁸ is one of the profoundest themes of erotic lyric throughout the ages (Dante, Petrarch, Novalis, Zhukovsky, Solov'ev, Ivanov, and others).²²⁹

This consummation of the infinite, intense, always open philosophical theme and of the possible ethical act (the possible life) is

---

^{gg}Such as faithfulness, purification, etc., which entered, in an aesthetically regenerated form, into the composition of Dante's lyric poetry.
^{hh}They might have been present in the author's, Pushkin's, soul, although his biography makes this supposition doubtful. The same theme is found in Zhukovsky's poetry.²²⁷

accomplished through the author's act of relating the event (the yet-to-be-achieved meaning of which constitutes the theme) to the given human being—the hero. This hero, moreover, may coincide *as a human being* with the author *as a human being*, and that, in fact, is what occurs most of the time. But the hero of a work can never coincide with the author—the *creator* of that work, for otherwise we would not get a work of art at all. If the author's reaction merges with the reaction of the hero (such merging may, after all, sometimes occur cognitionally and ethically), it is immediately directed upon objects and meaning: the author begins to act and cognize together with the hero, but loses the artistic, consummating vision of the hero. We shall see that to a certain degree this occurs quite often. A reaction that relates to an object immediately and, consequently, the intonation of an utterance as well, can be productive cognitionally and ethically, but not—aesthetically. An aesthetic reaction is a reaction to another reaction, a reaction not to objects and to meaning in themselves, but to objects and to meaning as they are for a given human being, i.e., as correlated with the values of a given human being. In our poem, the lyrical hero incarnates the cognitive-ethical theme, the faith and hope [indecipherable]. What sort of a hero is he and what is the author's relationship to him? At this point we shall make only a few preliminary remarks.

Let us begin with the author's relationship to the hero, for it is the author's creative relationship that actually determines an object. In our example, the author's relationship to the lyrical hero is purely and immediately formal-aesthetic: the hero's cognitive-ethical, value-toned experiencing (his *object*-related reaction) constitutes an immediate object of the author's purely aesthetic, formative, celebrating reaction. One could say that the experiences of the hero are immediately embodied here in image and rhythm, and that is why it seems that there is no author or no hero—a single, axiologically experiencing person. Meanwhile, as we shall see, in narrative literature (especially the novel), and sometimes in lyric as well (Heinrich Heine), the hero and his experiencing (his object-related emotional and volitional reaction as a whole) are not embodied in a purely ethical form in an immediate way, but are first determined by the author from a cognitive-aesthetic viewpoint. That is, before reacting to them immediately from an aesthetic-formal standpoint, the author reacts to them cognitionally and ethically, and only then does he proceed to consummate the cognitionally and ethically determinate hero (morally, psychologically, socially, philosophically, [indecipherable,] etc.) in purely artistic terms; and he does this even where the hero is profoundly autobiographical. Moreover, this cognitive-ethical determination of the hero is always intensely interested, intimately personal in character. In fact, this cognitive-ethical determination is so intimately and deeply bound up with the subsequent act of aesthetic forming that even for abstract analysis they are almost indistinguishable, for what occurs here is an almost immediate transition, a transition that is almost imperceptible to our reason, from one creative standpoint into another. Even if one actually tried to separate the formal-aesthetic device from the cognitive-moral evaluation in heroization, humor, satire, irony, i.e., even if one tried to isolate the purely formal-artistic device of heroization, humorization, satirization—one would never succeed in doing it [indecipherable], nor is doing it essential for accomplishing the task of analysis. The fact that analysis inevitably involves *both* form and content simultaneously is confirmed here with particular clarity. In addition, these phenomena show in a particularly clear-cut way the role of the author and the living event constituted by his relationship to the hero.

What is peculiar to pure lyric is that the hero's object-related reaction is insufficiently developed and is not founded on an essential principle: the author agrees, as it were, with its cognitive-ethical side, without engaging in an examination, evaluation, and generalization of it in principle, and the formal consummation of it is accomplished with painless ease. In this respect as well, lyric is akin to unmediated song, in which a lived experience itself sings or celebrates itself: grief not only grieves objectively (ethically), but at the same time sings or celebrates itself, not only weeps, but also sings its own weeping (aesthetic self-consolation). There is, of course, a division into hero and author here, as in any expression, for only the unmediated inarticulate wail, the cry of pain, does not know it, and in order to understand this phenomenon it is necessary to make that distinction and become aware of it in full, except that here this relationship has a merely special character. That is, it is a relationship that is desired, desired without any agitation: the hero is not afraid and not ashamed of being expressed, and the author does not have to struggle with him— they are born for each other, as it were, in the same cradle.

What must be said, however, is that this immediacy of lyric has its limits. The lyrical event of inner life may degenerate into an episode of inner life and, on the other hand, it may become false: what occurs again and again is that the relationship between hero and author is neither thought through nor felt through fully, that hero and author misunderstand each other, that they are afraid of looking directly into each other's eyes and of clearing up their relations candidly, and this produces dissonant tones, tones undissolved in the whole. What is also possible is synthetic[?] lyric, which does not enclose itself in self-contained individual poems. Lyrical books, or at least lyrical cycles, constitute another possibility (cf. Dante's *Vita nuova*, Petrarch's sonnets to some extent; in modern times, this is approached by Ivanov and by Rilke's *Stunden-Buch*).[230] To achieve this integration of lyrical poems into a large whole, unity of theme is not enough; what is necessary first and foremost is the unity of the hero and his attitude (in some cases, it is even possible to speak of the lyrical hero's character). More about this later.

In any case, our proposition concerning the unmediated, purely aesthetic relationship of hero and author remains, on the whole, in force in relation to pure lyric: the hero's emotional-volitional attitude and his cognitive-ethical directedness from within himself do not have a distinctly object-related character and are not founded on an essential principle. This applies to the hero of our poem as well (we cannot examine him in detail at this point): the position in which he is placed in relation to the author is not founded on an essential principle, and the author does not evaluate and does not generalize that position, but affirms it immediately in beauty[?] (lyrical acceptance).

Yet in narrative literature, or even in lyric, the same theme (its cognitive-ethical side) could be differently incarnated through a different hero, placed in a different position in relation to the author. We should recall that the same kind of theme (or a theme that has almost the same general, cognitive-ethical direction) is [indecipherable] in a completely different way in the figure of Lensky in Pushkin's *Eugene Onegin*: "He sang of *parting* and *sadness*, of *something*, and of the *misty* distance . . ." [II:10.7–8]. "For him, the purpose of our life was an *alluring riddle*; he *racked his brains* over it and suspected *marvels*" [II:7.11–14].[231] Here the theme is completely devoid of its cognitive-ethical authoritativeness, so that it becomes merely a constituent of the artistic characterization of the *given* human being (Lensky)—a characterization formulated in humorous-parodistic tones. Here the author's reaction has conditioned not only the choice of words, but also the choice of intonation for the entire emotional-volitional, cognitive-ethical, object-related position of the hero, who is determined and evaluated by the author not just in artistic-formal terms, but first and foremost in cognitive-ethical terms (he is generalized almost to the point of constituting a *type*), and this [indecipherable] penetrates and permeates the purely aesthetic, consummating form. Form is also inseparable from evaluation in Lensky's own poem,[232] "Whither, oh whither have you fled . . ." [VI: 21–22]—that parody of bad Romanticism. This evaluation, permeating the entire form-and-content structure of Lensky's poem, is then moved outside the poem and expressed directly: "Thus did he write, *limply* and *obscurely* . . ." [VI: 21.1]. Here the author's relationship to the hero is not immediately lyrical.

(What must constantly be kept in mind is the following: the emotional-volitional reaction is inseparable from its object and from the image of that object, i.e., it is always object-related and image-related in character. On the other hand, the object, too, is never given to us purely as an indifferent object: after all, the mere fact that I have started speaking about an object, that I have turned my attention upon it, singled it out, or that I have simply experienced it, means that I have *already* assumed an emotional-volitional position, a valuational attitude, in relation to it.)

In this sense, the emotional-volitional reaction of the author finds its expression not just in rhythm and intonation, but in the very choice of a hero, in the choice of theme and plot [*fabula*], in the choice of words for expressing the latter, in the choice and construction of images, etc. Intonation is not marked in a work at all; it is surmised, and when we read with our eyes, it is not expressed in a sound-image, although there *is* a physiological and [indecipherable] equivalent of it—in the expression of eyes and lips, in the expressive play of features, in breathing, etc., but these are not adequate, of course. The same must be said about the emotional-volitional position and reaction of the hero as well: it also finds its expression in *all* of the moments which constitute a work of art. If, on the other hand, we have isolated one of these constituent moments, namely, intonation, then we did so only because intonation expresses in particular the emotional-volitional reaction, the tonality of an object; it has no other function. In fact, all of the elements that we isolate in words and in an artistic whole (object, image, rhythm, intonation, etc.) can be isolated only in abstraction. In reality, they are fused into a concrete, integral unity; they interpenetrate and condition each other mutually.

That is why in a dramatic dialogue as well the emotional-volitional position of the hero is expressed not only by the intonation of his words, but also by the choice of words, by their object-related meanings and images, except that these moments also perform other functions at the same time. Furthermore, not only the reaction of the hero but also the encompassing reaction of the author—his attitude in relation to the whole and the parts—is expressed not only through rhythm, but also through the place which a given utterance of the hero occupies in the dialogue, and through the position of the entire dialogue within the whole—through the intonational coloration of the dialogue, and sometimes through its object-related meanings and images as well.

When we speak of the cognitive-ethical determination of the hero, which precedes and conditions his determination in artistic-formal terms, we should not represent him to ourselves as discursively finished, especially since, in relation to the whole of the hero, it is the ethical and not the cognitional approach that indisputably predominates, whereas the philosophical-cognitional moment predominates in relation to the theme and to particular constituents of the hero, to his [indecipherable] with respect to world view. The whole of the hero (the total, comprehensive expression of the hero) is purely ethical in character (insofar as one may speak of a nonaesthetic whole at all). It is a whole of an emotional-volitional order and not of a discursive order: [indecipherable], shamefulness, [indecipherable] nullity, saintliness, authoritativeness, rightfulness of a person, love, etc.

Let us repeat once again that such cognitive-ethical determinations are also indistinguishable from the formal-aesthetic determinations [indecipherable]; the concrete human being does not [indecipherable] at all anywhere except in art, and also in life, but here, too, he is aestheticized to a considerable extent. The mere fact that a cognitive-ethical determination relates to the *whole* human being, that it encompasses all of him, already constitutes a moment that is aesthetic. An ethical determination defines a given human being from the standpoint of what-is-yet-to-be-accomplished; the center of value, moreover, is in the latter. All one need do is transpose him into what-is-given and the determination becomes completely aestheticized. One could say that, before assuming a purely aesthetic position in relation to the hero and his world, an author must assume a lived-life position, a purely cognitive-ethical position.

All of the elements we have examined in the artistic whole constituted by our poem—the object-related constituents (homeland, foreign land, distance, long time); the object-related and meaning-governed whole (nature); the sculptural-pictorial images (three fundamental ones); inner space, inner temporal rhythm, inner time; the emotional-volitional positions of author and hero, and the intonational [indecipherable] corresponding to those positions; outer temporal rhythm, rhyme, and outer composition (none of which could be subjected here to a special formal analysis); and, finally, the theme—that is, all of the concrete and unique elements of the poem as well as the architectonic ordering of them in a unitary artistic event are actualized around the axiological center constituted by a human being *qua* hero. Being has been rendered totally human here in a once-occurrent event: everything that exists and has validity here is merely a constituent in the event of a given human being's life, of his fate. With that, we can end our analysis of the poem.

In our analysis, we forestalled to some extent what will be dealt with later in our inquiry: we spoke not only of the given human being who constitutes the center of aesthetic vision, but also of the determining of the hero, and we even touched upon the author's relationship to the hero.

A given human being constitutes the condition of possibility for any aesthetic vision whatsoever, regardless of whether that vision finds its determinate embodiment in a finished work of art or not, except that it is only in a work of art that a determinate hero appears, in which case, moreover, some of the constituents may be aestheticized even when they do not have an immediate relation to such a hero, but relate to a human being in general, as in our example, where nature is immediately vivified independently of the plot [*fabula*] that integrates it into the event of a determinate hero's life. The hero is no longer the condition of possibility for aesthetic seeing. Rather, he constitutes a concrete *object* of aesthetic seeing, although an object *par excellence,* inasmuch as it expresses the very essence of aesthetic seeing. But a human being may be approached, after all, from a standpoint other than that of the value of human givenness as such (the *Homo sapiens* of biology, the human being of an ethical act, the human being of history), and conversely: any object may be viewed from the standpoint of human givenness, and such viewing will be aesthetic, except that there will be no hero proper in it. Thus *aesthetic* contemplation of nature is rendered human ("humanized"),[233] yet it has no determinate hero (nor a determinate author, for that matter; in such a case there is an author who coincides with the contemplation[?], but he is extremely passive and receptive[?], even though the degree of passivity is variable). Another possibility is a work of art without a determinately expressed hero: description of nature, philosophical poetry, the aestheticized aphorism, the fragment of the Romantics, etc. Works without a hero are particularly frequent in the other arts: almost all of music, ornament, arabesque, landscape painting, *nature morte*, all of architecture, etc.

It is true that the boundary between a human being (the condition for aesthetic vision) and a hero (the object of aesthetic vision) often becomes unstable, for aesthetic contemplation as such tends toward isolating from within itself or bringing forth a determinate hero. In this sense, every act of aesthetic seeing includes within itself a tendency toward a hero, the potentiality of a hero. In every aesthetic perception there slumbers, as it were, a determinate image of a human being, as in a block of marble for the sculptor. Not only the ethical-historical moment, but also the purely aesthetic moment in the mythological approach to the world compelled one to see dryads inside trees and oreads inside stones, compelled nymphs to rise from the waters, compelled one to see in the events of nature events of the life of determinate participants.

It is only in relation to a determinate hero that one can fully determine [indecipherable] of the event and the emotional-volitional position of the author. One can assert, therefore, that there is no aesthetic vision and there are no works of art without a hero, and the only thing we must do is distinguish between an actual, expressed hero and a potential hero who strives to break through the shell, as it were, of a given object of aesthetic vision. In fact, to ascertain the author's axiological position in relation to an aesthetic whole and all its particular moments, it will be important, when there is no determinate hero, to actualize the potentialities of a hero that are inherent in the object of vision, to actualize them to the point where they form a determinate image—determinate at least to a certain degree. We shall see later that the half-philosophical, half-artistic conceptions of the world (such as those of Nietzsche and, in part, Schopenhauer) are founded on the living event of the author's relationship to the world, a relationship similar to that of the artist to his hero, and that a proper understanding of such conceptions requires to a certain degree an anthropomorphic world—as the object of their thinking. Nevertheless, in the course of our inquiry we shall continue to draw a strict distinction between a hero proper and a human being—the condition for aesthetic vision—who constitutes the *potentiality* of a hero, for the structure of an actual hero has a quite special character and comprises a whole series of highly important constituents which are unknown to a potential hero. Besides that, an actual hero is placed into a world that has been partially aestheticized by the potential hero and does not abolish[?] the work of the latter (just as in our example, where nature has been aestheticized). Furthermore, the form-and-content determinants of the varieties of hero (character, type, personage, positive hero, lyrical hero, and their subdivisions) are almost completely inapplicable to the potential hero, since they related primarily to the constituents of his actualization in the actual hero.

Until now, our account has clarified only the general functions of a human being—the condition of artistic vision, which is possible even where there is no determinate hero; our account has only to some extent anticipated the function of an actual hero in a work, inasmuch as a given human being and a determinate hero do, in fact, gravitate toward each other and often pass into each other without any mediation. A given human being constitutes the form-and-content center of value in artistic vision, but a determinate hero may not even be present in the center of a given work of art: he may be entirely absent, he may withdraw into the background in favor of the theme (as happens in our poem, where a determinate countenance of the hero is not essential). But it is precisely because of the intimate closeness of a determinate hero to the very principle of artistic vision ("humanization")[234] and because of the utmost distinctness of the author's creative position in such a hero that one should begin an analysis with the hero, and not with the theme. Otherwise, we may easily lose the principle of the incarnation of a theme through a human being as potential hero. That is, we may lose the very center of artistic vision and substitute a prosaic argument for its concrete architectonics.

What should also be said is that language, which the verbal artist finds to a considerable extent as something already on hand, is profoundly aestheticized, profoundly mythological and anthropomorphic, and that it gravitates toward the center of value constituted by a human being. Hence, aestheticism deeply permeates all our thinking, and philosophical thought, even at its loftiest, continues to be human in an intensely partial way even today (this is justified, but only within certain limits, which are often violated). Language or, rather, the world of language also has its own potential hero, as it were, who is actualized in an utterance of lived life within myself and within the other. And it is only when aesthetic directedness becomes specialized and detaches itself from other tendencies that, in the very process of detaching itself from and contending with the other tendencies, it begins to differentiate itself internally and, as a result of this internal differentiation, a hero appears as well as his author, and the living event constituted by their differentiation, contention, and mutual relations spills over into a finished work of art and crystallizes in it.

Let us sum up the results of the present section.

Aesthetic creation overcomes the infinite and yet-to-be-achieved character of cognition and ethical action by referring all constituents of being and of yet-to-be-achieved meaning to a human being in his concrete givenness—as the event of his life, as his fate. A given human being constitutes the center of value in the architectonics of an aesthetic object; it is around him that the uniqueness of every object, its integral concrete diversity, is actualized (from the standpoint of meaning, the object's diversity is fortuitous and fateful); it is round him that various objects and constituents are integrated into a temporal, spatial, and meaning-governed whole constituted by the consummated event of a particular life. Everything that enters into an artistic whole represents a value, not a value yet to be achieved and valid in itself, but a value that possesses actual validity for a given human being in his particular fate—as that in relation to which he has in actuality assumed an emotional-volitional, object-related position. A given human being is the condition of aesthetic vision; if he turns out to be a determinate object of that vision (and he always tends, tends essentially, toward that), he constitutes the hero of a given work. Every concrete value in an artistic whole is rendered meaningful in two value-contexts: in the context of a hero (the cognitive-ethical context) and in the encompassing and consummating context of an author (the cognitive-ethical plus the formal-aesthetic context). Moreover, the two contexts interpenetrate, although the context of the author seeks to encompass and close the context of the hero.

The choice of every referential meaning and the structure of every image and of every intonational-rhythmic tone are conditioned and permeated by both value-contexts as they interact with each other. The aesthetically formative reaction is a reaction to another reaction, a valuation of another valuation.

Author and hero meet in life; they enter into cognitive-ethical, lived-life relations with each other, contend with each other (even if they meet in one human being). And this event, the event of their life, the event of their intensely serious relations and contention, crystallizes in an artistic whole into an architectonically stable yet dynamically living relationship between author and hero which is essential for understanding the life of a work. The concrete formulation of the problem constituted by this mutual relationship will occupy us in the next section.

Notes

(Notes by the Russian editors are marked with an asterisk.)
Note: Bakhtin worked on this study in aesthetics at the very beginning of the 1920s, but did not finish it: following the section "The Problem of the Author," the ms. contains the title of a further section that remained unwritten—"The Problem of the Author and Hero in Russian Literature." The opening part of the ms. (including the title) is missing.

The study was published for the first time in 1979 in a collection of Bakhtin's works edited by Sergei G. Bocharov: *Estetika slovesnogo tvorchestva* [Aesthetics of Verbal Creation] (Moscow: Iskusstvo, 1979), pp. 7–180 (annotated by S. S. Averintsev and S. G. Bocharov). In this publication, the title "Author and Hero in Aesthetic Activity" was chosen by the editor, and the opening section—"The Problem of the Author's Relationship to the Hero"—is actually the second section.

Part of the first section (its second half) appeared in 1986 in two publications: in *Filosofija i sotsiologija nauki i tekhniki: Ezhegodnik 1984–1985* (Moscow: Nauka, 1986), pp. 138–157, and in M. M. Bakhtin, *Literaturno-kriticheskie stat'i* (Moscow: Khudozhestvennaja literatura, 1986), pp. 5–25. In the present translation this fragment of the first section is included in the form of a supplement.

1. "The author's relationship to the hero" should be taken here and throughout in a dynamic sense: the way in which the author acts toward and interacts with the hero (including the attitude he manifests in his comportment toward the hero). On "author" and "authorship," see S. Averintsev in *Kratkaja Literaturnaja Entsiklopedija* (1978), vol. 9, cols. 28–30; W. Schwemme, "Autor," *Historisches Wörterbuch der Philosophie* (1971), vol. 1, cols. 721–723. See also the section on "The Problem of the Author" in the present essay; section IV of the article on "The Problem of Content, Material, and Form in Verbal Art" in the present volume; M. M. Bakhtin, *The Dialogic Imagination*, trans. Caryl Emerson and Michael Holquist (Austin: University of Texas Press, 1981), pp. 252–257, 27–28; M. M. Bakhtin, *Speech Genres and Other Late Essays*, trans. Vern W. McGee (Austin: University of Texas Press, 1986), see index. Cf. also Jan Mukařovsky's essays "The Poet" and "The Individual and Literary History," in Jan Mukařovsky, *The Word and Verbal Art*, trans. John Burbank and Peter Steiner (New Haven: Yale University Press, 1977), and "Personality in Art," in Jan Mukařovsky, *Structure, Sign, and Function*, trans. John Burbank and Peter Steiner (New Haven: Yale University Press, 1978).

2. "Essentially necessary" is one way in which I shall translate the adjective *printsipial'nyj*—the Russian equivalent of the German *prinzipiell*. Other translations of the adjective used throughout this translation are "principled," "founded on a necessary principle," and "essential and fundamental."

3. The section on "The Problem of the Author and Hero in Russian Literature" remained unwritten. On the author-hero relationship in Dostoevsky and Tolstoy, see M. M. Bakhtin, *Problems of Dostoevsky's Poetics*, trans. Caryl Emerson (Minneapolis: University of Minnesota Press, 1984), chap. 2, and "Predislovie" ("Preface to *Resurrection*"), in L. N. Tolstoy, *Polnoe sobranie khudozhestvennykh proizvedenij*, ed. by K. Khalabaev and B. Eikhenbaum (Moscow-Leningrad: Gosizdat, 1930) vol. 13, pp. iii–xx.

4. Bakhtin's preferred word for parts of a whole is "moment," which I render in this translation as "constituent," "constituent feature," or "moment." On the concept of "moment," see Edmund Husserl, *Logical Investigations*, trans. J. N. Findlay (London: Routledge and Kegan Paul, 1970), vol. 2, investigation 3, chap. 2.

5. "To intonate": to pronounce or perform (sing, play, recite) with a particular intonation. The term is used by B. M. Eikhenbaum in his study of the "melodics" of Russian lyrical verse, *Melodika russkogo liricheskogo stikha* (Petersburg: OPOJAZ, 1922). On the concept of intonation in Russian musicology, see Gordon D. McQuere's articles on Yavorsky and Asafiev in Gordon D. McQuere, ed., *Russian Theoretical Thought in Music* (Ann Arbor, Mich.: UMI Research Press, 1983). See also Yu. Borev

and T. Radionova, "Intonatsija kak sredstvo khudozhestvennogo obshche-nija," *Kontekst 1982* (Moscow: Nauka, 1983), pp. 224–244.

6. "To consummate" (to bring to the utmost degree of completion or fulfillment, to accomplish) is intended to convey the definitiveness implied by the Russian *zavershit'* (cf. German *vollenden*). Other translations of Bakhtin use "to finalize" instead of "to consummate."

7. "Intuitable" is used here as an equivalent of the German *anschaulich*, that is, the opposite of conceptual or abstract—what is given in intuition, what is apprehended perceptually, as an individual object.

8. "Image" should be understood here and throughout in the sense of a plastic (sculptural) as well as pictorial configuration or figure.

9. On the ideality of meanings, see J. N. Mohanty, "Husserl's Theory of Meaning," in Frederic A. Elliston and Peter McCormick, eds., *Husserl: Expositions and Appraisals* (Notre Dame: University of Notre Dame Press, 1977), pp. 27–33.

10. See Nikolai Gogol', "Author's Confession" (1847), "Four Letters to Various People on the Subject of *Dead Souls*" (in his *Selected Passages from Correspondence with Friends*, 1847), and "To the Reader from the Author" (preface to the second edition of the first volume of *Dead Souls*, 1846).

Ivan Goncharov (1812–1891), Russian novelist, is the author of *Oblomov*. See his articles "The Intentions, Problems, and Ideas of the Novel *The Precipice*" (1876) and "Better Late Than Never" (1879).

11. Transgredient (from L. *transgredi, transgressus*, step across, step over): Jonas Cohn and Wilhelm Windelband use "transgredient" as the opposite of "immanent." See Jonas Cohn, *Allgemeine Ästhetik* (Leipzig: Engelmann, 1901), p. 27 (Cohn points out that the use of "transcendent" would be misleading, since in the Kantian tradition the term means "beyond the limits of possible experience"); Wilhelm Windelband, *An Introduction to Philosophy*, trans. Joseph McCabe (New York: Henry Holt, 1921), pp. 124–125. Johannes Volkelt uses "transgredient" in correlation with "transsubjective": "transsubjective" is that which lies outside the sphere of my current (*jeweilige*) consciousness; "transgredient" is that which lies outside the immediate being of my current act of thinking. See Johannes Volkelt, *Gewißheit und Wahrheit* (Munich: Beck, 1918), p. 160. Cf. also Helmut Plessner, *Die Stufen des Organischen und der Mensch* (1928) in his *Gesammelte Schriften* (Frankfort am Main: Suhrkamp, 1981), vol. 4, pp. 129–130.

12. Chatsky is the main hero in *Woe from Wit* (1824), a comedy in verse by Aleksandr Griboedov (1795–1829), a Russian dramatist and diplomat.

13. "What exists" or—Being (*bytie*).

14. "Validity"—*znachimost'*: used as an equivalent of the German *Geltung*. In some cases I translate *znachimost'* as "significance." See

Wilbur Marshall Urban, *The Intelligible World* (New York: Macmillan, 1929), pp. 149ff., 153ff.; Wilhelm Windelband, *An Introduction to Philosophy*, trans. Joseph McCabe (New York: Henry Holt, 1921), pp. 182–183; Rudolf Eisler, *Wörterbuch der philosophischen Begriffe*, 4th ed., 3 vols. (Berlin: E. S. Mittler & Sohn, 1927–1930), vol. 1, pp. 495–499.

15. Event of life: in the sense that life is an ongoing event, and not in the sense of an event in life. On "event" (German *Geschehen*), see Windelband, *An Introduction*, 5.

16. Bakhtin's formulation is "verbal creation," not "verbal art." The basal category for Bakhtin is creation or creative activity. Cf. A. F. Losev, "Dialektika tvorcheskogo akta," *Kontekst 1981* (Moscow: Nauka, 1982), pp. 48–78; Erich Rothacker, "Das Wesen des Schöpferischen," in his *Mensch und Geschichte* (Bonn: Athenäum, 1950), pp. 166–193. See also N. Berdyaev, *Smysl tvorchestva* (Moscow: Leman and Sakharov, 1916), which was translated by D. A. Lowrie as *The Meaning of the Creative Act* (New York: Collier, 1962).

17. See Charles E. Gauss, "Empathy," in the *Dictionary of the History of Ideas* (1973), vol. 2, pp. 85–89; Herbert S. Langfeld, *The Aesthetic Attitude* (New York: Harcourt, Brace and Howe, 1920), chap. 5; K. E. Gilbert and H. Kuhn, *A History of Esthetics*, revised and enlarged (Bloomington: Indiana University Press, 1954), pp. 537–540; Lev Vygotsky, "Vchuvstvovanie," *Bol'shaja Sovetskaja Entsiklopedija*, 1st ed. (1929), vol. 13, cols. 660–661. Cf. also Edith Stein, *On the Problem of Empathy*, trans. W. Stein (The Hague: Nijhoff, 1964); and F. A. Elliston, "Husserl's Phenomenology of Empathy," in Elliston and McCormick, eds., *Husserl*, pp. 213–231.

18. Theodor Lipps, *Ästhetik: Psychologie des Schönen und der Kunst*, 2 vols. (Hamburg and Leipzig: Voss, 1903–1906). For introductory information about Lipps (1851–1914), see *The Encyclopedia of Philosophy*, ed. Paul Edwards, 8 vols. (New York: Macmillan, 1967), and *Neue Deutsche Biographie* (Berlin: Duncker and Humboldt, vol. 1, 1953; vol. 15, Locherer-Maltzahn, 1987). For critical expositions of his aesthetics, see Langfeld, *Aesthetic Attitude*; Moritz Geiger in *Zeitschrift für Ästhetik* 10 (1915), 68–73; and Paul Moos, *Die deutsche Ästhetik der Gegenwart* (Berlin: Schuster and Loeffler, 1920), vol. 1.

19. Jean-Marie Guyau, *L'Art au point de vue sociologique* (Paris: Alcan, 1889). On Guyau, see F. J. W. Harding, *Jean-Marie Guyau (1854–1888), Aesthetician and Sociologist* (Geneva: Droz, 1973).

20. Hermann Cohen, *Ästhetik des reinen Gefühls*, 2 vols. (Berlin: B. Cassirer, 1912), see index under "Liebe" in vol. 2. On Cohen (1844–1918), see *The Encyclopedia of Philosophy* and *Neue Deutsche Biographie*.

21. "Identify" ourselves, etc.: this formulation is a paraphrase of the meaning of *vzhivat'sja*, an equivalent of the German *sich (in ein Gedicht, eine Rolle) einleben*. Cf. the expression "to live a part."

22. Excess (*izbytok*): that which exceeds the limits of anything. A possible alternative translation could be "surplus."

23. Projected world—*zadannyj mir: zadannyj* is equivalent to the German *aufgegeben* (set as a task to be accomplished). The world of cognition is not a world that is *given*, but a world that is to be methodically determined. The distinction goes back to Kant, for whom Noumena and Ideas are *aufgegeben* in contrast to what is given (*gegeben*). See *Kritik der reinen Vernuft*, B 7, 344, 527f. Elsewhere I shall translate *zadannyj* (set as a task) and *zadannost'* (what is set as a task) as "what is yet to be accomplished or achieved" or "what is set as a task (to be accomplished)." See "Aufgabe, aufgegeben," in *Historisches Wörterbuch der Philosophie*, vol. 1, col. 618.

24. Yet-to-be or yet-to-come—*predstojashchij:* what "stands before (someone)" in time, that is, lies ahead or is yet to occur in the future. Cf. German *bevorstehen*.

25. "Axiologically" and "axiological" will be frequently used as translations of *tsennostno* and *tsennostnyj* (with respect to value, relating to value, from the standpoint of value). Cf. German *werthaft*.

26. His lived life has the character of an ongoing event.

27. See note 2.

28. Bakhtin contracts the Russian phrase *nakhodit'sja vne* (to be situated or located outside the bounds of someone or something) into a noun—*vnenakhodimost'* (the state of being situated outside the bounds of). It should be stressed that this situatedness outside (the bounds of) the hero is a *position* assumed *in relation* to the hero or *toward* the hero. Other translators have preferred to render *vnenakhodimost'* as "extopy" or "extra-location."

29. See note 23.

30. "Unique" in the sense of once-occurrent. "Event of being (or Being)": Being constitutes an ongoing event, has the character of an event. Cf. German *Seinsgeschehen*. See note 15 and the first section of "The Problem of the Author" in the present text.

31. The author's *vnenakhodimost':* see note 28.

32. Axiological validity, i.e., validity with respect to value or the validity of a value. See notes 14 and 25.

33. "Consolidation" (*oplotnenie*) in the sense of forming into a body. A more literal rendering would be "to gain body (bodiliness, corporeity)."

34. See note 24.

35. See note 23.

36. See note 23.

37. Connatural: of the same nature, like in kind.

38. Artistically significant constituents: constituents that possess artistic validity. See note 14.

39. Pierre in *War and Peace* and Levin in *Anna Karenina*.

40. The author's *reaction* to the hero as well as *reflection* upon that reaction.

41. "Pseudo-Classicism": a post-Romantic term for the eighteenth-century Russian version of French seventeenth-century and eighteenth-century Classicism.

42. Aleksandr Sumarokov (1717–1777), was a poet, dramatist, journalist, and critic; Jakov Knjazhnin (1742–1791), a dramatist, poet, and translator; Vladislav Ozerov (1769–1816), a dramatist. The three authors may be viewed as representing three phases (beginning, middle, and end) in the history of Russian Neoclassical tragedy.

43. Spatial image (see note 8) and temporal rhythm. On rhythm, see "The Temporal Whole of the Hero," section 3, in the present text.

44. On the phenomenological concept of "horizon," see C. Van Peursen in Elliston/McCormick, eds., *Husserl*, pp. 182–201 and 234 (bibliography). Bakhtin's term for "horizon" is *krugozor*, compass of vision (cf. German *Gesichtskreis*).

45. Outsideness (*vnenakhodimost'*): my situatedness outside all other human beings. See note 28.

46. To avoid ambiguity, I shall use the Latin form *subiectum* instead of "subject."

47. Event of being: being is an ongoing event. See note 30.

48. Projecting myself, etc.: a paraphrase of *vzhivanie*. See note 21.

*49. Cf. Bakhtin's remark on the Romantic world of Byron in his lectures on the history of Russian literature given in the 1920s (lecture notes of R. M. Mirkina): "The fundamental peculiarity of Byron's creative work is the clear-cut distinction between the representation of the hero and the other characters. Their life proceeds on different planes. The hero is drawn by Byron lyrically, from within; the secondary characters are drawn epically—they live an external life. One cannot become conscious of one's own exterior from within oneself. The outward expressedness of others is something we come to know first of all. That is why the hero captivates and absorbs us in his inner life; the other characters we *see.*" This is a typical example of the combination of general philosophical aesthetics and literary analysis that distinguishes Bakhtin's mode of thinking.

Cf. also the likening (in the same lectures) of Dostoevsky's artistic world to the world of fantasizing or dreaming: "The world of our fantasizing, when we think of ourselves, is quite distinctive: we are in the role of both author and hero, the one controlling the other. We accompany the hero all the time, his inner experiences captivate and absorb us. We do not contemplate the hero, we co-experience with him. Dostoevsky involves us in the world of the hero, and we do not see the hero from outside." And further: "That is why Dostoevsky's heroes on stage produce an entirely different impression from the one they produce when we are reading. It is in principle impossible to represent the specificity of Dostoevsky's world on stage. . . . There is no independent and neutral place for us; an objective seeing of the hero is impossible. That is why the footlights destroy a proper apprehension of Dostoevsky's works. Their theatrical effect is—a dark stage with voices, and nothing more." It should be noted that this description of Dostoevsky's world was significantly rectified in Bakhtin's book on Dostoevsky—*Problemy tvorchestva Dostoevskogo* [Problems of Dostoevsky's Creative Work] (Leningrad: Priboj, 1929): the likening to the world of fantasizing corresponds, in essentials, to the world of the hero alone, whereas "the cognizant and judging 'I' and the world as its object are present [in Dostoevsky's works] not in the singular but in the plural. Dostoevsky overcame solipsism. He reserved idealistic consciousness not for himself but for his characters, and not only for one of them but for them all. Instead of a single cognizant and judging 'I,' the center of Dostoevsky's work came to be occupied by the problem of the interrelationship of all these cognizant and judging 'I's to one another." [See Mikhail Bakhtin, *Problems of Dostoevsky's Poetics*, trans. Caryl Emerson (Minneapolis: University of Minnesota Press, 1984), pp. 99–100.]

* 50. Cf. C. G. Jung's concept of mask-face (persona), which is defined as "that which in reality one is not, but which oneself as well as others think one is." [See C. G. Jung, *Collected Works*, (New York: Pantheon, 1959), vol. 9, part 1, p. 123.]

51. Rembrandt's *Self-Portrait* (1665) in the Wallraf-Richartz Museum in Cologne (oil on canvas, 82.5 × 65.5 cm). For a color reproduction, see Pascal Bonafoux, *Rembrandt: Self-Portrait* (New York: Rizzoli, 1985), p. 125.

52. Mikhail Vrubel' (1856–1910), Russian painter. See his *Self-Portrait* (1905) in the Russian Museum in Leningrad (charcoal, water-color, gouache on paper, 57.9 × 53.5 cm) or his *Self-Portrait* (1904) in the Tretyakov Gallery in Moscow (charcoal, sanguine on primed paper, mounted on cardboard, 35.5 × 29.5 cm). For reproductions, see S. Kaplanova, comp., *Vrubel* (Leningrad: Aurora, 1975), illustration no. 54 and frontispiece.

* 53. Pushkin's poem "Mon Portrait," written in French (1814).

54. Irtenev in *Childhood, Boyhood,* and *Youth,* and Levin in *Anna Karenina.*

* 55. Cf. the New Testament maxim: "Bear ye one another's burdens, and so fulfill the law of Christ" (Galatians 6:2).

56. Heinrich Rickert (1863–1936), German philosopher, one of the leaders of the southwest German school of Neo-Kantianism. Rickert differentiates the pure, nonobjectifiable *subiectum* from the psychophysical and psychological *subiectum*: the *subiectum* is, first, the animate body, then—the psychic *subiectum*, and finally (in distinction to the first two, which are real)—the epistemological *subiectum*, which is nonreal (*irreal*) and nonindividual. See Heinrich Rickert, *Der Gegenstand der Erkenntnis* (Tübingen: Mohr, 1921; the first edition appeared

in 1892), chap. 1, sections 6 ("Die realen Subjekte") and 7 ("Das erkenntnistheoretische Subjekt"). For an introduction to Rickert's philosophy, see Guy Oakes, "Introduction," in his abridged translation of Rickert's *Limits of Concept Formation in Natural Science* (Cambridge: Cambridge University Press, 1968).

* 57. The concept of Romantic irony, as worked out by Friedrich Schlegel, presupposes a victorious liberation of an "I" of genius from all norms and values, from its own objectifications and productions—an incessant "overcoming" of its limitedness, a ludic elevation above and beyond itself. Irony is a sign of the total arbitrariness of any state of one's spirit, for "a really free and cultivated person ought to be able to attune himself at will to being philosophical or philological, critical or poetical, historical or rhetorical, ancient or modern: quite arbitrarily, just as one tunes an instrument, at any time and to any degree." [See Friedrich Schlegel, *Lucinde and the Fragments*, trans. Peter Firchow (Minneapolis: University of Minnesota Press, 1971), p. 149, no. 55 in the "Critical Fragments"). On Romantic irony, see Ernst Behler, *Klassische Ironie, romantische Ironie, tragische Ironie* (Darmstadt: Wissenschaftliche Buchgesellschaft, 1972), and the articles by Walzel, Immerwahr, and Szondi in Helmut Schanze, ed., *Friedrich Schlegel und die Kunsttheorie seiner Zeit* (Darmstadt: Wissenschaftliche Buchgesellshaft, 1985).]

58. On the notion of the loophole, see also Bakhtin's *Problems of Dostoevsky's Poetics*, pp. 232–235, 241, 258, 277–278.

59. The domain of aesthetic activity is more extensive than that of artistic creation; not all forms of aesthetic activity can be reduced to artistic activity. Cf. Max Dessoir, *Ästhetik und allgemeine Kunstwissenschaft* (Stuttgart: Enke, 1906), p. 4: "Our admiring and loving devotion to certain phenomena of nature bears all the marks of aesthetic comportment, and yet need not be touched by art. Even more. In all intellectual and social domains a part of the creative power finds its expression in aesthetic forming; the products of such forming, though not works of art, are enjoyed aesthetically. Since countless facts of everyday experience show us that taste can develop and function independently of art, we must recognize that the scope of the aesthetic sphere is broader than that of the sphere of art." See Max Dessoir, *Aesthetics and Theory of Art*, trans. S. A. Emery (Detroit: Wayne State University Press, 1970).

60. "Overshadowing" (*episkiasis, obumbratio*): the Russian word for "overshadowing" implies the power to shelter, protect, and bless or bestow blessings. The term derives from the Bible, cf. Luke 1:35: "The power of the Highest shall overshadow thee." See Gerhard Kittel, *Theological Dictionary of the New Testament*, ed. Gerhard Friedrich, trans. and ed. G. W. Bromiley (Grand Rapids, Mich.: Eerdmans, 1971), vol. 3, pp. 399–400.

61. Cf. Henri Bergson, *Matter and Memory*, trans. N. M. Paul and W. S. Palmer (London: George Allen and Unwin, 1911).

62. Legal person: a human being or a body corporate as the holder of rights and obligations recognized by the law. Cf. Hans Kelsen, *Pure Theory of Law*, trans. Max Knight (Berkeley: University of California Press, 1967), pp. 171–174; E. N. Trubetskoi, *Entsiklopedija prava* (New York: Chalidze Publications, 1982; reprint of the 1901 edition); Hermann Cohen, *Ethik des reinen Willens*, 2nd rev. ed. (Berlin: B. Cassirer, 1907), pp. 78, 80, 224–225, 229–230.

* 63. A reminiscence from the closing lines of F. Tyutchev's poem "O chëm ty voesh', vetr nochnoj?" [Whereof are you wailing, wind of the night?], published in 1836.

64. On the "idea of man," see Cohen, *Ethik des reinen Willens*, pp. 210–211.

* 65. Cf. S. S. Averintsev's independently developed characterization of the attitude to bodiliness in antiquity in his *Poetika rannevizantijskoj literatury* [Poetics of Early Byzantine Literature] (Moscow: Nauka, 1977), p. 62.

66. Faddei Frantsevich Zelinsky or Tadeusz Zielinski (1859–1944) was a Russian-Polish classical philologist, historian of religion, and philosopher of culture (1885–1920, professor of classical philology at Petersburg University; 1921–1935 at Warsaw University). See, for example, his article "Dionis v religii i poezii" [Dionysus in Religion and in Poetry], *Russkaja Mysl'* 36, 7 (1915). Cf. Katerina Clark and Michael Holquist, *Mikhail Bakhtin* (Cambridge, Mass.: Harvard University Press, 1984), pp. 30–33.

* 67. At the time Bakhtin wrote his study, it was generally accepted that the orgiastic cult of Dionysus appeared quite late—it came from Thrace on the very eve of the 6th century B.C. In our time, however, it has been established that the cult had Creto-Mycenaean origins.

* 68. Epicurus's maxim "Live unknown" was perceived in antiquity as a challenge to the publicness which was indissolubly associated with the city-state (*polis*) conception of human dignity. Plutarch wrote a highly pugnacious polemical essay—"Is 'Live Unknown' a Wise Precept?"—in which he addressed the following words to Epicurus: "If you remove publicity from our life as you might the illumination at a drinking party, so that every pleasure may freely be indulged without detection—'live unknown.' Yes indeed, if I am to live with Hedeia the courtesan and my days with Leontion and 'spit on noble action' and place the good in the 'flesh' and in 'titillations'; these rites require darkness, these require night, and for these let us have concealment and oblivion. . . . I hold that life itself and indeed a man's very birth and becoming are a gift of God to make him known. . . . But he who casts himself into the unknown state and wraps himself in darkness and buries his life in an empty tomb would appear to be aggrieved at his very birth and to renounce the effort of being" [Plutarch's *Moralia* (Loeb Classics), vol. 14, pp. 329, 331, 335, 339 (the translation is by B. Einarson and P. H. DeLacy)].

*69. This ascetic exercise is associated not with the name of a Stoic, but with that of a Cynic—Diogenes of Sinope: "And in summer he used to roll [in the tub in which he lived] over hot sand, while in winter he used to embrace statues covered with snow, using every means of inuring himself to hardship" [Diogenes Laertius, *Lives of Eminent Philosophers*, trans. R. D. Hicks (Loeb Classics), vol. 2, pp. 25 and 27].

*70. Cf. the mention of pity as an undesirable state of the soul along with envy, ill will, jealousy, etc., in the ethico-psychological system of the Stoic Zeno of Citium: Diogenes Laertius, 7.111–112.

*71. Porphyry's "On the Life of Plotinus" begins with the following words: "Plotinus, the philosopher our contemporary, seemed ashamed of being in the body." Bakhtin provides a very accurate analysis of the ethical implications of the extreme concentration of Neoplatonic thought on the *One*, on the idea of the *One* (so that the *Other* is posited by the *One* not as essentially *other*, but simply as another form of being of that same *One*, as a mere aspect of its meaning, as an emanational "outflow" of it).

72. The root-meaning of the Russian word for "kindness" (*dobrota*) is akin to that of the French *bonté* and the German *Gute*.

*73. Bakhtin's view of the genesis and ideational composition of early Christian anthropology has two aspects. On the one hand, it is necessarily conditioned by a certain sum of ideas which were characteristic for the science, philosophy, and historical-cultural essays as well as for the consciousness of the intelligentsia at the beginning of the twentieth century in general. Some of the authoritative thinkers of that time Bakhtin himself mentions by name, such as the brilliant professor of classical philology at Petersburg University and later at Warsaw University and an eloquent popularizer of his theories—F. F. Zelinsky [see note 66], and the coryphaeus of liberal Protestant theology and historian of the church—Adolf Harnack; others are present without being named openly. This is not the place to offer a critique of that sum of ideas; the point is to see as fully as possible the perspective from which the second—the original—aspect of Bakhtin's formulations becomes evident. Because, on the other hand, the consistently prosecuted connection of thoughts that proceeds from the antithesis of the "inner" and the "outer" body, the antithesis of *I-for-myself* and *I-for-the-other*, gives a specifically Bakhtinian meaning even to those passages in which, on the whole, Bakhtin simply summarizes anew the results of previous scholarship. Thus, the correlation of the threefold roots of Christianity—Judaic, Hellenic, and "Gnostic" (ultimately, either Iranian-dualistic or syncretic-dualistic; cf. the once fashionable problem of the Mandaeans, which had such a hypnotic effect on Alfred Loisy and Oswald Spengler)—was one of the favorite topics of discussion at that time. Today this topic is as important as it was in the past, although it goes without saying that the approach to it has been significantly modified both by new materials (first and foremost, by the Dead Sea Scrolls) and by a shift in methodological orientations. In Harnack's works (of which *Das Wesen des Christentums* and *Dogmenge-schichte* came to enjoy special popularity) the genesis of church doctrine, worship (together with religious art), and church organization is described as a gradual substitution of the cultural elements of Hellenism for the "pure teaching of Christ." Harnack's conception, however, presupposes a forceful emphasis on the difference between "initial" Christianity (which is still "pure") and "early" Christianity (which is already Hellenized) and, therefore, on an opposition between the "essence" of Christianity and the obscuration of that "essence" by Hellenism. For Zelinsky, on the other hand, "initial" Christianity (including the teaching of Jesus) is already, in its very essence, a Hellenistic phenomenon, and he is particularly insistent about the Greek origins of the idea of Jesus the Son of God. See F. F. Zelinsky, *Iz zhizni idej* [Studies in the Life of Ideas] (Petersburg: Akademija, 1922), vol. 4, pp. 15–16, and *Religija ellenizma* [The Religion of Hellenism] (Petrograd, 1922), p. 129.

To understand the logic of Bakhtin's formulations properly, some additional comments are required. Bakhtin's interpretation of the Old Testament world view sums up concisely a number of his own and others' hypotheses. Bakhtin succeeded in overcoming the abstractness of the old ideas about "ethical monotheism" (which go back to Moses Mendelssohn and were to be repeatedly revived later on, as in Hermann Cohen's *Die Religion der Vernunft aus den Quellen des Judentums* [Religion of Reason Out of the Sources of Judaism; Leipzig: G. Fock, 1919]); he succeeded in seeing the pervasive "bodiliness" in the Old Testament (cf. the central place of *Leiblichkeit* in Martin Buber's interpretation of the Bible; see Martin Buber, *Werke*, vol. 2, *Schriften zur Bibel* [Munich: Kosel; Heidelberg: Lambert Schneider, 1964]), without in any way succumbing to the extreme of sensual *magismos* which is characteristic for the interpreters associated with the "philosophy of life" [*Lebensphiloso-phie*], both outside Judaism (in Russia—V. V. Rozanov) and within it (cf. O. Goldberg, *Die Wirklichkeit der Hebräer* [Berlin: 1925]. The "bodiliness" of the Old Testament is described for the most part as "inner bodiliness," i.e., not as a bodiliness contemplated from outside, but as a bodiliness felt from within in the mode of needs and in the mode of satisfaction, although *not* as the individual bodiliness of one human being, but as the collective bodiliness of a consecrated ethnic community— "the unity of the people as an organism." In this connection, it is worth noting that the German-Jewish philosopher and translator of the Bible Franz Rosenzweig was seriously considering the possibility of rendering the Hebrew phrase "holy people" (*goi gados*), as in Exodus 19:6 and 24:3, for example, with the German phrase *heiliger Leib*, i.e., "holy body" (see Buber's letter to Will Herberg, dated January 25, 1953, in Martin Buber, *Briefwechsel aus sieben Jahrzehnten* [Heidelberg: Lambert Schneider, 1975], vol. 3, p. 326).

*74. Bakhtin is referring to the Old Testament prohibition of images:

"Thou shalt not make unto thee any graven image, or any likeness of any thing that is in heaven above or that is in the earth beneath, or that is in the water under the earth" (Exodus 20:4).

75. See notes 66 and 73.

76. Adolf Harnack (1851–1930) was a German Protestant theologian. Cf. note 73. On Harnack, see J. Macquarrie in *The Encyclopedia of Philosophy*, ed. Paul Edwards, and F. W. Kantzenbach in *Theologische Realenzyklopädie* (1985), vol. 14, pp. 450–458.

*77. In the Old Testament, Yahweh says to Moses: "Thou canst not see my face: for there shall no man see me, and live" (Exodus 33:20). Cf. also Judges 13:22: "And Manoah said unto his wife, We shall surely die, because we have seen God." In the New Testament, however, we read (in a passage whose context implies the Old Testament experience of the divine): "It is a fearful thing to fall into the hands of the living God" (Hebrews 10:31).

*78. This idea is developed in Saint Paul's epistles: "For as the body is one, and hath many members, and all the members of that one body, being many, are one body: so also is Christ. For by one Spirit are we all baptized into one body, whether we be Jews or Gentiles, whether we be bond or free; and have been all made to drink into one Spirit" (1 Corinthians 12:12–13; in accordance with the logic of the argument further on in the text, the quotidian necessity of caring even for the "uncomely" and "less honorable" parts of the body is advanced as a norm for loving relations within the church community, in which greater care must be shown for the less perfect). That is why a Christian's union with Christ has not only a spiritual aspect, but also an essential bodily aspect: "Now the body is not for fornication but for the Lord; and the Lord for the body. . . . therefore glorify God in your body, and in your spirit, which are God's" (1 Corinthians 6:13 and 20). The sacrament or mystery of such union is comparable, within certain limits, to the unclosing of an individual's bodily self-enclosedness in the conjoint life of spouses or of man and woman in general, who are transmuted, according to the Bible (Genesis 2:24), into "one flesh" (cf. above Bakhtin's statement about sexual "merging into one inner flesh"). Within the bounds of the Christian world view, this comparability does not abolish, but, on the contrary, provides a crucial foundation for the ascetic principle of preserving the chasteness of one's body: "Know ye not that our bodies are the members of Christ? shall I then take the members of Christ, and make them the members of an harlot? God forbid. What? Know ye not that he which is joined to an harlot is one body? for two, saith he, shall be one flesh. But he that is joined unto the Lord is one spirit. Flee fornication. Every sin that a man doeth is without the body; but he that commiteth fornication sinneth against his own body" (1 Corinthians 6:15–18).

*79. In Ephesians 5:22–23 the relations of Christ and the church (i.e., the community of all believers) are described as an ideal paradigm of the relations of husband and wife in the "great mystery" of marriage. From this perspective, husband and wife constitute an "icon" of Christ and the church, as it were. On the other hand, in Revelation, the Heavenly Jerusalem, symbolizing the "Church Triumphant" (i.e., the community of believers in eternity, on the other side of earthly conflicts), is called more than once the wife and bride of the Lamb (i.e., Christ): "for the marriage of the Lamb is come, and his wife hath made herself ready" (Revelation 19:7); "And I John saw the holy city, new Jerusalem, coming down from God out of heaven, prepared as a bride adorned for her husband" (Revelation 21:2).

*80. The sermons of St. Bernard of Clairvaux on the Song of Songs, which interpret the sensuous images as a description of ardent spiritual love of God, continued a tradition founded by early Christian thinkers (especially by Gregory of Nyssa), and, in their turn, gave an impulse to the motifs of *Gottesminne* in German and Dutch mysticism in the late Middle Ages (Hildegard of Bingen, Mechthild of Magdeburg, Meister Eckart, Heinrich Seuse, Jan van Ruysbroeck, and others). [For a modern translation, with introductions, of St. Bernard's *Sermones supra Cantica Canticorum*, see Cistercian Fathers Series, nos. 4, 7, 31, and 40: *The Works of Bernard of Clairvaux*, vols. 2–3, 11–12: *On the Song of Songs* 1–4 (Kalamazoo, Mich.: Cistercian Publications, 1971–1980).]

*81. The mysticism of St. Francis of Assisi is distinguished by popular freshness and cheerfulness: nature is a bright and mysterious world, calling for man's love; the cunning of the devils is impotent and deserves ridicule; the doctrine of the predestination of the soul to perdition is a satanic invention. Personifying the sun and the moon, fire and water, the Christian virtues and death, St. Francis spoke to them, as in a fairy tale, calling them brothers and sisters; the lived experience of this brotherhood of all God's creatures, which conjoins the world of man and the world of nature, finds expression in the "Song of the Sun," a moving lyrical poem in popular language. That same brotherhood includes, as a part of nature, "brother Ass"—St. Francis's own body, which is sternly bridled in accordance with the rules of asceticism, but is not rejected, not condemned, and not despised: "brother Ass"—this designation of the body expresses a gentle humor which qualifies the enthusiasm of asceticism. While remaining within the confines of the Christian view of the world, St. Francis anticipated that need for the renewal of medieval culture which engendered the Italian Renaissance. Hence his importance for two forerunners of the Renaissance—the painter Giotto di Bondone and the poet Dante Alighieri. Personal devotion to the memory of St. Francis was a fact of both Giotto's and Dante's biographies: it was not without reason that Giotto named one of his sons Francis and one of his daughters— Clara (the name of the foundress of the Franciscan nuns), while Dante, it would appear, belonged to the Franciscan Tertiaries, i.e., he was a member in a confraternity of lay men and women connected with the Minorites. Giotto's realism, which dealt a blow to medieval conventionality, was formed during his work on the *Legend of St. Francis*, which is full of vivid and colorful scenes (frescoes in the Upper Church at Assisi). [In his essay on "Giotto and St. Francis," G. K. Chesterton wrote: "Some modern writers on the first Franciscans talk as if Francis was the first to invent the idea of the Love of God and the God of Love; or at least was the first to go back and find it in any of the Gospels. The truth is that anybody could find it in any of the creeds and doctrinal definitions of any period between the Gospels and the Franciscan movement. But he would find it in the theological dogmas as he would find it in the Byzantine pictures, drawn out in stark and simple lines like a mathematical diagram, asserted with a sort of dark clarity for those who can appreciate the idea of logical content and balance. In the sermons of St. Francis, as in the pictures of Giotto, it is made popular by pantomime. . . . Thus we find that St. Francis was in many ways the actual founder of the medieval miracle play; and there is all this suggestion of a stiff thing coming to life in the tale of his contact with the Bambino, illustrated in one of Giotto's designs" (G. K. Chesterton, *The Common Man* [London: Sheed and Ward, 1950], p. 103).] Heartfelt words praising St. Francis were put by Dante into the mouth of Thomas Aquinas (*Paradiso* XI); numerous invocations of his name appear in other passages of the *Divine Comedy*.

82. *Paradiso* XIV.61–66: "So quick and eager seemed to me both the one and the other choir to say *Amen* that they plainly showed their desire for their dead bodies—not perhaps for themselves alone, but for their mothers, for their fathers, and for the others who were dear before they became eternal flames" (John D. Sinclair). The passage follows Solomon's reply to the question (asked by Beatrice in Dante's name) about the appearance of the blessed after the resurrection of the body. Edmund G. Gardner, *Dante and the Mystics* (London: Dent and Sons, 1913), p. 121, argues that Dante's choice of Solomon as the expounder of the doctrine of the resurrected body was influenced by St. Bernard's interpretation of the Song of Songs. Cf. also Romano Guardini, "Leib und Leiblichkeit in Dantes 'Göttlicher Komödie,'" in *Anteile: Martin Heidegger zum 60. Geburtstag* (Frankfurt/Main: V. Klostermann, 1950), pp. 154–177.

*83. See note 177.

84. On the significance of glory or fame in the Renaissance, see Jacob Burckhardt, *The Civilization of the Renaissance in Italy*, trans. S. G. C. Middlemore, part 2, chap. 2.

85. "Outsideness": see note 28.

*86. Bakhtin has in mind, first of all, the "rehabilitation of the flesh" slogan which was characteristic of the ideology of "Young Germany" but was prepared by the thought of the Romantics; one should note especially the esoteric mysticism of sex, and of organic life in general, in Novalis (cf. his *Fragments*), as well as Friedrich Schlegel's unprecedentedly bold yet absolutely serious affirmation of sensuality, without any lasciviousness, in his novel *Lucinde* (1799), which caused a sensation in its time. Until then, sensuality was assigned a particular place—sometimes even a highly important one (cf. the mores of the Rococo period)—but a place that was immutably fixed, and the tone of lasciviousness was a token of that fixation. Romanticism destroyed that fixation.

87. Cf. the concept of the other (*der Andere*) in Cohen's *Ethik des reinen Willens*, pp. 211–214, 248–249.

88. Can become aesthetically valid or—can gain aesthetic validity or force. See note 14.

89. "Expressive" and "impressive": Bakhtin uses here the Russian adaptation of the Latin forms rather than the Russian loan-translations of these adjectives. To maintain the parallelism with "expressive," I retain the form "impressive" in the sense of "impressional," i.e., relating to impression.

90. On "empathizing" (*Einfühlung*), see note 17. "Co-experiencing" renders the Russian *soperezhivanie*, which (in the present context) is an equivalent of the German *Miterleben*. The term *Miterleben* was particularly favored by Karl Groos, for whom "empathizing" was only a special case of "inner co-experiencing" (*das innere Miterleben*); cf. Karl Groos, *Der ästhetische Genuß* (Giessen: J. Ricker, 1902), chap. 5, especially pp. 183–192.

91. Cf. Lossky's "Vosprijatie chuzhoj dushevnoj zhizni" (1914) [Perception of the Inner Life of Others] in his *Osnovnye voprosy gnoseologii* [Fundamental Problems of Epistemology] (Petrograd: Nauka i shkola, 1919), and his later article "Perception of Other Selves," *Personalist* 29 (1948), 149–162. See also Ludwig Binswanger's critical survey in his *Einführung in die Probleme der allgemeinen Psychologie* (Amsterdam: E. J. Bonset, 1965; reprint of the Berlin edition of 1922), chap. 4, sections 1 and 2 (*das fremde Ich*). On Lossky, see *The Encyclopedia of Philosophy*.

92. In his *Weltanschauungslehre* (Jena and Leipzig: E. Diederichs, 1905), vol. 1, pp. 170–171, Heinrich Gomperz criticized Stephan Witasek's theory of *Vorstellungsgefühle*, i.e., feelings we represent to ourselves or reproduced feelings. See S. Witasek, "Zur psychologischen Analyse der ästhetischen Einfühlung," *Zeitschrift für Psychologie* 25 (1901), 1–49, and his *Grundzüge der allgemeinen Ästhetik* (Leipzig: Barth, 1904), pp. 66 ff. Stephan Witasek (1870–1915), Austrian philosopher and psychologist and a pupil of Meinong, introduced Meinong's *Gegenstandstheorie* into aesthetic studies. On Gomperz, see *Neue Deutsche Biographie*.

93. See note 17. Wilhelm Perpeet, "Historisches und Systemmatisches zur Einfühlungsästhetik," *Zeitschrift für Ästhetik* 11 (1966), 193–216, provides a revision of the historical genealogy of *Einfühlung*: the traditional genealogy, tracing the concept back to Herder, Novalis, Jean Paul, Lotze, is a historical error. See also his "Einfühlungsästhetik," in *Historisches Wörterbuch der Philosophie*, vol. 2, pp. 397–400. On Fr. Th. Vi-

scher, Lotze, Wundt, and Lipps, see *The Encyclopedia of Philosophy*; on Robert Vischer and Johannes Volkelt, see *Enciclopedia Filosofica*, 2nd ed. (Florence: Sansoni, 1969), vol. 6.

94. See Karl Groos, *Der ästhetische Genuß*, chap. 5, especially pp. 192 ff. Aesthetic co-experiencing (*Miterleben*) is the "play of inner imitation": "ich nehme an, daß beim vollen Geneißen motorische Vorgänge von imitatorischem Charakter wirksam sind" (p. 193). On Groos, see *Neue Deutsche Biographie*.

95. See Karl Groos, *Der ästhetische Genuß*, chaps. 1 (aesthetic experience as play) and 6 (aesthetic illusions). Konrad Lange (1855–1921) was known for his *Illusionstheorie* of art as "conscious self-deception"; see his *Das Wesen der Kunst*, 2nd ed. (Berlin: G. Grote, 1907).

96. See note 20. Cf. the following reviews of Cohen's *Ästhetik:* Walter Kinkel in *Deutsche Literaturzeitung* 33 (1912), cols. 1669–1178, 1733–1740; G. Falter in *Archiv für Geschichte der Philosophie* 25 (1912), 379–396; P. Stern and A. Buchenau in *Zeitschrift für Ästhetik* 8 (1913), 291–303 and 615–623.

97. Cf. O. Schuster, "Die Einfühlungstheorie von Th. Lipps und Schopenhauers Ästhetik," *Archiv für Geschichte der Philosophie* 25 (1912), 104–116.

98. On Fiedler, Hildebrand, and Hanslick, see *Neue Deutsche Biographie*; on Riegl, see O. Pächt in *Burlington Magazine* 105/722 (1963), 188–193, and Hans Sedlmayr, *Kunst und Wahrheit* (Hamburg: Rowohlt, 1958), chap. 2.

99. On the Idea in Hegel, see Charles Karelis in *Hegel's Introduction to Aesthetics*, trans. T. M. Knox (Oxford: Clarendon Press, 1979). "Content aesthetics": Bakhtin is referring to the German *Inhalts-* or *Gehalts-ästhetik* (as opposed to empirical or formalist aesthetics); cf. "Gehalt," in *Historisches Wörterbuch der Philosophie*, vol. 3, cols. 140–145.

100. For criticism of expressive aesthetics in general and of empathy in particular, see Paul Moos, *Die deutsche Ästhetik der Gegenwart mit besonderer Berücksichtigung der Musikästhetik* (Berlin: Schuster and Loeffler, 1920); Charles Lalo, *Les Sentiments esthétiques* (Paris: F. Alcan, 1910); Emil Utitz in *Jahrbücher der Philosophie* 1 (1913), 324–328, 340–345.

101. While Hermann Cohen may be assigned to "expressive aesthetics," he does not accept the principle of empathy; see his *Ästhetik des reinen Gefühls*, vol. 1, pp. 185–186. Johannes Volkelt's views on empathy are analyzed in Roman Ingarden, *Studia z estetyki* (Warsaw: PWN, 1970), vol. 3, pp. 113–128.

102. Physiognomic and "gestural": it expresses inner states through outward movements of the face and the body.

103. On isolation (from the surroundings or from ongoing life) as a first precondition of form, see Cohn, *Allgemeine Ästhetik*, p. 35: "The aesthetic value is purely intensive; the object that corresponds to it is, in its

turn, an object which stands there as a complete, self-contained whole. One can say, therefore, that the isolation of the aesthetic object is a correlative concept of the pure intensity of aesthetic value. That is why even in nature we favor delimited vistas, so long as the point is not the distinctive impression of a boundless plain, of an exalted expanse. And even the aesthetic enjoyment of boundlessness requires a certain isolation, which is provided not by a changing abundance of manifold objects but only by a homogeneous content in the entire overviewable space—a wide treeless plain or the watery desert of the sea. Art produces a certain isolation by the sole fact that it is art; it promotes this isolation further by the use of additional special means. These include, first of all, a clear-cut boundary demarcating the work of art in space and time. Gottfried Semper writes: 'The frame is one of the most important basic forms of art. There is no self-contained picture without a frame, no measuring-standard of magnitude without it.' The tendency of many novella-writers to enclose their story by means of a frame, and thereby to move it a stage further away from life, rests on similar grounds. We want to see a work of art in such a way that nothing else disturbs its particularity. Statues stand out in the most pleasing way against a background that is colored divergently yet uniformly, e.g., against the background of green hedges. Every reproduction gains an advantage when it is glued, by itself, on a yellowish sheet of paper. A similar effect is produced by the expectant pause before the raising of the curtain, by the special space, and by the distinctive lighting in a theater performance. Richard Wagner's idea of a *Festspiel*, whose spectator would be entirely detached from the ordinary interests and environments of his life, also belongs here to some extent. Besides this closing-off (*Abschließung*), the arts also further isolation by the fact that their special means of representation do not produce a full semblance of naturalness, and necessitate a stylization that diverges, to some extent, from nature. Thus, statues may be colorless or at least not colored naturalistically. . . . Verse in poetry and elevated prose produce a similar effect. We are not claiming that the significance of such special means of representation is exhaustively explained by isolation, but there can be no doubt that a part of their significance is related to isolation." The fundamental importance of isolation is developed further by the art historian Richard Hamann, in the first edition of his *Ästhetik* (Leipzig: Teubner, 1911). Isolation is also a fundamental category in Hugo Muensterberg's theory of art; see his *Psychology and Life* (Boston: Houghton Mifflin, 1899), pp. 200 ff.; *Grundzüge der Psychologie* (Leipzig: Barth, vol. 1, 1900), pp. 121–124; *The Eternal Values* (Boston: Houghton Mifflin, 1909), part 3. See also Lev Vygotsky, *Psikhologija iskusstva* (Moscow: Iskusstvo, 1968), p. 134.

104. The Pythagoreans—Aristotle: in the development of the concept of harmony in antiquity (harmony in the sense of a concordant conjunction of contraries), the Pythagoreans mark the beginning, whereas Aris-

totle's analysis of the concept represents a closing synthesis; for passages on harmony in Aristotle, see Troy Wilson Organ, *An Index to Aristotle in English Translation* (New York: Gordian Press, 1966), under "harmony."

105. In its original form, the proverb is "a spoonful of pitch [i.e., something very bitter] in a barrelful of honey [is enough to spoil the sweetness of a whole barrel of honey]"; cf. the French *un peu de fiel gâte beaucoup de miel.*

106. Plastically significant positions: positions that have plastic validity or force. See note 14.

107. My being-outside (*vnenakhodimost'*): my situatedness outside him. See note 28.

108. The aesthetic object proper is the object constituted in *aesthetic* perception; it must be distinguished from the "material" artifact. See below in the section entitled "[Inner and Outer Form]." On the aesthetic object in this specific sense, see Waldemar Conrad's trailblazing phenomenological study "Der ästhetische Gegenstand," *Zeitschrift für Ästhetik* 3 (1908), 71–118, 469–511, as well as Roman Ingarden, "Aesthetic Experience and Aesthetic Object," *Philosophy and Phenomenological Research* 21 (1961), 289–313, and Mikel Dufrenne, *The Phenomenology of Aesthetic Experience,* trans. E. S. Casey et al. (Evanston: Northwestern University Press, 1973), part 1 (Phenomenology of the Aesthetic Object).

109. Makar Devushkin in Dostoevsky's *Poor Folk* (1846); see Devushkin's letter of July 8.

110. "Reincarnated" himself, i.e., embodied himself in another person or transformed himself into another person. On "reincarnation" in art, see I. I. Lapshin, "O perevoploshchaemosti v khudozhestvennom tvorchestve" in his *Khudozhestvennoe tvorchestvo* (Petrograd: Mysl', 1922), pp. 5–140.

111. Character: see part 4 in the section "The Whole of the Hero as a Whole of Meaning."

112. Rhythm: see part 3 in the section "The Temporal Whole of the Hero."

113. The enacted life event: the enacted life is an event.

114. On aesthetic *Scheingefühle,* i.e., feelings called forth by aesthetic *Schein,* see Eduard von Hartmann, *Philosophie des Schönen* (Berlin: Duncker, 1887), pp. 39–46.

115. The first explanation (extension of *Ichwert*) goes back to Lipps, the second (partaking in *das Menschlich-Bedeutungsvolle*)—to Johannes Volkelt.

116. On sympathy, see the fundamental study of Max Scheler, *Zur Phänomenologie und Theorie der Sympathiegefühle und von Liebe und Haß* (Halle: Niemeyer, 1913), and the second, enlarged, edition, *Wesen und Formen der Sympathie* (Bonn: Cohen, 1923).

117. Cf. the opening part of the next section, "The Temporal Whole of the Hero."

118. German verbs meaning "to shape, give a form to, fashion."

119. The German word *Ausdruck* (or *expression* in English) could be literally translated as "a pressing out from inside."

120. Cf. also the German *Darstellung*.

121. Imposed as a task: not *gegeben* but *aufgegeben*. See note 23.

122. Outsideness: one's own situatedness outside others. See note 28.

123. Isolation (from ongoing life): see note 103.

*124. [In the original: an act of forgiving *gratis*.] Cf. Saint Augustine's argument that grace is called *gratia* in Latin as an indication of its being bestowed *gratis*.

*125. Bakhtin gives a thorough analysis of this theory in *Formal'nyj metod v literaturovedenii* (Leningrad: Priboj, 1928), pp. 59–76. [See P. N. Medvedev/M. M. Bakhtin, *The Formal Method in Literary Scholarship*, trans. Albert J. Wehrle (Baltimore: Johns Hopkins University Press, 1978), part 2, chap. 1 (The Formal Method in European Art Scholarship).]

126. See notes 92 and 98.

127. See note 108 on this fundamental distinction.

128. Representation in the sense of the German *Vorstellung*.

129. Feeling-tone (German *Gefühlston*): the feeling-tone of a sensation, i.e., the feeling associated with a sensation.

130. Essentially necessary: founded on principle (German *prinzipiell*). See note 2.

131. The event of being: being is an ongoing event. See note 30.

132. Independent of meaning: they are independent or outside the bounds of the meaning to which the hero is directed from within himself in living his life.

133. "Interpretation" in the sense of "giving a meaning to, rendering meaningful."

134. Consolidating: taking on bodily consistency.

135. Fundamentally and essentially: a valuation that is new in principle (German *prinzipiell*).

136. Storyline significance: significance for determining a storyline or plot.

137. Independently of the purpose and the meaning toward which the other is directed from within himself in living his own life.

138. A quotation from Horace, *Odes* 3.30 (*Exegi monumentum*), lines 6–7: "I shall not altogether die, but a mighty part of me (*multaque pars mei*) shall escape the death-goddess" (C. E. Bennet).

139. Dante: see note 82.

140. "Narrowness of consciousness" (German *Bewußtseinsenge*): the psychological fact that only a part of the simultaneously received impressions can be consciously experienced.

141. "Philosophy of culture" is a translation of the German term *Kulturphilosophie*, which designates an influential trend in German philosophy in the first third of the twentieth century, especially the Neo-Kantian

contributions to the foundation of "cultural sciences" (in distinction from the "natural sciences"). See Wilhelm Perpeet, "Kultur, Kultur-philosophie," *Historisches Wörterbuch der Philosophie,* vol. 4, cols. 1314–1318.

142. Hermann Ebbinghaus (1850–1909) was an eminent German experimental psychologist. See R. A. Makkreel, *Dilthey* (Princeton, N.J.: Princeton University Press, 1975), pp. 206–209, on Ebbinghaus's dispute with Dilthey about, *inter alia,* the role of hypotheses in psychology.

143. Essentially necessary, i.e., founded on a necessary principle (German *prinzipiell*).

144. In ancient Greek prosody, *arsis* denoted the metrically unaccented part of a foot, while *thesis* denoted the metrically accented part of a foot.

145. "Purposive without purpose": the formulation is from Kant's *Critique of Judgement,* #15 ("Zweckmässigkeit ohne Zweck"). Cf. Eva Schaper, *Studies in Kant's Aesthetics* (Edinburgh: Edinburgh University Press, 1979), pp. 125–126, 128–129, 131–132; Paul Guyer, *Kant and the Claims of Taste* (Cambridge, Mass.: Harvard University Press, 1979), p. 238.

146. "Playing a fool"—I shall use this phrase as a stopgap translation of *jurodstvo,* i.e., the deliberate striving to act provocatively like a "holy fool." On the motivations and behavior of "holy fools" (in the original religious context), see G. P. Fedotov, *The Russian Religious Mind* (Cambridge, Mass.: Harvard University Press, 1966), chap. 3.

147. Bakhtin uses here the plural of *znachimost'* ("validity," German *Geltung*): validities of meaning or meaning-validities (German *Sinngeltungen*), as opposed, for example, to value-validities (anything that bears the validity or force of a value). See note 14.

148. To die as an intelligent being or (closer to the original) to die as spirit.

149. Folly or insanity: that is, the act of exceeding the bounds of reason.

150. "No sureties from heaven": a quotation from the closing lines of V. Zhukovsky's poem "Zhelanie" (1811), which is a rendering of Schiller's "Sehnsucht" (1803); cf. "Du mußt glauben, du mußt wagen, / Denn *die Götter leihen kein Pfand; /* Nur ein Wunder kann dich tragen / In das schöne Wunderland."

151. Aesthetically significant: he comes to bear aesthetic validity.

152. See note 173 below.

153. "An uttered thought is a lie"—an oft-quoted line from F. Tyutchev's poem "Silentium!" (published 1833).

154. "Sophianic"—a term from "Sophiology," a philosophical-theological trend in modern Russian philosophy of religion. See Lev Zander, "Sophiologie," *Die Religion in Geschichte und Gegenwart,* 3rd ed., vol. 6, col. 147; L. Ganchikov, "Sofiologia," *Enciclopedia Filosofica,* vol. 5, cols. 1522–1523.

155. Features or—constituents; Bakhtin uses his preferred term—moments.

156. Being is an ongoing event, an event that is unitary and unique.

157. On isolation as a precondition of aesthetic perception, see note 103.

158. On repentance, see Max Scheler, "Reue und Wiedergeburt," in his *Vom Ewigen im Menschen* (Leipzig: Der Neue Geist Verlag, 1921).

159. Confessional self-accounting, i.e., confession as an accounting rendered to oneself for one's own life.

160. For a selection from Tolstoy's diaries (from 1847 to 1910), see *Tolstoy's Diaries*, ed. and trans. R. F. Christian, 2 vols. (London: Athlone Press, 1985).

161. See note 146.

* 162. Bakhtin has in mind here three New Testament texts that are connected by unity of meaning. First, the parable of the Pharisee and the publican (Luke 18:13). Second, the healing of the daughter of the woman of Canaan (Matthew 15:28). Third, the story of the father of the possessed child who "said with tears, Lord, I believe; help thou mine unbelief" (Mark 9:24).

* 163. Psalm 51:7 and 10.

164. See note 80.

165. Book of Life: an expression found both in the Old Testament and the New Testament to signify the record or list of the names of those destined to be saved. Cf. *New Catholic Encyclopedia*, 17 vols. (New York: McGraw-Hill [1967–1979]), vol. 2, pp. 697–698.

166. Theomachy and anthropomachy: a fighting against or opposition to the divine will or to human beings. Or as Bakhtin defines it in the same sentence—"the refusal to accept a possible judgment by God or by man."

167. See note 146.

168. Cf. Psalm 51:5: "Behold, I was shapen in iniquity; and in sin did my mother conceive me."

169. Note the definition of *fabula* immediately below.

170. Its own purpose: literally, the particular task it sets itself.

171. Self-regulatedness: conforming to its own law(s). Cf. German *Selbstgesetzlichkeit*.

172. See note 108 about the "aesthetic object."

173. Cf. at the end of the Russian Orthodox service for the dead (*Panikhida*): "Grant rest eternal in blessed repose, o Lord, to Thy servant [ ], who is fallen asleep, and make his memory to be eternal (*sotvori emu vechnuju pamjat'*)." See Vladimir Solov'ev, *Sobranie sochinenij*, 2nd ed. vol. 8 (St. Petersburg: Prosveshchenie, n.d.): *Opravdanie dobra*, chap. 19, section 2, pp. 450–452; Pavel Florensky, *Stolp i utverzhdenie istiny* (Berlin: Rossica, 1929), pp. 195–202; Helmut Gollwitzer, *Krummes Holz—aufrechter Gang*, 3rd ed. (Munich: Chr. Kaiser, 1971), p. 58 ("göttliches Gedenken").

174. Luke 18:9–14.

175. "The Story of My Adversities"; cf. *The Story of Abelard's Adversities*, trans. J. T. Muckle (Toronto: Pontifical Institute of Mediaeval Studies, 1964).

176. See note 166.

* 177. *Secretum* (other titles: *De contemptu mundi, De secreto conflictu curarum mearum*)—a dialogue by Francesco Petrarca, written 1342–1343 and reworked 1353–1358. The participants in the dialogue are Petrarch himself, personified Truth, and Saint Augustine. The content of the dialogue is a discussion of Petrarch's way of life; he is both condemned as a sinner (by Truth and by Saint Augustine, but in part also by himself) and defended or, rather, noncritically described as an objective given that is not subject to change (Petrarch's basic position as a participant in the dialogue). Cf. M. Gershenzon's article in: Petrarka, *Avtobiografija: Ispoved', Sonety* (St. Petersburg: n.p., 1914).

178. See note 160. At the time Bakhtin wrote his study, Tolstoy's later diaries were available only in excerpts.

179. Fragment of the diary Pushkin kept from November 24, 1833, to February 1835.

180. See note 103 on "isolation."

181. "Interpreted" in the sense of "given meaning, rendered meaningful."

182. "Storm and Stress"—German *Sturm und Drang*: a literary and intellectual movement in Germany (from the end of the 1760s to the beginning of the 1780s). Cf. Roy Pascal, *The German Sturm und Drang* (Manchester: University Press, 1954).

183. Life's "fabular" possibilities, i.e., the manifold *fabulas* inherent in life.

184. *Dolce stil nuovo*, Guinicelli (Guinizzelli): see Karl Vossler, *Medieval Culture*, trans. W. C. Lawton, 2 vols. (New York: F. Ungar, 1958; reprint of 1929 edition), vol. 1, pp. 305–309, vol. 2, pp. 91–94; Hugo Friedrich, *Epochen der italienischen Lyrik* (Frankfurt/Main: V. Klostermann, 1964), chap. 2.

* 185. A most important event in Petrarch's life was his being crowned on the Capitoline with a laurel wreath for his poetic achievements. His imagination is affected by the consonance between the name of his beloved and the word "laurel"—a symbol of enthusiastic, passionate love of glory. [See Hugo Friedrich, *Epochen*, pp. 196–201 ("Laura-Symbolik").]

186. Friedrich Heinrich Jacobi (1743–1819), a leading representative of the "philosophy of feeling." See *The Encyclopedia of Philosophy*.

187. "Philosophy of life"—a rendering of the German term *Lebensphilosophie*, denoting a widespread movement in twentieth-century philosophy, the most important representatives of which were Wilhelm Dil-

they and Henri Bergson. See "Lebensphilosophie," *Historisches Wörter-buch der Philosophie*, vol. 5, cols. 135–141, especially #5.

188. See note 185.

189. Protagonist—the first actor (combatant, pleader) in ancient Greek drama. Thespis is said to have introduced a single actor's part to the original choral drama; Aeschylus added a second actor (deuteragonist), and Sophocles—a third (tritagonist).

190. On the postulation of immortality by love, cf. the supplementary section.

191. Cf. Albert J. Wehrle, "Decadence in Russian Literature," in *Modern Encyclopedia of Russian and Soviet Literature*, ed. Harry B. Weber, vol. 5, pp. 81–99.

192. Konstantin Sluchevsky (1837–1904) was a Russian poet and prose writer; Innokenty Annensky (1856–1909), a Russian poet, playwright, literary critic, and translator of Euripides.

193. See note 146.

194. On Andrei Bely (1880–1934), author of the novel *Petersburg*, see Vladimir E. Alexandrov, *Andrei Bely: The Major Symbolist Fiction* (Cambridge, Mass.: Harvard University Press, 1985).

195. See note 103 on "isolation."

196. Outside the meaning toward which he is directed from within himself in living his own life.

197. "Retribution"—a narrative poem by Russian poet Aleksandr Blok (1880–1921). Cf. Pavel Medvedev, "Tvorcheskij put' A. A. Bloka," in *Pamjati A. A. Bloka* (Petersburg: Poljarnaja Zvezda, 1922), p. 65: "[Blok] presents and interprets his heroes not as lyrically isolated monads, but— against the background of everyday existence, in the circumstances of family life, on the plane of history. [He] tends to understand the personality of his hero and the complex parabola of his fate as a 'retribution of history, milieu, period.'"

198. Cf. "Idee," in *Historisches Wörterbuch der Philosophie*, vol. 4, col. 123.

199. See note 146.

200. The heroine of "Poor Liza" (1792), short story by Nikolai Karamzin (1766–1826)—a classic of Russian Sentimentalism.

201. "Humor" in the special sense in which it is understood in German philosophical aesthetics; cf. W. Preisendanz in *Historisches Wörterbuch der Philosophie*, vol. 3, cols. 1232–1234.

202. See note 146.

203. Medieval "realism" (as opposed to "nominalism"): the scholastic doctrine that universals have objective existence (they are more than subjective concepts or mere names).

204. *Blago-obrazie*: the beauty of outward appearance as a manifestation of inner goodness. The word is a loan-translation of the Greek *eu-*

schemon; cf. *Theological Dictionary of the New Testament,* ed. Gerhard Kittel; trans. G. W. Bromiley, vol. 2, pp. 770–772. Cf. the Classical Greek ideal of *kalokagathia;* see *Historische Wörterbuch der Philosophie,* vol. 4, cols. 681–684.

205. Independently of the meaning toward which a human being is directed from within himself in living his own life.

206. What has been described in the preceding sentences is the transition from aesthetic vision to art specifically. On the distinction of "aesthetic" and "artistic," see note 59.

207. The event of a work of art, i.e., a work of art is an event.

208. The event of the world, i.e., the world constitutes an event.

209. That is, according to the conception which substitutes a "literary context" for the author's actual creative context.

*210. This synoptic note of Bakhtin's will become clearer in connection with the analogous thought in his article "Problema soderzhanija, materiala i formy v slovesnom khudozhestvennom tvorchestve": "There are works which really have nothing to do with the world, but only with the word 'world' in the literary context; that is, works which are born, live, and die on the pages of periodicals, without ever breaking out from the pages of contemporary periodical publications, without ever taking us outside their bounds in any respect" (M. M. Bakhtin, *Voprosy literatury i estetiki* [Moscow: Khudozhestvennaja literatura, 1975], p. 35).

211. The event of a world, i.e., the latter is an event.

212. See notes 192 and 194.

213. See note 201.

214. "Viewability" of life or its "intuitability"; cf. German *Anschaulichkeit.* See note 7.

215. "Negligible": of so little extent or consequence as to be practically nonexistent and so requiring or deserving little or no attention. The Russian adjective *nichtozhnyj* accentuates the idea of nothingness or nullity (cf. German *nichtig*).

216. "Parting"—*Razluka* (the poem has no title in the ms.): "Dlja beregov otchizny dal'noj . . ." (written on November 27, 1830, in Boldino). The poem is in memory of Amalia Riznich, one of Pushkin's loves in Odessa, where he lived from July 1823 to August 1824. She was the daughter of an Austrian banker; her mother was Italian. In May of 1824, she left Odessa for Italy and died of consumption in Genoa in May 1825.

217. Bakhtin cites the text of the poem according to S. A. Vengerov's edition of Pushkin's works (Petersburg: Brockhaus-Efron, 1909), vol. 3, p. 164 (no. 654). In the Centennial ("1837–1937") edition, lines 19 and 23 read: "Where the shadow of olive-trees lies on the waters," "And with them—the kiss of our meeting." See Pushkin, *Polnoe sobranie sochinenij* (Leningrad: Akademija nauk SSSR, 1948), vol. 3, pp. 1, 257.

218. See P. V. Annenkov's edition of Pushkin's works: *Sochinenija Pushkina* (Petersburg: 1855), vol. 1, p. 289.

219. *Arsis* and *thesis:* see note 144.

220. The normal dialogue meter in Greek tragedy was the iambic trimeter.

221. Elegies of 1823 and 1824: elegies written in Odessa.

222. "Conjuration"—*Zaklinanie* (written October 17, 1830, in Boldino). A poem in three 8-line stanzas, in iambic tetrameter.

223. Barry Cornwall, pseudonym of Bryan Waller Procter (1787–1874) was an English poet and dramatist. On Pushkin's interest in his works, see N. V. Yakovlev's article in *Pushkin i ego sovremenniki,* 28 (1917), 5–28. Pushkin's "Conjuration" was prompted by Barry Cornwall's poem "An Invocation" ("If, at this dim and silent hour, / Spirits have a power / To wander from their homes of light . . ."].

224. Boldino: from September to December 1830, Pushkin lived on the estate of Boldino, in the southeastern corner of the Nizhny Novgorod province (now the Gor'ky province). This was the most creative autumn in his entire life (known as "the Boldino autumn"): he wrote some thirty short poems (including "Parting" and "Conjuration"); he finished *Eugene Onegin* in its first form (nine cantos); he wrote a short mock epic, *The Cottage in Kolomna,* the five prose *Tales of Belkin,* and four short tragedies (*Mozart and Salieri, The Stone Guest, The Feast during the Plague,* and *The Covetous Knight*).

225. "The Poor Knight": "Byl na svete rytsar' bednyj . . ." A ballad in fourteen quatrains, in trochaic tetrameter, written in 1829. S. A. Vengerov's edition includes it under poems written in 1830.

"Farewell"—*Proshchanie:* "V poslednij raz tvoj obraz milyj . . ." (written on October 5, 1830, in Boldino): a poem in three 5-line stanzas, in iambic tetrameter.

"The Stone Guest"—*Kammenyj gost'* (finished on November 4, 1830, in Boldino): a verse tragedy in four scenes.

226. "We shall once more join our lips in a passionate kiss": a variant reading of lines 15–16 not found in the ms.

227. Vasily Zhukovsky (1783–1852), a distinguished Russian poet and translator. See Irina Semenko, *Vasily Zhukovsky* (Boston: Twayne Publishers, 1976), pp. 21–23, 25.

228. S. Averintsev identifies these phrases as citations from the poem *Iov* ("Job") by Vyacheslav Ivanov (1866–1949), a classical scholar and a leading poet and theorist of Russian Symbolism. See Ivanov's collection of poems *Nezhnaja Tajna* [Tender Mystery] (Petersburg: Ory, 1912), pp. 29–30.

229. See Novalis's *Hymnen an die Nacht* [Hymns to the Night], written in 1799 and published in 1800.

Zhukovsky: see note 227.

Vladimir Solov'ev (1853–1900) was an influential Russian philosopher and poet. See his long poem "Three Encounters"—*Tri vstrechi* (1898), and related shorter poems ("U tsaritsy moej . . . ," "Vsja v lazuri . . .").

Cf. Fedor Stepun, *Mystische Weltschau* (Munich: Carl Hanser, 1964), pp. 41–48.

Ivanov: see note 228. Cf. his collections of poetry *Cor Ardens* (Moscow: Scorpion, 1912), vol. 2, part 4 ("Love and Death"), and *Nezhnaja Tajna*. Cf. Fedor Stepun, *Mystische Weltschau*, pp. 258–262.

230. Dante's *Vita nuova* was composed between 1292 and 1300, and first published in 1576.

Petrarch's sonnets: "Sonnets to Laura" in his *Canzoniere* (published in 1470).

Ivanov: see collections cited in preceding note.

Rainer Maria Rilke's collection of poems *Das Stunden-Buch* [Book of Hours] was written in 1899–1903 and published in 1905. The book is based on the fiction that it was written by a Russian monk.

231. The citations from *Eugene Onegin* are based on Vladimir Nabokov's translation. On Lensky, see also M. M. Bakhtin, *The Dialogic Imagination*, trans. Caryl Emerson and Michael Holquist (Austin: University of Texas Press, 1981), pp. 43–44, 322, 329.

232. Lensky's last elegy, composed on the eve of his duel with Onegin.

233. Humanized: provided with human qualities, given a human character, conformed to human nature; represented as a human being, personified. Cf. German *vermenschlichen*.

234. See preceding note.

SUPPLEMENT:
THE PROBLEM OF CONTENT, MATERIAL, AND FORM IN VERBAL ART

The present study attempts a methodological analysis of the fundamental concepts[1] and problems of poetics[2] on the basis of general systematic aesthetics.

The starting point for our study was provided by certain Russian works on poetics; their basic propositions undergo critical examination in our opening chapters. However, here we shall not consider and assess trends and particular works considered as a whole and in their historical determinateness. Our principal interest is restricted to the purely systematic value of their basic concepts and propositions. Surveys of works on poetics of a historical or informational nature are not considered in our investigation, as they are not always appropriate to studies which set for themselves purely systematic goals, where only theoretical positions and arguments can have significance. We have also freed our study from the superfluous ballast of citations and references, for they lack any direct methodological significance in studies of a nonhistorical nature, while in a compressed work of a systematic nature they are entirely superfluous. For the qualified reader, they are unnecessary, and for the unqualified, useless.

I. The Study of Art and General Aesthetics

Work of the most serious and productive kind is being carried out in Russia at the present time in the field of the study of art. Russian scholarly literature has been enriched in recent years[3] by valuable works on the theory of art, especially in the area of poetics. One can, in fact, speak about a certain flowering of art study in Russia, especially by comparison with the preceding period, when the domain of art was a principal refuge for various kinds of scientifically irresponsible chatter with pretensions to profundity. All those ideas and considerations, which appeared to be profound and productive in life, but which could not be included in any single discipline, i.e., could find no place in the objective unity of cognition (so-called wandering revelations), were usually expressed and brought into a fortuitous external order apropos of art in general or of one particular work or another. This aestheticized, half-scientific thought, which sometimes by misunderstanding called itself philosophical, always clung to art, sensing its (not entirely legitimate) blood relation to it.

The situation is now changing. Recognition of the exclusive right of scientific thinking in the domain of art study is becoming common even in lay circles. One can almost speak of another extreme, of a vogue for science, of superficial imitation of science, of a prematurely self-confident scientific tone where the time of real science has not yet come. For the striving to construct a science, at any cost and as quickly as possible, frequently leads to an extreme lowering of the level of problematics, to the impoverishment of the object under study, and even to the illegitimate replacement of this object—in this case, artistic creation—by something entirely different. As we shall see below, the new Russian poetics has not always succeeded in avoiding this pitfall. Constructing a science concerned with some particular domain of *cultural creation*, while preserving all the *complexity, fullness, and distinctiveness of the object under study*, is an extremely difficult undertaking.

Despite the indisputable fruitfulness and significance of many Russian works on poetics published during the past few years, the general scientific position taken by the majority of them cannot be accepted as entirely correct and satisfactory. This criticism applies especially to works by representatives of the so-called Formal or Morphological Method,[4] although it can be extended to include some studies that do not accept this method entirely but share with it certain general presuppositions. The excellent works of Professor V. M. Zhirmunsky[5] are a case in point.

The unsatisfactory nature of the scientific position assumed in these works on poetics is, in the final analysis, the product of an incorrect or, at best, a methodologically indeterminate relationship between the poetics they are constructing and general, systematic, philosophical aesthetics. This is a common transgression of the study of art in all its branches, committed in the very cradle of this discipline: a negative attitude to general aesthetics, a rejection in principle of the guiding role of general aesthetics. The scientific study of art is, in fact, often defined by way of contraposition to philosophical aesthetics known to be nonscientific. Constructing a system of scientific judgments about a particular art (in the present case, verbal art) *independently of questions concerned with the essence of art in general*—such is also the tendency of contemporary works on poetics.

If the question of the essence of art is understood to mean the metaphysics of art, then one would really have to agree that scientific knowledge is possible only where studies are conducted independently of such questions. But, fortunately, it is no longer necessary at all to engage in serious polemics with metaphysics, and the independence claimed by poetics has assumed an entirely different, more unfortunate, meaning, which can be defined as a pretension *to construct the science of a particular art independently of the cognition and systematic determination of the distinctive nature of the aesthetic within the unity of human culture.*

Such a pretension is, in essence, completely unrealizable: without a systematic concept of the aesthetic in its distinctness from the cognitive and the ethical as well as in its interconnectedness within the unity of culture, it is impossible even to isolate the object to be studied by poetics (the works of verbal *art*) from the mass of verbal works of other kinds. This systematic concept is, of course, invariably brought in by scholars, but in a completely *uncritical* manner.

It is sometimes maintained that this concept can be found in the object under study immediately, that the student of literary theory has absolutely no need to turn to systematic philosophy to obtain a concept of the aesthetic, that he will find it in literature itself.

It is true that the aesthetic is in some way given in a work of art itself—the philosopher does not just invent it. But only systematic philosophy with its methods is capable of developing a scientific understanding of the distinctive nature of the aesthetic, of its relation to the ethical and the cognitive, its place within the whole of human culture, and, finally, the limits of its application. The concept of the aesthetic cannot be derived in an intuitive or empirical manner from a work of art: the concept would be naive, subjective, and unstable. For a confident and exact self-determination, it needs to determine itself in mutual relation to other domains within the unity of human culture.

No cultural value, no creative point of view, can remain (nor should it remain) at the stage of simple givenness, bare factuality of a psychological or historical kind. It is only a systematic determination within the unity of culture as a unity of meaning that is capable of overcoming the factuality of a cultural value. The autonomy of art is founded and guaranteed by its participation in the unity of culture, by the fact that art occupies here not only a distinctive but also a *necessary and irreplaceable position.* Otherwise, this autonomy would be simply arbitrary; on the other hand, it would be possible to impose upon art any goals or purposes that are alien to its bare factual nature. Art could find no objection, for bare nature can only be exploited. A fact and purely factual distinctiveness have no right to speak; to receive that right, they must become *meaning.* But it is impossible to become meaning without participating in a unity, without accepting the law of unity: isolated meaning is a *contradictio in adiecto.* Methodological discord in the study of art can be overcome not by creating a new method, still another method—one more participant in the general struggle among methods that will simply exploit the factuality of art in its own way, but only by way of a systematic philosophical grounding of the fact and the distinctiveness of art in the unity of human culture.

Deprived of the basis provided by systematic philosophical aesthetics, poetics becomes unstable and fortuitous in its very foundations. Poetics *systematically defined* must be *an aesthetics of artistic verbal creation.* This definition emphasizes its dependence on general aesthetics.

The absence of a systematic philosophical, general aesthetic orientation, the absence of a constant, methodically thought-through regard for the other arts, for the *unity of art—as a domain of unified human culture*—leads contemporary Russian poetics[a] to extreme simplification of its scientific task, to super-

---

[a] There are, of course, Russian works among those recently published and dealing with poetics and the methodology of literary history that take a position which is more correct in our view. An excellent article by A. A. Smirnov[6] deserves special attention ("Puti i zadachi nauki o literature" [Paths and Tasks in the Study of Literature], *Literaturnaja mysl'* 2

ficiality and incompleteness in encompassing the object under study. Researchers feel confident only when they are moving on the very periphery of verbal art, and they repudiate all those problems that draw art out onto the broad highway of unified human culture, problems that cannot be resolved outside of an inclusive philosophical frame of reference; poetics *clings to linguistics*, fearing to move more than one step away (the majority of the formalists and V. M. Zhirmunsky) and sometimes striving to become simply a branch of linguistics (V. V. Vinogradov).⁷

Linguistics as an auxiliary discipline is, of course, indispensable to poetics, which, like any special aesthetics, must take into account not only general aesthetic principles but also the nature of the material (in our case, verbal material). Here, however, linguistics has begun to assume an altogether inappropriate dominant position—almost the same position that general aesthetics ought to occupy.

This phenomenon is highly characteristic of theories about art that place themselves in opposition to aesthetics. In the majority of cases, they assess incorrectly the significance of the material in artistic creation, and this overestimation of the material element is conditioned by certain considerations on the level of principle.

At one time, a classic slogan was proclaimed: there is no art, there are only particular arts. This proposition asserted, in effect, the *primacy of the material* in artistic creation, for it is precisely material that separates the arts, and if it acquires methodological ascendancy in the mind of the aesthetician, it *isolates*⁸ the arts. But what conditions this primacy of the material, and is it justified methodologically?

In its effort to form a scientific judgment about art independently of general philosophical aesthetics, art study has found material to be the firmest basis for scientific consideration. After all, an orientation toward the material creates a seductive closeness to positive empirical science. Indeed—space, mass, color, sound—all these are received by the student of art (and the artist) from the appropriate branches of the mathematical natural sciences, and the word he receives from linguistics. It is in the soil of

---

[1923]). In many respects, our ensuing argument will agree with the positions and conclusions reached in this article.

the natural sciences that a tendency is nourished to understand *artistic form* as the *form of a given material* and nothing more, as a combination achieved within the bounds of a material in its natural-scientific and linguistic determinateness and regularity. This conception would enable judgments of art study to be positively scientific, and in some cases to be directly demonstrable mathematically.

In this way, the study of art ends up creating a presupposition of a *general-aesthetic character*—a presupposition which is completely understandable psychologically and historically on the basis of what we have said, but which can hardly be considered legitimate and capable of being proven systematically. Developing in some degree what we have said above, we could formulate this presupposition as follows: *aesthetic activity is directed toward a given material,* it *gives a form to that material alone:* an *aesthetically* valid form is *the form* of a given *material*—conceived from the standpoint of natural science or that of linguistics. The assertions of artists that their creative work is value-related, that it is directed toward the world, toward reality, and that it has to do with human beings, with social relations, with ethical, religious, and other values—all such assertions are no more than *metaphors,* for in reality the only thing that is directly available to the artist is the material (physico-mathematical space, mass, sound as defined by acoustics, the word as defined by linguistics), and he can assume an artistic position only in relation to the given, determinate material.

This presupposition of a general-aesthetic character that implicitly or explicitly constitutes the foundation of many individual studies and of whole movements in the domain of disciplines concerned with the particular arts gives us the right to speak of a special general-aesthetic conception, uncritically presupposed by them. We shall call that conception—*material aesthetics.*

Material aesthetics is, as it were, the *working hypothesis of those movements in the study of art* which pretend to being independent of general aesthetics. The Formalists as well as V. M. Zhirmunsky[9] are guided by it: it is the very presupposition which unites them.[b]

---

[b] This presupposition, which we have formulated as distinctly and forcefully as possible, often appears in more moderate forms. A characteristic

It is not superfluous to note here that the so-called Formal Method is in no way connected either historically or systematically with Formal Aesthetics (the aesthetics of Kant,[10] Herbart,[11] and others, in distinction to Content Aesthetics—the aesthetics of Schelling,[12] Hegel,[13] and others) and does not share its aims. On the plane of general aesthetics, the Formal Method must be defined as one of the varieties (a somewhat simplified and primitive variety, one must say) of the aforementioned material aesthetics, whose history is the history of the *Kunstwissenschaften* in their struggle for independence from systematic philosophy.

In assessing the work done in the field of *Kunstwissenschaft*, it is essential to separate that general conception of material aesthetics, which—as we hope to show below—is completely unacceptable, from those purely concrete, particular observations, which may possess scientific significance in spite of that false general conception (to be sure, only in the domain where artistic creation is conditioned by the nature of a given material).[c]

One could say that material aesthetics—as a working hypothesis—is harmless and, given a methodically clear-cut awareness of the limits of its applicability, it can even be productive in studying *technique* in artistic creation. But it becomes unmitigatedly harmful and inadmissible when it is taken as a basis for understanding and studying artistic creativity as a whole, in all its aesthetic distinctiveness and significance.

When the pretensions of material aesthetics are not confined to the technical aspects of artistic creation, they result in a whole series of fundamental errors and insurmountable difficulties. We

---

variant of these is V. M. Zhirmunsky's conception which gives prominence to the *thematic constituent;* however, the theme is introduced by him merely as a *constituent of the material* (the meaning of words), and, in some of the arts, whose material lacks this constituent, the theme is absent.

[c] One encounters in the works of the Formalists many observations of scientific value side by side with completely illegitimate assertions—for the most part, of a general nature. Such works as V. M. Zhirmunsky's *Rhyme, Its Theory and History* and B. V. Tomashevsky's[14] *Russian Metrics* possess scientific value of the highest order. In general, the study of technique in works of verbal art began for the first time on the basis of material aesthetics both in the West European and Russian literature on aesthetics.

shall analyze the most important of them. Moreover, in the course of all that follows, we shall consider material aesthetics not in relation to the disciplines concerned with the particular arts, but as an independent general-aesthetic conception, which indeed it is. And it is precisely as such that it must be subjected to discussion and criticism: will it be able to satisfy those requirements which are absolutely obligatory for any conception in general aesthetics?

A. *Material aesthetics is incapable of founding artistic form.*

The basic position of material aesthetics with regard to form gives rise to a whole series of doubts and, on the whole, is quite unconvincing.

Form, understood as the form of a given material solely in its natural-scientific (mathematical or linguistic) determinateness, becomes a sort of purely external ordering of the material, devoid of any axiological constituent. What fails to be understood is the *emotional-volitional tension of form*—the fact that it has the character of expressing some axiological relationship of the author and the contemplator *to* something apart from the material. For this emotional-volitional relationship that is expressed by form (by rhythm, harmony, symmetry, and other formal moments) is too intense, too *active* in character to be understood simply as a relationship to the material.

Any feeling, deprived of the object that gives it meaning, reduces to a bare factual state of the psyche, an isolated and extracultural state. If, therefore, form expresses a feeling that relates to nothing, then such a feeling becomes simply a state of the psychophysical organism, a state devoid of any intention that opens the closed circle of bare psychic givenness. It becomes simply pleasure which, in the final analysis, can be explained and understood only in purely hedonistic terms—for example, in the following way: a given material in art is organized in such a way as to become a stimulus of pleasant sensations and states in the psychophysical organism. Material aesthetics, if it is consistent, must arrive at such a conclusion, although it does not always do so in fact.

A work of art, understood as *organized material,* as a thing, can have significance only as a physical stimulus of physiological and psychological states or it must assume some utilitarian, practical function.

With a consistency peculiar to any primitivism along with a

dose of nihilism, the Russian Formal Method uses such terms as "to feel" the form, "to make" a work of art, and so forth.[15]

When a sculptor works with marble, he unquestionably also works the marble in its physical determinateness. But the creator's artistic self-activity is not directed to marble in its physical determinateness, nor does the form actualized by the artist relate to it, even though the actualization itself can at no moment do without the marble. But then it also cannot do without the chisel, which certainly does not in any way enter into the artistic object as one of its constituents. The sculptural form created is an *aesthetically* valid form of *man and his body:* it is in this direction that the intention of creation and contemplation proceeds, whereas the artist's and the contemplator's relationship to the marble as a determinate physical body has a secondary, derivative character, governed by some sort of primary relationship to objective values—in the given case, to the value of corporeal man.

Of course, it is unlikely that anyone would prosecute the principles of material aesthetics so consistently in application to marble as we do in our example (and it is really true that marble— as a material—has a more specific, a narrower sense than is usually given to the term "material" in material aesthetics). In principle, however, the situation is no different when instead of marble one has in view the sound of acoustics or the word of linguistics; the situation simply becomes somewhat more complex and less obviously absurd at first glance—especially, of course, when the material is constituted by the word, the object studied by a human science—linguistics.

The usual metaphorical expressions to the effect that artistic form sings or celebrates someone, that it adorns, transfigures, justifies, affirms someone or something, etc., are to some degree scientifically justified, precisely because artistically valid form really does relate to something, it is really directed axiologically toward something *apart from the material* to which it is attached and with which it is, after all, indissolubly connected. Evidently, it is necessary to admit the moment of *content*, which would allow us to understand the sense of form in a more essential way than the crudely hedonistic interpretation.

But there is, after all, a free or unbound beauty, and there is objectless art, in relation to which material aesthetics would seem to be perfectly legitimate.

Without entering into a detailed discussion of this question at this time, we shall note here only the following: the free arts are free only from the purely cognitive determinateness and object-related differentiatedness of their content—music, for example. But in the free arts as well, form is equally free from an immediate primary relationship to the material—to the sound of acoustics.

In general, one must do what is not always done: draw a rigorous distinction between content—an indispensable moment or constituent, as we shall see, in the aesthetic object[16]—and cognitive, object-related differentiatedness—a moment that is not obligatory in it. Freedom from the determinateness of a concept is not equivalent to freedom from content; objectlessness is not lack of content. In other domains of culture as well, there are values which do not admit in principle of any object-related differentiation and any limitation by a determinate, stable concept. Thus, a moral action actualizes (at its highest level) a value which can only be accomplished and cannot be expressed and cognized in an adequate concept. Music is devoid of object-related determinateness and cognitive differentiatedness, yet it has a deep content: its form takes us beyond the bounds of accoustic sound, and certainly not into an axiological void. Content here is, in its essence, ethical (one could also speak of the free, unpredetermined object-relatedness of the ethical tension that is encompassed by musical form). Contentless music as organized material would be nothing else but a physical stimulus for the psychophysiological state of pleasure.

Thus, in the objectless arts as well, form can hardly be validated as the form of a given material.

B. *Material aesthetics is incapable of founding the essential difference between the aesthetic object and the external work, between the articulation and interconnections within that object and the material articulations and interconnections within the external work, and it displays everywhere a tendency to confound these moments or constituents.*

For aesthetics as a science, the work of art is, of course, an object of cognition. But this cognitive relationship to the work has a secondary character, whereas the primary relationship must be a purely artistic one. What aesthetic analysis must be directed toward immediately is not the work in its sensuous givenness, which is ordered solely by cognition, but—that which the work is for the artist's and the contemplator's aesthetic activity directed toward it.

The object dealt with in aesthetic analysis is, therefore, the *content of aesthetic activity (contemplation) directed toward a work.*

This content we shall call henceforth simply—the *aesthetic object,*[17] in distinction to the external work itself, which admits of other approaches as well, and among these, first of all, the primary cognitive approach, i.e., sensory perception ordered by *concepts.*

The first task of aesthetic analysis is *to understand the aesthetic object in its purely artistic distinctiveness and to* understand *its structure,* which we shall call henceforth the *architectonics* of the aesthetic object.

Furthermore, aesthetic analysis must address the work in its primary, purely cognitive givenness and understand its construction completely apart from the aesthetic object: the aesthetician must become a geometer, a physicist, an anatomist, a physiologist, a linguist, just as the artist must to some degree. Thus, a work of verbal art must be understood in its entirety and in all its constituents as a phenomenon of language, i.e., purely from the standpoint of linguistics, without any regard for the aesthetic object it actualizes, solely within the bounds of those scientific regularities which govern its material.

And, finally, the third task of aesthetic analysis is *to understand the external material work as that which actualizes an aesthetic object, as the technical apparatus of aesthetic execution.* It should be clear that this third task presupposes the fact that one has already cognized and studied both the aesthetic object in its distinctiveness and the material work in its extra-aesthetic givenness.

In accomplishing this third task, one has to work by means of the *teleological method.*[18]

The structure of a work, understood as a structure that actualizes the aesthetic object, we shall call the *composition* of a work. Of course, the goal-directed composition of the material work of art does not coincide at all with the appeased, self-sufficient being of the aesthetic object. Composition could also be defined as the sum total of the factors that produce an artistic impression.

Material aesthetics[19] does not comprehend with sufficient methodic clarity its own secondary character, and it does not carry out to the end the preliminary aestheticization of the object it studies. That is why it never has to do with the aesthetic object in its absolute purity, and it is in principle incapable of understanding the distinctiveness of the aesthetic object. In accord with its fundamental presupposition, material aesthetics cannot go beyond the work as organized material.

Strictly speaking, what is fully accessible to material aesthetics is only the second of the tasks of aesthetic analysis we noted above, that is, not yet properly the aesthetic study of the nature of a work, but the study of a work as an object of natural science or of linguistics. The analysis of a work as a compositional, goal-directed whole cannot be accomplished satisfactorily by material aesthetics, because it lacks any understanding of the distinctiveness of the aesthetic object. The latter is brought in, of course, from the researcher's lived experience of aesthetic contemplation, but it is brought in quite uncritically and without any awareness of the methodological significance of doing so.

The failure to distinguish the three moments indicated above— (a) the aesthetic object, (b) the extra-aesthetic, material givenness of a work, (c) the teleologically understood composition of a given material—introduces into the work done by material aesthetics (and this applies to almost all *Kunstwissenschaft*) a great deal of ambiguity and confusion. It leads to a constant *quaternio terminorum*[20] in its conclusions: what one has in view is sometimes the aesthetic object, sometimes the external work, and sometimes the composition. The investigation vacillates for the most part between the second and the third moment, jumping from one to the other without any consistency in method. But what is worst of all is the fact that *the uncritically understood goal-directed composition of a work is declared to be the artistic value itself, the aesthetic object itself.* In doing so, cognitive judgment and inferior technical evaluation (inferior because it is not fully understood methodologically) are substituted for artistic activity (and for contemplation).

C. *There is in works of material aesthetics an inescapable and constant confusion of architectonic and compositional forms, so that the former are never clarified in principle or defined with precision, and are thus undervalued.*

This shortcoming of material aesthetics is conditioned by the very essence of this conception, and within its limits is insurmountable. It is closely linked, of course, to the particulars discussed under sections A and B above. Here are a few examples of the methodological delimitation of architectonic and compositional forms.

Aesthetic individuality is a purely architectonic form of the aesthetic object itself: what is individualized is an event, a person, an aesthetically animated object, and so on. The individuality of the author as creator possesses a special character and also enters into the aesthetic object. But the form of individuality can by no means be ascribed in the very same (i.e., purely aesthetic) sense to a work as organized material—to a painting, a verbal whole, and so on. The attribution of individuality to them can have only a metaphorical significance, that is, by making them the object of a new, elementary work of verbal art, of a metaphor, by poeticizing them.

The form of self-sufficiency, of self-containment, belonging to everything consummated aesthetically, is the purely architectonic form least of all capable of being transferred to the work as organized material. The latter is a compositional teleological whole in which every constituent and the entire whole are goal-directed, they actualize something, they serve some end. To call, for example, the verbal whole of a work "self-sufficient" is possible only if one uses a bold, purely Romantic metaphor.

The *novel* is a purely compositional form of the organization of verbal masses; through it, the architectonic form of the artistic consummation of a historical or social event is realized. It is a variety of the form of *epic consummation.*

Drama is a compositional form (dialogue, division into acts, etc.), but the *tragic* and *comic* are architectonic forms of consummation.

Of course, it is possible to speak of the compositional forms of comedy and tragedy as varieties of the dramatic when we are interested in devices for the compositional ordering of the verbal material and not in cognitive-ethical values: the terminology here is unstable and incomplete. We must bear in mind that every architectonic form is realized through specific compositional devices; on the other hand, essential architectonic forms in the realized object correspond to the most important compositional forms (to genre forms, for example).

The *form of the lyrical* is architectonic, but there are compositional forms of lyric poems.

Humor, heroization, type, character are purely *architectonic* forms, but they are realized, of course, through specific compositional devices. The *narrative poem*, the *tale*, the *novella* are purely compositional, generic forms. The *chapter*, the *stanza*, the *line* are purely compositional articulations (although they can be understood from a purely linguistic perspective, that is, independently of their aesthetic telos).

Rhythm can be understood in both ways—that is, as both an architectonic and a compositional form. As a form of ordering acoustical material which is empirically apprehended, heard, and cognized, rhythm is compositional. But rhythm is architectonic when it is emotionally directed, when it relates to that value of inner striving and tension which it consummates.

Between the architectonic forms noted here in an altogether unsystematic manner, there are, of course, essential gradations which we cannot examine now. What is important to us is the fact that all of them, *in contrast to compositional forms, enter into the aesthetic object.*

Architectonic forms are forms of the inner and bodily value of aesthetic man, they are forms of nature—as his environment, forms of the event in his individual-experiential, social, and historical dimensions, and so on. They all are achievements, actualizations; they serve nothing, they are tranquilly sufficient unto themselves. They are forms of aesthetic being in its distinctiveness.

The compositional forms, organizing the material, have a teleological, implemental character, a "restless" character, as it were, and they are subject to a purely technical evaluation: to what extent have they adequately fulfilled their architectonic task? The architectonic form determines the choice of the compositional form. Thus, the form of tragedy (a form of the event, and to some extent that of a person—the tragic character) selects the appropriate compositional form—the dramatic form. It does not follow from this, of course, that architectonic form exists somewhere in a finished state and can be realized apart from compositional form.

On the grounds of material aesthetics, it is completely impossible to describe the essential and fundamental distinction that exists between compositional and architectonic forms, and a tendency often arises to dissolve architectonic forms in compositional forms. An extreme expression of this tendency can be seen in the Russian Formal Method, where compositional and genre forms seek to swallow up the entire aesthetic object, and where, in addition, no rigorous distinction is drawn between compositional and linguistic forms.

The situation changes little in essence when architectonic forms are referred to thematics and compositional forms to stylistics, to the instrumentation of composition (in a narrower sense than the meaning we attach to this term); both are assumed to exist side by side in a work (the distinction between the aesthetic object and the external work is absent) and they are distinguished only as *forms of ordering different sides of the material* (see, for example, the works of V. M. Zhirmunsky).[21] What is absent here as well is a fundamental and essential methodical distinction between compositional and architectonic forms, and an understanding of their belonging to completely different planes. To this is joined a rejection of the thematic moment in some of the arts (e.g., music), thereby creating an abyss between thematic and nonthematic arts. One must note here that thematics in Zhirmunsky's sense is very far from coinciding with the architectonics of the aesthetic object; true, the majority (but not all) of the architectonic forms are found in it, but along with them it includes some things that are quite alien to the aesthetic object.

The fundamental architectonic forms are common to all the arts and to the entire domain of the aesthetic; they constitute the unity of this domain. There exist analogues (conditioned by common architectonic tasks) among the compositional forms of the various arts; but it is here that the particular properties of the materials come into their own.

A correct formulation of *the problem of style* (one of the most important problems of aesthetics) is impossible without a rigorous distinction of architectonic and compositional forms.

D. *Material aesthetics is incapable of explaining aesthetic vision outside of art:* the aesthetic contemplation of nature, the aesthetic elements in myth and in world views, and, finally, everything called aestheticism, that is, the illegitimate transfer of aesthetic forms into the domain of ethical action (personal-experiential, political, and social) and into the domain of cognition (the quasi-scientific, aestheticized thought of such philosophers as Nietzsche).[22]

A characteristic feature of all these manifestations of aesthetic vision outside art is the absence of a determinate and organized material, and, consequently, of technique. Form here, in the majority of cases, is not objectified and not fixed. It is precisely because of this that these manifestations of aesthetic vision outside art do not achieve methodological clarity and a full measure of independence and distinctiveness. They are confused, unstable, hybrid. The aesthetic realizes itself fully only in art, and therefore one must orient aesthetics toward art. It would be methodologically absurd to begin an aesthetic construction with the aesthetics of nature or of myth. But aesthetics *must* explain these hybrid and impure forms of the aesthetic. This task is extremely important both philosophically and practically. This task can serve as a touchstone for the productiveness of any aesthetic theory.

With its understanding of form, material aesthetics lacks even an approach to such phenomena.

E. *Material aesthetics is incapable of founding the history of art.*

There can be no doubt, of course, that a productive elaboration of the history of one art or another presupposes an elaborated aesthetics of the given art. But one must give special emphasis to the basal significance of general, systematic aesthetics—in addition to the significance it has in the construction of any special aesthetic. For only general aesthetics sees and validates art in its essential interaction and interdetermination with all other areas of cultural creativity, within the unity of culture, and within the unity of the historical becoming of culture.

History knows no isolated series: an isolated series as such is static, and a change in the elements within such a series can only be a systematic articulation or simply a mechanical disposition of series, but certainly not a historical process. It is only the establishment of interaction and interdetermination of the given series with other series that creates the historical approach. One must cease to be just oneself, in order to enter history.

By isolating within culture not only art but the separate arts, and by considering the work not in its artistic life but as a thing, as organized material, material aesthetics is able at best to found only a chronological table of changes in the technical devices utilized by a given art, because isolated technique can have no history at all.

These, then, are the basic, inescapable shortcomings and insurmountable difficulties confronting formal aesthetics. All of them are illustrated rather well by the Russian Formal Method and are a consequence of the primitivism inherent in its general-aesthetic conception, and a somewhat sectarian belligerence apparent in it.

All the shortcomings we have noted in the five points above are conditioned in the final analysis by the methodologically false thesis noted at the outset of this section, namely, that one can and should construct a science of art independently of systematic philosophical aesthetics. The result is the absence of a solid basis for scholarship. In order to escape the sea of the subjective in which aesthetic judgments, deprived of this scientific basis, are drowning, art study is striving to find shelter in those scientific disciplines that concern themselves with the material of a given art, just as in the past (and sometimes now as well) art study has clung for the same reasons to psychology and even physiology. But this escape is fictitious: a judgment is genuinely scientific only where it does not go beyond the bounds and becomes a proper judgment of aesthetics; it turns out to be immersed as much as in the past in those waves of the subjective and the fortuitous from which it hoped to be saved.

In such a situation, the fundamental assertion of art study turns out to be, before all else, an affirmation of the significance of material in artistic creation. This is a general aesthetic judgment, and, whether willing or not, it must face criticism from the perspective of general philosophical aesthetics. Only general aesthetics can validate this kind of judgment, and it can repudiate it as well.

The points we have examined make the premise of material aesthetics highly dubious and suggest in part the direction for understanding more correctly the essence of the aesthetic and its constituent features. Our task in succeeding sections is to develop this direction toward a general aesthetics, but mainly in application to verbal art.

After defining the moment of content and correctly establishing the place of material in artistic creation, we shall have in hand a correct approach to form. We shall be able to understand how form is, on the one hand, really material, and how it is realized entirely in a given material and is bound to it; and, on the other hand, we shall understand how *form takes us axiologically be-*

yond the bounds of the work as organized material, as a thing. This will clarify and reinforce all we have noted above in the form of suppositions and indications.

II. The Problem of Content

The problem of any particular domain of culture taken as a whole, whether it be cognition, ethics, or art, can be understood as the problem of this domain's boundaries.

Any creative point of view, whether potential or factually extant, becomes convincingly necessary and indispensable only in correlation with other creative points of view. It is only at that place on their boundaries where a genuine need arises for this point of view, for its creative distinctiveness, that it finds its solid foundation and justification. From within itself alone, outside its participation in the unity of culture, it is merely naked fact, and its distinctiveness may present itself as simply arbitrary and capricious.

However, a domain of culture should not be thought of as some kind of spatial whole, possessing not only boundaries but an inner territory. A cultural domain has no inner territory. It is located entirely upon boundaries, boundaries intersect it everywhere, passing through each of its constituent features. The systematic unity of culture passes into the atoms of cultural life—like the sun, it is reflected in every drop of this life. Every cultural act lives essentially on the boundaries, and it derives its seriousness and significance from this fact. Separated by abstraction from these boundaries, it loses the ground of its being and becomes vacuous, arrogant; it degenerates and dies.

In this sense, we can speak about the concrete systematicness of every cultural phenomenon, of every individual cultural act, about its *autonomous participation* or its *participative autonomy.*

It is only in this concrete systematicness, that is, in its unmediated responsibility and orientation within the unity of culture, that a phenomenon ceases to be simply an existing, naked fact, that it acquires validity and meaning, and becomes a kind of monad, as it were, reflecting everything in itself and being reflected in everything.

Indeed: no creative, cultural act has anything to do with completely random and unordered matter that is completely indifferent to value (matter and chaos are in general relative concepts). Rather, it always has to do with something already evaluated and somehow ordered, in relation to which it must responsibly assume its own valuational position. Thus, the act of cognition finds reality already organized in the concepts of prescientific thinking; more importantly, it has already been evaluated and ordered by ethical actions (practical, quotidian actions, political or social actions). The cognitive act finds reality confirmed by religion and, finally, it proceeds from an aesthetically ordered image of an object, from a vision of that object.

Thus, that which is found to be on hand by cognition is not a *res nullius* but the reality of ethical actions in all their variety, and the reality of aesthetic vision. With regard to this reality, the cognitive act must assume everywhere an essential position, which must not, of course, be the result of a random encounter but which can and must be systematically grounded in the essential nature of cognition and that of other domains.

The same must be said about the artistic act: it, too, lives and moves not in a vacuum but in an intense axiological atmosphere of responsible interdetermination. The work of art as a thing is obtrusively demarcated in time and space from all other things. A statue or a painting crowds everything else out physically from the space it occupies. The reading of a book begins at a specific time, occupies several hours, filling them up, and ends at a specific time—this in addition to the fact that the book itself is firmly held together by its binding. But a work is alive and possesses artistic validity in its intense and active interdetermination with a reality that has been identified and evaluated by a performed action. The work is alive and valid as an *artistic* work, of course, and not in our psyche. In the psyche, it is also present only empirically as a psychic process, localized in time and in accord with psychological laws. A work is alive and valid in a world which is also both alive and valid—cognitively, socially, politically, economically, and religiously.

The common opposition of reality and art, or life and art, and the effort to discover some essential link between them are perfectly legitimate, but they require a more precise scientific formulation. Reality placed in opposition to art can only be the reality of cognition and of ethical actions in all their variety—the reality of practical living (economic, social, political, and properly moral).

It should be noted that, on the plane of ordinary thinking, the reality placed in opposition to art (although in such cases the word usually favored is "life") is already essentially aestheticized; it is already an artistic image of reality, but one that is hybrid and unstable. Very often those who criticize new art for breaking with reality contrast it in fact with the reality of older art, of "Classical art," imagining that it represents some sort of neutral reality. But the aesthetic as such should be contrasted, as rigorously and distinctly as possible, to the reality of cognition and performed action before it is aestheticized, and consequently, unified. One should remember that this reality becomes a concretely unified life or reality only in aesthetic intuition, and it becomes a yet-to-be-accomplished systematic unity only in philosophical cognition.

One should likewise avoid the illegitimate, methodologically unjustified limitation which willfully specifies only one constituent or another of the extra-aesthetic world. Thus, natural necessity from the standpoint of science is opposed to the freedom and imagination of the artist; or, more often, only the social or the contemporary political constituent is specified, and sometimes even the naive, unstable reality of practical living.

It must be also remembered once and for all that no reality *in itself*, no *neutral* reality, can be placed in opposition to art: by the very fact that we speak of it and oppose it to something, we determine it and evaluate it in some way. One must simply come to see oneself clearly and understand the actual direction of one's evaluation.

All of this can be expressed briefly as follows: *reality can be contraposed to art only as something good or something true in opposition to beauty.*

Every cultural phenomenon is concretely systematic; that is, it occupies some essential position in relation to the already given reality of other cultural standpoints and thereby participates in the to-be-achieved unity of culture. But the relations of cognition, action, and artistic creation to the reality they find to be on hand differ profoundly from one another. Cognition does not accept the ethical evaluatedness and the aesthetic formedness of being, but thrusts itself away from them. In this sense, cognition finds nothing to be already on hand; it begins from the very beginning— or rather, the moment of the prior givenness of something valid apart from cognition remains beyond it and passes into the realm of factuality—historical, psychological, personal-biographical, and other factuality which is fortuitous from the perspective of cognition itself.

Preveniently encountered evaluatedness and aesthetic formedness of reality do not enter cognition. Reality, as it enters science, casts off all its axiological garments in order to become the naked and pure reality of cognition, where only the unity of truth is sovereign. Positive mutual determination within the unity of culture takes place only in relation to cognition as a whole in systematic philosophy.

There is a unitary world of science, a unitary reality of cognition, outside of which nothing can become cognitively valid. This reality of cognition is not consummated and always open. Everything that exists for cognition is determined by cognition itself and—in principle—is defined in all respects; everything obstinate, everything that, as it were, resists cognition in the object, that is as yet unidentified in it, is obstinate for cognition only as a purely cognitive problem and not at all as something of extracognitive value—as something good, holy, useful, and so on. Cognition does not know such axiological resistance.

Of course, the world of ethical actions and the world of beauty themselves become objects of cognition, but, in doing so, do not introduce their own valuations and their own regularities into cognition. In order to become cognitively valid, they must subordinate themselves entirely to the unity and regularity of cognition.

Thus, the cognitive act relates in a purely negative way to the preveniently encountered reality of actions and aesthetic vision, thereby actualizing the purity of its own distinctiveness.

The following specific features of cognition are conditioned by this, its basic character: the cognitive act takes into account only the prior work of cognition that it finds on hand, and it certainly does not assume any independent position in relation to the reality of actions and artistic creation in their historical determinateness. More than this, the separateness and the uniqueness of the cognitive act and of its expression in a separate, individual work are not valid from the point of view of cognition: *in the world of cognition, there are in principle no separate acts and no separate works*. Rather, it is indispensable to bring in other points of view in order to discover a way to approach them and to make essential the historical singularity of the cognitive act, and the isolatedness, completeness, and individuality of a scientific work. At the same time (as we shall see below), the world of art must in its essence divide into separate, self-sufficient, individual wholes—works of art—each of which occupies an independent position in relation to the reality of cognition and performed action. This creates the immanent historicity of a work of art.

Ethical actions relate somewhat differently to the preveniently encountered reality of cognition and aesthetic vision. This relation is usually expressed *as the relation of the ought to reality*. It is not our intention to examine this problem; we shall only note that here, too, the relation is negative in character, although this character differs from that in the domain of cognition.[d]

We turn now to artistic creation.

The basic feature of the aesthetic that sharply distinguishes it from cognition and performed action is its receptive, positively accepting character, which enters into the work (or, to be exact, into the aesthetic object) and there becomes an indispensable constitutive moment. In this sense, we can say that in actuality life is found not only outside art but in it, within it, in all the fullness of its value-bearing weightiness—social, political, cognitive, and so on. Art is rich—it is not arid, not specialized. The artist is a specialist only as a master-craftsman, that is, only in relation to the given material.

Of course, aesthetic form transposes this identified and evaluated reality to another axiological level, subordinates it to a new unity and orders it in a new way: it individualizes, concretizes, isolates, and consummates it, *but it does not alter the fact that this reality has been identified and evaluated,* and it is precisely toward this prior identification and evaluation that the consummating aesthetic form is directed.

Aesthetic activity does not create a reality that is wholly new.[e] Unlike cognition and performed action, which create nature and

---

[d] The relation of obligation or the ought to being has a *conflictual* character. From within the world of cognition, no conflict is possible, for in that world one cannot meet with anything axiologically different in kind. Not science but a scientist can enter into conflict, and do so, moreover, not *ex cathedra*, but as an ethical *subiectum* for whom cognition is *the performed act of cognition*. The split between the ought and being has validity only from within the ought, i.e., for the ethical act-performing consciousness; it exists only for that consciousness.

[e] What we might call the secondary nature of the aesthetic in no way reduces, of course, its independence and distinctiveness alongside the ethi-

social humanity, art celebrates, adorns, and recollects this preveniently encountered reality of cognition and action (nature and social humanity). It enriches and completes them, and above all else *it creates the concrete intuitive unity of these two worlds*. It places man in nature, understood as his aesthetic environment; it humanizes nature and naturalizes man.

In this acceptance of the ethical and the cognitive into its proper object resides the distinctive *kindness* of the aesthetic, its *mercifulness*. It does not choose, as it were, anything, it does not divide anything, does not abolish anything, does not push away and detach itself from anything. These purely negative moments exist in art only in relation to its material. Toward it, the artist is stern and merciless: the poet casts away words, forms, and expressions without pity, and he selects only a few; fragments of marble fly away from beneath the sculptor's chisel. But the inner man in the first case and corporeal man in the second are only enriched: ethical man is enriched by nature positively affirmed, while natural man is enriched by ethical meaning.

Almost all of the kind, accepting and enriching, optimistic categories of human thinking about the world and man (not religious, of course, but purely secular categories) are aesthetic in character. The eternal tendency of such thinking to represent what ought to be and what is set as a task as already given and extant somewhere is also aesthetic—the tendency that created mythical thinking, and, to a significant degree, also metaphysical thinking.

Art creates a new form as a new, axiological relation toward that which has already become reality for cognition and action: in art, we recognize everything and we remember everything (in cognition, we recognize nothing and remember nothing, contrary to Plato's formula).[23] But this is precisely why the constituent of novelty, originality, unexpectedness, freedom has such significance in art, for here there is a background against which novelty, originality, freedom can be apprehended—the recognized and coexperienced world of cognition and action. It is this world that looks and sounds in a new way in art, and it is in relation to this

---

cal and the cognitive. Aesthetic activity creates its own reality in which the reality of cognition and action is positively accepted and transfigured: this is what constitutes the distinctiveness of the aesthetic.

world that the artist's activity is perceived—as free. Cognition and performed action are primary, that is, they create their own objects: for the first time, that which is cognized is not recognized and not remembered in a new light, but determined for the first time, and an action lives only by that which does not yet exist. Here everything is new from the outset, and that is why there is no novelty here; here everything is *ex origine,* and that is why there is no originality here.

The characteristic of the aesthetic noted above—its positive acceptance and concrete unification of nature and social humanity—also explains the distinctive relationship of the aesthetic to philosophy. We observe in the history of philosophy a constantly recurring tendency toward a substitution of the yet-to-be-achieved unity of cognition and action by the concrete intuitive, and as it were *given,* present-on-hand *unity* of aesthetic vision.

After all, the unity of cognition and ethical action, of being and obligation, is a concrete, living unity given to us in our unmediated seeing, in our intuition. Is not this intuitive unity perhaps the sought-after unity of philosophy? This represents in fact a great temptation for thought, a temptation which has created beside the single high road of the science of philosophy parallel—not roads, but isolated islands of individual, artistic-philosophical intuitions (even if sometimes brilliant in their own way).[f] The quasi-philosophical unity discovered by these aestheticized, intuitive conceptions relates to the world and to culture in the same way that the unity of aesthetic form relates to content in a work of art.[g]

---

[f] Another distinctive variant of the intuitive-aesthetic unity of cognition and action is myth. Myth is much closer to art than intuitive philosophy, because in myth the ethical moment predominates over the cognitive one (which is, moreover, almost completely devoid of internal differentiation), and because of a greater freedom to give an aesthetic form than there is in intuitive philosophy (the moment of isolation or detachment in the presentation of the mythic event is stronger, although it is, of course, incomparably weaker than in art; the moment of aesthetic subjectivation and personification is stronger, as well as some other constituent moments of form).

[g] Philosophy can make use of the intuitive image of unity as an auxiliary means, something like a drawing in geometry, and as a heuristic hy-

One of the most important tasks of aesthetics is to discover an approach to aestheticized philosophemes, *to create a theory of intuitive philosophy on the basis of the theory of art.* Material aesthetics is least of all capable of carrying out such a task: in ignoring content, it lacks even an approach to artistic intuition in philosophy.

The reality of cognition and ethical action that enters (as an already identified and evaluated reality) into the aesthetic object and is subjected there to concrete, intuitive unification, individuation, concretization, isolation, and consummation, i.e., to a process of comprehensive artistic forming by means of a particular material—*this reality we call* (in complete agreement with traditional word usage) *the content of a work of art* (or to be exact—*of the aesthetic object*).

Content is an indispensable constitutive moment in the aesthetic object, and artistic form is correlative to it; *outside this correlation, artistic form has no meaning at all.*

Outside its relationship to content, that is, to the world and its constituent moments, to the world as the object of cognition and ethical action, form cannot be aesthetically valid and cannot fulfill its basic functions.

The position of the author-artist and his artistic task can and should be understood in the world in connection with all the values of cognition and ethical action: it is not the material that is unfied, individualized, rendered whole, isolated, and consummated; it has no need of unification, for there is no rupture in it, and no need of consummation, to which it is indifferent, for, in order to need consummation, the material must participate in the axiological and meaning-related movement of an action. Rather, what is united, individualized, rendered whole, isolated, and consummated is the comprehensively experienced axiological makeup of reality—*the event of reality.*

Aesthetically valid form is the expression of an essential relation to the world of cognition and action. However, this relation is not cognitive and not ethical: the artist does not intervene in the event as an immediate participant in it, for then he would

---

pothesis. In life, too, we work at every step with the help of a similar image of unity.

become someone who is engaged in cognition and who acts ethically. The artist assumes an essential *position outside* the event as a contemplator who is disinterested but who *understands the axiological sense of what is coming to pass*—as a contemplator who does not experience the event but co-experiences it, for, without co-evaluating to some extent, one cannot contemplate an event as an *event* specifically.

This *situatedness outside* (but not indifference) allows artistic self-activity to unite, give a form to, and consummate the event *from outside*. This unification and consummation are in principle impossible from within cognition itself and an action itself: the reality of cognition, as long as it remains true to itself, cannot unite with obligation (the ought), and obligation, so long as it preserves its distinctiveness, cannot unite with reality. What is needed is an essential axiological position outside the cognizing consciousness and outside the obligated and act-performing consciousness, a position from which it is possible to effect that unification and consummation (consummation from within cognition itself and an action itself is impossible).

Aesthetic form, as an intuitively uniting and consummating form, descends upon content from outside—content in its potential fragmentation and its constant state of being-set-as-a-task, of being unsatisfied (which are actual outside the bounds of art in ethically experienced life)—and transposes it to a new axiological plane, to the plane of detached (isolated) and consummated being, axiologically self-contented being—to the plane of beauty.

Form, embracing content *from outside, externalizes it, that is, embodies it.* Thus, the traditional classic terminology remains fundamentally accurate.

Two tendencies are evident in the rejection of content as a constitutive moment in the aesthetic object in contemporary poetics, tendencies that are not always strictly distinguished and have not yet received a distinct formulation: (1) content is merely a constituent of form, that is to say, the cognitive-ethical value in a work of art has a purely formal significance; (2) content is merely a constituent of the material. We shall touch briefly on the second tendency in the following section, which is devoted to material in art. Here we shall discuss the first of these attempts.

Before all else, one must note that the content is given in the artistic object as totally formed, totally embodied; otherwise, it would be an objectionable prosaism and not a moment that has been dissolved in the artistic whole. It is impossible to isolate some real moment in a work of art that would be pure content, just as there is no pure form either: content and form interpenetrate, they are inseparable. However, for aesthetic analysis, they are not fused, that is, they are validities of a different order: if form is to have a purely aesthetic significance, the content it embraces must have a potential cognitive and ethical significance. Form needs the extra-aesthetic weightiness of content, for without it form could not realize itself as form. But can one say on this basis that content is a purely formal moment?

Without dwelling on the outward logical (terminological) absurdity of using the term "form" when completely denying content (since form is a concept correlative to content, which is precisely *not* form), there is, of course, a more essential methodological danger in such an assertion: in it content is understood as something replaceable from the point of view of form—form is not concerned with the cognitive-ethical validity of content, and this validity is completely fortuitous in the aesthetic object. Form relativizes content completely; this is the sense of the assertion which makes content a moment of form.

The fact is that such a situation can actually occur in art: form can lose its primary relation to content in its own cognitive and ethical validity; content can be reduced to the level of a "purely formal moment." Such an enfeeblement of content diminishes first of all the artistic significance of form: form is deprived of one of its most important functions—the intuitive unification of the cognitive and the ethical, which has such great significance, especially in verbal art. The function of isolation and the function of consummation are also enfeebled. In such instances, too, we are still dealing with content as a constitutive moment in the work of art (for otherwise we would not have a work of art at all), but with content at second hand, attenuated content, and, as a consequence, with an attenuated form: we have to do quite simply with so-called literature. It is worth considering this phenomenon, since some Formalists are inclined to consider "literature" the only kind of artistic creation in general.

There are works which indeed do not deal with the world, but only with the word "world" in a literary context, works which are born, live, and die on the pages of magazines, without ever going beyond the pages of contemporary periodical publications, and in no way taking us beyond their bounds. The cognitive-ethical moment of content, which is nevertheless indispensable to them as a constitutive moment in the work of art, is not taken by them immediately from the world of cognition and from the ethical reality of performed action, but from other artistic works, or it is constructed by analogy with them. The issue here, of course, is not the presence of artistic influences and traditions, which will invariably be present in the very highest art. Rather, the issue concerns an inner relation to the assimilated content: in those literary works of which we are speaking, content is not co-identified and co-experienced, but is assimilated according to external, purely "literary" considerations. Artistic form does not come together here with content in all its cognitive and ethical weightiness face to face, as it were. Rather, one work of literature comes together with another, which it imitates or which it "makes strange,"[24] and against the background of which it is perceived as something new. Here form becomes indifferent to content in its immediate, extra-aesthetic validity.

Besides the reality of both cognition and performed action, the artist of the word also finds literature to be already on hand: it is necessary for him to fight against or for old literary forms, to make use of them, to combine them, to overcome their resistance or to find support in them. But, at the heart of all this movement and struggle within the bounds of a purely literary context, there is a more essential, determining primary struggle with the reality of action and cognition: in his work, if it is significant and serious, every artist is *the first artist*, as it were; *he must immediately assume an aesthetic position with regard to the extra-aesthetic reality of action and cognition*, even if only within the bounds of his purely personal ethical-biographical experience. Neither the work of art as a whole nor any constituent of it can be understood in terms of abstract literary regularities alone. It is indispensable as well to take into account the level of meaning, that is, the possible regularities of action and cognition, since aesthetically valid form encompasses not a void but the persistent, autonomous directedness of life to meaning. In the work of art, there are, as it were, two ruling powers and two lawful orders determined by these powers; each constituent moment can be determined within two systems of value, that of content and that of form, for in each valid constituent both of these systems are in a state of essential and axiologically intense interaction. But aesthetic form completely encompasses, of course, the possible internal regularities of action and cognition and subjects these regularities to its own unity: it is only when this condition is satisfied that we can speak of a work as a work of art.

How is content realized in artistic creation and in contemplation, and what are the tasks and methods of an aesthetic analysis of it? Here we must touch briefly upon these problems of aesthetics. The following remarks in no way exhaust this subject and merely outline the problem. What is more, we shall not discuss at all the compositional realization of content by means of a determinate material.

(1) One must distinguish clearly between the cognitive-ethical moment, which truly is content, that is, a constitutive moment in a given aesthetic object, and those judgments and ethical assessments which one can construct and utter concerning content, but which are not part of the aesthetic object.

(2) Content cannot be purely cognitive, completely devoid of an ethical constituent. Even more, one can say that the ethical has essential primacy in content. Artistic form cannot realize itself in relation to pure conceptualization and pure judgment: a purely cognitive moment will inevitably remain isolated as an undissolved prosaism in a work of art. Everything cognized must be correlated with the world in which human action is performed, it must be fundamentally linked with the acting consciousness, and only in this way can it enter into the work of art.

It would be utterly wrong to conceive of content as a cognitive, theoretical whole, as a thought, an idea.

(3) Artistic creation and contemplation gain mastery of the ethical constituent of content directly *by way of co-experiencing or emphathizing and co-evaluating,* and certainly not by means of theoretical understanding and interpretation, which can only provide a means for empathizing. Only the *event* of an action *in its living performance from within the acting consciousness itself* is immediately ethical (an action of thinking, doing, feeling, desiring, and so on). It is precisely this *event* that is completed from outside by artistic form, but certainly not its theoretical transcription in the form of ethical judgments, moral norms, maxims, judicial rulings, and so on.

A theoretical transcription, a formula of an ethical action, already constitutes its transposition to the plane of cognition, that is, a secondary constituent, while artistic form (e.g., the form actualized by a story about the action, or the form of its epic heroization in a narrative poem, or the form of its lyrical embodiment, etc.) has to do with the action itself in its primary ethical nature, gaining mastery of this nature by way of co-experiencing with the willing, feeling, and acting consciousness; the secondarily cognitive moment can have here only the auxiliary significance of a means.

It must be emphasized that the artist and the contemplator do not co-experience at all with the psychological consciousness (strictly speaking, it is impossible to co-experience with it), but with ethically directed, acting consciousness.[h]

What are the tasks and possibilities of the aesthetic analysis of content?

Aesthetic analysis must disclose before all else the constituents of the content immanent to the aesthetic object, without in any way going beyond the bounds of this object as it is realized in the processes of creation and contemplation.

Let us turn to the cognitive constituent of content.

The constituent of cognitive recognition everywhere accompanies the activity of artistic creation and contemplation, but in the majority of cases it is completely inseparable from the ethical constituent and cannot be expressed in an adequate judgment. The potential unity and the indispensability of the world of cognition shine, as it were, through every constituent of the aesthetic object, and although such unity never achieves fullness of actualization in the work itself, it joins with the world of ethical striving, bringing about that distinctive, intuitively given unity of the two worlds, which, as we have indicated, is an essential constituent of the aesthetic as such.[i] Thus, behind every word, behind

---

[h] Empathy and sympathetic co-evaluation are not in themselves aesthetic in character. The content of the act of empathizing is ethical: it is the moral or practical-quotidian axiological attitude (emotional-volitional attitude) of another consciousness. This content of the art of empathizing can be interpreted and reworked in various directions: it can be made an object of cognition (psychological or philosophical-ethical cognition), or it may condition an ethical action (the most widespread form of interpreting the content of empathizing: sympathy, compassion, help), or, finally, it may be made an object of aesthetic consummation. Later on we shall have to consider in greater detail the so-called aesthetics of empathy.

[i] We shall subsequently illuminate the role of the creative personality of the author as a constitutive moment in artistic form; it is within the

every phrase of a work of poetry, one can sense a potential prosaic meaning, a prosaic slant, that is, a potential, total referredness to the unity of cognition.

The cognitive constituent illuminates, as it were, the aesthetic object from within; like a sober stream of water, it mixes with the wine of ethical tension and artistic consummation. But it is very far from condensing and solidifying to the point that it becomes a determinate judgment. Everything is recognized but not everything is identified in an adequate concept.

If this all-pervasive recognition did not exist, the aesthetic object (i.e., that which is artistically created and apprehended) would evade all the interconnections of experience, both theoretical and practical, just as the content of a state of complete narcosis blanks out (there is nothing to recall about the content of this state, nothing to say, and it cannot be evaluated, i.e., the state can be evaluated, but not its content). In the same way, artistic creation and contemplation, if they were deprived of any participation in the potential unity of cognition, if they were not penetrated by it and not recognized from within, would become simply an isolated state of amnesia, about which it is possible to learn only *post factum*, from the time elapsed, that it had occurred.

This internal illuminatedness of the aesthetic object can rise, in the domain of verbal art, from the level of recognition to the level of *determinate cognition* and profound insights, which can then be isolated by aesthetic analysis.

However, having isolated some particular cognitive insight from the content of the aesthetic object (for example, Ivan Karamazov's purely philosophical insights into the significance of the suffering of children, the unacceptability of God's world, and so on, or Andrei Bolkonsky's philosophico-historical and sociological judgments about war, about the role of the individual in history, and so on),[25] the investigator must remember that all these insights, no matter how profound they may be in themselves, are not given in the aesthetic object in their cognitive isolatedness and that it is not to them that artistic form is referred and not them that it consummates immediately. These insights are necessarily connected with the ethical constituent in content, with the world of per-

---

unity of his activity that the cognitive and ethical moment finds its unification.

formed action, the world of event. Thus, Ivan Karamazov's insights perform purely characterological functions; they are a necessary constituent in Ivan's moral position in life, and they are also related to Alesha's ethical and religious position, and they are thereby drawn into the event, to which the novel's consummating artistic form is directed. Similarly, Andrei Bolkonsky's judgments are expressions of his ethical personality and his position in life, and they are woven into the imaged event not only of his personal life, but of social and historical life as well. In this way, what is cognitively true becomes a constituent of ethical performance or accomplishment.

If all these judgments were not necessarily bound in one way or another to the concrete world of human action, they would remain isolated prosaisms, which sometimes occurs in Dostoevsky's work, and in Tolstoy's as well (for example, in *War and Peace*, where toward the novel's end the cognitive, philosophico-historical judgments completely sever their bond with the ethical event and organize themselves into a theoretical treatise).[26]

The cognitive moment which occurs in descriptions and in natural-scientific or psychological explanations of what has transpired is linked to the ethical event in a somewhat different way. But it is not our purpose to indicate all the methods for binding the ethical and the cognitive in the unity of content of the aesthetic object.

In emphasizing the bond between the cognitive moment and the ethical, one ought to note, however, that the ethical event does not relativize the judgments that enter into it, and it is not indifferent to their purely cognitive depth, breadth, and truthfulness. Thus, the moral events of the life of the "man from underground," which were artistically shaped and consummated by Dostoevsky, need the purely cognitive depth and consistency of his world view, which is an essential moment of his position in life.

Having isolated the theoretical constituent of content in its purely cognitive weightiness within the bounds of the possible and the necessary, aesthetic analysis proper must further understand that constituent's link with the ethical constituent and its significance within the unity of content. Of course, it is possible to make of this isolated cognitive constituent the object of theoretical examination and evaluation independent of the work of art, relating it not to the unity of content and of the entire aesthetic object as a whole, but to the purely cognitive unity of some philosophical world view (usually the author's). Such studies have great philosophical and historical-cultural significance, but they lie beyond the bounds of aesthetic analysis proper and must be rigorously distinguished from it. We shall not discuss the distinctive methodology of such studies.

Let us turn to the tasks that pertain to the analysis of the ethical moment in content.

The methodology here is much more complex: aesthetic analysis, to be scientific, must somehow transcribe the ethical moment, which contemplation comes to master through co-experiencing (empathizing) and co-evaluation. In carrying out this transcription, one must turn away from artistic form and, first of all, from aesthetic individuation: it is essential to separate the purely ethical personality from its artistic embodiment in an individual, aesthetically valid body and soul; it is essential to turn away as well from all constituents of artistic consummation. Such transcription is difficult, and in some cases (e.g., in music) completely impossible.

The ethical moment of a work's content can be conveyed and partially transcribed by way of a retelling: it is possible to relate in different words the experience, the action, and the event which has been artistically consummated in the work. A retelling of this sort, given a methodologically correct comprehension of the task at hand, can have great significance for aesthetic analysis. Indeed, although the retelling still retains an artistic form (the form of a story), it simplifies it and reduces it to a simple means for empathizing, abstracting as far as possible from all the isolating, consummating, and calming functions of form (of course, a story cannot abstract from them completely). The result is that, although empathy has grown weaker and paler, the purely ethical, responsible character of what is co-experienced (which is incapable of being consummated and which participates in the unity of the event of being) stands out more clearly—its ties with the unity from which form detached it stand out more clearly. This can also make it easier for the ethical constituent to pass into the cognitive form of judgments (ethical ones—in the narrow sense, sociological ones, and others), that is, the purely theoretical transcription of it within those bounds in which such a transcription is possible.

Many critics and literary historians have displayed great mastery in exposing the ethical moment by means of a methodologically thought-through semi-aesthetic retelling.

A pure theoretical transcription can never comprise the ethical moment of content in all its fullness; empathizing alone can accomplish that. But it can and it ought to strive for this as its unachievable limit. The constituent of ethical performance itself either is performed or is contemplated artistically, but it can never be adequately formulated theoretically.

Having transcribed (within the limits of the possible) the ethical moment of content that is consummated by form, aesthetic analysis proper must understand the significance of the entire content within the whole of the aesthetic object, that is, it must understand it as the content of precisely this given artistic form, and the form as the form of precisely this given content, never passing beyond the bounds of the work. But the ethical moment, like the cognitive, can be isolated and made the object of independent analysis, philosophico-ethical or sociological. It can also be made the object of contemporary moral or political evaluations (secondary evaluations and not the primary co-evaluations which are indispensable to aesthetic contemplation as well). Thus, the sociological method[27] not only transcribes the ethical event in its social aspect—the event co-experienced and co-evaluated in aesthetic contemplation—but it also passes beyond the bounds of the object and draws the event into broader social and historical interconnections. Such studies can have great scientific significance, and for the literary historian they are indispensable, but they do go beyond the bounds of aesthetic analysis proper.

The psychological transcription of the ethical constituent also does not relate directly to aesthetic analysis. Artistic creation and contemplation are concerned with ethical subjects, the subjects of action, and with the ethical-social relationships among them (it is to them that artistic form, which consummates them, is axiologically directed); artistic creation and contemplation are in no way concerned with psychological subjects or with the psychological connections among them.

It should be noted, without developing this proposition further, that in certain cases (e.g., in perceiving a musical work) the intensive deepening of the ethical moment is perfectly acceptable methodologically, while its extensive expansion would destroy the given artistic form. The ethical moment has no downward boundaries that could be illegitimately breached: the work does not predetermine and cannot predetermine the depth of the ethical moment.

To what degree can the analysis of content have a strictly scientific character (a universally valid character)?

In principle, it is possible to achieve a high degree of scientific validity, especially when the corresponding disciplines— philosophical ethics and the social sciences—have themselves achieved as high a degree of scientific validity as is possible for them. But, in point of fact, the analysis of content is extraordinarily difficult, and it is impossible to avoid a certain degree of subjectivism, a result conditioned by the very essence of the aesthetic object. But the investigator's scientific tact can always keep him within the proper limits and force him to make reservations about what is subjective in his analysis.

This in its basic features is the methodology for the aesthetic analysis of content.

III. The Problem of Material

In resolving the problem of the significance of material for the aesthetic object, one must consider the material in its perfectly exact scientific determinateness, without enriching it with any moments alien to that determinateness. Ambiguity with regard to the material occurs especially often in the aesthetics of the word; virtually anything one might like is understood by the "word," right up to "the Word, which was in the beginning." The metaphysics of the word (true, in its more subtle forms) is encountered especially often in studies on poetics written by poets themselves (in Russia, by Vyacheslav Ivanov,[28] Andrei Bely,[29] and Konstantin Bal'mont);[30] the poet takes the word as already aestheticized, but thinks of the aesthetic moment as belonging to the essence of the word itself, in this way transforming it into a mythical or metaphysical entity.

By endowing the word with everything peculiar to culture, that is, with all cultural validities—cognitive, ethical, and aesthetic— it is very easy to arrive at the conclusion that there is nothing else in culture but the word, that all of culture is nothing more than a phenomenon of language, that the scholar and the poet are to an equal degree concerned only with the word. But, by dissolving logic and aesthetics or even just poetics in linguistics, we destroy the distinctiveness not only of the logical and the aesthetic, but, to an equal degree, that of linguistics as well.

It is possible to understand the significance of the word for cognition, for artistic creation, and in particular for poetry (which interests us here most of all) only after having understood its purely verbal, linguistic nature completely apart from the tasks of the cognition of artistic creation, religious worship, etc., all of which are served by the word. Linguistics is not indifferent, of course, to the peculiarities of scientific, artistic, or religious language, but for it these are purely linguistic peculiarities of the language itself. On the other hand, to understand their significance for art, for science, and for religion, linguistics cannot manage without the guiding directions of aesthetics, the theory of cognition, and the other philosophical disciplines, just as the psychology of cognition must rely upon logic and epistemology, and the psychology of artistic creation—on aesthetics.

Linguistics is a science only to the extent that it masters its object, language. The language of linguistics is determined by purely linguistic thinking. A single, concrete utterance[31] is always given in a value-and-meaning cultural context, whether it be scientific, artistic, political, etc., or in the context of a situation from everyday personal life. Each separate utterance is alive and has meaning only within these contexts: it is true or false, beautiful or ugly, sincere or deceitful, frank, cynical, authoritative, etc.—there are no neutral utterances, nor can there be. But linguistics sees in them only a *phenomenon of language*, and it *relates them only to the unity of language*, and not at all to the unity of a concept, of practical life, of history, of the character of a person, etc.

No matter what significance some historical utterance may have for science, for politics, or in the personal life of some individual, for linguistics, it does not represent a shift in the domain of meaning, it does not represent a new perspective on the world, or a *new artistic form*, or a crime, or a moral feat. For linguistics, it is merely a phenomenon of language, and perhaps a new linguistic construction. And the meaning of the word, its referential significance, is for linguistics merely a constituent of a *linguistically determined word*, properly extracted from the meaning-and-value cultural context in which the word in reality was heard.

Only in this way, by isolating and liberating the *purely verbal* constituent of the word and by creating *a new verbal unity* with its concrete subdivisions, does linguistics master methodologically its object—language *indifferent* to extralinguistic values (or, if one prefers, it creates a new, purely linguistic value to which it relates every utterance).

Only in consistently freeing itself from metaphysical bias (from substantialization and real objectivization of the word), from an overinvestment in logic, from psychologism, and from aestheticism does linguistics work its way through toward its object, posit it methodologically, and thereby become for the first time a scientific discipline.

Linguistics has not succeeded in mastering its object methodologically to the same degree in all areas: it is only beginning to master it in syntax,[32] and with difficulty; very little has been done as yet in the area of semantics; nothing has been worked out yet in the department concerned with the study of large verbal entities—long utterances from everyday life, dialogue, speech, treatise, novel, and so on—for these utterances as well can be and must be defined and studied in purely linguistic terms, as verbal phenomena. The examination of these phenomena in old manuals of poetics and rhetoric and in their contemporary variant—descriptive poetics—cannot be considered scientific owing to the previously noted mixing of the linguistic point of view with those completely alien to it—logical, psychological, aesthetic. The syntax of large verbal wholes (or—composition as a department of linguistics, as distinct from composition which takes into account an artistic or a scientific task) still awaits its foundation and validation: scientifically, linguistics has still not moved beyond the complex sentence. The complex sentence is the most extended phenomenon of language that has been scientifically examined by linguistics: one gets the impression that the methodically pure language of linguistics suddenly comes to an end at this point, and what begins at once is science, poetry, and so on, and yet the purely linguistic analysis can be continued further, no matter how difficult it is and how tempting it may be to introduce here points of view that are alien to linguistics.

It is only after linguistics masters its object fully and with complete methodological consistency that it will be able to work productively for the aesthetics of verbal art, in its turn using without fear the services of the aesthetics of verbal art. Until that time, "poetic language,"[33] "image," "concept," "judgment," and similar terms will remain temptations and a great danger for linguistics. And linguistics has good reason to fear them: they have far too long muddied and continue to muddy the methodological purity of this discipline.

What significance, then, does *language conceived in a strictly linguistic sense* have for the aesthetic object of poetry?[34] This question does not concern at all the linguistic peculiarities of poetic language (as some are inclined to reinterpret this problem), but concerns the significance of the language of linguistics in its entirety as material for poetry, and this problem is purely aesthetic in character.

Language for poetry, just as for cognition and for an ethical action (and its objectification in law, in the state, etc.), is merely a *technical moment*. In this there is a perfect analogy between the significance of language for poetry and the significance of nature studied by natural science as the material (and not the content) of visual arts: physicomathematical space, mass, the sound of acoustics, etc.

But poetry utilizes the language of linguistics technically in an altogether special way: poetry needs language *in its entirety, in all its facets and all its constituents*—poetry does not remain indifferent to *any nuance* of the word studied by linguistics.

Language in its entirety is not needed by any domain of culture save poetry. Cognition certainly does not need the complex distinctiveness of the word's phonic dimension in its qualitative and quantitative aspects; it does not need the diversity of possible intonations; it does not need the feeling of the movement of the articulatory organs; etc. The same must be said about other domains of cultural creativity: none can do without language, but they select very little from it.

Language reveals all of its possibilities only in poetry, since here maximal demands are placed upon it: all its aspects are strained to the extreme, and reach their ultimate limits. Poetry squeezes, as it were, all the juices from language, and language exceeds itself here.

But in placing such demands on language, poetry nevertheless *overcomes it as language, as a linguistically determinate entity.* Poetry is no exception to the general proposition concerning all the arts: *artistic creation, determined in relation to its material, constitutes an overcoming of that material.*

Language in its linguistic determinateness does not enter into the aesthetic object of verbal art.

This occurs in all the arts: the extra-aesthetic nature of the material (in distinction to content) does not enter into the aesthetic object. That is, physicomathematical space, the lines and figures of geometry, the movement of dynamics, the sound of acoustics, etc., do not enter into it. The artist as craftsman and the discipline of aesthetics have to do with them, but primary aesthetic contemplation does not. These two moments must be strictly distinguished: in the course of his work, the artist must deal with the physical, with the mathematical, with the linguistic, and the aesthetician must deal with physics, mathematics, and linguistics. But all this technical work carried out by the artist and studied by aesthetics (without which there would be no works of art) does not enter into the aesthetic object created by artistic contemplation, that is, into aesthetic being as such, into the ultimate goal of creativity: all of this is removed at the moment of artistic apprehension, just as the scaffolding is removed when a building is completed.[j]

To avoid misunderstanding, we shall provide here an exact definition of technique in art: by the technical moment in art, we mean everything that is absolutely necessary for the creation of a work of art in its natural-scientific or linguistic determinateness (this includes the entire makeup of a finished work of art as a thing), but that does not enter immediately into the aesthetic object—is not a component of the artistic whole. Technical moments are factors of the artistic impression, but they are not aesthetically valid components of the content of that impression, i.e., of the aesthetic object.

Must we perceive or feel the word in the artistic object precisely as the word in its linguistic determinateness? Must we feel the word's morphological form precisely as morphological?—the syntactic as syntactic?—the semantic order as semantic? Must we apprehend the poetic whole in artistic contemplation as a verbal whole, and not as the consummated whole of an event, of a certain striving, of an inner tension, etc.?

Of course, linguistic analysis will find words, sentences, etc.; physical analysis would find paper and printer's ink of a determi-

---

[j] From this it does not follow, of course, that the aesthetic object exists somewhere and somehow in an already finished state prior to the creation of the work and independently of it. Such a supposition is, of course, completely absurd.

nate chemical composition, or it would find sound waves in their physical determinateness; the physiologist would find appropriate processes in the sense organs and nerve centers; the psychologist would find appropriate emotions, auditory sensations, visual representations, and so on. All of these scientific judgments by specialists, and particularly the judgments of the linguist (and, to a much lesser degree, of the psychologist), will be needed by the aesthetician as he studies the structure of a work in its extra-aesthetic determinateness. But it is obvious to the aesthetician and to any artistic contemplator that all these constituents do not enter into the aesthetic object, that object to which our immediate aesthetic evaluation relates (it is beautiful, it is profound, etc.). All these constituents are noted and determined only by the secondary, explanatory scientific judgment of the aesthetician.

If we were to attempt to define the composition of the aesthetic object of Pushkin's poem "Remembrance" (1828),[35] we would say that the following enter into its composition: the city, the night, recollections, remorse, etc.—it is with these *values* that our artistic activity has to do immediately, it is toward them that the aesthetic intention of our spirit is directed. The ethical event of recollection and remorse has been aesthetically shaped or formed and consummated in this work (artistic forming includes the constituent of isolation and fiction, i.e., of incomplete reality), but not words, not phonemes, not sentences, and not semantic series. All these lie outside the content of aesthetic perception, that is, outside the artistic object, and they may be needed only for the secondary, scientific judgment of aesthetics, insofar as the question arises as to how and by which constituents of the extra-aesthetic structure of the external work the given content of artistic perception is conditioned.

Aesthetics must determine the immanent composition of the content of artistic contemplation in its aesthetic purity, i.e., the aesthetic object, in order to decide what significance the material and its organization in the external work have for it. Proceeding in this manner, aesthetics must inevitably establish, with regard to poetry, that language in its linguistic determinateness does not enter into the aesthetic object, it remains outside it *while the aesthetic object itself* is composed of artistically shaped content (or of content-bearing artistic form).

The artist's enormous labor over the word has the ultimate goal of overcoming the word, because the aesthetic object arises on the boundaries of words, on the boundaries[36] of language as such. But this overcoming of the material is purely *immanent in character.* That is, the artist frees himself from language in its linguistic determinateness not through negation but by way of *perfecting* it *immanently:* the artist conquers language, as it were, with its own verbal weapons—he forces language, in the process of perfecting it linguistically, to surpass itself.

This immanent overcoming of language in poetry is sharply distinguished from the purely negative overcoming of language in the domain of cognition—algebraization, the use of conventional signs in place of words, abbreviations, and the like. *Immanent overcoming is the formal determination of the relationship to material not only in poetry but in all the arts.*

The aesthetics of verbal art must not skip over linguistic language either, but must utilize all the work of linguistics to understand, on the one hand, the *technique* of the poet's creation on the basis of a correct understanding of the place of material in artistic creation, and, on the other hand, the distinctiveness of the aesthetic object.

As we have pointed out, the aesthetic object, as the content of artistic vision and its architectonics, is a completely new ontic formation that is not of a natural-scientific order (nor of a psychological order, of course) and not of a linguistic order: it is a distinctive aesthetic existent, which arises on the boundaries of a work by way of overcoming its material—extra-aesthetic—determinateness as a thing.

On the one hand, words in a poetic work combine into the whole of a sentence, a period, a chapter, an act, etc., and, on the other, they create the whole of a hero's appearance, his character, his situation, the condition of his life, his actions, etc. And, finally, they create the whole of an aesthetically shaped and consummated ethical event of a life, and in doing so, they cease to be words, sentences, verses, chapters, etc. That is to say, the process of realizing the aesthetic object, i.e., of realizing the artistic task in its essence, is a process of consistently transforming a linguistically and compositionally conceived verbal whole into the architectonic whole of an aesthetically consummated event.[37] At the same time, of course, all the verbal interconnections and interrelations of a linguistic and compositional order are transformed into extraverbal architectonic event-related interconnections.

A more detailed study of the aesthetic object and its architectonics is not part of our present task. Here we shall only touch
briefly on those misunderstandings which have arisen in contemporary Russian poetics in connection with the theory of the image and which have the most essential relation to the theory of
the aesthetic object.

The "image" in the aesthetics of Potebnya's followers[38] seems
unacceptable to us, because there is much closely associated with
it that is superfluous and untrue, and, despite the image's old and
venerable tradition, poetics would do well to part company with
it. But the criticism of the image as the fundamental constituent
in poetic creation that has been advanced by some Formalists and
developed with especial clarity by V. M. Zhirmunsky seems completely wrong to us methodologically, although at the same time
it is highly characteristic for contemporary Russian poetics.

The significance of the image is denied here on the ground that
it is not distinct *visual representations* of the objects spoken of in
the text that arise during artistic perception of a poetic work but
only random, changeable, and subjective fragments of visual representations, from which it is, of course, completely impossible
to construct an aesthetic object. It follows that clear-cut images
do not arise and even that they cannot arise in principle. How, for
example, are we to represent to ourselves the "city" in the poem
by Pushkin noted above—as a foreign city or as a Russian one, as
a large or a small one, as Moscow or at Petersburg? This is left to
the subjective will of each reader:[39] the work provides us with no
directions that are necessary to construct a single concrete visual
representation of the city. But if this is so, then the artist has
nothing to do with an object but deals only with words, in the
present instance, with the word "city," and no more.

*The artist has to do only with words, because words alone are
something determinate and undoubtedly present-on-hand in
the work.*

This kind of argumentation is highly characteristic for material
aesthetics, which is still not entirely free from a psychologistic
bias.[40] First of all, it should be noted that exactly the same kind of
argumentation could be used in the domain of epistemology (and,
in fact, this has been often done): the scientist, too, has to do only
with words and not with objects or with concepts. For one can,
after all, show without difficulty, using analogous devices, that
there are no concepts present in the scientist's psyche, but only

unstable, subjectively random formations and fragments of representations. What we get here is nothing more or less than the re-
vival of old psychological nominalism applied to artistic creation.
But it is possible to show just as convincingly that words in their
linguistic determinateness are also not present in the psyche of
the artist or of the scientist—or, even more, that there is nothing
in the psyche except for psychic formations which are as such
subjective, and which, from the perspective of any domain of
meaning (cognition, ethics, aesthetics), are equally fortuitous and
inadequate. "Psyche" one should understand only as the object
studied by the empirical science of psychology, posited methodically by that science, and possessing its own purely psychological
regularities.

But despite the fact that everything in the psyche is only psychological and that it is quite impossible to experience nature, a
chemical element, a triangle, etc., psychically in an adequate way,
there are objective sciences where we have to do with nature,
with an element, with a triangle, and, moreover, scientific thought
has to do with *these objects themselves*—it is directed to them
and establishes interconnections among them. The poet, too, in
our example, has to do with the city, with recollection, with remorse, with the past and the future as *ethical aesthetic values,*
and, what is more, he has to do with them in an aesthetically responsible way, although there are no values in his soul, but only
psychic experiences. The components of the aesthetic object of
the *given work* are "the city's wide and silent streets," "the shadow
of night," "the scroll of memory," etc., *but not visual representations, not psychic experiences in general, and not words.* The artist (and the contemplator) has to do, moreover, precisely with
"the city" as expressed by the Church Slavonic form of the word
(*grad*):[41] the connotation of the Church Slavonic form relates to
the ethical-aesthetic value of the city, giving great significance to
that value, and it becomes the *characterization of a concrete
value*[42] and as such enters into the aesthetic object, i.e., it is not
the *linguistic form* that enters into the aesthetic object but *its
axiological significance* (psychological aesthetics would say "the
emotional-volitional moment corresponding to that form").

These components are joined together to form the unity of an
axiologically valid event of life, aesthetically shaped and consummated (outside aesthetic form, it would be an ethical event that is
in principle incapable of being consummated from within itself).

This ethical-aesthetic event is completely determinate and artistically unambiguous: we could call its components—images, understanding by this term not visual representations, but fully shaped moments of content.

It should be noted that one cannot *see* an image in the visual arts either: it is, of course, completely impossible to see *with the eyes alone* a represented human being *as a human being*, as an ethical-aesthetic value, an image, to see his body as a value, the expression of his exterior, and so on. In general, in order to see *something*, to hear *something*—that is, *something* objectively determinate or only axiologically valid, axiologically weighty— the external senses are not enough—it is not enough to have only "an unseeing eye and a noisy ear," in the words of Parmenides.[43]

Thus, the aesthetic component (we shall call it for the present an image) is neither a concept, nor a word, nor a visual representation, but a distinctive aesthetic formation which is realized in poetry with the help of the word, and in the visual arts— with the help of visually apprehended material, but which does not coincide anywhere with the material or with any material combination.

All the misunderstandings (like the one we examined above) that arise around the nonverbal aesthetic object (and the nonmaterial one in general) can be ultimately explained by the completely illegitimate effort to find a purely empirical equivalent for the aesthetic object that would be localized in space and time like a thing; or even by the effort totally to empiricize the aesthetic object cognitively. There are two empirically present-on-hand constituents in artistic creation: the external material work and the psychic process of creation and perception (of sensation, representation, emotion, etc.). In the first case, we have a natural-scientific (mathematical or linguistic) regularity, and, in the second, a psychological one (the associative interconnection, etc.). The investigator clings to them, fearing to go beyond their bounds in any respect, usually assuming that beyond them lie only metaphysical or mystical essences. But these efforts to achieve a total empiricization of the aesthetic object always prove to be unsuccessful, and, as we have shown, methodologically they are completely illegitimate. For it is precisely the distinctiveness of the aesthetic object as such and the distinctiveness of the purely aesthetic interconnection of its constituents, that is, its architectonics, which it is important to understand. Neither psychological nor material aesthetics is capable of accomplishing that.

There is absolutely no reason to be afraid of the fact that the aesthetic object cannot be found either in the psyche or in the material work of art. It does not become in consequence some sort of mystical or metaphysical essence. The multiform world of action (the being of the ethical) finds itself in the same situation. Where is the state located? In the psyche? In physicomathematical space? On the pages of constitutional records? And where is the law located? Nevertheless, we do deal responsibly with the state and with the law. What is more, these values give meaning and order not only to empirical material but also to our psyche, enabling us to overcome its bare psychic subjectiveness.

This same tendency toward extra-aesthetic empiricization and psychologization of the artistic object explains the attempt (noted above) to understand content as a constituent of the material (of the word): when attached to the word as one of its aspects (alongside the phoneme, the morpheme, and others), content appears to be more scientifically palpable, more substantive materially.

We shall not return to the question of content as an indispensable constitutive moment; we shall say only that scholars are usually inclined to understand under the thematic constituent (which is absent in some arts and present in others) only the constituent of object-related differentiation and cognitive determinateness, which is not peculiar to all the arts; but this constituent in no way exhausts content. However, in some cases (e.g., V. M. Zhirmunsky, although the first, narrower understanding of thematics is not foreign to him), contemporary poetics subsumes under thematics virtually the entire aesthetic object in its non-material distinctiveness and with its architectonic (event-related) structure. But, at the same time, this object, introduced uncritically, is squeezed into the linguistically determined word and set there alongside the phoneme, the morpheme, and other moments, and thereby, of course, one radically distorts its purity. But how we are to harmonize the world of thematics, the world of events (i.e., shaped content), in a unitary whole, with the linguistically determined word—poetics does not answer this question, and in fact does not even pose it in the form appropriate to a question of fundamental principle. Meanwhile, the world of thematics broadly understood and the word of linguistics exist on completely different planes and in different dimensions. It is worth adding that thematics renders the aesthetic object and content extraordinarily theoretical: the ethical constituent and the feeling appropriate to it are undervalued, and the purely ethical constituent and its cognitive transcription fail to be distinguished.

That is how the significance of material in artistic creation is defined: while it does not enter into the aesthetic object in its material, extra-aesthetic determinateness, it is indispensable for the construction of the aesthetic object as a technical element.

From this it does not follow at all that the study of the work's material structure (as a purely technical matter) must occupy only a modest place in aesthetics. The significance in specialized aesthetics of studies of the material is very great—just as great as the significance that the material work and its creation have for the artist and for aesthetic contemplation. We can agree fully with the assertion that "technique, in art, is everything"—understanding it in the sense that the aesthetic object is realized only by way of creating a material work (aesthetic vision outside art is hybrid precisely because here one cannot achieve complete organization of the material—as, for example, in the contemplation of nature). Prior to this creation and independent of it, the aesthetic object does not exist—it is realized for the first time together with the work.

One should not give the word "technique" a disparaging meaning when it is used in reference to artistic creation: technique here cannot and should not be severed from the aesthetic object, for it is vivified and moved in all its constituents by that object. In artistic creation, therefore, technique is by no means mechanistic; it may appear mechanistic in bad aesthetic studies which lose the aesthetic object, making technique self-sufficient and severing it from purpose and meaning. To offset such studies, one must emphasize the auxiliary character of the work's material organization, its purely technical nature, not in order to denigrate it, but rather to give it meaning and life.

Thus, a correct resolution of the question of the significance of material will not render works on material aesthetics unnecessary, nor will it lessen their significance in the least; rather, it will provide these works with principles and give them a *correct methodological direction*. Of course, they will have to give up their pretension that they are capable of explaining artistic creation exhaustively.

It should be noted that with regard to some of the arts aesthetic analysis must be limited almost exclusively to the study of technique, methodologically understood, of course, as technique only: this is the situation of the aesthetics of music. The aesthetic analysis of particular works has almost nothing to say—beyond the most general definition of its distinctiveness—about the aesthetic object of music that arises on the boundaries of acoustic sound. Judgments that go beyond the bounds of an analysis of a musical work's material composition become in the majority of cases subjective: they are a free poetization of the work, or an arbitrary metaphysical construction, or a purely psychological discussion.

A special kind of methodologically aware subjective-philosophical interpretation of musical compositions is possible that could have great cultural significance; but it would not be scientific, of course, in the strict sense of the word.

We cannot outline here a methodology of material compositional analysis, even in the general terms in which we presented the methodology of the analysis of content; that would be possible only after a more detailed study of the aesthetic object and its architectonics, by which the composition is determined. Here we must limit ourselves to no more than what we have said.

IV. The Problem of Form

Artistic form is the form of content, but a form which is realized entirely in the material—is attached to the material, as it were. Form must therefore be understood and studied in two directions: (1) from within the pure aesthetic object, as architectonic form, axiologically directed toward content (the possible event) and referred to it; (2) from within the compositional material whole of the work—this is the study of the technique of form.

In the case of the second direction, form must never be interpreted as the form of a given material (this would fundamentally distort correct understanding). Rather, form is only realized in the material and with its help, and, in this respect, apart from its aesthetic purpose, form is also conditioned by the nature of the given material.

The present section is a brief introduction to the methodology of the *aesthetic* analysis of form as *architectonic* form. Form is all too often understood merely as "technique"; this is typical of both Formalism and of psychologism in the study of art. We consider form, however, on the aesthetic plane proper, an artistically valid form. The fundamental question to be dealt with in this section is the following: how does form, being realized entirely on the basis of the material, nevertheless become the form of content, relating axiologically to the content? Or, in other words, how does compositional form (the organization of a given material) realize architectonic form—the unification and organization of cognitive and ethical values?

Form is dematerialized and taken beyond the bounds of the work as organized material, only upon becoming the expression of the axiologically determinate creative activity of an aesthetically active *subiectum*. This constituent of the activeness of form (mentioned in the first section above) will be examined more closely here.[k]

In form I *find myself*, find my own productive, axiologically form-giving, activity, *I feel intensely my own movement that is creating the object*, and I do so not only in primary creation, not only during my own performance, but also during the contemplation of a work of art. *I must to some extent experience myself as the creator of form, in order to actualize the artistically valid form as such.*

In this lies the essential distinction between artistic form and cognitive form. The cognitive form does not have an author-creator: I find the cognitive form in the object, and I do not feel in it either myself or my own productive activity. It is this that conditions the distinctive, compelling necessity of cognitive thinking: it is active, but does not feel its own activity, because feeling can only be individual, related to a person, or, to be exact, the feeling of my own activity does not enter into the object-related content of the act of thinking itself, remaining outside it like a subjective psychological addendum, and no more: *science as an objective, object-related unity does not have an author-creator.*[1]

---

[k] The understanding of form as the expression of activity is by no means foreign to art studies, but it can receive a solid validation only in an aesthetics that is systematic in its orientation.

[1] The scholar or scientist as the author actively organizes only the external form of exposition; the separateness, completeness, and individuality

I must experience form as my own active, axiological relationship to *content*, in order to experience form aesthetically: in form and through form, I sing, recount, and depict; through form, I express my love, my affirmation, my acceptance.

Content is contraposed to form as something passive and in need of form, as something receptive, accepting, something that is encompassed, made firm, loved, and so on. As soon as I cease being active in form, content—the content calmed and consummated by form—immediately rebels and appears in its pure cognitive-ethical validity, that is, artistic contemplation ceases and is supplanted by purely ethical co-experiencing or by cognitive reasoning, by theoretical agreement or disagreement, by practical approval or disapproval, etc. Thus, in nonartistic perception of a novel it is possible to suppress form and to make the content active in its cognitive-problematic or its ethical-practical direction. It is possible, for example, to co-experience the adventures, the successes, and the failures of the heroes; it is also possible to reduce music to a simple accompaniment to one's fantasies, as an accompaniment to one's free, elementary, ethical tension, making it the center of gravity.

So long as we simply see or hear something, we do not yet apprehend artistic form; one must make what is seen or heard or pronounced an expression of one's own active, axiological relationship, one must *enter as a creator into what is seen, heard, or pronounced*, and in so doing overcome the material, extracreatively determinate character of the form, its thingness. Form ceases to be outside us as perceived and cognitively ordered material; it becomes an expression of a value-related activity that penetrates content and transforms it. Thus, in reading or hearing a work of poetry, I do not leave it outside myself, as someone else's utterance which must be simply understood. Rather, I make it to a certain extent my own utterances about the other, I make my own the rhythm, the articulatory tension, the internal gesticulation (the creating movements) of the story, the descriptive activity of metaphors, etc., as an adequate expression of my own axiological relationship to content. That is, I am directed in perception not toward words, not toward phonemes, not toward rhythm; rather,

---

of a scientific work, which express the creator's aesthetic, subjective activity, do not enter into cognition of the world.

I am actively directed with the words, the phonemes, and the rhythm toward content—I encompass it, give it a form, and consummate it (the form itself, taken in abstraction, is not self-sufficient, but renders the shaped content self-sufficient). I become active in the form, *and through form I assume an axiological position outside content as cognitive-ethical directedness*, and this makes possible for the first time the consummation and, in general, the realization of all the aesthetic functions of form with regard to content.

Thus, form is the expression of the active, axiological relationship of the author-creator and of the recipient (who co-creates the form) to content; all the movements of the work in which we can feel ourselves, our own activity in its axiological relation to content, and which are overcome in their materiality, must be assigned to form.

But how can form, as an expression through the word of a subjective active relationship to content, become a *creative* form that *consummates* content? What makes verbal activity, or activity in general—which *in reality does not go beyond the bounds of the material work*, engendering and organizing only the material work—an activity that gives form to cognitive-ethical content, a fully consummating form?

Here we must touch briefly on the primary function of form in relation to content—that of *isolation or detachment.*

Isolation or detachment relates not to the material, not to the work as a thing, but to its significance, to its content, which is freed from certain necessary connections with the unity of nature and the unity of the ethical event of being. This detachment from connections does not destroy the fact that the isolated content has been identified and ethically evaluated: that which is detached or isolated is recognized by the memory of reason and the memory of will, but it can be individualized and becomes in principle capable of being consummated, inasmuch as individuation is impossible in a state of relatedness to and inclusion in the unity of nature, while consummation is impossible within the unitary, irreversibly occurring event of being. That is, content must be detached from the future of the event, so that consummation (self-sufficient presence-on-hand, the self-contained present) would become possible.

The content of a work is, as it were, a segment of the unitary open event of being that has been isolated and freed by form from responsibility to the future event, and that is why it is as a whole self-sufficiently calm, consummated, having absorbed isolated nature as well into its calm and self-containment.

Isolation out of the unity of nature destroys all the material elements of content. The form of materiality became possible for the first time on the basis of the natural-scientific conception of unitary nature: outside it, an object could be perceived only animistically and mythologically—as a force and a participant in the event of life. Isolation once again dematerializes: an isolated thing is a *contradictio in adiecto*.

So-called fiction in art is only a positive expression of isolation: an object that is isolated is by the same token a fictive object—that is, it is not actual within the unity of nature and has not existed within the event of being. In regard to the negative moment, fiction and isolation coincide. What is emphasized in the positive moment of fiction is activeness, the authorship characteristic of form: in fiction, I feel myself more acutely as actively making up the object, I feel my freedom (conditioned by my situatedness outside) to give a form to and to consummate the event without any impediment.

It is only possible to make up something subjectively valuable and valid in the event, something humanly significant, but not a thing: a made-up thing is a *contradictio in adiecto*.

In music, as well, isolation and constructedness cannot be axiologically related to the material: it is not the sound of accoustics that is isolated and not the mathematical number of the compositional order that is made up. What is detached and fictively irreversible is the event of striving, the axiological tension, which actualizes itself thanks to that without any impediment, and becomes consummated.

The so-called defamiliarization [*ostranenie*] of the Formalists is fundamentally the function of isolation that is not very clearly expressed methodologically and is incorrectly referred in most cases to the material: what is defamiliarized is the *word* by way of destroying its habitual place in a semantic series. Sometimes, however, defamiliarization is related to the object as well, but is understood in a crudely psychologistic way—as the removal of the object, the value, and the event from the necessary cognitive and ethical series.

Isolation makes possible for the first time positive realization of artistic form, for what becomes possible is not the cognitive and not the ethical relationship in the event, but the free shaping of content; what is freed is the activeness of our feeling of the object, of our feeling of the content, together with all the creative energies of this feeling. Isolation is thus the negative condition of the personal, subjective (not psychologically subjective) character of form; it allows the author-creator to become a constitutive moment of form.[m]

On the other hand, isolation foregrounds and defines the significance of the material and its compositional organization. The material becomes a *condition:* in working the material, the artist is working the values of the reality isolated, and thereby overcomes the material immanently, without going beyond its bounds. The word, the utterance, ceases to expect and to want anything real beyond its own bounds—action or correspondence to reality, that is, actualization in reality or verification and confirmation (the overcoming of subjectiveness). Through its own strength, the word transposes the consummating form into content. Thus, a request in the lyric—an aesthetically organized request—begins to be sufficient unto itself and does not need satisfaction (it is satisfied, as it were, by the very form of its expression); a prayer ceases to have need of God, who could hear it; a complaint ceases to need assistance; repentance ceases to need forgiveness, and so on. Making use of the material alone, form brings any event and ethical tension to fullness of completion. With the help of the material alone, the author assumes a creative, productive position with regard to content, that is, with regard to cognitive and ethical values. The author enters, as it were, the isolated event and becomes the creator in it, without becoming a participant. Thus, isolation makes the word, the utterance, and the material in general (the sound of acoustics, etc.) formally creative.

How does the creative individuality of the artist and the contemplator enter the material—the word—and over which of its aspects does it primarily gain control?

We distinguish in the word as material the following moments or constituents:[n] (1) the phonic side of the word, the musical con-

---

[m] Isolation is, of course, the first product of this activity; isolation is, as it were, the author's assumption of control.

[n] We approach the linguistic word here from the standpoint of the compositional realization through it of artistic form.

stituent proper; (2) the referential meaning of the word (with all its nuances and variations); (3) the constituent of verbal connection (all the relations and interrelations that are purely verbal); (4) the intonational (on the psychological plane—the emotional-volitional) constituent of the word, the axiological directedness of the word that expresses the diversity of the speaker's axiological relations; (5) the feeling of verbal activeness, the feeling of the active generation of signifying *sound* (included here are all motor elements—articulation, gesture, facial expression, etc.—and the whole inner directedness of my personality, which actively assumes through utterances a certain value-and-meaning position). We emphasize that the point here is the feeling of generating the signifying word. This is not a feeling of bare organic movement that generates the physical fact of the word, but a feeling of generating both meaning and evaluation, that is, a feeling of moving and assuming a position as a whole human being—of a movement into which both the organism and the meaning-directed activity are drawn, because both the flesh and the spirit of the word are generated together in their concrete unity. All of the four preceding moments are reflected in this, the fifth moment; the latter is that aspect of the other four which is turned to the speaker's personality (the feeling of generating sound, generating meaning, generating connections, and generating evaluation).

The form-giving activity of the author-creator and the contemplator takes possession of all the aspects of the word: with the help of these aspects, he can realize the consummating form that is directed upon content, and, on the other hand, they all serve the expression of content as well. In each of these moments or constituents, the creator and the contemplator feel their own activity—a selecting, constructing, determining, consummating activity—and at the same time, they feel something upon which this activity is directed, something which is already there. But the *governing* moment, the focal point of the form-giving energies here, is, of course, the fifth moment, and then, in sequential order of importance, the fourth (i.e., evaluation), the third (connections), the second (signification), and, finally, the first (sound), which absorbs into itself, as it were, all the other moments and becomes *the bearer of the unity of the word in poetry.*

The governing constituent in the cognitive utterance is the referential, object-related meaning of the word, which strives to find its necessary place in the objective (object-related) unity of

cognition. This objective unity governs and determines everything in a cognitive utterance, casting out mercilessly everything
unrelated to itself. In particular, the feeling of assuming an active
position by that which has been said is cast out: it is not referred
to the objective unity and does not penetrate it as creative, subjective volition and feeling, and it is least of all capable of creating
the unity of the cognitive utterance.

The feeling of verbal activity in the performed act (verdict,
agreement, pardon, supplication) is by no means the governing
constituent. The verbal act is related to the unity of the ethical
event and is there defined as necessary and obligatory.

It is only in poetry that the feeling of the activity of generating
a signifying utterance becomes the form-giving center, the bearer
of the unity of form.

What breaks through into the open first of all from this focal
point is rhythm (in the broadest sense of the word—verse rhythm
as well as prose rhythm) and, in general, *any ordering of an utterance that is not object-related in nature, any ordering that returns the utterer to himself, to his own acting, generating unity.*

The unity of an ordering based upon the return of what is similar, even if it is the return of similar moments of meaning, is the
unity of an activity which returns to itself, finding itself anew.
The center of gravity lies not in the meaning that has returned
but in the return of the activity of movement (internal and external movement, that of body and soul) that engendered this
meaning.

The unity of all the compositional moments that realize form,
and, first of all, the unity of the verbal whole of a work (as a formal unity), is founded not in what is said but in how it is said, in
the feeling of the *activity* of meaningful speaking, which must
constantly feel itself as a *unitary activity*, independently of the
object-related and meaning-related unity of its content. What is
repeated, what returns, what establishes connections are not constituents of meaning immediately (in their objectiveness, i.e.,
their complete detachment from the speaking personality of a
subiectum), but—constituents of the relational self-activity, of
the living self-sensation of the activity. The activity does not lose
itself in the object, but again and again feels its own subjective
unity within itself, within the tension of its corporeal and inner
position: *the unity is not of the object and not of the event; it is*

the unity of encompassing, embracing the object and the event. Thus, the beginning and the end of a work are, from the perspective of the unity of form, the beginning and the end of activity: I begin something, and I end something.

The objective unity of cognition knows no ending as something which possesses positive validity: it is not science that begins and ends, but the scientist. The end, the beginning, and a considerable number of the compositional moments of a learned treatise reflect the activity of its author-*subiectum*, that is, they are *aesthetic* moments, which do not penetrate into the open, infinite, and beginningless world of cognition.

All the compositional divisions of the verbal whole (chapters, paragraphs, stanzas, lines, words) express form only as divisions; the *stages* of verbal generating activity are periods of a unitary tension, they are moments or constituents that achieve a certain degree of completeness not of content itself, and so are not *defined from within it*, but are rather moments of the activity of encompassing content *from outside*, moments determined from the author's activity that is directed toward content, although they, of course, penetrate content in an essential way, shaping it in an aesthetically adequate manner, rather than doing violence to it.

The unity of aesthetic form is thus the unity of the position assumed by acting body and soul, by the whole acting human being, who relies on himself. As soon as this unity is transposed into the content of activity—into the objective unity of cognition and the meaning-related unity of the event—form is destroyed as *aesthetic* form. This is how rhythm loses its form-giving power, as well as consummating intonation and other formal moments.

However, this activity of generating the signifying sound (the word)—an activity that feels itself and in this feeling possesses its own unity—is not sufficient unto itself, it is not satisfied only with itself; it is taken beyond the bounds of the acting organism and psyche, it turns outside of itself, inasmuch as this activity is the activity of loving, elevating, denigrating, lauding, lamenting, etc. That is, it is an axiologically determinate attitude (on the psychological plane, it has a determinate emotional-volitional tonality). For it is not simply sound that is generated, after all, but signifying sound; the activity of generating the word penetrates and becomes aware of itself axiologically in the intonative aspect of the word—gains mastery of evaluation in the feeling of active intonation.⁰ Under the intonative aspect of the word, we understand its capacity to express all the diversity of the speaker's axiological attitudes toward the content of an utterance (on the psychological plane—the diversity of the speaker's emotional-volitional reactions). Moreover, whether or not this aspect of the word is expressed in actual intonating when speaking or is experienced only as a possibility, this aspect is nevertheless aesthetically weighty. The author's activity becomes the activity of *expressed valuation*, which colors all aspects of the word: the word abuses, caresses, is indifferent, denigrates, embellishes, etc.ᵖ

Further, the generating activity gains mastery of signifying verbal connections (simile, metaphor; the compositional utilization or syntactic connections, repetitions, parallelisms, and the interrogative form; the compositional utilization of hypotactic and paratactic connections, etc.): *the feeling of the activity of connecting constitutes the organizing moment here as well*, but it is a feeling that has already been determined axiologically. Thus, a simile or metaphor relies on the unity of the activity of evaluation; that is, the connections enclose the world's intonative aspects, which are not indifferent, of course, to referential meaning (on the psychological plane—metaphor, simile, and other poeticized verbal connections are based upon the emotional-volitional interrelations and upon the kinship of words). The unity is created not by logical thought but by the feeling of valuational activity. These are not object-related, necessary connections that leave the feeling and willing *subiectum* outside themselves, that have no need of him; they are purely subjective connections that need the subjective unity of the feeling and willing human being. However, metaphor and simile also presuppose the potential objective unity and connection, and the unity of the ethical event, against the background of which one can feel their constructive activity. That is, metaphor and simile encompass the persis-

---

⁰The order (which we shall indicate below) in which the moments of the word are mastered by the activity of the author and the contemplator is by no means the order of actual perception and creation.

ᵖWe have in mind the purely aesthetic axiological intonation of the author, in contrast to the ethical "realistic" intonation of an actual or potential person-as-hero who experiences events ethically and as an interested party, but not aesthetically.

tent cognitive-ethical directedness, and the valuation expressed in them becomes that which really gives a form to the object and de-materializes it. Detached from the feeling of the author's connect-ing and form-giving activity, metaphor dies, that is, ceases to be poetic metaphor, or it becomes a myth (as a purely verbal meta-phor, it can also serve the purposes of cognitive utterance).

All syntactic verbal connections, in order to become composi-tional connections that realize form in the artistic object, must be permeated by the unity of the feeling of connecting activity, which is directed toward the unity (realized through composi-tional components) of object-related and meaning-related connec-tions of a cognitive or ethical character, that is, by the unity of the feeling of tension and form-giving encompassing from outside of cognitive-ethical content.

Even the object-related, referential meaning of the word is en-veloped by the feeling of the *activity of choosing meanings*, by a distinctive *feeling of the subject-creator's initiative with regard to meaning* (this initiative does not exist in cognition, where one cannot be an initiator, where the feeling of the activity of choice is cast out, beyond the bounds of the world of what has been cog-nized). But this feeling of choice is not in relation to that which is chosen, it embraces its cognitive and ethical autonomy.

Finally, the feeling of activity also takes possession of the phonic side of the word. The bare accoustical side of the word has a rela-tively minor significance in poetry. The movement that generates acoustical sound, and is most active in the articulatory organs, although it also takes hold of the whole organism—this move-ment, either actually realized during one's own reading, or experi-enced only as a possible movement—is incommensurably more important than what is *heard*. What is heard is reduced almost to the auxiliary role of eliciting the generative movements corre-sponding to it, or to the even more external auxiliary role of being a token of meaning, or, finally, of serving the basis for intonation, which needs the acoustical extension of the word but is in-different to its qualitative phonic makeup, and as the basis for rhythm, which has, of course, a motive character. In the novel, and generally in the larger prosaic verbal wholes, the phoneme yields almost completely its auxiliary functions (to designate sig-nification, to elicit movement, to be the basis for intonation) to the grapheme. In this lies an essential distinction between poetry and music. In music, the movement creating sound is of secondary importance in comparison to the acoustical side of the sound being heard (except for vocal music, which in this respect is still close to poetry, although the acoustical aspect here is nevertheless incomparably more important than in poetry). But this sound-creating movement is still organic here, and we can say that the actively creating inner body of the creator-performer-listener is drawn, as a moment, into the artistic form.

In instrumental music, the movement generating sound ceases almost entirely to be organic: the movement of the bow, the striking of keys with the fingers, the exertion necessary for wind instruments, etc., all remain to a significant degree outside form; and only the tension corresponding to this movement, the force of the expended energy, as it were, completely detached from the inner organic feeling of the striking or moving hand, is absorbed into the sound itself, and there, purified, it is caught by the understanding ear, and becomes an expression of the activity and tension of inner man, who generates the axiologically valid sound, regardless of both the organism and the instrument-thing. In music, all the compositionally valid moments are absorbed by the acoustical aspect of the sound. If in poetry the author, who realizes the form, is the speaking human being, then in music he is the immediate producer of sound, and most definitely not the performer (on the piano, the violin, etc.), that is, he is not the producer of sound in the sense of performing a movement by means of an instrument. The creative activeness of musical form is the activeness of the signifying sound itself—the axiological movement itself of that sound.

The term "instrumentation" as a designation for the ordering of the qualitative side of the acoustical material in poetry must be extraordinarily infelicitous. Properly speaking, it is not the acoustical aspect of words that is ordered, but the articulatory, the motor aspect, although this articulatory order does find its reflection in the phonic makeup, just as it does in the graphic makeup.

The significance of the creating inner organism is not the same in all kinds of poetry. It is maximal in lyric, where the body, generating the sound from within itself and feeling the unity of its own productive exertion, is drawn into form. The involvement of the inner organism in form is minimal in the novel.

Of course, the activity that generates the word remains the fundamental principle governing form in the novel as well (if the novel is truly artistic). But this activity is almost completely devoid of organic, corporeal moments: this is an activity of a purely spiritual generation and selection of meanings, connections, axiological relations; this is the inner tension of consummating spiritual contemplation and encompassing large verbal wholes, chapters, parts, and, finally, the whole novel. Especially evident here is the feeling of intense, axiologically remembering activity, of emotional memory. It is here that the constitutive moment of form—the internally active human being as creator—enters form: he sees, hears, evaluates, connects, selects (even though there is no actual exertion of the external senses and of the bodily organs); he remains one in his feeling of activity throughout the entire novel, beginning and ending it—as a whole of the productive and self-aware inner tension.[q]

The unity of form is the unity of the active axiological position of the author-creator, realized by means of the word (its act of assuming a position through the word), but relating to content. This position, assumed through the word and the word alone, becomes productive and creatively consummates content thanks to the isolation of content, to its nonactuality (to be more precise and philosophically rigorous—an actuality of a special, purely aesthetic order). Isolation is the first step taken by the form-giving consciousness, the first gift bestowed by form upon content, making possible for the first time all the subsequent, purely positive, enriching gifts bestowed by form.

All the moments of the word that realize form oppositionally become the expression of the author's creative relation to content. Thus, rhythm, attached to the material, is placed outside its boundaries and begins, of its own accord, to penetrate content as a creative relation to content, transposing it to a new axiological plane—the plane of aesthetic being. The novel's form, having become the expression of the author's attitude, creates the architectonic form, which orders and consummates the event, independently of the unitary, invariably pure event of being.

In this lies the profound distinctiveness of aesthetic form: it is

---

[q]The indicated creative activity of the author—the creator of form—must be rigorously distinguished from the passive, imitative movement (actual or potential) which is sometimes necessary for ethical empathy and co-experiencing, just as ethical intonation must be distinguished from the consummating aesthetic intonation.

my organically moving, evaluating, and meaning-giving activity, and at the same time it is the form of an event and its participant standing over against me (his individuality, the form of his body and soul).

The individual human *subiectum* experiences himself as a creator only in art. A positively subjective creative personality is a constitutive moment in artistic form; here its subjectiveness finds a distinctive objectification and becomes a culturally valid, creative subjectivity. And it is here as well that the distinctive unity of the organic—corporeal and inner man, his soul and his spirit—is realized, but a unity that is experienced from within. The author, as a constitutive moment of form, is the organized activity, issuing from within, of the integral whole human being, who realizes his task completely, without presupposing anything external to himself for the consummation. It is an activity of the entire human being, from head to foot: he is needed in his entirety, as one who breathes (rhythm), moves, sees, hears, remembers, loves, and understands.[r]

This activity (*organized from within*) of the creator's personality differs essentially from the passive personality (*organized from outside*) of the hero, of man as the object of artistic vision, determined in body and soul: his determinateness is a visible and audible, a shaped determinateness—it is the image of a human being, his externalized and embodied personality. The personality of the creator, meanwhile, is both invisible and inaudible, and is experienced and organized only from within, as a seeing, hearing, moving, remembering activity—as an embodying activity, and not as an embodied activity—which is only afterward reflected in the shaped object.

The aesthetic object is a creation that includes its creator within itself. The creator finds himself in it and feels intensely his own creative activity in it. Or put differently: it is a creation as it looks from the eyes of the creator himself, who freely and lovingly created it (true, this is not a creation from nothing, for it presupposes

---

[r] Only the methodologically rigorous understanding and study of the author as a moment in the aesthetic object can provide the foundations for the methodology proper to the study of him from the psychological, biographical, and historical points of view.

the reality of cognition and action which it only transfigures and shapes).

The basic task of aesthetics is the study of the aesthetic object in its distinctiveness, avoiding the substitution for it of some intermediate stage in the path of its realization. Above all, it is necessary to understand the aesthetic object synthetically, in its wholeness, to understand form and content in their essential and necessary interrelationship: form as the form of content, and content as the content of form—to understand the distinctiveness and law of their interrelationship. Only on the basis of this understanding is it possible to outline the proper direction for the concrete aesthetic analysis of particular works. It should be clear from all we have said that the aesthetic object is not a thing, since its form (or to be exact, the form of its content, for the aesthetic object is shaped content), in which I feel myself as an active *subiectum*, and into which I enter as a necessary constitutive moment, cannot be, of course, the form of a thing, of an object.

Artistically creative form, first and foremost, gives a form to the whole human being; and it gives a form to the world only as the world of man, either by humanizing and vivifying it directly, or by bringing it into an axiological connection with man so immediate that the world loses its own axiological independence, becoming only a moment in the value of human life. As a result, the relation of form to content in the unity of the aesthetic object has a distinctively *personal* character, and the aesthetic object is a distinctive, realized event of the action and interaction of creator and content.

In verbal artistic creation, it is particularly evident that the aesthetic object has the character of an event—here the interrelation of form and content has an almost dramatic character, and what is especially evident is the author's entering (as a human being with a body, a soul, and a spirit) into the object. Not only is the inseparability of form and content evident, but also their not merging into one, whereas, in the other arts, form penetrates more into content, becomes materialized, as it were, in it, and is harder to separate from it and to express in its abstract distinctness.

The explanation is to be found in the character of the material in poetry, the word, by means of which the author (the speaking human being) can immediately assume his creative position, whereas, in the other arts, alien bodies enter the process of creation as technical intermediaries (musical instruments, the chisel, etc.). In addition, the material does not take possession of the whole active human being as comprehensively. Having passed through these mediating foreign bodies, the activity of the author-creator becomes specialized, one-sided, and therefore less separable from the content to which it has given a form.

Notes

(Bakhtin's own notes appear in numbered sequence within the body of the text.)

1. The whole essay, of course, is devoted to elucidating the topics listed in its title. But at this initial point it may help to keep in mind that, roughly speaking, "content" is used by Bakhtin to refer to what a work is about at the level where it can be restated in terms *outside* the work (but, as will become apparent below, content is not the same as "theme," which is an even more generalized concept); "material" is the particular matter out of which a work is constructed (i.e., stone, paints, tones, words—the latter being the focus of the present essay); "form" is the relation in a particular work of "content" to "material." In addition to these three categories that have traditionally been understood as constituting a work of art, Bakhtin introduces in this essay the very important category of "aesthetic object," about which more below. At this point, suffice it that the aesthetic object is related to content, but is not coincidental with any of the three categories of the title.

2. That is, the purpose of this essay is not to sketch a poetics as such, i.e., "a totally intelligible structure of knowledge attainable about poetry [understood in the broadest sense to include what is usually called prose as well] which is not poetry itself, or the experience of it, but poetics" (Northrop Frye, *The Anatomy of Criticism* [Princeton: Princeton University Press, 1957], p. 14). By attempting to ground poetics in a "systematic aesthetics," Bakhtin both continues his earlier work as we have it in the other texts included in the present anthology and sets himself off from the Russian Formalists, who are the primary target of this polemical piece.

3. The decade from 1914, when Shklovsky published his *Resurrection of the Word*, to 1924, when this essay was intended to be published, was indeed a golden age of critical thought in Russia, encompassing major works not only by the Formalists, but by leading representatives of the so-called sociological school, and of the poetic schools of Symbolism and Futurism as well. Bakhtin refers to most of these in this essay. The

important thing to keep in mind at this point is the central role that the task of rethinking poetics played in Russian intellectual life of the time, and Bakhtin's attempt to join the dialogue.

4. Bakhtin is referring, of course, to members of the Leningrad "OPOJAZ" group, preeminently Viktor Shklovsky (1893–1984) and Boris Eikhenbaum (1886–1959), and members of the Moscow Linguistic Circle, such as Roman Jakobson (1896–1982), who worked closely together from 1915–1916 on, and who collectively have come to be known as the Russian Formalists, although in 1924 their membership—and even their methodology—was so much in flux that there was still discussion about who "belonged" to the Formalists and what they should be called as a group ("morphological school" was a variant, because of the Formalist insistence on studying the formal "grammar" of literature, rather than its semantics or history—although this emphasis shifted later). See Victor Erlich, *Russian Formalism, History-Doctrine*, first published in 1954 by Mouton in the Hague, which has gone through several editions since. For a more technical account, see Peter Steiner, *Russian Formalism: A Metapoetics* (Ithaca: Cornell University Press, 1984).

5. Viktor Maksimovich Zhirmunsky (1881–1971) was a leading Russian literary scholar and professor at Leningrad University from 1919. Somewhat older and more conservative than the Formalists, he nevertheless shared—especially in the early twenties—certain interests with them (although in later years he openly opposed their early work). He wrote on both Russian and West European literature (most importantly on Goethe) and was a founder of the modern study of comparative literature in the Soviet Union. Although Zhirmunsky's classic *Introduction to Metrics: Theory of Verse* (an English translation was made in 1966 in Mouton's Slavistic Printings and Reprintings series, no. 58) was not published until a year after Bakhtin finished this essay, by 1924 the major outlines of his position had been made clear in such works as *The Composition of Lyric Verse* (1921), a series of programmatic articles on Blok (1921) and Bryusov (1922), a long review of Eikhenbaum's *The Melody of Verse* (1922), and *Rhythm, Its History and Theory*. Zhirmunsky's own attempt to define his relation to the Formalists had also appeared ("On the Question of the Formal Method," 1923).

6. Aleksandr Aleksandrovich Smirnov (1883–1962) was a leading Russian literary scholar and professor at Leningrad University from 1913 to 1958. He began his career as a specialist on the medieval literature of Western Europe, but in the 1930s concentrated on the Renaissance, especially on Shakespeare, whose complete works in Russian he edited, and on whom he wrote a remarkable book (*Shakespeare*, published posthumously in 1963). The specific article to which Bakhtin here refers appeared in an almanac that also contained pieces by such "fellow travelers" of the Formalists as Zhirmunsky and Boris Viktorovich Tomashevsky (1890–1957). It is all the more remarkable, then, that Smirnov's piece

polemically opposes the Formalists, and on many of the same grounds as Bakhtin. The article is indebted in some of its assumptions to Heinrich Rickert (1863–1936), especially to *Kulturwissenschaft und Naturwissenschaft* (1899; the fifth edition had appeared the year before publication of Smirnov's article; see also note 56 to "Author and Hero in Aesthetic Activity"). Smirnov's assumptions, based as they are on Neo-Kantianism, even if of a kind different from the Marburg version that was so important for the young Bakhtin (Smirnov worked in the tradition of the so-called southwestern school of Windelband to which Rickert belonged), may account for some striking similarities between his work and that of Bakhtin. In a footnote to his article (p. 91), Smirnov says he is working on a book devoted to the "methodology of literary history based on the theory of poetry and the artistic word," a project, like so many in the twenties, that never was completed.

7. Viktor Vladimirovich Vinogradov (1895–1965) was a longtime professor of Russian at Moscow University and a powerful member of the Soviet Academy; he was reputed to have aided Stalin in writing the articles in 1950 that brought the influence in Soviet linguistics of Marr-ism to an end; his work on the Ushakov dictionary, his great *Outline of a History of the Modern Russian-Literary Language from the XVII to the XIX Centuries* (1938), and his *The Russian Language* (1947) make him the most important academic philologist of the Soviet period. In the 1920s, Vinogradov published a number of literary studies, the most important of which for Bakhtin in 1924 were "The Subject and Composition of Gogol''s Story 'The Nose,'" (1921); "The Style of the Petersburg Poem 'The Double'" (1922); and "On the Problems of Stylistics" (1923). Vinogradov is frequently used by Bakhtin as an example of the limitations of an unphilosophically grounded stylistics.

8. "Isolation" is a key factor in Bakhtin's aesthetics—see note 103 to "Author and Hero in Aesthetic Activity."

9. In Zhirmunsky's "On the Question of the Formal Method," his introductory article to a Russian translation of Oskar Walzel's *The Problem of Form in Poetry* (1923), exception is taken to the Formalists' emphasis on the reaction of readers, a move which psychologizes both literary texts and the history of literature. Above all, thematics get slighted, argues Zhirmunsky: "The study of poetry as art requires attention to be paid to its thematic aspect, the very *selection* of the theme as well as to its *construction*, compositional elaboration, and combination with other themes" (quoted from the second printing of this essay in Zhirmunsky's *Questions in the Theory of Literature* [1928], p. 169).

10. Reference here is to Kant's third critique, *The Critique of Judgement* (1790), which sought to link the worlds of nature and freedom that had been separated in the first two critiques, thus making Kant the first modern philosopher to make his aesthetic theory an integral part of his philosophical system. For the next hundred years, it would be customary

for German thinkers to think of aesthetics as an integral part of any philosophy claiming to be systematic. In 1923 (during the period he was
working on this essay), Bakhtin gave a series of lectures on the relation of
Kant's third critique to the philosophy of religion. Only fragmentary
notes of these lectures taken by some of his listeners remain.

11. Johann Friedrich Herbart (1776–1841) was a leading systematic,
antirationalist philosopher of the early nineteenth century, who, after occupying Kant's old chair at Königsberg, taught for many years at Göt-
tingen. Herbart, whose influence in the history of psychology and educa-
tion was enormous, had elaborate ideas about the role of concepts in
philosophical practice; the last division of concepts he calls "aesthetics,"
including ethics under that heading.

12. Friedrich Wilhelm Joseph von Schelling (1775–1854) was a leading
Idealist philosopher, a central figure in German Romanticism whose importance is out of all proportion to his neglect in the anglophone world.
Schelling went through several phases; he deals with aesthetics throughout, but the most important statements on the subject are to be found
in his *System of Transcendental Idealism* (1800) and his lectures at
Munich University brought together as *On the Relation of the Plastic
Arts to Nature* (1807; translated into English as *The Philosophy of Art* in
1845). For a more current translation, see F. W. J. Schelling, *The Philosophy of Art*, ed. and trans. Douglas W. Stott (Minneapolis: University of
Minnesota Press, 1989). See also Werner Marx, *The Philosophy of F. W. J.
Schelling*, trans. Thomas Nenon (Bloomington: Indiana University Press,
1984).

13. Georg Wilhelm Friedrich Hegel (1770–1831) deals with aesthetics
in both the *Phenomenology of Mind* (1807) and *Encyclopedia*, the outline of his system that Hegel provided to students, which went through
several versions, but most sustainedly in the *Lectures on Aesthetics* published by his students after his death. Bakhtin opposes the "formal aesthetics" of Kant and Herbart to the "aesthetics of content" of Schelling
and Hegel in order to contrast the emphasis in the former on architectonics, as opposed to a primary concern for thematic meaning in the
latter.

14. Boris Viktorovich Tomashevsky (1890–1957) was a close associate
of the Formalists who (although originally trained as an electrical engi-
neer) became a leading theorist of versification and the study of motifs.
Bakhtin is here referring to *Russian Metrics* (1923), in which the basic
argument is that Russian verse should be studied not on the basis of metrical feet, but from the perspective of the verse line—i.e., that rhythm
should take precedence over metrics. See Steiner, *Russian Formalism*,
pp. 176–184.

15. Bakhtin is here referring to two of the most distinctive doctrines of
early Formalism, "perceptibility" (*oshchutimost'*) and "constructing"
(*sdelat'*). The concept of "palpable form" was given its classic formula-

tion by Shklovsky in his two essays on "Potebnya" (1916) and "Art as Device" (1917). The most important example of "constructing" is Boris Eikhenbaum's (1886–1959) essay "How Gogol' 's 'Overcoat' Was Made" (1919).

16. On this extremely important topic, see note 108 to "Author and Hero in Aesthetic Activity."

17. Note that "the problem of content" is being resolved in terms of "the aesthetic object."

18. "Teleological method" is the procedure of assuming that all data are parts, teleologically linked to a whole; the object of analysis is to define the relation of parts to whole—in other words, to seek the architectonics in a given subject of analysis.

19. For a more detailed account of what Bakhtin means by "material aesthetics," see M. M. Bakhtin/P. M. Medvedev, *The Formal Method in Literary Scholarship*, trans. Albert J. Wehrle (Cambridge: Harvard University Press, 1985), esp. chap. 6, "Material and Device as Components of the Poetic Construction."

20. Sheer proliferation of terms.

21. Cf. note 9.

22. For a radical interpretation of the central role of the aesthetic in Nietzsche's work, see Alexander Nehamas, *Nietzsche: Life as Literature* (Cambridge, Mass.: Harvard University Press, 1985).

23. Reference here is to Plato's doctrine of innate ideas, the assumption that knowledge is correct remembering, as in the *Meno,* where Socrates demonstrates to Meno that even the slave, who has never studied geometry, "innately" knows how to demonstrate the proposition about the square of the hypotenuse.

24. Reference here is to the Formalist doctrine of estrangement (*ostranenie*), first broached by Shklovsky in his 1914 manifesto, "Resurrection of the Word."

25. Reference here, of course, is to characters in Dostoevsky's *Brothers Karamazov* and Tolstoy's *War and Peace.*

26. On the problem of Tolstoy's interpolations on the meaning of history in *War and Peace,* see Isaiah Berlin's classic study, *The Hedgehog and the Fox: An Essay on Tolstoy's View of History* (London: Weidenfeld and Nicolson, 1959), and Gary Saul Morson's *Hidden in Plain View: Narrative and Creative Potentials in "War and Peace"* (Stanford: Stanford University Press, 1986).

27. "Sociological method" is a general term for several attempts made between 1900 to 1930 to found a new science of literature based on contemporary work in sociology; the most prominent of such critics were G. V. Plekhanov (1856–1918), V. M. Friche (1870–1929), P. N. Sakulin (1868–1930), and V. F. Pereverzev (1882–1968). Their work was increasingly attacked as "vulgar sociologism" by the party in the late 1920s, and

Pereverzev was arrested in 1938, spending the next eighteen years in prison (he was finally rehabilitated in the thaw of 1956).

28. Vyacheslav Ivanovich Ivanov (1866–1949) was a poet, critic, scholar, and chief theorist of the Russian Symbolist movement. Ivanov received his doctorate at the University of Berlin under Theodor Mommsen, and for most of his life taught classical history and literature in the Soviet Union and (after his departure from Russia in 1924) Italy. A founder of the vogue in Russia for Hellenistic thought, he was an influence on both Bakhtin's older brother Nikolai and on Mikhail Bakhtin himself, one of whose lectures on Ivanov has been published as "Vyacheslav Ivanov," in *The Aesthetics of Verbal Creation (Estetika slovesnogo tvorchestva;* Moscow: Iskusstvo, 1979, pp. 384–415). The most important collections of Ivanov's articles on aesthetics are *Following the Stars* (1909) and *Furrows and Landmarks* (1916). An important essay by Ivanov, "On the Latest Theoretical Research in the Area of the Artistic Word," was published in *Nauchnye izvestija* in 1922, as Bakhtin was doing the groundwork for "The Problem of Content."

29. Andrei Bely (pseudonym of Boris Nikolaevich Bugaev, 1880–1934) was a poet, novelist, and leading theorist of Russian Symbolism. Bely is chiefly important in this essay as the most powerful defender of the concept of poetics as a separate discipline, for his insistence on the need of readers (not just critics) to pay close attention to the formal features of literary texts. He pioneered the use of statistics in studying versification. Bely's 1910 *Symbolism* (particularly the chapter on "Lyric as Experiment") was an important influence on the Russian Formalists.

30. Konstantin Dmitrievich Bal'mont (1867–1942) was a poet, novelist, and translator, who influenced Russian Symbolism. As a critic, he celebrates the psychological, almost mystic effects of poetry, as in his 1915 book, *Poetry as Magic (Poezija kak vol'shebstvo).*

31. The argument against linguistics here, and particularly the isolation of the utterance as a metalinguistic phenomenon, foreshadows Bakhtin's later work on utterance and speech genres in *Marxism and the Philosophy of Language* (which was, of course, published under the name of Voloshinov in 1929; Eng. trans. available from Harvard University Press) and the essay called "Speech Genres" (1952–1953, included in *Speech Genres and Other Late Essays,* published by the University of Texas Press in 1986).

32. The very important third (and concluding) section of *Marxism and the Philosophy of Language,* "Toward a History of Forms of Utterance in Language Constructions: A Study in the Application of the Sociological Method to Problems of Syntax," is an attempt to overcome this deficiency in the study of syntax.

33. Poetic language, image, concept, and judgment are all major categories of the first stage of Formalism, most of which (particularly the idea

of "poetic language") were highly modified in later Formalist practice, if not always in theory.

34. A reference to the work of such linguists as Roman Jakobson, in whose work it is often difficult to distinguish between formal linguistic categories of grammar, syntax, phonemic structure, etc., of a poem and its aesthetic being (the categories defining it which lie outside linguistics as an academic discipline).

35. "When the noisy day is stilled for mortal man, and the translucent shadow of night, and sleep, the reward of the day's toil, descend upon the city's wide and silent streets, then hours of tormenting wakefulness drag on for me in silence: in the blankness of night, remorse, like a serpent's bite, burns more fiercely in my heart; fancies seethe; a throng of oppressive thoughts crowds my mind, weighed down by anguish; memory silently unfolds its long scroll before me; and, reading the chronicle of my life with loathing, I tremble and curse, and complain bitterly, and shed bitter tears, yet I do no wash away the sorrowful lines" (trans. D. Obolensky in *The Heritage of Russian Verse* [Bloomington: Indiana University Press, 1976], p. 98). It is interesting to note that Bakhtin, who is usually thought of as a student of the novel (and sometimes as one who puts prose ahead of poetry), should in his early work give such prominence to lyric poetry, particularly that of Pushkin.

36. The attention paid to boundary phenomena here is another indication of Bakhtin's early disposition toward dialogism.

37. This is arguably the key to Bakhtin's insistence on the role of architectonics in the analysis of the aesthetic object.

38. Aleksandr Afanasievich Potebnja (1835–1891) was a philologist, philosopher of language, and theorist of poetics. He made his reputation with an early book that is still of the greatest interest, *Thought and Language* (1862). Heavily influenced by Wilhelm von Humboldt (as was Bakhtin), Potebnja spent the rest of his life in relative obscurity at Khar'kov University in the Ukraine, where he led a group of philologists who have since come to be known as the Khar'kov school. Potebnja argued that poetry was "thinking in images" (see *From Lectures on the Theory of Literature* [*Iz lektsij po teorii slovesnosti*], published by his students after Potebnja's death in 1907). Although far from the first to do so, Potebnja was perhaps more sustained than most other theorists in defending the central role of imagery in all language activity, not just literature. Potebnja was a favorite target of the Russian Formalists. For more information on this fascinating figure, see John Fizer, *Alexander Potebnja's Psycholinguistic Theory of Literature*, Harvard Ukrainian Research Institute Monograph Series (Cambridge, Mass.: Harvard University Press, 1987).

39. This, in sum, is why Bakhtin emphasizes not "inner images" but the inner *word*.

40. In other words, for all their attempts to avoid it, the Formalists are still trapped in a psychologism of their own, a point taken up later in the Bakhtin/Medvedev volume at some length: *The Formal Method in Literary Scholarship*, pp. 159–174.

41. Russian has the possibility of substituting Old Church Slavonic forms in order (usually) to achieve a more solemn effect. Pushkin was particularly given to the selective use of such forms, as in this example, where instead of the modern word for city, *gorod*, he uses the OCS form *grad*.

42. Bakhtin is here deploying a concept that will play an important role in his theory of the novel under the term "image of a language" (*obraz jazyka*): see *The Dialogic Imagination*, trans. Caryl Emerson and Michael Holquist (Austin: University of Texas Press, 1981), pp. 49, 65, 300, 355ff.

43. Parmenides of Elea (b. 515 B.C.), perhaps the greatest of the pre-Socratic philosophers, whose work is available only in fragments quoted by later thinkers. Bakhtin is here referring to FR. 7 of *On Nature*, in which the goddess warns Parmenides against the way of knowing typical of most mortals, which is to assume that "things both are and are not," i.e., a thing may be and then cease to be, or a thing may be here, but not there. Ordinary habits of speech and our organs of perception (unassisted by reason) make such assumptions plausible. The goddess argues that only through thought can the falsity of the assumption that "things both are and are not" be overcome. Therefore, the goddess insists on the primacy of reason as opposed to just our eyes and ears.

44. A term (*instrumentovka*) used by Yury Nikolaevich Tynyanov (1894–1943) in his *Problems of Verse Language* (1924). A translation of this important work exists in English under the title *The Problem of Verse Language* (with an afterword by Roman Jakobson), trans. Michael Sosa and Brent Harvey (Ann Arbor: Ardis, 1981), cf. esp. pp. 112–119. Tynyanov was one of the most systematic, erudite, and creative of the Formalists, as well as a major historical novelist in his later years.

Index